Engendering Forced Migration

REFUGEE AND FORCED MIGRATION STUDIES
General Editors: Barbara Harrell-Bond and Roger Zetter

ENGENDERING FORCED MIGRATION
Theory and Practice

Edited by

Doreen Indra

Berghahn Books
NEW YORK • OXFORD

First published in 1999 by

Berghahn Books

Editorial offices:
55 John Street, 3rd Floor, New York, NY 10038 USA
3, NewTec Place, Magdalen Road, Oxford, OX4 1RE, UK

© 1999 Doreen Indra

Library of Congress Cataloging-in-Publication Data

Engendering forced migration : theory and practice / edited by Doreen
Indra.
    p.   cm. – (Refugee and forced migration studies : v. 5)
    Includes bibliographical references and index.
    ISBN 1-57181-134-6 (alk. paper). – ISBN 1-57181-135-4 (alk. paper)
    1. Forced migration. 2. Women refugees. 3. Women immigrants.
I. Indra, Doreen Marie. II. Series.
HV640.E56 1998   98-28455
325–dc21   CIP

British Library Cataloguing in Publication Data

A catalogue record for this book is available from the British Library.

Printed in the United States on acid-free paper.

Cover photo: UNHCR/H. Timmermans/1994

Contents

List of Tables

Acknowledgments

The contributions of many individuals went into the creation of this volume. I would like to express my thanks to the seventeen chapter authors for their hard work and patience, and especially for their tolerance for my many editorial interventions. Thanks here also go to Robert Paine, who helped make it possible to include Lisa Gilad's chapter posthumously.

The Fifth International Research and Advisory Panel Conference on Forced Migration (9–12 April 1996) in El Doret, Kenya, brought together a number of those whose chapters are now found here. I am therefore grateful to the conference organizers, Khalid Koser and Lois van Willigen, and to the conference hosts, Monica Kathina and others at the Centre for Refugee Studies, Moi University. The conference was financially supported by the UNHCR, the Dutch Ministry of the Interior, and the Swiss Agency for Development and Cooperation. Material assistance was provided by Stichting Pharos, Moi University, the Refugee Studies Programme at the University of Oxford, the University of Sussex, and the University of Utrecht. Thereafter, Richard Black, Barbara Harrell-Bond, Eftihia Voutira, and Helene Moussa provided important support and encouragement in the formative days of this project.

At the University of Lethbridge, I am particularly indebted to Norman Buchignani for discussing with me every aspect of the volume's development, for helping editorially, and for the emotional labor he contributed to the completion of this work. This volume is much stronger because of him. I would like to express my gratitude to Connie Donoghue and Marlene Hollwey for their insightful comments, humor, and sheer endurance in assisting in editing and word-processing in the late stages of the project. I would also like to acknowledge Dean Bhagwan Dua for his continuing support of my work.

I am very grateful for the support of Berghahn Books. Marion Berghahn must have been dismayed by the initial size of the manuscript, yet along with Janine Treves generously encouraged my efforts throughout. Shawn Kendrick did a masterful job of final copy editing and the value of her contribution cannot be overestimated.

I would like to acknowledge the UNHCR for their permission to use photographs from their journal, *Refugee*. Thanks also go to the Life and Peace Institute, Upsalla, for permission to develop Carolyn Nordstrom's chapter out of their 1997 report, *Girls and War Zones*.

My own research was financially supported by the Social Sciences and Humanities Research Council (SSHRC) of Canada under its standard grants program (#42154) and through its funding of the international Women in Conflict Zones network, and by the University of Lethbridge Research Fund.

Introduction

As in the evolution of many academic domains devoted to the study of phenomena that are also significant social issues, the study of forced migration initially was powerfully influenced by representations of refugees and flight driving from that social issues discourse. Research consequently focused on particular kinds of political refugees, not environmentally forced migrants and certainly not so-called 'economic migrants'. Conceptually, 'refugee' in most academic research up to the mid-1980s was essentially what it was in folk discourse, save in legal studies. The formative days of refugee studies was also characterized by a concentration on the comparatively short period when refugees attract the public eye through flight and acute trauma, and on the comparatively few who secured resettlement in rich countries. There was little sustained interest in the chronic national, international, and environmental forces generating such movements of people, or in empirical or theoretical parallels between those deemed political refugees crossing international borders and others. Researchers often nonproblematically used highly stereotypic social issues and bureaucratically generated representations of 'the' culture, experiences, and goals of refugees that would never have been acceptable in contemporary ethnographic treatments of people in source countries.

Even fifteen years ago, gender rarely surfaced in folk representations and practice concerning forced migrants. Refugees were sometimes spoken of as women, men, or children, but typically either in passing, in relation to idealized, traditional 'family' life and roles, or in regard to programs aimed specifically at family unification, women's health, or employment. 'Generic' employment and health programs were 'for everybody' and therefore were not usually seen as gendered. The 1951 UN *Convention Relating to the Status of Refugees* and subsequent elaborations that most governments used to determine formal refugee status then gave no support for gender as a factor in political oppression. There was almost no social issues or research interest in how many major forces affecting the lives of those who flee–and those who do not–are gendered as well as classed.

This is now rapidly, if inconsistently, changing on both fronts, with the research side often in the vanguard. This volume reflects a time of rapid expansion and high flux in the study of forced migration that is characterized by increasingly bold attempts to go beyond extant research paradigms, while simultaneously being powerfully informed by such paradigms.

The idea for this volume arose out of a mix of my ongoing research interests and a good opportunity. The International Association for the Study of Forced Migration (IASFM) was being hosted by Moi University, Eldoret, Kenya, in April 1996. I was asked by Khalid Koser and Richard Black to give a talk to initiate a full day of presentations on gender and forced migration–a radical increase over the number of such papers presented at the last IASFM meetings four years previously. Half of the authors represented here attended. Over the intervening months I worked extensively with these and other, invited authors to formulate and refine chapters reflecting both their interests and orientations, and a range of critical dimensions of study and practice dealing with forced migration and gender.

In retrospect, this editorial process highlighted and confirmed for me a number of important issues, tendencies, and tensions concerning gender and forced migration, some of which are now reflected in both the thematic structure of this volume and the specific content of each chapter. Perhaps the most central of these is a tension in dealing with the universal versus the specific concerning gender and forced migration through time and space. In the end, this tension may be epistemologically unresolvable without much more middle range theory. In the meantime, how it plays out and the center of gravity actually reached in discourse and practice have important consequences. How useful are the superinclusive, intransitive categories like refugee, woman, ascribed nationality, and citizenship that we have inherited from social issues discourse and forced migration practice, especially when their casual or politically strategic application so often leads to vacuously uninteresting, generic representations and to procrustean assistance programs that serve no one well? While little benefit derives from idiosyncratic, highly individualized representations of forced migrants divorced from the forces of their production, many of the authors here ably argue that the balance in research remains much too far on the macro side.

In doing so, they raise many allied questions concerning the boundedness and coherence of social systems, cultures, and lives, and the analytical frameworks we use to make sense of them. For example, Nordstrom, Giles, Smith, Gómez and others question the notion that the cultures and social systems impacting upon and forming forced migrant women and men are, or ever actually were, bounded, organic wholes. In doing so, they and others (for instance, Cammack, Matlou, Boelaert et al., Macklin, and Crawley) illustrate ways that particular societies, cultures, classes, political forces, laws, and programs are differently organized for women and men, and for various subcategories *of* women and men. At the same time, it is of some interest to note that every author (myself included) ultimately depends at least in part on such simplifying characterizations. Perhaps this is rhetorically driven because thereafter, everything taking place within such a categorical boundary "can be treated as one single event" (Brown 1989: 176) or phenomenon. Giles, Nordstrom, Matlou, and others highlight ways that what has been classically considered abnormal such as wartime, is immanent in or deeply part of 'normal' processes at work in peacetime. Going further, it is my impression that there is a broad consensus across the authors represented here that every 'noun' (personality, citizen, family, household, culture, etc.) articulating with forced migration is so situational and far from static that it may be usefully considered as a processual 'verb'. Many also question the utility and empirical clarity of other oppositions that have long informed refugee discourse: refugee/economic migrant, public/private, civilian/non-civilian, home/diaspora, and present/past.

Several also question whether and where it is appropriate to apply what are in the main Western-derived academic, bureaucratic, and media representations to gender and forced migration cross-culturally, noting the mixed consequences this has had in the past. Western social issue and social problem-generated images of refugees as powerless victims of forces beyond their control are well-entrenched. One of the pitfalls facing those now highlighting gender is the risk of quick foreclosure: that gender will be simplistically read as 'women' rather than as relations of power, privilege, and prestige informed by situated notions of maleness and femaleness; and that 'women refugees' will then be comfortably categorized as a comparatively invariant kind of 'multiple minority', victimized as 'women' in their source and host cultures and as 'refugees'. Systematic neglect of the class, subcultural, and situational variability among women would be an almost automatic consequence. Only gendered violence of particular sorts long associated with women's violation and men's honor, such as rape, would be considered, and only when immediately connected to 'war'.

Over the last twenty years, a great tension has developed in feminist studies concerning how to weigh the sometimes directly contradictory values of cultural relativism and universalized notions of individual human rights. This tension is now reflected in the study of gender and forced migration, and a spectrum of positions is reflected in this volume; Matsuoka and Sorenson, and McSpadden, for example, argue for a more compassionate and flexible institutional recognition of Eritrean and Ethiopian conceptions of masculinity even if these do not fit Western feminist ideals, while Cammack's treatment of crumbling aid agency resolve in the face of Taleban assertions about the place of Afghan women takes a very different line. Even so, the balance here is definitely on the side of the priority of individual human rights when rights and cultural expectations are in opposition.

The organization of the volume reflects these objectives and concerns. The first two chapters by Indra and Colson and my interview with Barbara Harrell-Bond deal in differing ways with the history of forced migration research, historical constraints, and future possibilities. In "Not a 'Room of One's Own'" I outline a number of historical parallels between successive feminist approaches to gender in development and forced migration research and talk some years later. Drawing illustrations from the evolution of gendered household entitlement theory in development studies, I also suggest that we might use the history of gender in development to avoid a number of unnecessary conceptual limitations and dead ends. Elizabeth Colson's "Gendering Those Uprooted by 'Development'" draws on her extraordinary, forty year longitudinal study of the Gwembe Tonga, who were resettled in 1958 after the building of Kariba Hydroelectric Dam on the Zambezi River. Colson pushes the bounds of research convention in several ways to construct representations of Gwembe Tonga women and men as complex actors in history, multiply constrained by gender, age, locality, and national policy. Colson also clearly demonstrates how the key relational dimensions of gender for these developmentally forced migrants vary significantly from place to place and over time. Barbara Harrell-Bond is the founder of one of the first centers for forced migration research, the Refugee Studies Programme (RSP) at the University of Oxford. In her interview she presents insights drawn from her ongoing experience with, and active role in the rise of refugee studies and gender studies within it. In outlining her own strongly held position about the need for a deep synthesis of research and practice, she well illustrates the complex and changing ways in which talk and action in forced migration discourse have historically reflected highly global Northern ways of seeing and responding.

Each of the next seven papers challenges and politicizes extant conceptual or practical boundaries. Carolyn Nordstrom's "Girls and War Zones" decries the invisibility of girl children in bureaucratic, media, and academic discourses of refugee-generating situations of acute, violent conflict. She shows how highly naturalized, doxic distinctions between peace and war zones mask underlying forces that mute, abuse, oppress, and destroy girls in both these nominally different domains. Wenona Giles's "Gendered Violence in War" considers how images of home ideologized by nationalists frame women as "mothers, wives, partners, workers, warriors, enemies, victims, or heroines, located in highly political and public spaces"–ideologies which differentially expose women in source countries, in flight, and in camps to certain forms of oppression. Diana Cammack sharply criticizes "Gender Relief and Politics During the Afghan War," showing how national and international media, Islamic organizations, academics, aid organizations, funders, and governments generated competing constructions of Afghan aid, war, gender, and nation. She also narrates how macropolitical considerations led a number of aid organizations to compromise their human rights charters and limit their aid programs aimed at women and girl refugees. Peter Marsden then draws on his long experience with the practical delivery of Afghan aid to respond to Cammack's chapter.

Patrick Matlou's "Upsetting the Cart" develops the thesis that while African "refugees are caused chiefly by political events, the international refugee regime, oddly enough, conceptualizes and treats them primarily as a humanitarian issue." Moreover, Matlou chronicles how gender-oriented violence is increasingly one of the main weapons of war in Africa and, hence, a major source of forced migrants. Charles David Smith's "Women Migrants of Kagera Region, Tanzania" challenges the long-established bureaucratic distinction between 'economic migrants' and political refugees. He shows how women, who most governments and aid organizations would class as 'economic migrants', face highly gendered "factors forcing them out [that] are political: their educational disadvantage, their inability to inherit land under customary law, and their exclusion from serious involvement in coffee production." "The Relevance of Gendered Approaches to Refugee Health" is a case study of health care provision in Hagadera, Kenya. In it, Marleen Boelaert and her medically trained co-authors investigate what many others merely assume: that a gendered approach is in fact relevant to emergency health programs. They concur, but also question whether the most effective route might then be "a matter of better, rather than more care"–care that does not simply address refugee women "from a biological perspective only," and that acknowledges "the fact that gender cannot be reduced to sex."

In "Post-Soviet Russian Migration from the New Independent States," Natalya Kosmarskaya considers the gendered implications of Russian speakers returning 'home' to Russia from the New Independent States (NIS) of the former Soviet Union. In doing so, Kosmarskaya shows that Western-informed models of refugee migration and settlement based on European evidence do not particularly fit well in this context, in which once comparatively privileged women and men are forced to move to the rural hinterland of Russia as the result of the collapse of empire and the loss of their associated privileges. Inés Gómez then considers ways in which Chilean women in the California diaspora use home-pedagogy to construct "A Space for Remembering" 'home', and for effectively conveying associated images and symbols to their children.

Atsuko Matsuoka and John Sorenson's "Eritrean Canadian Refugee Households As Sites of Gender Renegotiation" shows how strongly gendered Eritrean personal roles and expectations are often directly confronted by the changed economic, social, and political circumstances of Canadian exile, and why these changed circumstances undermine some men's self-identities and not others. Matsuoka and Sorenson also describe how a distinctive feminism has arisen among Eritreans during their long years of political and military struggle, and why some Eritrean women exiles claim that they "don't necessarily want to be like the feminists in the West." Lucia Ann McSpadden's "Negotiating Masculinity in the Reconstruction of Social Place" extends this inquiry to Eritrean and Ethiopian men in the US and Sweden. She shows how class-based, source country gender ideals powerfully drive diasporic men to succeed (as judged by freestanding, idealized source country standards), and how such attempts are sometimes frustrated by government programs that gauge refugee success in very different terms.

The balance of the volume is primarily concerned with the interplay of gender with issues of human rights, protection, and refugee determination in law and practice. In "The Human Rights of Refugees with Special Reference to Muslim Refugee Women," Khadija Elmadmad explores ways in which Islamic states might be able to complement secular, 'modern' international legal instruments relating to refugees with notions of asylum and protection derived from Islam. Audrey Macklin then presents "A Comparative Analysis of the Canadian, US, and Australian Directives on Gender Persecution and Refugee Status." Her thorough analysis explains how agents of these three governments have developed linked, yet differing, legal bases for partially incorporating gender as a criterion for refugee status. In "Women and Refugee Status," Heaven Crawley describes how UK asylum policy has moved in the opposite direction to a hard stance, rejecting any notion that modest suggestions made by the UNHCR on how gender might be incorporated into such criteria are binding on States Party.

Lisa Gilad's "The Problem of Gender-Related Persecution" and Sidney Waldron's response, "Anthropologists As 'Expert Witnesses,'" complete the volume. Lisa Gilad's chapter is included posthumously. I contacted Lisa Gilad early in the course of soliciting authors, and in the subsequent to-and-fro that inevitably follows, she sent me a draft paper on the use of anthropological input in establishing gender dimensions of refugee determination, along with a query on whether it could be a basis for a more developed treatment. Lisa's partner Robert Paine quickly replied to my affirmative response that she had tragically died in an automobile accident just a few days earlier. I have included her draft paper, which, because of the circumstances has only been lightly edited. Sidney Waldron, whose work Lisa uses as an extended example, has kindly provided a response.

List of Abbreviations

ACBAR	Agency Coordinating Body for Afghan Relief
AIG	Afghan Interim Government
ARC	Australian Relief Committee
BIA	(US) Board of Immigration Appeals
CHW	Community health worker
CRDD	Convention Refugee Determination Division
DACAAR	Danish Committee for Aid to Afghan Refugees
DIMA	Department of Immigration and Multicultural Affairs, Australia
ECPAT	End Child Prostitution, Child Pornography, and Trafficking in Children for Sexual Purposes
ELR	Exceptional Leave to Remain
EPLF	Eritrean People's Liberation Front
EPRDF	Ethiopian People's Revolutionary Democratic Front
EXCOM	Executive Committee of UNHCR
Frelimo	Front for the Liberation of Mozambique
FSU	Former Soviet Union
GAD	Gender and development
GAFM	Gender and forced migration
GIFM	Gender in forced migration
IAB	Immigration Appeal Board
IASFM	International Association for the Study of Forced Migration
ICRC	International Committee of the Red Cross
INGO	Intergovernmental organization
IRB	(Canada's) Immigration and Refugee Board
IRC	International Rescue Committee
MSF	Médecins Sans Frontières
NGO	Non-governmental organization
NIS	New Independent States (of the former Soviet Union)

NUEW	National Union of Eritrean Women
NWFP	Northwest Frontier Province, Pakistan
OAU	Organization of African Unity
ODA	British Overseas Development Agency
Renamo	Resistencia National Mocambicana
RHO	Refugee Hearing Officer
RPG	Refugee Policy Group
RRT	Refugee Rights Tribunal
RSP	Refugee Studies Programme, University of Oxford
SCF	Save the Children Fund
SNI	Shelter Now International
SPLA	Sudan People's Liberation Army
TBA	Traditional birth attendant
TPLF	Tigrayan People's Liberation Front
UNDP	United Nations Development Program
UNHCR	United Nations High Commissioner for Refugees
UNICEF	United Nations Children's Fund
UNOCHA	United Nations Office for the Coordination of Humanitarian Assistance in Afghanistan
UNOMOZ	United Nations Operation in Mozambique
USAID	US Agency for International Development
WAD	Women and development
WFP	World Food Program
WID	Women in development
WIFM	Women in forced migration

1

Not a "Room of One's Own"

Engendering Forced Migration Knowledge and Practice

Doreen Indra

Introduction

This chapter introduces some challenges to the more thorough integration of gender into forced migration research and practice. There are many ways in which this might be accomplished, none of which can be exhaustive or definitive. What I have done is to take a broadly historical journey through several research discourses on gender that highlight what I see as a range of pertinent framing, representational, and revisioning challenges facing forced migration studies and practice today. This approach has in turn required me to read 'gender issues in forced migration' differently than some may anticipate. One *could* take a quite circumscribed, topically bounded route through the relevant material. But if I were to take this route, I would be accepting as given one of the central framing assumptions I want to challenge: that 'gender' *is* simply one topic or topical frame among many in forced migration.

Instead I would like to explore the possibility of deeply *engendering knowledge* in the study and practice of forced migration, through its many topical dimensions. I see several of today's variously integrated gender discourses as providing potent ways of analytically approaching and practically addressing a wide range of social and cultural phenomena. To highlight this point, I have organized this chapter around two very basic assertions drawn from contemporary feminist theory in the social sciences: that neither in talk, research, analysis, policy, nor programming can 'gender' be equated solely with women, nor solely with women's activities, beliefs, goals, or needs; and that 'gender' is instead a key *relational* dimension of human activity and thought–activity and thought informed by cultural and individual notions of men and women–having consequences for their social or cultural positioning and the ways in which they experience and live their lives. As Colson reminds us in this volume, "Gender is a cultural artifact, however much it may play upon sexual characteristics, [and] the 'key *relational* dimensions' must of necessity vary from place to place and over time. How people respond to forced migration will be gendered, but it will vary given that they come to the experience with different 'cultural and individual notions.'"

The generality of this stance renders it impossible for me to provide here an exhaustive treatment of any of the most central gender issues in forced migration. What I do is broadly locate forced migration studies within a limited set of linked, evolving approaches to the study of gender. I begin with a brief historical overview of how gender emerged as a category of analysis in anthropology, and how it has "transformed research questions" and accepted knowledges there and in other disciplines (Beneria 1995: 1839). These comments are intended to be illustrative, evocative, and agenda-setting. I then turn to the gender and development literature, focusing primarily on ethnographically oriented development research, and occasionally drawing illustrations from my Bangladesh-based fieldwork on environmentally forced migration and associated literatures.[1] Thereafter, I draw some implications from this particular body of development thought and practice for gender and forced migration.

There are four broad reasons why I have used the ethnographically oriented theoretical and applied literature on development in this way. For one, first as a social and political issue, then as a theorized discourse, and finally as applied practice, gender made its appearance far earlier in the domains of development and development studies than in forced migration circles. Sustained concern with gender in forced migration studies is in its infancy, and awareness of the evolution of the much more mature development discourse may therefore guide us and help us avoid costly sidetracks and pitfalls. Second, theoretical discussion in ethnographically oriented feminist development research occurs in a tradition that is strongly empirically grounded, at least illustratively. Moreover, like forced migration studies, development studies necessarily span research and practice;

so does its theory. Third, front and center in forced migration are a large set of research, policy, and program issues which are in fact issues of development. Many of both the world's inter- and intranationally displaced women, men, and children at least temporarily experience poverty, disempowerment, stigmatization, and marginalization. The understanding, amelioration, or removal of these disabilities is central to forced migration research and practice—practice that, as is often recognized, may not meet its development goals. Likewise, both source and host country people and institutions drafted or self-selected to assist displaced people are increasingly drawn from those already involved in development, and it is therefore appropriate that those now involved in refugee studies better address this fact. In addition, development resources are always scarce and are particularly so in most countries facing significant forced migration challenges. They ought not to be squandered. Hopefully, we can learn much from costly historical failures to consider gender adequately in the larger context of world development. Finally, a greater awareness of the findings of locally informed and grounded development research with a feminist accent may further challenge ways in which talk and action concerned with forced migration continue to reflect overly global, Northern ways of seeing and responding (see interview with Harrell-Bond, this volume).

Most of the world's forced migrants are neither Northern natives nor are they located in Northern countries. But academics, other researchers, government policymakers, and international agencies from the North dominate much discussion and action involving forced migrants, and hence chiefly frame relevant institutions, agencies, programs, and communities in virtually every part of the world. They also appear to so powerfully inform current research with a macrolevel paradigm of forced migration that situational, individual, interpersonal, cultural, historical, and cross-contextual variability are often neglected; many research-generated representations of refugees consequently exhibit a dreary similarity that belies great on-the-ground variability. It is time to actively rethink how refugee studies and practice might unconsciously reflect these facts and tendencies—something already extensively discussed in feminist, ethnographically grounded development discourse.

Gender and Feminist Anthropology

Let me now turn to the evolution of feminist anthropological thought and its uneven impact on how refugees are framed. Again, a theme

I want to stress is that while it is a significant conceptual advance over not considering gender at all, gender *is not usefully equated simply with women.* For one thing, the latter practice often leads to topical containment and little change in how core debates are framed. To illustrate, a decade ago at conferences dealing with social issues it was almost obligatory to have a few 'special' sessions considering 'gender' *and* the conference's main theme: gender *and* ... unemployment, mental health, 'the' family, etc. Usually, one then found that most papers in these special sessions actually dealt solely or centrally with women or with concerns and activities conventionally associated with them. Most papers given outside this representational 'gender ghetto' were presented as if the issues raised were essentially genderless, or as if gender was one of a host of 'attributes' or 'dependent variables' that might qualify or affect how the main topic played out.

Many social policy statements and societal social problems discourses today are similarly partitioned, recently evolving specific, sometimes sharply delimited, subdomains dealing specifically with women. This practice makes a strong, ironic statement. The very process which validates greater consideration of women as a special case facilitates speaking of the rest of the topics considered at a conference, or in a policy statement or social problems discourse, as if they were, in their most central essence or manifestation, not gendered. Moreover, it allows these other topics to continue to be presented as mainstream, primary, and central—the big picture—framed as they are in 'universal' and 'general' categories. The 'little picture' is simply a qualification: how women impact upon or are specifically impacted by the phenomena under consideration.

This irony finds a parallel in the public and private sphere distinctions formed by much earlier Western liberal thought and theory—a parallel that is not coincidental. Today, whether clear public/ private distinctions have any remaining analytical utility is being hotly contested. Even so, for generations powerful ideologies naturalized this public/private divide, partially consigning women to the so-called 'private sphere' of household life and often framing women primarily in relationship to it. This facilitated addressing what were not so long ago claimed to be primarily public sphere issues such as access to human rights and privileges in 'universal' terms— issues unconsciously associated chiefly with the public practices and concerns of some men. It also masked many ways in which human rights issues powerfully articulate with a range of private concerns and with household and home. As several authors in this volume ably argue, and some clearly demonstrate, the unconscious naturalization of sets of women's roles and statuses identified with narrowly framed, highly political notions of household, home, and the private sphere has had profound consequences for forced migration research and practice and for affected migrants.

I concur with many who, in considering the private/public distinction, have also argued that these categorizing practices mute the significance of gender in many societal venues by containing and restricting discussion to a narrow range of 'women's issues' or to venues where women are present. Many people evidently still do not "see the issue of gender arising ... where men [are] with men," as Dorothy Smith notes in another context; neither is there as yet commonly a recognition of "the gender subtext of those spheres claiming gender neutrality" (Smith 1991).

Given this larger context, it is not hard to see why major refugee issues affecting many thousands of people continue to be discussed and addressed with little reference to gender; or under close scrutiny, are issues reflecting the concerns of Western men (and some women); or are issues where migrant women's concerns are being considered, but as a special, added-on case. To permute Virginia Woolf's phrase, forced migration *discourse* may now increasingly allocate a 'room of their own' to women and men wanting to discuss women's issues, *but most of the rest of the house remains genderless space.*[2]

I do not mean to be overly critical here. The rise of representational gender ghettos is most certainly an advance over not mentioning gender or women at all. The older tendency to talk in genderless, universal terms still maintains sufficient legitimacy that Liisa Malkki's otherwise sophisticated (1995) overview of research on refugees contains no mention of women or gender. We may perhaps be seeing a snapshot in time of an evolving way of better coming to terms with engendering forced migration: an evolutionary sea change that began in academic circles and spread to certain applied domains like development, where it has effected a revolution in discourse and a partial one in practice. It is now influencing forced migration theory. Hopefully, this signals many future changes in forced migration studies and practice.

Henrietta Moore (1988), Helen Callaway (1987), and others wrote of this tendency to identify gender with women in the first wave of feminist anthropological research arising in the early 1970s. That phase was characterized by a number of fine ethnographically based studies of women by women, and by challenges to many androcentric orthodoxies in anthropology reflecting Western associations of women with the private sphere and men with the public one—especially the then current 'man the hunter, farmer, factory worker;

woman the housewife' model of social life.[3] In retrospect, this was a necessary corrective response to a disciplinary orientation that historically had selectively portrayed or ignored women. The program then was to 'put the women back' into ethnographic representations, where before they had largely been absent. The way this was accomplished initially was to build another room onto an extant anthropological edifice, largely leaving the latter's basic architecture unchanged.

This renovation project had hardly begun before feminist theorists in many disciplines forcefully raised my second main point: that the historical 'problem' with research did not simply derive from the invisibility of women in it. In fact, women have been extensively written into kinship, marriage, socialization, and enculturation studies since the rise of fieldwork-based ethnography in the early 1920s. The issue was how were women and men represented and analytically characterized. 'The problem', then, was with how social theory informed empirical work by organizing how and what we see. Critically, what became central to feminist anthropology was not the study of women, per se, but of *gender*: of societally and culturally constructed notions of women and men, and how these notions structure human societies, including their histories, ideologies, economies, politics, and religions. This way of seeing gender as a fundamental organizing principle of everyday life highlights the point that gender matters greatly even in empirical situations where there are only men or only women, and where nothing is ever spoken of women or men, maleness or femaleness. To continue my building metaphor (and with due apologies to Virginia Woolf), while women and men may differentially occupy and use society's various rooms, gender is deeply incorporated into the architectural plans, furnishings and room assignments, as well as into the values and practices relating to spaces and places everywhere in the building.

The first analytical requirement demanded by this orientation is to take a gender relational approach to *all* research topics—*to disaggregate everything by gender*: concepts, methods, theories, folk ideas, bureaucratic practice, and policies. In advocating this, I concur with the central assertion of Malkki's recent review (1995: 497–500, 502, 504–6, 508–12), which is that the revisioning potential of most refugee research has been greatly limited by its unconscious incorporation of a wide range of historically generated Western folk conceptions about refugees, rights, nations, international aid, the good life, cultural loss, and the like. The additional point not made by Malkki is that these are all *gendered* social constructions, and are profitably examined as such.

Such a way of looking at all the "rooms of the house" clearly facilitates the achievement of greater understanding of the larger political contexts of their creation and use. As Foucault (1972) and many others have shown, neither language nor history are conceptually neutral. Following on this, the power to define and create classifications, institutions, and policies is neither disinterested nor ungendered (Starr 1992). Unpacking and revisioning such categories and relationships, many that are otherwise typically viewed as natural and self-evident, is a necessary first step, leading to a deeper understanding of who we are, and of general relations of power and process. By inserting disaggregating questions about gender into bureaucratic and social issues discourse such as those concerning forced migration, what were previously 'natural', taken for granted facts, structures, categories, policies, and procedures suddenly appear in a new light. They appear as 'unnatural', gendered social, cultural, and historical *constructions* that may at once be problematical to some, and vigorously challenged. New insights also may arise that allow us to become more reflexive about appropriate social action and how to work and plan more effectively for constructive social change (see Giles, this volume).

This process of disaggregating and unpacking categories opens up political entry points for those wishing to exert pressure on extant institutions to better address gender issues in what they do. As Jacqueline Castel (1992), Jacqueline Greatbach (1989), I (1987, 1989a, 1993), and more recently Lisa Malkki (1995) (though without reference to gender) have noted, one also can see this in the now more vigorously contested category 'refugee'. A concept whose genealogy begins in the North, 'refugee' is now being constructed in other ways elsewhere, especially in Africa. Once assessed in terms of generic, universalized, genderless standards, even some Northern governments now assert that gender oppression should be officially recognized as criterion for political/legal refugee status (see Macklin, Crawley, and Gilad, this volume).

During the last two decades, then, there has been a broad-based revolution in anthropological and some other social science approaches to women and gender—especially at the level of talk about doing research. At *that* level, my two main organizing points have long been axiomatic in ever-broadening domains in the social sciences. I should point out, however, that the program to study women more extensively in anthropological research is ongoing, and has not disappeared despite the tendency of theorists to increasingly stress the centrality of gender.

Much recent conceptual and theoretical discussion centers on the analytical weighting of the specific versus the general in research, especially when considering women. Feminists inside and outside anthropology argue that framing research with an axiomatic, invariant category "woman" risks a number of things: focusing on presumed, rather than research-supported similarities among women; masking or backgrounding differences between them, such as differences in class, social race, ethnicity, and power; naturalizing or essentializing women–that is, seeing (questionable) fundamental commonalities among women deriving from their putatively common biology, psychology, or social position; and unproductively deflecting attention away from context-specific social, political, and cultural constructions of gender.

Critically, there *is* increasing consensus that cultural, race, class, ethnic, national, and sexual orientation differences between women, women and men, and men must be given more significance. Di Leonardo notes (1991: 26) that while "the proposition that women are, across time and space, a single oppressed and virtuous class ... has remained popular among many Western feminists ...," strong resistance to such globalized and romanticized notions is having a profound effect. Southern women increasingly maintain that global and Northern-referenced representations of women have little or no relevance to their daily lived experience (Chakravorty Spivak 1987; Ogundipe-Leslie 1996). One sees this very clearly in worldwide feminist 'autoethnography'–that is, in ethnography done on and with people in one's own society. For example, Felicia Ekejiuba's (1995) work on women-centered 'hearth-holds' in rural Nigeria provides rich local data demonstrating the unique ways in which women, gender, and residence units are constructed there; she, Ogundipe-Leslie (1996), and Amadiume (1987) each show that in certain Nigerian contexts the analytical (Western) construct 'woman' has a poor fit with the gender categories and practices they observe in the field. In overview, effective resistance by feminists in Southern countries has forestalled the appropriation of feminist discourse by Northern, mainstream, totalizing ideologies and has changed the whole course of feminist theory and representational strategies. In this regard also, there remains much value in studying women in specific contexts *as women*; such an approach may help avoid the conceptual trap of women defining themselves against men as an Other–especially of being constructed both ethnocentrically and phallocentrically as an opposite of a stereotype of Western man.[4]

We also have to be aware of the conceptual trap prevalent in both popular and academic discourse of comparing images of Western 'liberated' women to a caricatured image of a backward and unenlightened Oriental Other. As Grewal's (1996: 23–84) critical analysis demonstrates, early British suffragist discourse and practice was powerfully informed by imperial representations of cloistered and oversexualized Oriental women. At a time when women of means like Virginia Woolf were increasingly able to pay for and claim title to rooms of their own, they also pointed to women in the East who, they believed, were constrained by rooms they merely inhabited.

Engendering Development

Certain patterns in the historical evolution of how gender has been approached in development discourse closely parallel those that characterize changes in academic feminist discourse in anthropology. These two domains have become increasingly interpenetrated. Bina Agarwal observes (1994: 3) in regard to changes in development circles that "what is notable is that it has been a process of negotiation and struggle involving multiple actors–academics and researchers, women's activist groups, government policy makers, and bureaucrats, and international agencies."[5] Beginning twenty-five years ago, findings from development research–particularly on women and particularly that done from an ethnographic perspective–have powerfully shaped more general academic theory and ways of thinking about gender. This is one of the few domains I know of where development-based research has strongly influenced the course of 'mainstream' anthropological thought, and where there is a powerfully effective synergy between applied and so-called "pure" research.

Though the search for landmark initiating or foundational landmark studies here is likely to be both controversial and ideological, Agarwal, Eva Rathgeber, Elizabeth Colson (this volume), and others have pointed to Ester Boserup's (1970) *Women's Role in Economic Development* as being seminal. I remember it as such. It was in this work that Boserup provided gender-specific evidence and gendered analysis to expose gaps in how the benefits and burdens of development were being distributed. She found many instances in which well-intentioned development projects left women impoverished. This work and its author are illustrative of the synergy to which I refer: a work by a Northern feminist academic, yet one about development disparities faced by women. I believe this work was persuasive because it was produced at a time when the intellectual groundwork for its ready acceptance had been laid. In contrast, Audrey Richards's (1932; 1939) pioneering work on women and labor development in East Africa had little similar impact. Effie

Voutira (1995) and di Leonardo (1991) likewise date "the explosive growth of research on the integration of women into development" to the mid-1970s, especially to the beginning of the UN Decade for Women in 1975.

Women in Development

Rathgeber (1990) characterizes development as moving from virtually no deep consideration of either women or gender through three overlapping perspectives. From about 1972 on, much talk arose about 'putting women into the development equation'. This approach is now associated with the acronym WID, or Women in Development. WID was initially—and today often remains—an add-on approach grounded in 'traditional modernization theory'. In particular, this approach has largely "accepted [the] existing social structures" (Rathgeber 1990: 491) both of the focal societies in question and of development programming. The chief goals are: to better integrate women into ongoing development initiatives, to ensure that they fare better under them, and to differentially allocate aid and development resources to women in great need. Much ethnographically based, development-oriented research informed by this orientation followed. Discussion and some research aside, changes in development *practice* lagged—even at an institution-building level. Rathgeber points out that "… the British ODA steadfastly refused to give special support to projects for women until the second half of the 1980s …" and that when USAID carried out

> an evaluation of its experience with women in development between 1973 and 1985 … the evaluation revealed that even in the 1980–84 period, by which time the WID Office had been established for several years, 40 percent of the projects evaluated made no mention at all of women. In the earlier period from 1972 to 1977, 64 percent of the projects analyzed had made no mention of women. (Rathgeber 1990: 498)

Voutira (1995) claims that the World Food Program (WFP) endorsed a WID approach only in the 1980s. WID today remains, however, the most common philosophy informing those development programs that recognize women or gender at all.

WID is conceptually and otherwise limited and is currently very controversial. Even so, I think WID programs remain practically useful in a wide range of contexts—as long as their limitations are understood. Food aid to some extremely poor, environmentally forced migrant women in rural Bangladesh where I have worked may have no transformative power concerning their position in society, and such aid has no sustainability. The program reflects little understanding of local gender dynamics, and an unintentional consequence is the enhancement of the power of local male brokers and politicians. Even so, the program does give some very poor women and others greater access to food at relatively low personal cost. Another small program there employs a score of indigent women to maintain rural earth roads. As this work puts these women in the public sphere of paid work and out of their 'normal place' and space, it may even have some subtle transformative consequences. Findings from what I have here loosely categorized as 'ethnographic' studies of such 'women's' programs around the world continue to provide a richly productive range of insights into structural and individual disparities faced by women.

At the same time, Bina Agarwal follows today's analytical consensus in saying that "the approach underlying these directives and programs treats gender as an additive category, to be added onto existing ones, with women as a special focus or target group, rather than seeing gender as a lens through which the approach to development should itself be re-examined" (1994: 4). She asserts that such programs make use of what Harding (1987) has called the 'add women and stir' approach to development, and argues that it is not surprising that, in general, most such programs aimed at sustainable development fail. This certainly seems the case for most narrowly framed 'women's projects' involving forced migrants, even today.

Rathgeber suggests that this WID model rapidly became outmoded in development *discourse*, even though it had great staying power in actual programming. Both Beneria (1995: 1840) and Rathgeber observe that "'trapped' within the constraints set up by the analytical framework and basic assumptions of the neo-classical models, it [the WID approach] was not conducive to ask, let alone answer, the kind of feminist questions about gender and asymmetric power relations that the women's movement generated" (Rathgeber 1990: 492). Agarwal concurs stating that programs guided by WID philosophies

> are essentially couched in welfare terms, under the umbrella of the 'basic needs' approach that gained currency in development thinking in the mid-1970s. This approach emphasizes the provision of 'basic' goods and services (such as food, health care, education) to the economically disadvantaged, but without seriously questioning the existing [gendered] distribution of [statuses, roles,] productive resources and political power.... Most governments typically deliver such programs in a top-down manner involving little dialogue with the people (especially women) themselves on the definition of their needs or the best means of meeting those needs. (1994: 4)

Women and Development

A neo-Marxist Women *and* Development or WAD discourse arose in the late 1970s as a critical response to WID. WAD highlighted the "relationship between women and development processes" (Rathgeber 1990: 492) and focused on the role of classical development in maintaining elite national and international structures of power. Focusing rather globally and concentrating on class relations, as Gisela Geisler (1993: 1966) asserts, WAD approaches, however, failed to go to the heart of on-the-ground gendered relations or women's roles in everyday social reproduction. WAD never gained much favor.

Gender and Development

Over the past ten years, development organizations have increasingly embraced a Gender and Development (GAD) orientation.[6] GAD is strongly informed by contemporary feminist anthropological theory. By emphasizing gender rather than women, it focuses more forcefully on "the social construction of production and reproduction" (Rathgeber 1990) and on the forces which form and inform gender relations and societal ideologies. Voutira (1995: 1) observes that in contrast to WID, GAD also moves "beyond a simple economic analysis ..." In "restituting the balance of material resources ..." it "... introduc[es] the concept of social justice and the improvement of the quality of life for men and women." GAD, in short, has much potential to revision societal gender relations.

As this is rather abstract, let me illustrate GAD analysis and its revisioning potential through reference to a single topical frame in development discourse—one highly relevant to forced migration as well—the analysis of women, gender, and households.

GAD Approaches to Household Analysis

Classical development research and practice typically treats households as wholes for the purposes of analysis and programming: as highly corporate and opaque, private sphere 'black boxes' to be addressed chiefly in terms of key 'inputs' and 'outputs'. Individual men and sometimes women certainly surface as producers and consumers, and unequal gender relations within households often are recognized. Yet neither WID nor analytical approaches predating it often consider internal, gender-based household structures of power, privilege, and prestige or patterns of production, reproduction, distribution, and consumption within households. Often, many unsupported assumptions are made about the existence of generalized household pooling and reciprocity (Geisler 1993: 1967). In this regard, Lourdes Beneria observes (1995: 1843) that "to argue that women's economic needs require a specific focus, distinct from those of men, is to challenge a long-standing assumption in economic theory and development policy, namely, that the household is a unit of congruent interests, among whose members the benefits of available resources are shared equitably, irrespective of gender."

When considered at all by classical development theory and practice, structural gender inequalities within households are often characterized as static, uncontested social and cultural systems, framed as the 'local context' of development.[7] Alternatively, the statuses and roles encompassing such inequalities may be seen as 'natural', nonproblematic public/private distinctions between women and men. Warren and Bourque (1991: 290) note that men are often nonproblematically framed as 'heads of households', who articulate with the public sphere in the name of a corporate household. This framing strategy was almost universally applied in Bangladesh development practice until very recently. Household men "then fall from view as members of households ... [at the same time] when focusing attention on women in households, their reproductive and domestic roles [as mother and wife] ..." are foregrounded.

This orientation can even be found in Amartya Sen's (1976; 1977; 1981) highly influential formulation of entitlement analysis, which he applied to the study of famine. One of Sen's central points was that in agricultural, exchange-based societies that lack extensive state social welfare systems, it is the unequal distribution and allocation of food *between* households rather than an overall "food availability decline" (FAD) (Sen 1976: 1273) that is the usual cause of starvation during famine. When a *household* cannot produce sufficient food itself and its "exchange entitlements" are inadequate, its members may starve, even while others prosper. Entitlement analysis of this sort was a major advance in famine studies, and has greatly influenced worldwide crisis food aid provision program strategies.

Two key assumptions of Sen's formulation relevant to this discussion also were sharply criticized: his globalizing use of households as aggregated units of analysis, and his unacknowledged association of entitlements with men's culture-specific, legal, public sphere claims. At the forefront here were academic feminists involved in reformulating development paradigms to more adequately understand the lives of women existing under contemporary conditions of chronic poverty and malnutrition, and to better characterize the increasing "feminization of poverty" (Pryer 1990: 125). Great advances in household analysis soon followed in some development circles, and only a few pertinent to forced migration can be identified here. Most centrally, disaggregating households by gender led some theorists to the revisioning of intra (within) household distributions of power, privilege, and prestige, moving things such as generalized sharing within a household from 'givens' to open questions. It is this revisioning potential upon which I concentrate—again illustratively.

Entitlement analysis evolved radically and quickly, especially in its application to households. Just in South Asia-oriented commentary alone, Agarwal (1986: 165), Kabeer (1990; 1988) Papanek (1990); Chowdhury and Bairagi (1990); Maloney (1988: 42–48), and eventually Sen himself (1983; 1988; 1990: 139) powerfully extended entitlement analysis to gendered, intrahousehold dynamics. This approach has been used extensively in South Asian development research in particular to analyze food production, distribution, and consumption patterns within and between households, both in everyday, crisis, and aid-provision contexts. Both the very significant role women had *always had* in household production, and gendered disparities in household food distribution (as well as access to health care, education, etc.) were immediately highlighted.

In South Asia and elsewhere, unpacking our understanding of households has also led to a better appreciation of men's roles in *reproduction* and to the ability to look at gender more centrally as a context-specific social construction. For example, in *Male Daughters, Female Husbands: Gender and Sex in an African Society*, Ifi Amadiume (1987: 185) shows instances where biological sex does not always cleanly align with gender, especially in regard to household roles; older women may, for example, take young female wives, who bear children for them. Others have demonstrated similar things in many other locales. Searle-Chattergee (1981) has, for instance, highlighted "Reversible Sex Roles" among Benares Sweepers where many women have secured paid work.

Moreover, this revisioning process has allowed researchers to query the coherence and universality of the notion of 'the' household itself, and to conceptualize more adequately households which do not match classical development images of this notion. A hitherto basic development unit of analysis and data collection, Western-based definitional characteristics of a normative household (a male husband, female mother(s), and children) are now often inscribed in national and international law. Ekejiuba (1995: 48) has dissented (along with many others, see Smith, this volume), insisting that development practice organized in terms of this household image is itself a transformative force that often leads to the further muting and subordination of women. Bridgit O'Laughlin (1995: 75) likewise notes that the "gender-based critique of household economics has been particularly important in clarifying studies of family and household in rural communities in Africa." The damage created by the naive application of normative notions of 'the' household to development–and by extension to forced migration practice–in both Southern and Northern contexts can only be imagined. In rural Bangladesh local cultural ideals of households *do* in certain ways crudely approximate this normative model. Even so, revisioning households in the fashion indicated here has led me quite a way from how I saw things before doing field research there. I had done gendered disaggregated studies of Southeast Asian refugee households earlier (1989a; 1989b), but looking back, I can see now that before entering the field in Bangladesh I had unconsciously accepted the subtext of classic rural Bangladesh development discourse–that the 'women-headed households' of forced migrants I was to study were deviant, powerless, and automatically in great need. This was the general view when, as Geisler notes, "female heads of household, previously almost non-existent in development theory and practice, were discovered by WID researchers in the 1980s," and were quickly characterized as a highly reified, globalized, pathological category, "bypassed by development, particularly vulnerable, and particularly poor" (1993: 1968).

With the subsequent rise of GAD, the world's many millions of so-called 'women-headed' and other nonnormative forms of household reappeared in a new light. I now see those in the part of rural Bangladesh where I work as being on a multidimensional continuum of differing household arrangements. At least in the vanguard of development analysis, this approach has swept away the taken-for-granted, static, gender status and role characterizations found so often in earlier work. Dynamic, interpersonal models involving intrahousehold 'bargaining' and decision-making renegotiation have replaced them.[8] This approach has also contributed to a tendency to view poverty as a process, as opposed to a state–to look on "the *means* by which basic needs are met rather than [just] on the *extent* to which they are met" (Kabeer 1991: 244). I do not believe that this way of theorizing nonnormative households has as yet made much of an impact on refugee studies, in which media and interest group representations of forced migrants as primarily women and children separated from their normal family structures and household men still hold powerful sway.

Once households were seen as socioculturally informed, dynamic, gendered structures, it was natural to extend the same kind of unpacking process to relations between household individuals and 'the outside'. Again, historically this largely was considered only in regard to nonproblematically conceived 'heads of households' who, except in 'deviant', 'broken', or 'disrupted' households, were always identified with men. Even today, many so-called 'household surveys' done in a development mode—including many carried out in forced migration contexts—are based solely on interviews with men identified as household heads. I know of a number done recently in Bangladesh in which interviewers actually skipped households because no such men were available within them! The perverse consequences of such practices are now obvious in enlightened development circles; they were not twenty years ago.

Following on this, it is not surprising that an increasing number of researchers have found that women have substantially wider community relations, too, and that many of these relations have potent consequences for everyday survival and development. Lacking information on women's extra-household relations, it is not surprising that a number of classic household-based economic audits in Bangladesh have been unable to show how absolutely poor people survive at all; so do some food accessibility audits done in refugee camps. The poorest households there appear to lack sufficient income, aid, and local production even to fulfill basic physiological needs.[9] My own work in rural Bangladesh purposely concentrated closely on very poor women's survival strategies, and perhaps because of this concentration has been able to show that even in this highly patriarchal context women have significant *inter*household social networks and entitlements (Indra and Buchignani 1997). In fact, among a number of these very poor, environmentally displaced households men have often exhausted their kinship-based entitlements, and effective claims asserted by women upon *their* kin frequently determine such basic things as where people find house plots upon which to rebuild their homes. In such cases these same claims thereafter often greatly increase the probability of economically supportive reciprocity between host and guest households. Women's activities outside the household are critical to the survival of the one out of five households of environmentally forced displacees in Bangladesh that would classically be termed 'women-headed'.

Gender and Forced Migration

Women in Forced Migration

There are of course many parallels to be found between the evolution of academic feminist theory, the treatment of women and gender in development, and the much shorter history of forced migration research. These are most evident in forced migration *discourse,* some of which has over the past twenty years followed the same trajectory as that of development. Noreen Spencer-Nimmons's (1994) recent doctoral dissertation, *The Emergence of Refugee Women as a Social Issue,* charts the worldwide rise of what I will call a Women *in* Forced Migration (WIFM) approach to gender issues. By this I mean to imply an explicit parallel with the Women in Development (WID) orientations initiated in the 1970s. As such, WIFM also brings to the fore the need to reform discussion and practice in order to put women more centrally into the forced migration picture.

Spencer-Nimmons shows that this helping institution and interest group-driven WIFM discourse dates from the mid-1980s at best– almost fifteen years after WID was first broached in academic and development circles. She sees the 1985 Decade for Women conference held in Nairobi as an early seminal event (1994: 139), with WIFM gaining significant institutional recognition only from 1988 on. In that year, the Deputy High Commissioner for the UNHCR brought together "more than 150 participants from forty countries who represented over 100 organizations" (Spencer-Nimmons 1994: 319) to discuss refugee women's issues.

Though the general domain of forced migration remains highly fragmented and diverse, I think it is fair to say in overview that WIFM continues to gain strength and influence in research and in the institutional charters of organizations dealing with aid, refugee determination, resettlement, and development. Slowly, it is becoming a fully legitimate, institutionalized element of forced migration discourse. York University's landmark *International Conference on Gender Issues and Refugees: Development Implications* held in Toronto in 1993 exemplifies this rising trend and some of its limitations: while most of the speakers stressed the centrality of gender or its important revisioning potential for a wide range of phenomena relating to forced migration, most presenters also dealt solely with refugee women in need.

I can draw on no overall surveys of the frequency with which WIFM approaches have become integrated into forced migration *programming*–development oriented or otherwise. My overall sense of things is anecdotal, and is drawn from what aid- and development-oriented program plans, reports, and proposals are available to me. The evidence I have suggests that there remains a significant gap between WIFM's incorporation into forced migration bureaucratic charters, research, and discourse and its incorporation into forced migration aid and development practice. This also parallels the uneven history of WID, which, while already considered outmoded by many development theorists, continues to be resisted by others who still formulate and implement development programs without any reference to women at all. It is my impression that most aid and development projects involving forced migrants either remain completely gender neutral (in the negative sense) or else evoke women in policy statements and program guidelines but not in on-the-ground activities. It also appears to me that today's WIFM programs are much more likely to appear in certain contexts rather than others: more often in long-term food provision or supplementation than either in aid-related situations of acute distress or in long-term development initiatives. At the same time, the prevalence of a Women in Forced Migration approach to the provision of aid and to development programming does appear to be increasing, albeit slowly.

GAFM Today

What is the status today of Gender and Forced Migration (GAFM), the forced migration analogue to Gender and Development (GAD)? What is happening in development studies is instructive, and I believe argues strongly that a fully gendered orientation would have significant revisioning potential in forced migration research and practice. Moreover, it is ethically compelling. A key dimension of forced migration—whether politically, economically, environmentally or developmentally driven—is just that: it is *forced*. A majority of the world's forced migrants are at least temporarily unable to control key dimensions of their existence. Those dealing both in practical and representational ways with forced migrants inevitably are placed in positions of power over such individuals. Whether they wish it or not, they and forced migrants often are unequally located in structures of interpretation, representation, decision-making, policy generation, and program delivery. In other, nonrefugee contexts, it has been repeatedly shown how easily the powerful impose their grids of understanding and formulas for action upon the comparatively disempowered, even when this is not intentional.

At the same time, I do not believe that the acceptance of a deeply rooted Gender and Forced Migration approach would, by itself, necessarily automatically lead to a significant alteration of this asymmetry of power in practice. Both feminist anthropology and development research inspired by these principles demonstrate that a GAFM orientation *could* be highly decentering, which *could* in turn lead to greater self-consciousness among researchers and practitioners about how external, taken-for-granted expectations, concepts, ideologies, and world-views are imposed in forced migration contexts. In this regard, the philosopher Elizabeth Minnich (1990: 16, quoted in Beneria 1995: 1839) is correct in asserting that "... the old errors and exclusions and hierarchies are by no means 'only' conceptual; they reveal and perpetuate the articulated hierarchy in intrapsychic, education, social, historical, and political relations that have very serious consequences indeed." Such revisioning or reconceptualizing changes often do work themselves into, and often temporally lead, structural change.

Simply revisioning 'the' household alone in forced migration discourse and research would lead minimally to some pressure to revision refugee aid and development practice; the latter could not thereafter so easily be done in good conscience without a situational, interpretative understanding of local migrant women's and men's world-views and everyday lives. Such situated, interpretative understandings have some probability of generating practical programs that would be less likely to mute and speak for forced migrant women and men than programs typically do today.

At a more general level, a GAFM approach could help forced migration researchers become less frequently the conceptual captives of international folk and agency discourse. Malkki (1995) rightly identifies the unconscious use of folk social problems discourse to frame research as a major impediment to the theoretical development of anthropological research on forced migration, imbuing research with persistent essentialist, globalizing, functionalist biases. I believe that a GAFM approach may allow forced migration researchers to be more sensitive to situationality and variability, so that, in the end, each research-generated representation of forced migrants tells, if not a different tale, then at least a gendered, meaningfully different local variant of the story. Establishing this as the standard for research will be a struggle. There will be many who find a GAFM approach unnecessary or an actual impediment to 'getting on with the job' of collecting baseline information used to facilitate the provision of assistance to forced migrants. Moreover, it is methodologically hard to *do* research that does not representationally conform to one of the pervasive, almost mythological themes of refugees that have developed over the last fifty years: hard to collect sufficiently detailed local level data that is both valid and reliable; hard to maintain the variability of collected data through the analysis phase; and hard to write.

Beyond revisioning, the more extensive use of engendered knowledge in forced migration practice could induce and guide meaningful structural change. GAFM does not conceptualize group or institutional cultures as ungendered, uncontested wholes. Neither does it take gendered structures of power as givens—either structures of power among helpers or those being helped. These cultures and power structures are themselves therefore potential objects of both study and change. In many cases, even representing cultural frames and structures of power within, say, aid organizations and forced migrant 'ethnic groups' as open to observation and reformation will be highly threatening. Practice based on a GAFM orientation in particular will negotiate highly difficult moral terrain, as it requires both researchers and practitioners to articulate between a variety of different and not necessarily complementary ethical and cultural systems. I think that the firm establishment of a GAFM orientation in forced migration discourse and research will take quite some time. Its meaningful incorporation into development programming generally has come slowly, and this remains a distant goal for programs dealing with forced migrants. In the meantime, a Gender in Forced Migration (GIFM) approach to practice will always be more appropriate to a wide range of situations than a GAFM orientation, and the further development of targeted 'women's programs' in such situations ought to be strongly supported.

I believe we should, if nothing else, recognize these facts, and not assume that the increased use of the word 'gender' in forced migration circles means that there now exists a broad-based commitment to further gender practical programming. The latter will of course face much bureaucratic resistance, some of which will itself reflect prevailing gender ideologies. In addition, the thorough implementation of GAFM into actual programs requires much more fundamental institutional change and much greater up-front knowledge of the empirical situation than does an 'add women and stir' strategy. Elizabeth Minnich (1990) observes that "this is [one reason] why the transformation is a difficult one: it addresses deeply ingrained prejudices and it challenges deeply entrenched 'ways of knowing', of theorizing and of 'doing science'." It also challenges comfortable, highly containable, increasingly status quo ways that bureaucracies have found to 'add women' to otherwise unchanged policies and to some programs.

Beyond a Room of One's Own

To return a final time to my architectural analogy, the fashioning of a forced migration house as an engendered space is an obvious advance over providing women an attic room of their own. It is highly useful to know where all the people and furnishings are located, and to know that one should pause to reorient oneself when moving from room to room. Still, this must inevitably remain an odd house: one without any commonly understood, readily available floor plan shared either by occupants or outsiders, and, especially, one where there is likely to be sharp, fundamental disagreement about possible renovations.

Both the revisioning and revolutionary dimensions of GAFM call for one thing about which there *is* growing consensus: the need for much greater situationally specific, diversity-maintaining, in-depth knowledge of individual women and men who are forced migrants, and of the class, ethnic, cultural, subcultural, national, and transnational systems with which they articulate. This cannot possibly be achieved only through nonreciprocal, outsider-controlled research. The development of rigorous, theoretically grounded and locally based and staffed programs of forced migration knowledge collection and analysis clearly remains a high priority.

And yet I do not believe that this alone will suffice. There is also a need for reciprocal, international research and for training ties between locally based programs and those elsewhere, so that the gendered knowledge thereby produced can more often share in the best of both opportunities: local grounding and participation in a polysemic, international discourse that is revisioning gender around the world.

Notes

1. I will illustrate my discussion through reference to my own ongoing fieldwork with rural, environmentally displaced Bangladeshis in Kazipur Thana of Siraj-ganj District. These several thousand individuals and their families and communities—most of them desperately poor—living alongside the ever-wandering Jamuna River are among the many millions of people in Bangladesh who have at one time or another been displaced by environmental factors, that is, by river-bank shifting and land erosion.

2. For a review of this issue, see Pamela A. De Vos (1993).

3. This orthodox, highly male-centered "man the hunter" view of the hunting and gathering societies ancestral to all of us was usefully challenged by feminists stressing the centrality of "women the gatherer." The classic view of foraging societies as centrally organized around male hunting along with more contemporary views are epitomized by chapters in Lee and Devore (1968). For an early rebuttal of the classic view, see Sally Linton (1971).

4. Many scholars have reminded us that Western thought is often framed in an oppositional mode. This has been well researched in terms of defining woman against

the definition of man. In this regard Kamuf and Miller (1990: 121, 133) query whether by focusing on the relations between women and men Western feminist research in this vein has accomplished "the last project of phallocentricism."

5. Agarwal notes here (1994: 278) "the building up of gender-specific empirical evidence and analysis, especially since the mid-1970s, which exposed a systematic gender gap in how the benefits and burdens of development were being distributed."

6. Geisler (1993) identifies feminist anthropologists involved in development as key "voices of dissent" from the forming WID paradigm. To quote Rathgeber (1990: 493–4) once more: "[GAD] ... finds its theoretical roots in socialist feminism and has bridged the gap left by the modernization theorists by linking the relations of production to the relations of reproduction and taking into account all aspects of women's lives. Socialist feminists have identified the social construction of production and reproduction as the basis of women's oppression and have focused attention on the social relations of gender, questioning the validity of roles that have been ascribed to both women and men in different societies. Although they have not trivialized the importance of greater female participation in all aspects of social, political, and economic life, their primary focus has been on an examination of why women systematically have been assigned to inferior and/or secondary roles. Socialist feminists have combined an analysis of the impact of patriarchy with some aspects of a more traditional Marxist approach in attempting to address this concern."

7. Geisler (1993: 1968) goes further and argues that the identification of women's problems in WID programs often shifts the key orienting issue from inequality to such things as income disparity under highly contained status quo terms.

8. Advocates now counsel the application of entitlement analysis to "bargaining" (Sen, 1990: 123) between poor household women and men that highlights both gender inequities and women's "'agency' as opposed to [just] their well being" (Sen, 1990: 148). While "this often appears" as what Kandiyoti (1988: 275) terms "the patriarchal bargain," which implies fundamental subjugation of women to men "... it also suggests fluidity and re-negotiation" (Kabeer 1990: 138). It also involves a recognition that, received ideologies about the centrality of the family and household notwithstanding, women may have "self-interests other than the collective interest of the domestic group" (Papanek 1990: 181).

9. See Jiggins (1986) for a general discussion of poor women's responses to seasonal variations in income and food availability.

2

Gendering Those Uprooted
by 'Development'

Elizabeth Colson

Gender, Development, Refugees, and Resettlement

The Gendered Literature

Boserup long since pointed out that households or families are composed of individuals whose productive roles and ability to benefit from production are determined or at least strongly influenced by the structure of gendered relationships (1970). This has become at least a rhetorical commonplace among those who critique development projects, especially those that purport to serve agricultural populations, and the literature on the roles of women in agriculture and as wage earners and how these are affected by centralized planning is now vast (see for example, Adepoju and Oppong 1994; Afsar 1991; Ahmed 1984; Beneria 1982; Chilvers 1992; Creevey 1986; Dauber and Cain 1981; Davidson 1988; Dixon, 1980; Gladwin 1991; Guyer 1986b; Lele 1986; Mencher and Okongwu 1993; Moser 1989; Poats, Schmink, and Spring 1988; Savane 1986; Spring 1979; Staudt 1990; Tinker 1990).

The gendered refugee is less common, and the refugee literature is still biased toward undifferentiated 'people' without gender, age, or other defining characteristics except ethnicity. Even so, some writers have focused on the way women and children are affected by the events leading to flight; the traumas of the flight itself; and the way basic gender and age identities become reorganized as men, women, and children are affected by life in refugee camps or elsewhere in exile (see for example, Ahearn and Athey 1991; Allman et al. 1989; Burton 1982; Callaway 1987; Daley 1991; Gilad 1990; Harrell-Bond 1986: 266–82; Indra 1987, 1989a; Kibreab 1995; Lipsky and Nimol 1993; Martin 1993; McSpadden and Moussa 1993; Moussa 1993; Reynell 1989; Salinas 1989; Simon and Brettell 1986; Spring 1982; Taft 1987). Armstrong, for one, who worked in refugee camps in Tanzania, maintains that women in such camps commonly find themselves newly disadvantaged: "Their position remains one of under-privilege, overwork, and exploitation" (1991: 218). He notes how women in the Tanzanian camps are affected by the absence of a support network provided by relatives, the alienation due to the likelihood that they do not share a common language with their hosts, the sheer labor load involved in building and maintaining the camp, and the uncertainties of provisioning when they live on distributed food. Moreover, what they like about their new environment may be transitory, as the schools and health services provided by international agencies in the early days of a camp are then handed over to local governments (1991: 219–20).

Oddly, given this awareness that 'gender counts', when people are uprooted because their land is wanted for *economic* reasons usually associated with visions of national development, their multiple identities tend to disappear: they become the ungendered uprooted, or are dealt with as undifferentiated families or households. As Koenig (1995: 22) says, "the particular effects of involuntary resettlement on women have been relatively ignored, beyond the general recognition that women suffer more than men from the problems of resettlement projects." Wali (1989), in her fine study of the Bayano displacement in eastern Panama, finds at least a partial exception to this caveat.

Of the thirteen authors who contributed to the recent volume on the consequences of development-induced displacement (McDowell 1996), only one suggests that women are among those displaced or that individuals at different points on the life cycle may respond differently (Thangaraj 1996). The displaced are almost equally ungendered in the 1985 volume edited by Cernea on putting 'people' first and in the 1993 volume edited by Cernea and Guggenheim, although the latter purports to deal with anthropological approaches to involuntary resettlement. Only Aberle, who writes of the Navajo having been forced to move as a consequence of the settlement of the Hopi/Navajo land dispute, makes it plain that Navajo women were "particularly devastated by relocation" and that older relocated women "lost one of their most important functions" when they no longer had stock to supervise (Aberle 1993: 169, 171). Guggenheim, writing of resettlement in Mexico caused by a large hydroelectric project, notes that in the absence of men, women took on the role of family representative in public meetings where those resettled met with government administrators and technicians (Guggenheim 1993: 231). These authors only hint at the many ways that gender roles are affected in relocation by disruption of status and power hierarchies, geographical dispersal of kin and friendship networks, new residence patterns, loss of economic resources, differential access to new resources, shifts in work patterns, exposure to strangers with different lifestyles, and different expectations.

Koenig has tried to pull together what is known about how gender affects those involved in involuntary resettlement, but because of the paucity of data she has had to attempt to extrapolate from what is known from refugee studies and the study of those recruited to agricultural resettlement schemes (1995: 22). She is concerned to show how subsequent access to resources reflects previous economic resources and access to political power and involvement in the planning for resettlement. She finds that women who made gains after resettlement were likely to have been involved in earlier negotiations about the move and to have had class positions that gave them control over material resources and social networks. Those with the most power gained most, those with the least power lost most. In an earlier, unpublished but presented paper, she concluded that "those most at risk are female-headed households, particularly those without male kin" (1992: 5).

But much of her evidence came from studies of refugees and voluntary agricultural settlement schemes: for evidence on the gendered impact of forced resettlement in conjunction with a major development project, she relied largely upon findings from the study of Gwembe Tonga of Zambia, whose land was taken for the building of Kariba Hydroelectric Dam and the creation of Kariba Lake (Colson 1971; Colson and Scudder 1975; Scudder 1969; Scudder and Colson 1972).[1]

The Development-Uprooted

Does the experience of women uprooted by a large-scale development project differ from that of women refugees or women whose families have a choice of whether to go or stay?

Women forced to move because of development share with refugees the trauma of uprooting, though they are less likely to be subject to enemy violence or the death of children and other close kin in flight. They also have more opportunity to relocate with some possessions in an orderly departure and may be moved with neighbors and kin, thus maintaining long-established social ties. They *should* arrive less traumatized in their new locations. On the other hand, refugees may have realistic hopes of return once the crisis is over while those whose lands are flooded or otherwise preempted for development are told they cannot go home again. Where governments accept some responsibility for those uprooted due to development, the processes of resettlement in a new area often have characteristics common to the placement of refugees in long-lasting holding camps or the settlement of voluntary immigrants on official agricultural schemes. Among the latter, wives accompanying husbands who volunteered to join the scheme may have had little option and feel as dispossessed as those officially labeled as involuntary resettlers.

Koenig (1992: 6) believes that gender differentiation "would appear to play itself out quite differently in urban and rural areas," due, perhaps, to the greater number of female-headed households in urban areas. I know little of what happens to women forced to resettle because of urban renewal or other urban projects that disrupt communities, and I shall not attempt to deal with them here. Instead, I am concerned with rural women and with those who find themselves moved to new areas officially designated as resettlement areas. Robert Chambers, basing his observations primarily on experience with voluntary agricultural settlements, pointed out long ago that "The lot of women is often worsened by settlement. It is true that there have been cases where they have benefited ... But such cases are exceptional" (1969: 174). He goes on: "Not only have women often lost their traditional sources of income, but their husbands have usually acquired a monopoly of new income ... and bitter family quarrels have arisen from the husbands' new economic monopoly ..." (1969: 175). Brain, who looked at resettlement schemes in Tanzania in the late 1960s, concluded that "women were far worse off on the settlement scheme than in their traditional societies" (1976: 265). Bernal (1988: 131–3), writing specifically of irrigation schemes in the Sudan, argued that resettlement schemes based on irrigation have a profound effect on family dynamics, as women lose rights over land and the resources needed to work the land while income from the land is vested in the male designated as household head.

Yet some recent studies have come to less negative appraisals of the gendered impact of agricultural schemes. McMillan (1995: 93–95) found that planners of resettlement schemes in Burkina Faso ignored women's previous control over fields and their own labor, and that women on the scheme now relied upon gifts from husbands or other kinsmen to make good the drop in their own earnings. On the other hand, crops they did grow were no longer used primarily to feed the family, the man who had been allocated land now accepting this responsibility. Such money as women earned, including that earned through the sale of produce, was used for personal needs or investment. She concluded: "[T]he actual impact of the AVV [scheme] was less negative and more complex than could be deduced from an analysis based on a point-in-time survey limited to the agricultural project itself" (1995: 95). In the Sudan, some Shukriya Arab women settled on the New Halfa irrigation scheme certainly preferred living on the scheme to life in their old area, stressing the availability of water, money, and shops (Salem-Murdock 1989: 14– 15, 109).

But the Shukriya had chosen to come. Nubian women on the same scheme who had been forced from their homes by the building of the Aswan Dam continued to mourn their lost homeland along the Nile. Married Nubian women had initially favored resettlement because they thought the promised economic opportunities would allow labor migrant husbands to earn a living locally; those opportunities, however, had not been realized. Their husbands were once more migrants, and they were left in a land for which they had no love (Fahim 1983: 41, 67–68).[2]

All this suggests that those resettled are concerned about a wide range of issues with gender implications. These encompass but, as Koenig says (1995: 31), are not confined to economic issues. Resettlement involves a reordering of gender relationships across a wide spectrum, but that reordering emerges from previous assumptions about gender and the gendered experience of those involved, as Indra stresses in this volume. People are usually aware of expectations structuring formal gender roles. They may or may not be aware of underlying assumptions. There is little appreciation for how previous experience arising from behaving in accordance with gendered expectations limits or advantages people when they are faced with new challenges. This is what I propose to examine here, using data from the experience of the Gwembe Tonga of Southern Zambia, who were displaced in 1958 when Kariba Dam was completed and Kariba Lake flooded much of their territory.

The Kariba Resettlement

Gender Definitions at Resettlement

In 1956, Gwembe Tonga occupied that portion of the Middle Zambezi Valley known as the Gwembe Valley. The majority of the fifty-five thousand inhabitants of Gwembe District cultivated rich soils on either side of the Zambezi River, which formed the boundary between what were then Northern Rhodesia and Southern Rhodesia and today are Zambia and Zimbabwe. About sixty miles of rough terrain rising through the Zambezi escarpment separated the river villages from the commercial development taking place on the western plateau, with its railway line, highway, European settlement, and railway townships. At the beginning of the 1950s the absence of roads and wheeled transport isolated Gwembe residents from participation in the cash crop economy already in place on the plateau.

In Gwembe villages, gender together with age served to structure most relationships in the years immediately before the building of Kariba Dam, which was completed in 1958. Gendered relationships then current were accepted as traditional, although they reflected the demands of the colonial system and had emerged during the twentieth century while the territory was under colonial rule (Colson 1960; Scudder 1962). Able-bodied men between the years of about eighteen and forty-five migrated to work outside the Gwembe Valley (about 40 percent being absent at any one time) because they needed a cash income for taxes and a minimum of imported goods; cash was hard to earn in Gwembe. Women stayed home to maintain homesteads, manage stock, work fields, and care for children. Girls looked forward to early marriage and a life in the village, usually one within their home neighborhood where they would have the support of their own kin. Few women ever traveled more than ten miles from home. Boys looked forward to trips to cities or mines in southern Africa interspersed with periods at home during which they would marry a number of wives and beget children. Only in middle age would they be able to remain permanently in the village supported by inherited and self-cleared fields, the labor of wives, and cash payments from working sons and sons-in-law.

Most women had fields given to them by their own kin. These they controlled and could pass on to their own heirs. They also expected to be allocated land by their husband and to work in fields reserved to the husband. In case of divorce, they kept their own fields but lost allocated land, as they also did if they refused to be inherited by a dead husband's kinsman. Produce was stored in separate granaries—grain from the husband's field went into his granary whether or not he had been home to work the crop, while each wife had granaries in which she stored produce from her own fields and allocated fields.

A woman expected to feed herself, her children, her husband, and any other dependent from her own granaries, and only when her supplies were exhausted were the husband's granaries broached. Grain surplus to subsistence therefore vested largely in the husband. A husband also used the surplus and his wives' labor to provide the hospitality that widened and reinforced his social relationships. A man invested his surplus primarily in additional wives and livestock, or exchanged it for other goods. A woman also invested in livestock, but had less to invest because her fields had to feed her household. At death, the surviving spouse was protected against the claims of the other's heirs, for the survivor kept food stored in his or her granaries and any food still growing in his or her fields. In case of divorce, the wife took the food in her granary when she moved to her kin.

New fields above the Zambezi River or its tributaries were cleared by men when needed, though women could and did use an axe when necessary. Whoever cleared a field or organized a work party to clear a field claimed it and had the right to allocate it to others. Newly cleared land, therefore, vested in individual men, but might be allocated to women who had use-only rights. When rivers realigned and new river gardens became potentially available, either men or women might move in to clear reeds and sand, and thus both women and men acquired individual rights in such fields and could reallocate them as they pleased.

Houses and other structures were built by male labor, though women and children cut and brought thatching grass and mudded dwelling houses. A woman owned her house only if she was single. Both men and women planted, cultivated, and harvested most crops, but because of male labor migration, much field work fell to women and children. Gathering, fishing, hunting, and crafts were gendered activities.

Men controlled their own labor and that of dependent sons and sisters' sons, who, however, tried to establish their independence as they established their marriages. Men gained control over female labor largely through marriage: they could give orders to their wives, within limits. Widows, divorcées, and unmarried girls attached to their households were a potential but less reliable source of labor. Women could expect assistance from their husbands, but their greatest control over male labor was derived from their right to make demands on the husbands of their daughters during the early years of a marriage. Sons-in-law could be called upon to clear a field, build a field shelter, or build a house or granary. Sons and other male matrilineal kin were potential but unreliable sources of labor. Extra labor was organized through work parties, for which one needed resources in grain for food or for the making of beer.

Before resettlement, primary schools existed in a few villages, but few boys and even fewer girls attended for more than a year or two.

Boys learned something of the larger world through their work experiences. Girls had no such opportunities. In the years before Kariba Dam was built, almost no strangers visited Gwembe Valley, and women met only those from their immediate vicinity. Girls usually married within their birth neighborhoods and relied upon the continued presence of their kin to protect their interests while they lived in homesteads headed by their husbands and worked under the husband's authority—although with a good deal of autonomy during his long absences at work.

While gendered relationships governed much of their lives, they thought of gender as operating through their roles as daughters, sisters, mothers, etc., as well as through the role of wife. Through these roles they expected to gain status and satisfaction and behave as responsible people. The men in their lives were again judged as they fulfilled their obligations as fathers, brothers, sons, husbands, etc.

Class differences were minimal. Gwembe ethics emphasized an egalitarian ideology, with adults, especially men, having much autonomy. When decisions had to be made, whatever level of social group was concerned, those involved sat together for discussion, negotiation, and decision. Men sat separately, usually in kinship groups facing each other, while women sat to one side. Men first discussed, but then formally communicated their discussion and conclusion to the women, who in turn had their say. This was taken back to the men who took the women's advice into consideration. Senior women expected to be heard, and even junior women and men thought they had the right to be informed of decisions that affected them. One not informed usually refused to cooperate in what had been decided. The spirit world empowered both men and women. Both could be guardians of the spirits of the dead, and both could be mediums of spirits appealed to for rain and other communal benefits.

But in the system of authority inaugurated by the colonial government, only men served as chiefs, counselors, and headmen, and colonial officials dealt with the rest of the population through these authorities or through men as family heads. By definition, women were not included in the colonial-authorized local government, and since it did not address them directly and as individuals, they saw little reason to heed any of its orders.

In pre-resettlement times, therefore, broad gender assumptions existed that precluded women from learning much of the world outside Gwembe and gave them no training for dealing with a governmental hierarchy or its agents; this was irrespective of the gendered kinship definitions that related women to other women and to the males of their society. Their knowledge of European settlers, industry, and colonial government was filtered through the males who had the right to encounter such phenomena, which women saw as dangerous and alien: so dangerous and alien, indeed, that they expressed their anxieties in the form of possession cults through which they embodied such mysteries as airplanes, railways, colonial government, aliens, and the experiences men encountered while at work (Colson 1969, 1977; Luig 1992).

Uprooting and Its Aftermath

When a community is uprooted, role expectations are stretched, as people either cannot or refuse to meet obligations once assumed to be normal and yet are faced with situations outside their experience. This happens regardless of the divergent assumptions held by representatives of central governments or other planners of resettlement and those to be resettled.

In cases such as the Kariba Resettlement, resettlement was in fact a direct attack upon gendered relationships, since it represented a political defeat for those resettled. It was traumatic for all involved, though probably least so for youngsters who may well enjoy the turmoil and the excitement associated with the move and the exploration of a new terrain. Men and women, however, responded differently. Women bemoaned the move the longest, and found it hardest to adapt to loss of familiar surroundings. Men felt the immediate sting of defeat. It was they who had been expected to argue with officials and openly oppose the move. Some died in the one attempt to abort the move by force. Others went to prison for their defiance. All felt that they had lost face when their powerlessness was demonstrated to themselves and to the women who looked to them to defend their interests against outsiders.

Their frustration in turn vented itself upon the vulnerable: their wives and children. Wives and children, in turn, were more vulnerable because when resettlement disrupted old neighborhoods, women could be separated from kin who would normally give them refuge and negotiate for better treatment. Wives had been beaten before the move: a husband was assumed to have the right to discipline a lazy, disrespectful, or unfaithful woman. Even so, the wife had the right of appeal to her own kin. Given the initial crowded housing after resettlement, kin, even when available, were less likely to give sanctuary to beaten women. An increase in physical violence against women–gendered behavior though not gender dictated–was one immediate consequence of the Kariba resettlement. Similar behavior has been reported in refugee camps, and is probably to be expected whenever men are humiliated, frustrated, and unable to strike back at the powerful who have demeaned them. When, as in the Kariba case, the early years of resettlement are also associated with an increasing availability of alcohol, violence is even more likely.

Resettlement also reduced women's property rights. This was associated with a redistribution of land rights and access to other resources (Colson 1966, 1971). Elsewhere, such a reduction has often been attributed to gendered assumptions of administrators stemming from the West. In the Kariba case, these were less immediately influential than the gender assumptions that Gwembe people carried in their heads.

Officials planned initially to allocate land to heads of households (characteristically assumed to be male), as apparently has been the common practice in most resettlement schemes. This was contested, and men proceeded to demarcate and cut fields for themselves and sometimes for dependents. Women made almost no attempt to establish independent claims to fields in the new area, although they must have been aware that this made them vulnerable in the case of divorce or the death of a husband; they would then be left without land of their own and thrown back on relatives. They had the physical strength to clear land, and had cleared river fields in the old area. They had more time available than before the move, given that initially thereafter fields were small and they were no longer cultivating dry season gardens. It is doubtful that men could have prevented them from clearing. A handful of women in fact did arrange to have land cleared, saying they wanted to have land that they themselves controlled.

Other women lost out for two reasons: their own gendered perceptions of appropriate behavior and their lack of understanding of what had happened. The last was a consequence of their previous restricted exposure to industrial development and markets. Women assumed that men ought to clear fields and that a married woman had the right to a field supplied by her husband, either cut by himself or allocated from his inherited land. They also assumed that their use of the field would be protected as long as the marriage lasted. A woman could acquire more secure rights by exercising her claims to a son-in-law's labor, and an unmarried woman could usually inveigle male kin to give her a portion of a cleared field. In the circumstances of resettlement, however, when all fields initially required clearing, it was almost impossible for a woman to obtain a field except as a wife. It was a time of heavy labor demands for rebuilding homesteads and clearing land. Men gave priority to clearing and building for themselves and their wives. They resented claims of women kin and urged widows and divorcées into marriages, often with men considered bad marriage bets. They ignored such responsibilities if women kin were settled at a distance.

Administrative decisions did have long-term implications for gender relationships, and these affected land rights indirectly. The colonial government had agreed that compensation should be paid for houses and, on a per capita basis irrespective of age or sex, for loss of production. There was no payment for lost land. Administrators were used to dealing with men, and they proceeded to hand payments to heads of homesteads or male taxpayers, who in some instances received very substantial sums by Gwembe standards. Some gave a small part of their per capita payment to wives and children for clothing or other requirements, but women received little in comparison with the amount appropriated by their male representative. The latter used a good deal of this money to buy food before new fields came into production, but many also invested in more wives and in scotch carts, plows, and cattle.

During the years when people had to reestablish themselves on the land, men therefore financed work parties to clear fields using grain brought from the old areas or bought with compensation money. Women's grain had usually been consumed by the family immediately after resettlement, and women received only a minor fraction of the compensation money. They usually lacked grain for work parties, and if they had grain they usually preferred to use it in brewing, which brought them an immediate cash return (Colson and Scudder 1988).

Personal experiences, affected by gender expectations, also influenced women's willingness to invest in fields, which they regarded as ephemeral assets that would soon be abandoned. Men had more experience with industry and technology, and were more willing to believe that the Europeans could build a dam and that Kariba Lake, once formed, would be permanent–though there were skeptics enough among them. A year or so after the move, even the most skeptical males accepted that they must clear fields to produce food for the next season or so, even if they thought they might eventually recover their old fields. Moreover, as husbands, they had an obligation to provide their wives with land to cultivate. To clear fields was to establish rights in them. In contrast, women held out the hope that the lake would be transitory; ten and fifteen years after resettlement they still asked when the dam would be destroyed and the old area reemerge. In the short run, they had no need to worry about depending on their husbands for fields; they had always depended on their husbands for fields. Their tenure would be secure enough so long as their marriages lasted, and if they divorced, then a new husband would provide a new field which would tide them over until they could go home.

Other government actions, some ostensibly gender neutral, also tilted the balance in favor of male control of land. Resettlement areas were cleared of tsetse fly, making it possible to cultivate with plow oxen. The government also trained men to undertake net-fishing in the forming lake and employed local people to build roads, schools, and wells in resettlement areas. The employed were men, for only men were accustomed to work for wages. From compensation payments, fishing, and wage labor, men acquired the capital to equip themselves for plow agriculture and for cultivating larger acreages.

For several years immediately following resettlement, women probably did less agricultural work than before the move, as fields were then small and cultivated only during the rains. Thereafter, fields expanded, and men increased demands on wives and other dependents for field labor. At the same time, an improved road system and the spread of small shops and buying stations made it easier to sell produce. Men who controlled fields and plowing equipment could assert rights over all produce and any cash income derived from what were now family enterprises.

In the late 1960s, the independent Zambian government expanded agricultural extension work and credit and encouraged moves into cotton farming. Extension services and credit were primarily directed at men, who in turn delegated much of the field labor to wives and dependents–while they received the check and claimed the right to spend it arbitrarily. Some men went so far as to forbid wives to grow food crops because they wanted their labor for cotton.

How extension services were delivered reflected gender assumptions held both by Zambian males influenced by Western education and by representatives of international organizations. In turn, women were vulnerable to this form of exploitation because they had earlier made decisions based on their own gender expectations and were influenced by the way these had restricted their access to information crucial for underwriting their futures.

In 1957 most Gwembe women had fields of their own which gave them independent resources. By the 1970s, although many women had small vegetable plots over which they asserted independent rights, most younger married women said that they cultivated together with their husband and had no fields allocated to them for their own use. Cash cropping also made it possible for many men to remain permanently at home where they assumed a managerial position over the family work force. Younger women were unlikely to have their own granaries, even though some men saw homestead granaries as under their wives' control since the granaries held food to feed the household: the rest of the grain was sold from the field. In case of divorce or the death of a husband, ownership of the food supply was subject to litigation, while the husband's kin commonly claimed the fields upon his death.

An Expanding Horizon

In the 1970s, over ten years after removal, those women who remembered conditions in the old regime often said the old life was better because river fields were permanent and they had their own land and were surrounded by supportive kin. Younger women might well say they preferred the new area, and all liked some of what they saw as deriving from the move. They liked the new ease of movement, the existence of shops, the increased supply of money, and the sense of belonging to a national community.

Fears associated with the resettlement period, especially fears of unfamiliar surroundings, broke the ban on women leaving the area, and young women were permitted to accompany husbands who left for work. By the time the fears had subsided, it was accepted that women should migrate with husbands. Many who settled in towns turned to petty trading to increase the family income or to provide themselves with a personal income. By the 1970s women and children were traveling throughout Zambia to visit kin working in other provinces. A few Gwembe women had lived in Europe.

Younger women also had more exposure to education than the women of 1958. Resettlement coincided with a new interest in education on the part of the colonial government and a drive to increase the number of girls in school. Funds became available for scholarships for girls, and while the first generation of girls to enter secondary school had a dismal record of success—many becoming pregnant by teachers and school boys who denied responsibility—enough succeeded and found jobs to convince others, including parents, that girls should be sent on to school. In boarding schools, as in towns, they were exposed to different perceptions of appropriate gender relationships (Lungu and Sinyangwe 1987). A life based on agriculture and dependence on the land became but one alternative, rather than the destiny of every girl, and some women no longer defined themselves primarily as producers of food and producers of children. If the roles now available to them were still gendered, gender definitions had shifted.

In the meantime, within five years of resettlement Gwembe villagers (including women) had become incorporated into a market economy. Everyone now needed money, as had not been true in

1958. For the most part, people had more money, and this included single women. The creation of the Kariba Lake fisheries and the development of a small-scale labor market within the district attracted immigrants and encouraged a movement of people from one part of the valley to another. Marriage pools widened, and the increased number of potential husbands gave women a new bargaining power both as unmarried girls and as dissatisfied wives. Fish sales, local employment, and the sale of agricultural produce also created a market for skills associated with the old division of labor. Women sold cooked food and did still better by selling beer and, later, more potent drinks (Colson and Scudder 1988). Husbands might try to claim a share in the profits, but most women seem to have been able to retain much of what they made. This paid for clothes, school fees for children, and various other needs.

Much of what women earned went for immediate consumption, but they also invested against the future in stock (including cattle), rather than in land and agricultural equipment. They also began to claim rights as mothers against male kin, who had previously monopolized the maternal kin's share of their daughters' marriage payments. Men with property became more willing to forego such payments to forestall arguments with sisters' children who made claims on wealth said to have been generated from marriage payments for their mothers and sisters. Men settled in cities were also willing to be replaced by their sisters as holders of matrilineally acquired property. Before resettlement, few women owned cattle, even though many owned sheep and goats. Now many women have cattle and goats over which husbands exercise no claims.

Women have also learned to put a cash value on their labor, even if this is family labor. A few have brought suit, on divorce, for a share of any money paid for the crop they helped to grow on fields claimed by their husbands. They are also aware that legislation passed in 1989 (championed by women living elsewhere in Zambia) gives wives more substantial rights to inherit on the death of a husband. While most are afraid to claim their rights under this act, some are prepared to argue their case before the local court, which in some instances has awarded them land and cattle.

Before resettlement, women had claims to inherit land and movable property as members of their own matrilineage, and had minimal use rights to property vested in a husband. Husband and wife maintained separate estates, and a woman's rights in land, produce, and stock were not confused with the rights a man obtained over his wife's labor. The vesting of fields and control of agricultural produce and its profits in male household heads that occurred after resettlement has had the unexpected long-term consequence of redefining male estates as the property of the *household,* giving a wife a new stake in the joint enterprise. But her gain as a wife is at the cost of the rights that women exercise in other gendered roles as mothers, sisters, and sisters' daughters, and that males have exercised as a man's brothers and sisters' sons. Overall, women's right to the inheritance of male property is increasing at the expense of males, but by virtue of their role as wives rather than as maternal kin.

What we do *not* know is how much of all of this would have come about without resettlement, as a consequence of the political and economic choices made as Zambians pursued modernization and immersed themselves in a market economy. Certainly, changes in the inheritance law were initiated by elite women and their supporters, only a tiny number of whom had originated in Gwembe. The increasing economic differentiation occurring throughout Zambia had alerted them to the inequity involved when male claims on the labor of their wives and children resulted in estates over which wives and children had no claim.

Gendered Responses

Indra recognizes that gender structures much of what happens in circumstances of forced resettlement because gender is "a key *relational* dimension of human activity and thought –activity and thought informed by cultural and individual notions of men and women" (Indra, this volume).

Since gender is a cultural artifact, however much it may play upon sexual characteristics, the "key *relational* dimensions" must of necessity vary from place to place and over time. How people respond to forced migration will be gendered, but it will vary given that they come to the experience with different "cultural and individual notions." We can also be certain that migration and resettlement are transformative experiences that must lead to a reevaluation of those very cultural and individual notions that inform gender constructs. But how they will change over time is something we need to examine more thoroughly.

Too few studies of forced resettlement associated with large-scale technical schemes have looked at those affected as gendered individuals. In consequence, data from the study of the Kariba resettlement have been relied upon too heavily by those trying to generalize about this form of forced resettlement. It is difficult to generalize even for those Gwembe Tonga resettled within Zambia, given the varied experiences they brought to resettlement and the varied resources of the areas in which they were settled (Colson and Scudder 1975). Gwembe Tonga resettled within Zimbabwe show even greater contrasts, as they faced a different political regime that restricted access to land, employment, schools, and other possibilities until the 1980s (Reynolds 1991). We need a good many more studies that spell out what happens to different populations, with different initial resources, who encounter different conditions and make compromises over time.

Koenig (1995) has made a start by suggesting key factors on which to concentrate when she hypothesizes that responses of any one population will vary with differential access to resources in political and economic power and to knowledge and—crucial factors in determining individual outcomes. It is also possible to spell out some probable gender consequences when rural people are forced to resettle and are resettled as communities in areas made available to them: (1) Women are vulnerable to greater physical violence from husbands and other close male kin, given the frustrations of the period and that anger is projected onto available targets. (2) Women's rights to property are likely to be undercut by their own ideas of appropriate behavior as well as by deliberate policy decisions. (3) Gendered assumptions about familial roles will restrict access to economic resources so that women are likely to make their gains through using existing skills to occupy less lucrative economic niches not immediately usurped by male competitors. (4) Since resettlement almost invariably brings migrants into greater contact with outsiders and greater immersion in a market economy, old ideas about gendered relationships will be profoundly changed as people live in new areas and compare their lives with those whom they see as more privileged. (5) The processes of renegotiating relationships will be anything but easy, for those with power rarely cede it willingly, especially if the power remaining to them is control of women.

Notes

1. Research among Gwembe Tonga in Zambia in relationship to the proposed resettlement was initiated in 1956 by Thayer Scudder and myself, and we have since then made repeated visits to the Gwembe Valley and interviewed many who have now settled elsewhere. Mary Elizabeth Scudder was associated with the field research in 1962–63, 1972, and 1981–82. In 1987–88 Jonathan Habarad participated in the study, and more recently Sam Clark, Lisa Cliggett and Rhonda Netting-Gillette have initiated their own research in conjunction with the study. The Institute for Economic and Political Studies of the University of Zambia (formerly the Institute for African Studies, and before that the Rhodes-Livingstone Institute) has been the main sponsor of the Gwembe Study within Zambia since its inception in 1956. In addition, research by myself or Scudder has been supported by the University of California, Berkeley; the California Institute of Technology; the Joint Committee on Africa of the Social Science Research Council and the American Council of Learned Societies; the National Institutes of Health; the Food and Agriculture Organization of the United Nations; the John Simon Guggenheim Memorial Foundation; Harvest Help; and the National Science Foundation.

2. For the Nubian resettlement see also Fahim (1981), but in that volume he had little to say on differential gender impacts.

3

Interview with Barbara Harrell-Bond

Doreen Indra

Q. *Before becoming involved in refugee studies you had established yourself studying more conventional anthropological subjects in Sierra Leone. How did you come to do the field research on African forced migrants that was the basis for your book,* Imposing Aid?

A. Well, first of all, I have never been "established" as a "conventional anthropologist" in the sense of having a 'my' people approach, nor did I ever study "conventional" anthropological subjects! My first research was in fact in a housing estate in Oxford, Blackbird Leys. It was the last, largest, most 'progressive' housing estate built in Britain and was intended for working-class migrants. The housing shortage in Oxford was a consequence of the migration of workers from other parts of the United Kingdom as well as some from the Commonwealth who had come to Oxford to work in the motor [automobile] industry. So Blackbird Leys was built to house those people referred to as the 'overspill' population in Oxford. In fact, by the time the houses there got built, most people moving to Blackbird Leys had been born in Oxford, and most of those working in the motor industry had bought houses in villages around the city.

I did this research with Barry Machin. We used a range of "conventional" participant observational methods of anthropology in what was then an unconventional setting for anthropological studies. Our work built on a tradition of family studies in Britain—perhaps the work of Young and Willmott (1957) is the most well known.

At the time, expecting that I would return to the US with my family, I had planned to concentrate or specialize on family studies in urban communities. When our return to California did not work out as expected, I applied for a position in Anthropology at the University of Edinburgh, which sent me to Sierra Leone to conduct a study of marriage and the family among the elite. This study was comparative with one carried out by Christine Oppong in Ghana and another of marriage and family in a town outside Edinburgh, Scotland. That project was the brainchild of Professor Kenneth Little, whom you will know had always been out in front in anthropology in the UK in such fields as race relations, urban studies, and women's studies. There are many, Christine and myself included, who are direct beneficiaries of Kenneth Little's commitment to giving women chances to start careers in anthropology, a field which was then much more dominated by men than it is today, and in researching topics which today would probably fall under 'women's studies'.

My research in Sierra Leone was to test 'Bott's hypothesis' concerning the impact of migration and urbanization on conjugal roles, as measured by the extent to which domestic tasks were shared between husbands and wives as a consequence of the absence of an extended family. I had already found Bott's hypothesis 'wanting' in my study of Blackbird Leys (Harrell-Bond 1969). After having conducted preliminary fieldwork in the town of Bo (where Kenneth had presumed I would concentrate), I used this article to support doing a much more comprehensive study of marriage among professionals in Sierra Leone.

It was in the course of this two-year field study that I became interested in family law. Sierra Leone had a plural personal legal system that recognized marriage and inheritance law under customary, statutory (based on the British system), and Islamic law (Harrell-Bond and Skinner 1977a). After writing up this research (Harrell-Bond 1975b), I was employed by the Afrika-Studiecentrum in Leiden, Holland, to lead a team study to provide the government of Sierra Leone with the information it needed to reform its family law (Harrell-Bond and Rijnsdorp 1975). The Dutch government funded my research and publications for five years.

My own part of this research concentrated on family cases heard in the illegal courts in Freetown, which were headed by tribal headmen, so I then proposed a further study of this institution, which I carried out with two historians, Professors Alan Howard and David Skinner (Harrell-Bond, Howard, and Skinner 1977). Our work, which looked at the impact of migration on the social structure of Freetown, resulted in a revisionist history which challenged the tendency of researchers to rely solely on Christopher Fyfe's interpretation of the role of the Creoles in shaping Sierra Leone society (Harrell-Bond and Skinner 1977b).

It is important to point out that one of the groups whose migration history we were following was the Fula, whose market networks spread across West Africa. At the time of our research there were unknown thousands of Fula in Sierra Leone who had fled Sekou Toure's socialist Guinea. Although our book did mention one individual who was *refouled* [forcibly returned to one's country of origin], we never referred to Fula as refugees because they were not labeled as such; the government of Sierra Leone had refused to allow UNHCR to set up a humanitarian relief program for them. Today we would have called them refugees, but as far as the Sierra Leone government was concerned, they were resident aliens who were allowed to mix freely in the country.

In retrospect, the Fula case was important for other reasons. For one thing, it disproved the theory that no state can afford to give asylum to the 'enemies of its friends'. While hosting refugees from Guinea, Siaka Stevens, and Sekou Toure continued to enjoy very close relations. After all, Stevens had been himself a refugee in Guinea; once he took power in Freetown, he signed a mutual defense treaty with Toure. When his position was under threat, Stevens asked Sekou Toure to send soldiers.[1] At the same time, Fula refugees were allowed to circulate freely.

With hindsight, I regret our lost opportunity of studying in more depth the relations between these refugees and their hosts, because it is one of only two such African examples that I know of where a host state not only did not ask for international assistance but actually rejected it, and where it was a matter of state policy that the affected people were genuinely free to integrate themselves. The other was Guinea, which served as a host to many refugees from the liberation war in Guinea Bissau (Adeji 1990). Such a study would have been invaluable, especially given the progressive expansion of the activities of the humanitarian regime, or what Alex de Waal calls the "humanitarian internationale." Today it would be hard to convince most host states that they might be better off without relief programs for the refugees they host.

One of the effects of these years of research and writing on Sierra Leone with historians and lawyers was to experience the value of team work across disciplines. Another effect of the more than one year that I spent in the Public Records Office and the Collendale library of old newspapers was to acquire a deep appreciation for archival research. EP–Professor Evans-Pritchard–always taught us that anthropology *is* history, but it is very interesting to *do* a historical study as an anthropologist *with* historians. From Leiden I moved to a position in the Faculty of Law, University of Warwick. My task was to supervise lawyers conducting sociolegal research for advanced degrees. I also participated in a "Vienna Group," an institution in Austria which brought researchers from the Eastern bloc together with European researchers in various projects. Ours was a comparative study of methods of dispute treatment, which brought me back to research in Britain (Harrell-Bond and Smith 1983). While at Warwick I also became involved in a study of planning law and organized a conference which resulted in a book entitled *The Imposition of Law* (Harrell-Bond and Burman 1979). I totally forgot about that book's title later on when I was writing *Imposing Aid* (1986)!

In the process of collecting materials on planning law, I encountered an issue in Gambia which faces many countries in the South: the introduction of tourism as a development project, in this case encouraged by the World Bank and United Nations Development Program (UNDP). In fact, the only 'planning' going on in Gambia was tourism (Harrell-Bond and Harrell-Bond 1980). One of the side effects of tourism there was the introduction of male prostitution to sell services to European women. Many (even elderly) Scandinavian women appropriated young Gambian males, taking them back home as 'pets'. When racism was still a taboo subject in Sweden, one could see graffiti ("Nigger go home") on walls in Uppsala and young Gambians with their bell-bottom trousers walking the streets of Stockholm. My publications on this topic caused quite a stir, especially in Gambia. In fact, a friend in UNDP pleaded with me not to publish my analysis of what were essentially racist documents in which his organization and the World Bank were convincing Gambians that tourism would be their 'window on the outside world' and would be the catalyst for getting over all their 'traditional' values like polygamy, land tenure systems, and extended family obligations, while becoming modernized through the 'market economy'.

For about three years I then spent much of each year researching throughout West Africa and writing on any subject I chose, as well as lecturing in the US universities which were members of the American Universities Field Staff of which I was an Associate. Driving slowly through West Africa with only women in the car was very informative. We went through areas and encountered hazards that I am sure we survived only *because* we were women. I think that experience was a very important preparation for the demands that I faced at the Refugee Studies Programme (RSP). I was in Ghana in 1979 at the time of the coup that put Jerry Rawlings in power the first time (Harrell-Bond 1982).

I realize that you must be getting impatient, but I am coming to the answer to your question. In Guinea Bissau, I met the Polisario Front representative and learned more details about the Saharawi war for self-determination. I decided it was important to inform American students of the invasion in 1975 and the occupation of this former Spanish colony by Morocco. After all, this war was being supported militarily by the US Back in Oxford, where I continued to live with my children, OXFAM asked if I would be interested in visiting Algeria to write an update on Saharawi refugees (Harrell-Bond 1981). Now 1981 was also the year of a devastating earthquake in Algeria, so I had a chance to see at first hand the emergency responses of the Algerian Red Crescent and military. This was an illuminating example of local institutions handling a horrific crisis without outside personnel. Their capacity—including that of the soldiers—to decide priorities, to provide comfort to the bereaved, to work and even to cry together was impressive.

I mean that, about crying together. Many of those actively working in the distribution of tents and blankets were themselves bereaved. They also knew what was best for the kids who were orphaned, which was to keep them in the city where they were born rather than 'adopt' them around the country. "We do not want to diminish our children," they said. "We know what happens to adopted children households in Algeria. [The children] become servants." However, Northern NGOs then 'knew better', and OXFAM refused to support this part of their program.

I read a lot of agency documents about refugees in advance of this visit to the Saharawi camps in the Sahara Desert. None of them prepared me for what I observed in the camps near Tindouf. Surviving under extreme conditions in an incredibly difficult climate, people were actively using their time in exile to prepare themselves to be part of a twentieth-century state. Women's equality was a most dominant theme of life in the Saharawi camps. The educational program was organized to allow every woman to participate. Women also had to learn to protect and defend the camps, so they had military training which was initially taught by men, but by 1981 included women instructors. They also learned to drive and repair vehicles. The health program, like everything else in the camps, was organized around a series of committees of which everyone sixteen and over was a member. Schools were called "palaces for children."

When I returned, I had long discussions with OXFAM staff concerning why the refugees they were assisting appeared so different from these Saharawi refugees. OXFAM literature had described their refugees as suffering from a dependency syndrome, unmotivated to become self-sufficient, and so on. It was during these discussions that one staff member said of their emergency relief work, "We are so busy saving lives that by the time we get time to *think*, we have made so many mistakes that it is too late." It was out of these discussions that I got curious as to just how humanitarian organizations in general operate in an emergency. I hypothesized that one of the main problems of refugees is their helpers or, perhaps better put, the manner in which refugees are helped. Late that year a research position at Queen Elizabeth House was advertised which included refugees as a topic for which one could apply. I was appointed in January 1982, and the Refugee Studies Programme (RSP) was founded soon afterwards.

Q. *How would you characterize the general state of academic refugee studies at the time you were researching for your book,* Imposing Aid?

A. Strong interest in refugee studies which focuses on refugees' own experiences existed before my book was published. This was well illustrated at the first RSP conference, *Assistance to Refugees: Alternative Viewpoints.* Concerning the state of the literature, there were already a few important studies (some of which I cited in my book). However, with the exception of refuge law, which had been well developed theoretically, I suppose the general state of academic studies could be best characterized as *very* scattered. Volume 15 of the *International Migration Review* (1981) brought together a number of works. Peter Loizos had done a study of his own people who became refugees, but I have to admit I did not discover him and his book in time (1981). There were just enough people publishing on refugees to hold a 1982 conference in Khartoum, which was organized largely by Ahmed Karadawi. While a very few like Barry Stein had become specialists in refugee studies, most individuals conducted one-off projects on refugees and then went on, or back, to their main topics of interest.

It is also interesting to note how some people who had published specifically on refugees had done their research by 'accident'; they had planned a study in a place which happened to include a refugee population. This was the case with anthropologists such as Renee Hirschon, Art Hansen, and Anita Spring. But at least when they discovered that people in the sites of their research *were* refugees, they focused their research on them *as* refugees. I have been amazed at how many researchers (and development economists have been particularly noteworthy in this regard) still conduct research in 'refugee-affected' areas and do not even seem to notice how the economies of the places they are studying are affected by the cheap labor available because of their presence.

When we started the *Journal of Refugee Studies*, the majority of the papers submitted were on Southeast Asian refugees, written by American or Canadian academics, as there were a growing number of studies of the Southeast Asians who were being resettled in the North. It was tough initially to make this journal global and multidisciplinary in perspective. Although I knew Elizabeth Colson's groundbreaking study, *The Social Consequences of Resettlement* (1971), I must admit that I was not thinking of the relevance of other such studies of people internally displaced by development projects, which were available at the time. This is still a problem: the failure of researchers to cross-reference each other's work when they are studying uprooted people who are labeled differently. What I *did* know was that no one had ever before made an independent field study to evaluate a humanitarian operation mounted in response to a refugee emergency. It was my curiosity concerning how humanitarian agencies function in an emergency and how emergency assistance could be improved to benefit both refugees and their hosts that I was focusing on.

It is also important to note how difficult access to refugees was for independent academics in the early 1980s. I had first intended to study Chadians on the Nigerian/Cameroon border, and in December 1981 I drove up to Maiduguri. By the time I arrived, the camp was in the middle of a 'repatriation' exercise. What I quickly learned was that the Nigerian government had simply handed over responsibility to UNHCR and that if I did not have Geneva's blessing I might not be allowed to do research there. For someone who had already spent years in Africa conducting research with the agreement of local universities or governments, this came as a huge shock. Most academics are unaware that even today UNHCR and other UN organizations still largely control the logistics of transportation to, and communication with, many refugee situations.

I went to Geneva, and the advice I received was that I should go to the Sudan to become familiar with 'how UNHCR works' and then go on to Somalia to do the fieldwork. Once I arrived in Khartoum, I learned through gossip that the UNHCR representative in Sudan did not want me to go to the South. "There must be something there to see," thought I, and sure enough, when I went there in May 1982 there was a large emergency influx of refugees from

Uganda who had been surviving in the bush for very long periods of time, resisting flight across the border until it was almost too late to save their lives.

It is important at this point to clarify how my own thought developed in the process of undertaking the research for *Imposing Aid*, as this quite naturally set the tone for a lot of future work at the RSP. Remember, I was trained at Oxford in what is one of the most conservative schools of anthropology in the world. In my day, you were trained to do your research as a participant *observer*. You did not comment, and you certainly did not *interfere*. You described, you did not evaluate. Siaka Stevens had earlier tortured and killed some of my dear friends and many of what anthropologists refer to as their *informants*, but I never wrote or said a word in protest. I suppose in this sense, you are right, I was a pretty conventional anthropologist.

For the first six weeks of fieldwork, I approached research in southern Sudan in the same way, even though I was 'observing' scenes of suffering and death of such magnitude it is almost impossible to describe in words. When I arrived, Ugandans were pouring across the border and UNHCR did not have a bean, bucket, or blanket to provide them. Remember that in 1982 President Obote was in every donor's good books, and no one wanted to know that a worse force than Amin had been unleashed on the country. UNHCR's ability to mobilize assistance there was profoundly affected by international politics. In such situations, the political pressures on UN staff must be enormous. I remember what the North Africa desk officer at UNHCR told me in 1982, that Morocco regularly checked on what UNHCR provided the Saharawi refugees and that even tankers to haul water were challenged since they could be used for fuel for the war effort.

When I planned this research, it was well known that most refugees lived outside camps and were *not* formally assisted. Chambers (1979) had written his "What the eye does not see" article, highlighting their plight, which he assumed was much greater than those in camps. Despite my experiences the year before in Algeria, or perhaps because of them, my original research proposal did not question UNHCR's settlement approach. It specifically stressed investigating how UNHCR could become more efficient, and how camp administration could be more participatory and humane, and less wasteful. My fairly naive idea was that if we could just get the approach in the camps right, we would then be in a better position to address the problems of the larger numbers of unassisted refugees.

My research led not only to a change of mind, but also later to a change in heart. I came to see and argue with a certain degree of passion that I was wrong about both humanitarian aid and about camps. I even experienced personally the perverse effects of the perceptions of helpers, and of the sense of absolute 'power' over other people. These can take one over in a desperate refugee situation, and that is why I wrote a "confession," as an addendum to Chapter 2 of *Imposing Aid* (1986).

Contrary to what I had been led to expect by Chambers, my research showed that in many ways those living *outside* the umbrella of assistance were actually better off than those living under it. In terms of the enjoyment of their rights and physical protection, this was dramatically the case. In many instances, even the standard of living of the two groups was strikingly different. In fact, in times of crisis—for example, when World Food Program's lorries got stuck in the mud—it was the self-settled refugees who were feeding many of those who were living in the camps! Relationships between hosts and refugees were certainly much more peaceful outside the camps than in them. The hypothesis of the book was that too often the approach humanitarians take makes their assistance a liability rather than an asset. Using the participatory methods of an anthropologist allowed me to document the negative impact of aid on both refugees and their hosts, and thus demythologize it.

Engaging in demythologizing such a sacred arena as humanitarian work, is, as I have come to learn, a hazardous activity. However, as I was writing the book, I was still naive enough about bureaucratic interests in humanitarian work to believe that people who are employed in this field would welcome an opportunity to reflect on their actions and to change practices. Many did and do, but independent research which actually brings in the voices of the beneficiaries continues to be a threat to those in the aid establishment today. When the book came out in 1986, I was shocked to discover that it was being interpreted by some as a broadside against humanitarians. This was not my intent. The way *Imposing Aid* was written was also with the intention of 'blowing open' this new field for other academics to research. In this respect, one nice thing said about the book, which was gratifying, was that it was a book full of hypotheses waiting to be studied. I believed, and I still believe, that research on critical social problems such as forced migration belongs *in* the university.

The book *was* intended as a critique of the relief model then in place, and it was quite appropriate that the RSP was subsequently invited to do a mission in Uganda for the EC (European Community). This was supported by Lome III funds, which were targeted for investment in 'refugee' or 'returnee' affected areas. Dr. George

Kanyiehamba and I did this mission together.[2] It was during this research in Uganda that the fallacy of the notion that repatriation is the best answer for all refugees was brought dramatically home to me. Ugandans were being driven back by the war in southern Sudan, and the Rwandans in the camps in the Southwest were in dire straits. George had serious discussions with Museveni about naturalizing the Tutsi and getting them out from under a very authoritarian camp administration. Our report was very well received in Brussels, and the RSP was asked to be the advisor to the EC on its expenditure of Lome III (Article 204) and Lome IV (Article 255) moneys in Africa, starting with six countries.

However, the idea that with Lome funds it would be possible to develop alternatives to UNHCR's package had serious implications. What if assistance to refugees was shifted to an approach which would also help the hosts? My research has shown very clearly that using the funds refugees attract as well as their labor toward development was better than encamping refugees and keeping them on relief. It is very unwise to underestimate the bureaucratic interests which have developed in keeping the status quo, putting refugees in camps and keeping them there, or, as it is now done, pushing them home as destitute as they came and mounting yet more relief programs for them there. In the end the money–something like £200,000–was not forwarded. At the time, I remember, we had only money for six more weeks of life! OXFAM saved us from extinction.

More generally, I think it is worth saying that in the 1980s, many researchers (particularly students) had to make serious academic decisions that would affect their futures. If they were aligned with the RSP's developing tradition of critical research, which kept a 'rights' approach at the center of its work, they might not get a job with an NGO or UNHCR, and there were then few opportunities for academic careers in refugee studies. It is hard to believe the level of defensiveness that then existed toward independent scholarship.

In fact–you ask about the general state of refugee studies at the time–most academic research had been conducted by consultants, many of whom signed away their freedom to publish as part of their contractual arrangements with UNHCR. If one could still lay one's hands on these studies, they would be a rich source of comparative data. As but one case relevant to the theme of your volume, Ingrid Palmer[3] did a study on women refugees for UNHCR which she couldn't circulate. Robert Chambers was one of the few consultants to UNHCR who quite exceptionally had published some of his observations, and I must say that my correspondence with him during 1982–84 was extremely useful (Chambers 1979: 381–92).

Q. *What empirical topics were prevalent then? What theoretical traditions or themes do you recall as figuring prominently in refugee studies at that time?*

A. Without doing a computer search in our library, it is hard to recall exactly. Certainly, the early and mid-1980s were marked by a rush of studies from all kinds of directions, particularly in international relations. The Aga Khan study (1981) had come out, and it concentrated on the causes of refugee movements. One of the big topics of discussion beginning in 1982 was 'irregular movements', of people acting autonomously, migrating and trying to find employment in countries other than their first country of asylum. Europe (and the US and Canada) couldn't have that, and this was the beginning of serious restrictionism in the North. Even though, according to Gilbert Jaeger, there were then no more than two hundred thousand of these people on the move, worldwide. I remember Ahmed Karadawi getting very agitated on this subject, predicting that African states would follow suit and pass their own restrictive laws.

His predictions have since come true. Now most countries of the world believe, erroneously, that the principle of requiring refugees to remain in their 'first country of asylum' is international law. Worse still, beginning with Djibouti and more recently in Tanzania, forcible repatriation is hardly questioned. Where is the outcry over the use of the military to drive Rwandans home in December 1996?

By 1983, the Ford Foundation (Carmichael and Berresford 1983) had produced a booklet meant to stimulate research on refugees and migration. Research by Zolberg, Suhrke, and Aguayo (1989) had been funded by the Ford Foundation, and this team visited Oxford and other academic institutions in Europe in the mid-1980s to report on their research—which concentrated on causes. There was strong attention then also paid to the mental health problems of refugees in resettlement countries. Ron Baker organized a conference in London in 1981 on this subject and published the proceedings the next year. Work on cultural bereavement was then beginning to appear, primarily concerning the settlement of refugees in the North. Willie Shawcross's book (1984), *The Quality of Mercy*, addressed the situation in Thailand, and condemned the political failure of state and international responses to refugees.

Only because I was most aware of it, I recall that much work at the time was concerned with refugee policy. UNHCR was then pushing a developmental approach to refugees based on the ideas of Jacques Cuenod. Policy work also began to come from a wider range of institutions, including the Refugee Policy Group (RPG), which had begun about the same time as had the RSP, and the Center at York University (Canada).

Theoretically, a key problem for all of us at the time was that there was no focus for interdisciplinary work, and publications continued to be scattered. Researchers chiefly drew on theories from their own disciplines. There was no forum for academics from different disciplines to establish a coherent and collective vocabulary to refer to the different dimensions of the phenomenon that they were each describing in their disciplinary terminology. Even so, I am still bemused by those who decry the lack of theory in refugee studies, as if there ever could be a single grand theory which will encompass the whole field—especially when there is now a concomitant crisis of grand theory in all disciplines. As I always saw it, the main theoretical contribution of multidisciplinary research among populations in crises was to inform, correct, expand, and develop the theories of each discipline. Effie Voutira and I recently made that point vis-à-vis anthropology (Harrell-Bond and Voutira 1992). I don't think refugee theory should be compartmentalized. Neither does John Davis (1992) who, in his lecture in honor of Elizabeth Colson, attacks the false division between applied and mainstream anthropology and advocates a unified anthropology of suffering.

Slowly, the literature developed and was brought together. The RSP's first indexed directory of current research in 1987 was much less than one hundred pages long, yet two years later the second was nearly twice as long. We had to publish a third edition in 1993. Julian Davies (1990) compiled a resource guide for the RSP, for which he sent over a thousand questionnaires to centers of migration studies and interested academics around the world. If one looks through those four directories, you will see how few names persist in the subsequent editions. Still today, very few academics focus their academic careers on the subject of refugees. Those who did in the early 1980s took the risk that they would not find employment or would have to switch topics of research in order to get teaching positions. Happily, that situation now is beginning to change.

Once again, I would like to emphasize that the focus should be on using the new learning, which comes from studying populations in crisis from a multidisciplinary perspective to enrich the theories of the mainstream disciplines. When we started the RSP, we had no ambitions to create a new *discipline*. This is why Elizabeth Colson and I designed the master's course to be a *conversion* course: you come from your discipline, get exposed to concepts and theories and methods and content from other disciplines, but you *return* (hopefully much better prepared) to your own discipline for advanced research on refugees.

Although this is getting ahead of your question, by now I believe that much of the ground work of professionalizing refugee studies has been done. The *Journal of Refugee Studies* is in its tenth year, and a professional organization, the International Association for the Study of Forced Migration (IASFM), has been founded.

Q. *In your book you did not specifically concentrate either on refugee women or on gender, either among refugees or in the provision of aid. Was this intentional or simply a reflection of the times?*

A. I mentioned before, the whole process of researching and writing *Imposing Aid* involved a personal transformation. The research for *Imposing Aid* was designed to be a critical analysis of an emergency relief program. I still believed then that humanitarians would appreciate findings from such a study, and would use them to improve their performance. I had intended to spend my time in the field only 'observing' the work of UNHCR and the NGOs. I *never* intended to do the kind of massive survey work among refugees that I ended up doing. It was only after seeing the incredible waste and damage caused by the foreign agencies operating there that I proceeded with the refugee survey. After a while–and getting really frustrated with the amateurism of much of what was going on–I sat with the Ugandans themselves and asked them, "What do these agencies need to know to do their job better?"

The research was not intended to be a study of gender per se, or what I had been trained to refer to as 'conjugal relations'! Since I had already established my credentials in the study of marriage and family, the fact that the book does not give greater attention to these issues can certainly not be understood as a 'reflection of the times'. What may be a 'reflection of the times' is that I did not use the term 'gender'.

Moreover, Doreen, I think you would agree that in relation to all of the subjects the book covers, for example, protection, food, health, education, psychological problems, etc., it gives equal attention to the particular problems of women and points out in that oft-repeated quotation, that the failure to consider women's special problems leads to entire programs going awry. I of course did call attention to the way in which the aid program disempowered women by making *men* the recipients of the rations in the context of a culture in which women were responsible for providing the food on the table. This has had an impact on the thinking of some humanitarian agencies, and it has stimulated a lot of research on methods of distributing food (Voutira et al. 1995). In fact, the situation in food distribution today has become almost reversed, so that the special problems of men now need to be highlighted.

Q. *Given an opportunity to do an update on* Imposing Aid *today, how would you address gender differently?*

A. I would write a completely different book. I would design a different kind of research, focusing exclusively on male/female relations in the context of a specific refugee situation. As I stated in *Imposing Aid*, many women were on their own and responsible for their households, or were designated head of a household because the husband was attached to a different household with another wife. The power women got from receiving and controlling rations themselves led to an increased number of divorces, and increasing domestic violence. We know from a great deal of more recent research that marital power relations are severely affected in exile, and it would now be both 'natural' and important to focus on this.

Q. *The RSP at Oxford was founded by two women: you and Belinda Allan. Oxford was not at that time particularly noted for its encouragement of women or of innovative social research on such topics as refugees or gender. How did the two of you being women affect the early development of refugee studies at Oxford?*

A. I think that gender relations in and around the RSP have been quite complex. Anyone who knows anything of the RSP would know that without Belinda Allan, we would have never succeeded. Given Belinda's and my involvement, the RSP was often seen as being run by women. In fact, the men *behind the women* made all the difference! One was Ahmed Karadawi, who must also be recognized as a founder. It was Ahmed's inspiration (in April 1982) that convinced me to seriously respond to the challenge of establishing a center at Oxford. Ahmed came to Oxford that year and kept the RSP seminars going while I was doing fieldwork; he also wrote his important article, *Obstacles to Assistance* (Karadawi 1983), and initiated the student field trips that have changed so many undergraduate lives. His subsequent contributions have been immense.

Another man behind the scenes was Hugh Pilkington. Back in 1982 he was perhaps one of the few people in the world who understood what we were up to. He used to send me support checks, saying, "I don't want any acknowledgment, but I know you need money for postage and telephone calls." I used to *run* to the University to deposit them. As you know, funding from the Hugh Pilkington Trust that was bestowed to us after he died, gave us the continuity that we needed. And of course, Sir Edward Heath has also been a wonderful supporter who made a critical contribution during our difficult early years.

Moreover, the RSP began in Queen Elizabeth House (QEH) when it was presided over by Arthur Hazlewood, *yet another man* and the Warden. He had given a home to women's studies years before, when their seminars were not welcome in anthropology. He did everything he could to promote what we were doing. Sometimes people did remark on the predominance of women in RSP's staff, but it was always possible to respond that, overall, Oxford was notorious for the few women it employed. Moreover, when I look back on the senior academics who devoted the most time to help establish the RSP, only one was a woman–Elizabeth Colson. The others were men–Sidney Waldron, Gil Loescher, and Emmanuel Marx.

Over the years I think that we have made significant gains with regard to the position of women in Oxford. For example, the Pedro Arupe Tutorship, which honors the Jesuit priest who founded the Jesuit Refugee Service, has been established at the RSP in cooperation with Campion Hall. It was assumed at first that it would always be filled by a man, but the second incumbent is Maryanne Loughrey.

But I can't really answer your question adequately without going into some of the other history of the RSP and its own survival strategies within Oxford. In my view, the *real challenge,* as Belinda and I experienced it, was not that we were women; it was to create a program of research and teaching in a multidisciplinary field that was not yet explicitly defined. Another serious and ongoing challenge to the Refugee Studies Programme was our desire always to link research with practice. This *was* a serious challenge to Oxford conventions, which at least for anthropology have always involved a rigid separation between so-called 'theoretical' and 'applied' research. In this respect, being part of QEH had its advantages. It was established in the 1950s (at the 'end of Empire', as they say) to provide just such links.

As I said, I don't believe we ever associated our primary challenges within Oxford with the fact that we were women, although I have to admit I once was encouraged by someone in the administration to complain officially on these grounds in relation to one particular don! I should say, by the way, when there were really serious difficulties, it *was* a woman, Lady Daphne Park, the former principal of Somerville College, who did step in and put some of the men in their place! She has continued to work behind the scenes on our behalf in more than one male-dominated arena.

Overall, maintaining an evenhanded, nonpartisan approach to very sensitive, highly political refugee issues at the RSP has been a real challenge, but I think we have been very successful in doing just that. It is in relation to this challenge that I want to give credit to the *tradition* which the University of Oxford represents. We may have had problems with individual dons, but whether or not it is always deserved, Oxford is known in the world as a place of 'detached' scholarship. As a result, we have never had problems either with British government interference or with the representation of other governments in RSP activities and programs.

Q. *Another pioneering Oxford program, the Centre for the Cross-Cultural Study of Women is at Queen Elizabeth House. What, if any, cross-fertilization has occurred between these two programs over the years?*

A. As I mentioned earlier, under Arthur Hazlewood's leadership Queen Elizabeth House had much earlier provided a home for seminars on women's studies. It was after Juliet Blair and some other women students in Anthropology began a series of seminars on women's issues that Shirley Ardener decided to develop this program, and it had been going for about a year as a Centre before the RSP began. Helen Callaway, a key member of the Centre, has written for RSP publications and served on the editorial board of the *Journal of Refugee Studies*. But although our two programs have been going on in the same institution—literally across the road from each other—there was never the kind of interaction that we always hoped for. If there was someone in residence at the RSP whose focus was on women's issues, they were welcomed at Centre seminars, but I was never successful in getting joint research going. In fact, you, Doreen, when you were a Fellow at the RSP actually took the greatest initiative in this respect, and we did have one joint meeting. No doubt part of the problem was that both programs were struggling to create a separate identity and both were highly dependent on 'soft' funding, which may have served as an impediment to greater collaboration.

Q. *Some of RSP's critics have argued, first, that the program has pretty much backstaged gender in its research and training, and second, that this is an indirect reflection of the priority you yourself place on gender issues in forced migration. Care to comment on this? Where do you prioritize the study of gender in refugee studies?*

A. I do not feel it necessary to defend my record of interest in gender relations per se; although many who know my work since 1982 are probably unaware of my previous research on conjugal relations. Of course, I don't really accept that the RSP backstaged gender–take a look in the library on the amount of RSP-based research done. But there are *many topics* which critics might well argue have been backstaged by RSP researchers, for example, the elderly, the adolescents, and research on psychosocial issues (particularly since interventions in this area are now in fashion and are often undertaken without any guidance from basic studies). As far as women are concerned (and whenever you say "gender" people think "women"), it is interesting to note the findings of a recent review of the program for Sudanese refugees in Ikafe. This report asserts that it was refugee women themselves who argued that they did not want to waste time talking about their special problems, since their major problems of food shortage, poor soils, and insecurity affected everyone.

It is true that the focus of much of the *early* research at the RSP was concerned with the macro- and microdimensions of the political economy of humanitarian assistance. I believe that anyone who actually spends time in a refugee camp anywhere in the world would understand the reason why these issues and social justice or human rights got priority and should continue to do so.

Q. *For many involved in forced migration, 'gender' has become a simple synonym for 'women': the inference being that if you study or acknowledge women you are addressing gender. But the current dominant feminist view is that gender is relational, and involves the study of both maleness and femaleness in thought and action. Do you have any ideas how people could be encouraged to more consistently employ this relational form of gender analysis?*

A. I think that is just the point. No one believes that those outside feminist circles who talk about gender studies are actually including men or considering the dynamics of relationships *between* men and women. Perhaps the earlier fashion of talking about *conjugal relations* was, in some ways, an advantage as it immediately forced researchers to focus on both sexes in, as you put it, relational terms. I don't know. Researchers need to focus relationally on roles, structures of power, domains of power, ideologies of flight and assistance, rights –*human rights*, family law practices and differential access to justice, and how all of these are affected by gendered resource bases, modes of livelihood, educational opportunities, social class, and so on, as well as by the differential experiences of women and men in forced migration.

Q. *Beyond being an object of study, in what key ways (if any) do you see that gender practically matters in the dynamics of oppression? What about in patterns of refugee flight? In the administration of humanitarian assistance? In resettlement?*

A. I wish I could summarize Foucault in a sentence or two, but I can't. In his work, the dynamics of oppression are closely intertwined with the history of Western sexuality. It would be important to see this kind of analysis being applied in refugee situations. I think that there is an urgent need for ethnographic documentation of the ways in which different groups of refugees divide and unite in different circumstances across age and gender: in flight, in detention, and in resettlement. Concerning the administration of humanitarian assistance, I think that the question of gender is important, but we are still trying to come to terms with the general structures of power that exist. I am sure that introducing gender as a variable in the analysis of the style and substance of bureaucratic authority would shed new light on the management of humanitarian assistance. As it stands, at least in Africa, most humanitarian assistance is camp administered, and most administrators are men. Gender relations therefore parallel conventional patterns of domination and division of labor between helpers and helped (see Cammack, Giles, and Indra, this volume). Concerning resettlement, there is already a great deal of work on the different patterns of adaptation by age and gender. You have done a great deal of that work yourself.

Q. *Can you think of any key instances or examples in recent years where the neglect of gender issues has had profoundly negative consequences?*

A. I assume that you are talking about in practice rather than research and that you are talking primarily about the situation of women. There are so many examples that it is difficult to know where to start. Perhaps the most disgusting has been the neglect of the protection of the physical safety of women and their children in situations where they are ostensibly under the protection of the international community through UNHCR: that is, where they are living—we might as well say it—detained in camps around the world. One of the RSP's first published studies by Josephine Reynell (1989) for the World Food Program on the Thai/Kampuchea border pointed out the way in which the Khmer Rouge military were terrorizing women after dark when the representatives of the humanitarian agencies involved were fast asleep far away from the camps they left promptly at 5 P.M.

The problems of not applying the exclusion clause to individuals among the Rwandan refugee populations is well known. What is not so well known is that the war in southern Sudan has been allowed to enter Sudanese refugee camps in Uganda. You will remember when we visited Ikafe and Rhino camps in 1996 that the SPLA (Sudan People's Liberation Army) was recruiting young men. SPLA soldiers are not routinely disarmed when they enter Uganda to visit their families in the camps, which has increased insecurity for both refugees and local people.

Everyone now knows that the requirements of fetching fuel and water renders women particularly vulnerable to the risk of rape and other assaults. Instead of addressing the problem in ways which reduce this risk, we chiefly have rape clinics in camps! As a case in point, Guglielmo Verdirame, who is doing a sociolegal study of protection in Kenya, has been informed that rape in Dadaab camps is now down to 'acceptable levels' [see Boelaert et al., this volume]. Most of the rapes there occur when women are fetching firewood, and Lamont-Gregory has made a strong case for including fuel as part of the aid package. While men are unlikely to voluntarily take over this aspect of 'women's work', if they were paid to do so, it would reduce this danger to women. Paying men would also increase their self-esteem vis-à-vis their wives and families, and could consequently reduce domestic violence.

Another area where gender issues have been neglected is in the UK: when a couple is seeking asylum here, usually only the credibility of the husband's claim is taken into consideration by their legal advisers, even when both were involved or implicated in the causes of their flight [see Crawley, this volume]. In cases where I have been asked to give advice, I have often found that the case has been lost because the husband is less able to present his case than his wife would have been, or the combined evidence of both would have been more persuasive. This also affects cases where an application for resettlement has been made on the grounds that a person cannot be protected in the country of first asylum. In one case in which I have been involved recently, after the husband escaped Uganda, the wife was arrested and gravely tortured by the military. Her experiences included being doused with fuel, which was then lit, burning her legs. Apparently no one had interviewed her, much less found a medical doctor to examine her scars or write a statement on her behalf. The husband admits he does not know if she was raped while held by the military because she is loathe to talk about her experiences with him. That she was found naked in a cell and released by another army officer is known.

Another more general aspect of this particular problem is that agencies act in ways that unwittingly empower the most conservative forces (usually the old men) within refugee populations through practices which are motivated by naive good intentions. Rather than monitoring the protection of refugees who get involved in legal problems, agencies encourage refugees to settle their own disputes to avoid their falling into the 'bad, bad hands' of the host's police. A lawyer just recently told me of a case where a woman found guilty of adultery was locked up with her infant for seven days by refugee elders. When the lawyer pointed this out, she was advised not to interfere, as this was the 'culture of the refugees'.

Again, in the name of cultural sensitivity, humanitarian agencies now encourage 'traditional' methods of dispute treatment which give license to many kinds of oppression by the 'elders'. This can include the charging of fines which, when the allegedly guilty cannot pay, lead to the appropriation of their property. In one camp I recently visited, an agency was actually *paying* one group to maintain such extrajudicial law and order, thus rewarding them for practicing their version of customary law. These 'courts' operate without *any* supervision. We found two lockups there, one holding three boys under eighteen, and the other, a mentally disturbed woman. They were guarded by a young man carrying a long whip which was (and is) also used as a form of punishment. In August 1996, we saw a similar sight: people tied up and receiving extra-judicial corporal punishment from their fellows. Those detained included a very young child. In a camp in Tanzania, UNHCR was paying Rwandan refugees to act as camp police after dark–in camps which were thought to be too unsafe for any official to remain in them.

Of course, collective punishment neglects gender issues. At this point, I think I should mention the two documented cases of collective punishment imposed on *all* Kakuma camp inhabitants because a few people had destroyed the food distribution corrals. It happened in 1994; food was withdrawn for twenty-one days from *everyone*, including pregnant women and lactating mothers. Again, such a collective punishment was imposed in 1996–food (and incentives) were withdrawn for fourteen days. I suppose you know that collective punishment is illegal even for armies in times of war.

Q. *Can you think of any recent examples where the active consideration of gender issues has had a clearly positive practical effect?*

A. Again, I presume you are talking about in 'real (refugee) life' and again about positive practical effects for women. I suppose that a major achievement in recent years is the practice of a few countries that now accept women as members of a 'social group' for the purposes of the [*1951*] *Convention* [*Relating to the Status of Refugees*] [see Crawley and Macklin, this volume], when they are escaping such practices as genital mutilation or forced marriage. Also, there is some impressionistic evidence that when women are given more control over ration distribution, the system works out to be more fair, and in some assistance programs this practice is becoming more usual.

I learned of a marvelous recent example from a Kenyan medical worker, who was extremely gender sensitive. Sudanese women require a higher rate of C-sections than should be the case, which is thought to be because of subnutritional diets when they are growing up. Husbands often object to the required surgery when a normal delivery is impossible. Medical personnel managed to gather a group of men who could understand the importance of this lifesaving intervention and employed them as 'male motivators' to convince the other men to accept its necessity.

Q. *A lot of those involved in the provision of assistance and protection in forced migration contexts claim that they can barely manage to fulfill their basic charters with the resources they have available, and that being forced to consider gender more fully would therefore be extremely dysfunctional and distracting. What do you think of this argument?*

A. What are these basic charters that they "barely manage to fulfill"? I suppose my first response would be that I would be quite satisfied if humanitarian agencies would simply begin to treat refugees as human beings, begin to be honest about the limits of international assistance, begin to share responsibility and decision-making power with refugees, and begin to incorporate human rights as a measure for their own actions. An essential problem is the persistent assumption on which humanitarian relief programs all over the world are based: that they, the helpers, are *rescuing helpless victims.* Their approach is based on a highly ideologized overestimation of their capacity to respond in the first place, and on the belief that without them, no one would survive.

What is highly dysfunctional is the ways in which assistance agencies consequently abuse their power over refugees whom they have assumed the responsibility for saving, rather than consulting with them as responsible equals. In this regard, a thesis has just become available, a field study of Dadaab refugee camps in Kenya. The author describes a situation in which, on the one hand, an NGO is promoting refugee participation, while on the other hand, the same population is being humiliated by being locked up in an enclosure for registration (M. Hyndman 1996). Those who control the power over the distribution of material assistance are often still unwilling to consult the beneficiaries at all, much less consider the different views of men, women, the old, or the young. If they did consult, they could avoid many mistakes that are repeated time and time again.

Q. *Over the last ten years, gender in forced migration has become a fashionable topic for discussion at conferences and is receiving really a lot of attention by the UNHCR and a range of NGOs—at least in the form of policy statements and the like. What effects of all this discussion do you see in practice?*

A. Certainly there is greater consciousness of women's issues, and more efforts are being made to integrate guidelines and policy statements into practice. In short, the rhetoric is moving downward to the level of those who are in face-to-face contact with refugees. At the same time, faraway in the field it is still largely rhetoric. For example, when I suggested it, the male Ugandan staff of one very gender-aware agency recently resisted handing power over food distribution to women, saying that the refugee men would not accept this. So I asked the men in question; they clapped their assent with the idea. They were not stupid. They knew that they would have much less temptation to sell the food for alcohol and that their kids would get fed if women had control of food.

One can observe that there are a few *more* women in key positions, but we do not have evidence yet that the efforts, for example, of such international organizations as the World Food Program, which aims to recruit women on a fifty/fifty basis, are actually going to change the hierarchical structure of policymaking or assistance programs. I just interviewed a woman in WFP who pointed out that, despite her eighteen years of service, she will never be promoted again because she has been too outspoken about human rights problems, in this case, the central 'right to life'—making sure that refugees have sufficient and nutritional food! She noted that at the beginning, she had access to the new head of WFP (who is a woman) but now middle-level staff restrict her access.

I keep being disappointed with having to face the fact that so much still depends on a particular individual happening to be in the right place at the right time. There are many of these individuals, but in talking about women, I want to mention one in particular: Dr. Whande, who works for UNHCR in Nairobi. She is the first person I know of who effectively noticed that African women (not unlike Bosnian women) have menstrual periods. Remember how much attention was given to getting sanitary towels to former Yugoslavians? Now such provisions are included in many assistance programs in other parts of the world.

Q. *Today, what key topical domains in refugee studies do you think would be most enriched by further inquiry into gender relations?*

A. Well, since I mentioned at the outset that my early research focused on *conjugal* relations, I think that a necessary corrective is to return to studying relationships *between* men and women. In addition, as I always suggest to NGOs everywhere, if you want to help women, help men. It would be very interesting to study families where women are active members of an 'empowerment' program addressing women *and* men. Perhaps such a program could also direct its work to better include men and help them adjust to a new power balance within the home.

Notes

1. Sekou was always under armed guard at both the State House and at his own residence.
2. At that time, Dr. Kanyiehamba was a refugee in Britain where he taught law. Following the mission, he stayed on in Uganda and has just been made a supreme court judge.
3. Ms. Palmer is an economist and was then at Sussex University.

4

Girls and War Zones

Troubling Questions

Carolyn Nordstrom

Introduction

This is a paper I did not want to write because I would be happier if the data did not exist.

Graburn (1987: 211)

The inception of this chapter dates to a day in 1990 when I was sitting in a hot and dusty town in Central Zambezia, Mozambique. The town had just been retaken by the Frelimo governmental forces after having been under rebel Renamo control for several years. Renamo was credited with the majority of human rights abuses during the war, and the Renamo commander in charge of this town had a particularly brutal reputation. During Renamo's occupancy, the town center had been destroyed, and a sea of small mud huts spread in all directions on the outskirts of the city ruins. I arrived shortly after the first Frelimo administrator. Disease and starvation were rampant; town leaders estimated that twenty-five people were dying each day. This was in part due to the fact that both Renamo and Frelimo used forced resettlement tactics to control the population, with the result that civilians were frequently denied access to farmlands. Virtually all trade routes had been destroyed by the war, and what resources did exist were often plundered by soldiers and armed bandits. The town's dirt runway allowed emergency cargo planes to land, so this town was the recipient of a one-week feeding program administered by several Western NGOs working with Mozambican emergency relief programs. The pilot of a cargo plane had given me *boleia*–a free ride.

I was sitting on the ground with several women of the town who had volunteered to assist in cooking food dropped off by the cargo planes. During our conversation on the war's impact, one of them asked me: "Do you notice anything?" I looked around, and it was obvious. "It must be over ninety percent boys here," I responded, and the women nodded. "Do the NGOs know this?" I asked. "No," the women shook their heads. "They simply do not notice." "Where are the girls?" The women explained that their absence was a result of the way the NGO set up its emergency relief food program. The 'organizational policy' of this Western-based aid institution insisted that mothers bring their children and sit under trees at the feeding center from sunup to sundown in order to secure three meals. They could not get food otherwise. The NGO failed to recognize that if the townspeople did not plant crops, they would starve in the up-coming months, long after the NGO feeding programs were gone. So girls were left at home to tend crops and care for elderly or inca-pacitated family members. Because the NGO also specified that no food could be taken from the feeding area (ostensibly fearing thiev-ery), nothing could be taken home for those left behind. "But what happens to the girls?" I asked again. The women shook their heads gently: they had wanted to make sure someone would take these stories back to policymakers, but beyond that, it was up to me to pursue the matter.

I knew children constituted a major percentage of war deaths in the contemporary world, as well as half of all forced migrants. Behind the rhetoric of soldiers fighting soldiers that fuels military propaganda and popular accounts of war, children are maimed, tortured, starved, forced to fight, displaced, and killed in numbers that rival adult civilian casualties and outnumber those of soldiers (UNICEF 1995a:2). The UN estimates that in the last decade alone, approximately two million children have died in wars and between four and five million have been physically disabled. More than five million have been forced into refugee camps, while twelve million have been left homeless. In 1995, twenty-eight million minors lived in war zones (UNICEF 1995a:13). Except for the statistics, these youthful casualties are largely invisible: most of the military texts, the political science analyses, and the media accounts of war do not discuss either the tactical targeting of children or war's impact upon them. Most representations of refugees and other forced migrants likewise focus almost entirely on adults. I had seen child victims of war—maimed in hospitals, lying dead in bombed out villages, living or dying of starvation in refugee camps and on the streets, and after their families and homes had been attacked. In cases like the feeding programs, I had seen mostly boys. Where were the girls?

The more I considered the question, the less of an answer I had. Political violence produces many war orphans, and many join the one hundred million street children of the world.[1] Yet programs to assist such youth find, and deal predominantly with, boys. Programs to help child soldiers focus predominantly on male youths. The faces looking up at us in media photos of war and flight and at on-site feeding programs are virtually all male. Girls surface primarily in one social frame: prostitution.

Children and girls are of course constantly used as symbols of war, starvation, forced displacement, and other calamities. Every war has the obligatory 'horror photo' of the child. The crying, radiation-burnt child in Hiroshima (*Life Magazine*); the naked napalm-burnt girl running down the village road in Vietnam (Associated Press); the 'one-of-the-world's-one-hundred-million-landmines-victims' with amputated legs in Africa (CNN); the small corpse in Bosnia after a Serb shell hit a civilian zone (Reuters). Each war has its obligatory 'horror story' that is too graphic, too barbaric, even for photos. The major battles I have witnessed and the wars I have studied all involved stigmatizing the actions of the 'other side' in the rape, maiming, and murder of women and girls. Images of victim girls function as political symbols: as policy justification, as military propaganda to engender nationalist loyalties, and to call people to arms (see Cammack and Matlou, this volume). But where are the millions of others whose plight is equally tragic yet who are outside the range of CNN crews, journalists' cameras, and the political gaze? In fact, the images of children in war are very circumscribed. Starvation among refugee children is a frequent topic of analysis and a recurrent photographic theme, while the rape of these children is a rarely considered topic. So also is discussion of the state torture of children. The forceful conscription of boy children into militaries is now a popular academic and documentary theme, while the contemporary slaving of girl war orphans is given little attention.

Troubling Questions

> *If children are loved and valued, why are they still being*
> *used as cannon-fodder?*
>
> UNICEF (1996a: 10–11)

Cynthia Enloe (1993, 1989) insists that we consistently ask: "Where are the women in politics, in conflict, and in political solutions?" But women were constantly visible to me in war zones: they told stories, traded, and set up healing programs. It was the girls who were largely, dangerously, invisible. Outside of families, they disappeared from sight: they had no apparent agency to direct their lives. They never spoke on the radio, their words were not found in the news, political scientists did not quote them, and NGOs did not interview them. When I started looking for girls in other war situations, I found silences and empty spaces, punctuated sporadically by the work of a handful of researchers focusing on children in general and girls in particular.[2]

In the war zones I have visited, girls are actors in the drama and tragedy of war along with adults. They are targeted for attack, they conceive of escapes, they endure torture, they carry food to the needy, they forge a politics of belief and action, and yet, in general accounts of war–excepting the few excellent ethnographies focusing specifically on children–I look for children actors, and instead find the view that girls, children, are chiefly acted *upon;* they are listed as casualties–they do not act. They are not presented as having identities, politics, morals, and agendas for war or peace.

Girls and War Zones: Following Threads in Mozambique

> *More than half a million children lost their lives to war-related*
> *causes in the last decade of war in Mozambique that ended in 1992.*
>
> UNICEF (1996b)

My study begins in the towns and villages hours by flight and days by foot from the nearest capital cities. It is here where war moves from the abstract to the enacted. In this section, I explore three contexts in which war impinges directly on the health and well-being of girls: the frontlines of war; locations beyond the borders of war zones proper; and, after the war, considerations of the peace process itself.

In War

One day in 1991, I visited a town in north central Mozambique. Controlled for several years by rebel Renamo forces, the area had been recaptured by local anti-Renamo militia and Frelimo governmental forces. In many ways, it faced similar circumstances as the town introduced above. A short window of opportunity opened up: the town had a dirt runway relatively free of landmines, Renamo was not attacking at the moment, and the plight of the war-ravaged citizens caught the eye of an NGO with sufficient funds and an airplane to fly emergency food and materials to the town for about a week. I flew in on a cargo plane packed with corn and oil.

When I sat listening to the local citizens talk of their experiences of the war and Renamo's occupation, one concern predominated: every woman and adolescent girl in the town had been sexually assaulted. Many had been forced into concubinage and 'marriage' at a soldier's whim and into providing manual labor. As but one consequence, the townspeople told me that virtually all the women and adolescent girls had sexually transmitted diseases. In a part of the world rife with HIV and AIDS, sexually transmitted diseases can mean a death sentence. There were no local clinics or pharmaceuticals available. Shortly thereafter, the war rolled over the town again; attracted by the strategic location of the town and the emergency supplies that had been flown in, Renamo forces renewed their attacks. It was no longer safe to fly, drive, or walk to the town. The emergency supply planes were diverted elsewhere, and government officials (favorite targets of Renamo) stopped their visits. With no telephones or communications equipment, the people's lives once again became invisible to the outside world.

In places like this, where war is the worst and suffering is at its greatest, the least is known. The sad truth is that no outsider knows what occurred in that town, or what happens in the thousands in the world like it when violence closes down links with NGOs, reporters, and researchers. In such instances, when we ask questions like 'where are the girls', or 'what is their experience of the war', no answer is possible. Even the most concerned of researchers cannot track the lives of girls in such towns under fire.

Following the plight of girls across time as well as war zones complicates an already difficult task. Hundreds of towns in Mozambique faced similar tragedies as the one described here, and millions of people were affected. In addition to the one million people killed in fifteen years of war, one-fourth of the total population fled their homes, and fully one-half of the population was directly affected by war in some way. War left some 200,000 to 300,000 orphans. During my fieldwork, I continually asked about the plight of orphans. The general response was that people took them into their own families and cared for them. There is a strong tradition of such care in Mozambique: more than once I visited friends whose families had grown by a child or two since the last time I saw them. But this is not the full story. Thousands of street children were visible on the streets of the major cities, and, again, virtually all of them were boys. When I pointed this out to people, their answers were vague. People speculated that girls were easier to tend and care for than boys and that orphan girls fit more readily into established families. I would silently add to myself, yes, and girls the world over do not have the option to flee in the same way boys do. But none of these explanations can be more than speculation for no one has followed the path of the hundreds of thousands of girls orphaned in war to find out what has happened to them.

Beyond War

In the midst of a war, in which public violence is often associated with armed forces, collective civilian actions stand out. In 1991, groups of civilians gathered in one of the suburbs of the capital city Maputo and proceeded to stop and overturn certain vehicles, beating their occupants. This was not seen as a riot but rather as civil indignation against illegal actions. The explanations circulating in the media focused on *feiticeiria:* indigenous medicine used to cause harm and to gain power at the expense of others. Body parts, often of children, are claimed to be the ingredients in the more powerful and dangerous medicines of *feiticeiria.* Periodically, unsubstantiated stories had surfaced throughout the country of a dead child who had 'clearly' been killed in order to make these medicines.

The general word on these disturbances in Maputo was that children from the area were being kidnapped and killed to make these medicines. Powerful people of questionable ethics, the story went, were making money by selling these body parts, and those buying the parts were gaining illicit power. A number of cars with South African registrations, known to travel the dangerous route from Maputo across the border to South Africa, were believed to be involved in this trade and were targeted in retaliatory attacks. This was during the period when the apartheid South African government was aiding Renamo's war in Mozambique. Like arms and military strategists, so it was said, body parts were moving across the border to the detriment of most Mozambicans.

A bit of investigation into the allegations of *feiticeiria* and 'body parts' racketeering showed that there was a different and more insidious truth behind these disturbances. A thriving industry had sprung up selling Mozambican children detached from their families into white South African homes as domestics: a clear, modern form of international slavery. Children were also channeled off into prostitution (including the making of pornography) and forced labor. The civilian attacks described above were indeed against the people running children across the border, but these children were alive.

What is curious about these events is that while the fanciful stories of selling 'body parts' in the pursuit of sorcery were widely circulated in the media, the actual selling of living children was not. A handful of industrious journalists documented the sale of children into white South African homes and businesses, but the stories did not make local front-page news, nor were they prominent in the international media. This may have been due in part to the concern local journalists had about implicating certain powerful local people. Networks that assist the selling of children internationally are not based on the work of a few alienated and amoral individuals. Allegations of such racketeering can ruin more than a journalist's career.

While framing the story as one of *feiticeiria* at least got the story out, the links between war, networks of profiteers, systems of illegal border transfers, and abusive child labor practices were largely lost. The end result was that little changed in these children's lives, and their realities were largely silenced. Yet, as UN investigations are now beginning to show, modern slavery is occurring around the world at a serious rate. Forced sexual labor is a multibillion dollar a year global industry. Girls figure predominantly but their stories are often muted. The beneficiaries of these illegal practices work to ensure that they remain invisible to public and judicial eyes.[3]

While these accounts are war-time accounts, their relevance does not end with war. The war in Mozambique has been over since the Peace Accord was signed in 1992, yet at this writing, girls sold into domestic and sexual service are still unaccounted for and many are still working in illegal and inhumane conditions. Their war is far from over. Even those who have escaped their servitude may find their ordeals have not ended. A significant number pressed into sexual labor contract AIDS. Others return home to find that their families no longer have a place for them. As the more carefully documented case of the comfort women of Korea shows, many may endure a lifetime of stigma. Some face this disapprobation with children produced by forced sexual relations–and so the effects of the war carry into the next generation, long after the fighting has been relegated to history.

After War

In perhaps one of the most profound ironies of war and peace-building, young girls also found themselves victims of sexual predation by peacekeepers in Mozambique. Thousands of peacekeepers passed through Mozambique in the two years from the signing of the Peace Accord in 1992 to the elections in 1994. Many peacekeepers were dedicated to their jobs and to the rights of the Mozambicans. However, a significant number abused the rights of girls (and boys), as M.M. Poston shows in her powerful study (1994). These criminal acts violated UN covenants on human rights, the protection of the child, and protection against sexual slavery of children.

Even so, systemic international toleration of the sexual exploitation of children is highlighted by the fact that no UN soldier has to date been prosecuted or convicted for abetting child prostitution or rape. Part of the problem, notes Fetherston (1995:19–23), is that neither the UN nor the country in which the soldiers are stationed, have jurisdiction over UN peacekeeping personnel. National governments who contribute the UN troops alone have this power, and they are notoriously reluctant to prosecute their soldiers for sexual misconduct. Perpetuating the problem is a pervasive attitude that soldiers have a right to act in this way. By way of illustration, Yasushi Akashi was head of the UN mission in Cambodia when he was reproached by various governmental and NGO representatives about the physical and sexual violation of women and girls by UN troops. He responded that he was "not a 'puritan'; that eighteen-year-old, hot-blooded soldiers had a right to drink a few beers and chase after 'young beautiful things of the opposite sex'" (Fetherston 1995: 22; Fetherston and Nordstrom 1995: 94–119). Akashi subsequently moved from Cambodia to head up the UN peacekeeping mission in former Yugoslavia, a powder keg of sexual violations.

There have always been men who prefer to have sex with underage girls and boys. Beyond the motivating cultural cliché of having sex with a virgin, some men are attracted by the power inequalities that having sex with children entails. But with the advent of AIDS, men have turned to younger and younger girls to avoid infection. Worse, I encountered a belief in Mozambique that a man infected with AIDS could rid himself of the disease altogether by having sex with a 'clean' (and this often meant virgin) girl, thereby passing the virus to her. In this way, younger and younger girls are themselves becoming infected, and preliminary medical research indicates that the younger the girl, the more susceptible she may be to HIV infection (Asia Watch and The Women's Rights Project 1993).[4] This mirrors the world scene, as a million children globally will be infected with HIV by the year 2000. By then, as many as ten million children will have lost one or both parents to AIDS (UNICEF 1995b: 43).

While soldiers of several nationalities were implicated in the sexual abuse of children in Mozambique, the Italians came into the spotlight. In 1993, Redd Barna of Norway and the International Save the Children Fund Alliances working in Central Mozambique sent a report to the United Nations, detailing their concern with the sexual abuse of children by UN soldiers and with the great increase in prostitution. As part of the investigation, a member of Save the Children Fund spoke to a fifteen-year-old prostitute who had just had an illegal abortion, and who said that UN soldiers paid extra for sex without condoms. This report more specifically condemned the Italian Blue Berets as among the worst offenders. Poston (1994: 35) writes that local Mozambican officials were aware of the behavior of Italian soldiers, but were afraid to make complaints about UN personnel. As Poston stresses, this is a clear indication of the power relations in operation: UNOMOZ (United Nations Operation in Mozambique) at the time was spending a million dollars a day in preparation for the 1994 elections. This abuse persists despite Article 34 of the UN's Convention on the Rights of Children which, as Save the Children Fund points out, prohibits the exploitation of children for sexual purposes (Phillips 1994, quoted in Poston 1994: 35).[5]

The plight of girls living in violent conditions therefore challenges us to question the artificial boundaries between peace and war. Rather than seeing 'war abuses' or 'child (s)exploitation' as outside the rules and boundaries of average or normal society, we should instead be asking what it is that makes such behaviors possible *wherever* they are found, and what patterns of in/tolerance link them. Following along this thread of thought, I will argue in the next section that what people tolerate in peace and in the domestic sphere configures what takes place in war.

On War Zones and Peace Zones

War and peace are classically opposed, mutually defining folk concepts that do not fit worldwide patterns of child risk, oppression, abuse, and neglect. When children's fates are considered analytically, the distinctions between war zones and peace zones are not only blurred, they are interfused. For example, the institutions that profit from the abuse of children are not specific to countries or regions, or to war or peace. The networks that make such trafficking possible are international. They are in every sense multinational industries with global linkages.[6] Such international systems are consciously constructed and used by people; they are maintained within societies and, irrespective of actual laws, are tolerated in significant ways within legal practice. In short, they exist—even flourish—across divisions and zones of contention.

It is here that profit is realized. Specific people benefit, or think they benefit, from exploiting or ignoring the exploitation of children. And yet, the majority of the world's citizens do not engage directly in these systems of abuse: the latter therefore cannot be deemed part of human (criminal) nature or the 'consequences of inequalities and war'.[7] To sharply distinguish war (zones) from peace (zones) therefore obscures many processes that lead to the abuse of children and, by extension, obscures their potential solution.

By challenging belief in the naturalness of separating war (zones) and peace (zones), the mechanisms supporting these systems of abuse become more clear. Social habits move fluidly across conflict zones with people whose actions also resonate across war and peace. This compels the question: would we as readily find the physical and sexual abuse of children in war if child prostitution did not flourish in many 'peaceful' countries, if domestic violence and adult-child incest were not so systematically ignored? Many of those who take (or fantasize taking) sex tours to patronize underage girls and boys are unlikely to find the abuse or exploitation of children in war *or* peace a significant cause for concern. Studies consistently show that domestic violence increases dramatically during war, and that people in uniform show significantly higher rates of domestic and sexual violations both in war and peace (Nordstrom 1996: 147–62; Ashworth 1986). To put the point bluntly: those who use physical and sexual violence against noncombatant youths in war ground their actions in part on prevailing cultural beliefs, and then carry these kinds of abusive actions and their associated meanings back into their own communities. That legal systems have so rarely prosecuted violators of children's rights and have often engaged in persecuting the victims themselves (Asia Watch and The Women's Rights Project 1993) illustrates how widespread such social practices permeate civil, judicial, governmental, and military structures.

Why Children?

So why, then, are children raped, maimed, starved, overworked, and killed across war and peace zones? Several avenues offer possible explanations. I have explored (para)militaries' use of dirty terror tactics against civilians during war to control populations through intimidation and fear (Nordstrom 1992a, 260–74; 1992b, 27–43; 1992c, 6–8; 1994; 1995). Dirty war tactics that target civilians have become common in the second half of the twentieth century (see Matlou, this volume) and do not appear to be abating as we move into the third millennium. From tortures conducted behind prison walls to mutilations conducted in public squares for whole towns to see, violations of human codes of ethics and morality are still routinely employed to break political will through sheer terror. A classic example of the use of terror is summarized in Lina Magaia's (1988) *Dumba Nengue: Run For Your Life. Peasant Tales of Tragedy in Mozambique.* It opens with the following true story.

> It happened at night, as it always does. Like owls or hyenas, the bandits swooped down on a village in the area of Taninga. They stole, kidnapped and then forced their victims to carry their food, radios, batteries, the sweat of their labor in the fields or in the mines of Jo'burg where many of those possessions had come from.
>
> Among the kidnapped were pregnant women and little children. Among the little ones was a small girl of nearly eight. And the hours went by and dawn broke and finally there was a halt. They put down their loads and the bandits selected who could return home and who had to carry on. Of those who had to keep going, many were boys between twelve and fifteen. Their fate was the school of murder–they would be turned into armed bandits after training and a poisoning of their conscience. Others were girls between ten and fourteen, who would become women after being raped by the bandits. Others were women who were being stolen from their husbands and children.
>
> To demonstrate the fate of girls to those who were going back, the bandit chief of the group picked out one, the small girl who was less than eight. In front of everyone, he tried to rape her. The child's vagina was small and he could not penetrate. On a whim, he took a whetted pocketknife and opened her with a violent stroke. He took her in blood. The child died. (Magaia 1988: 19–20)

As in this example, the ability to control terror is intended to lead to or symbolize the ability to control populations. As girls often represent the most vulnerable and innocent members of society, their abuse renders the most terror: society is most undermined by the violation of those considered most 'inviolable'. A society that is effectively undermined through terror, dirty war theory wrongly postulates, is a society whose members will be unable to marshal the personal or political will to resist.[8]

A second very obvious reason why children are maimed, molested, and killed in war has to do with the subjugation and humiliation of 'the enemy'. This is part of the symbolic war, fought out using the physical bodies of those least able to protect themselves and least implicated in the war effort. One intended message is that if a state is so weak as to allow this to happen to its children, how can it possibly have the political and moral strength to govern a population? In this regard, Mankekar summarizes the relationship between constructions of childhood—especially that of girls as the quintessential innocents—and nation in drawing attention to "the synecdochic relationship between the purity of girl-children and the purity of the nation ..." (1995: 4). "Significantly," she elaborates, "the purity of childhood seems to implicate nothing less than the moral state of the nation" (1995: 19). By extension, symbols of impurity of a nation's children strategically deployed in war implicate the impurity, even the viability of the nation itself.

Yet these explanations conveniently fail to address the fact that a number of people both in and out of war are perpetrating the same violence upon their own children, families, and communities. Contrary to conventional wisdom, it is therefore important to ask what exactly is the difference between a soldier abusing a youth in a rape camp during war and his abusing a youth in his own community. This question challenges both epistemological and ontological 'realities'. Moreover, I am increasingly finding a third reason for the abuse of children in war, or in peace. Beyond the constructions of terror and their relationship to sociopolitical power, beyond notions of purity and a nation's morality, there appears a tragic fact: children are abused by those with more power and strength simply *because they can be.*

To explain: many of the world's discourses on war (from Sun Yat Sen to Clausewitz, from *The Seven Samurai* to John Wayne) valorize the moral contest between *equals.* This characterization continues to pervade both popular and military ideologies. It is, however, a dangerous myth that hides a cowardly truth: violence is often directed against those who are perceived to be weak or who by their situation or nature cannot fight back. Global statistics on violence show that, whether in battle or in domestic life, the more powerful harm those who pose little threat. As noted, UN figures show that children's deaths outnumber soldiers' deaths in war today. The majority of war deaths likewise are noncombatants (see Matlou, this volume). The unarmed and undefended are the main targets of the armed. This trend extends into civil life: on the streets, muggers prey on low-risk victims; at home, men primarily abuse women, and adults abuse children. Ardent racism and homophobia also tend to be expressed in situations of unequal force. The same holds true in rape: it is estimated that underage boys are sexually assaulted with a frequency that is close to that of girls; women are raped by men (though in less numbers than girls) many times more often than men are raped by men. A look at the statistics on violence worldwide shows that girls suffer the most, in part, because they are the most vulnerable, least powerful, and easiest to silence. Children have little recourse to rectify their own problems in the face of these pathologies of power. While the major civil and human rights abuses children face are perpetrated by adults, children must rely on adults to protect their rights. Children do not have direct access to United Nations forums and decision-making consuls, to direct representation in courts of law, to the state's policy-forming committees, or to NGO grants. Children are bound by laws in which they have no input, and by legal practice which they do not influence. They are governed by institutions generated by and in the image of (some) adults. In fact, children may even find it difficult to elicit police or legal protection, find a hospital on their own, or learn about their rights.

War Zone Solutions

Much of the tragedy befalling children is preventable.... Brutality, violence, rape and torture—all would stop tomorrow if the will to stop them existed, or if the rest of us devised means to compel them to be stopped.

UNICEF (1995a: 11)

The world must foster a culture that dissuades combatants from directing violence against those who least deserve it and are least able to defend themselves.

Graca Machel, Chairperson of the *Study on the Impact of Armed Conflict on Children* (UNICEF 1996b)

The first step toward a solution is to lift the veil of silence that surrounds the treatment of girls in war. The prevailing silence, as I suggested earlier, is about politics and power: both are fundamentally implicated in any form of human rights abuse. Effective solutions cannot be implemented if we do not know how many girls are targeted in war, displaced, sold into forced labor, or harmed in their homes and communities—or if we do not know who is doing this and why. We need to ask: when the word 'human' is used, as in 'human rights violations', does it actually include children? When the word 'child' is used, does it really mean girls and boys, or just boys? Does 'children' mean youths, teenagers, or all children? Too often girls are considered *only* as silent victims of (sexual) assault—devoid of agency, moral conscience, economic potential, or political awareness. The focus on boys and specifically on older youths is often subtle: portrayals of 'child soldiers' tend to show boys twelve to fifteen years old; the fighting or torture of five-year-olds is seldom discussed. In the same vein, the category 'girl prostitute' tends to refer to twelve- to sixteen-year-olds, while the extensive sexual predation of younger children is infrequently referenced. The phrase 'child victim of war' seldom considers the experiences of infants. We cannot seek the answers until we begin asking the questions, and asking is not a simple thing.[9] Silence protects the gain made on child labor, the police and military who target children, and the child-sex tour operators and patrons. It also protects those who continue to provide state, aid, and development programs that ignore or mute children. Speaking out involves risk. It may involve speaking out against trusted or powerful leaders, entrepreneurs, government and military officials, friends and neighbors. It may involve the threat of retaliation or subjecting our own lives and assumptions to scrutiny. Even so, maintaining silence is uncomfortably close to complicity. Speaking out is, of course, only a first step, for as I have asserted throughout this chapter, we simply do not have adequate information on what happens to girls in war to pose effective solutions. We need to ask and to know: What percentage of casualties are girls? How many are tactically targeted for torture or terror-warfare? How many girls are in rape camps and refugee communities? What do they face, if they survive, when they return home? We also need to develop the means whereby girls can tell us their own stories of war, its impact, and potential solutions, rather than assume the right to speak for them.

Beyond this, we have to map the international systems of exploitation of children that, as I have argued, are deeply implicated in specific wartime practices. Who benefits, and how? If public opinion continues to see the exploitation of children as the random product of antisocial fragments of society or the sad consequence of war, and not as integral to 'normal' practice, the mechanisms by which this industry can be dismantled or made just will not become evident. Simultaneously, we need to move our analysis inward to the center of society. As suggested above, what people tolerate in peace determines what they will tolerate in war, and the injustices of war carry over into peacetime (see Giles, this volume). Those who tolerate domestic child abuse and underage sex tourism in peacetime are likely to tolerate (arguably similar) abuse of children in war as well. Where, then, do war zones end?

It is important to consider the very conceptual systems and habits of discourse that surround discussions of girls and human rights abuses. For example, analyses on conflict and war seldom conjoin the stories of girls raped or battered by enemy soldiers and girls raped or battered by friendly soldiers or familials. That these two sets of girls might well see their plights as similar is seldom considered. Why does the first constitute part of war's discourse, while the latter does not? Why has so little research investigated the similarities and differences–not as constructed or analyzed by researchers–but as *experienced* by girls themselves? I doubt that there is any political, social, or moral system that formally condones war practices that violate children. There are seventy thousand documents in the world today ensuring human rights (Clements 1992:10), and none tolerate the violation of noncombatant children. How can violations of children *within* one's own community be discussed in the same breath? These acts are equally reprehensible but the 'we' can no longer be differentiated from the 'they'. Solutions thus rest on recognizing the realities of justice and abuse that circle the globe, not as abstract categories but as they affect the lives of very real people. If countries are to deal effectively with children's rights, they will have to face serious introspection. Australia and Sweden, for example, have legislated that their citizens can be prosecuted for having sex with underage children in *foreign* countries. Governments, businesses, and private citizens alike face complex dilemmas here linking profit, free trade, international ethics, and personal morality (Dwyer 1995).

The next level of solutions in considering 'girls and war' involves the conventions and protocols ensuring human and children's rights. The Convention on the Rights of the Child is the most widely ratified international treaty in existence. By 1995, 168 countries were signatories. Yet it is easy for an adult to sign a protocol supporting the rights of children and to ignore that treaty in everyday practice. The letter of the law is rarely the dialogue of social practice. I am, therefore, more concerned with the *implementation* of children's rights protocols than their construction and ratification. It seems to me that one of the most important routes to better implementation is to give children a greater public voice. Consider the impact, for example, if media representatives interviewed children in war zones as well as adults; if children's solutions to violence were sought as seriously as those of officials; if children presented at formal bodies dedicated to the rights of children–bodies that included representatives who *are* children. And consider the impact if, in these examples, 'children' did not mean boys, or mostly teenage boys, but a full representative range of children.

At a more formal level, consider the impact if those working with non/governmental or research organizations more consistently addressed children as well as adults, girls as well as boys, peacetime as well as crises intervention. This is not as simple as it seems, as several innovative attempts to do so indicate. For example, I recently visited the Center for the Study of Violence and Reconciliation in Johannesburg, South Africa. While going into neighborhoods to counsel children affected by violence, Center specialists realized that they could not reasonably separate the sexual abuse of children, physical violence, and the impact of years of political violence. As the head of the Trauma Center explained:

> We are finding forty cases of incest a day at our centers. But these children often mention in the course of counseling that they saw someone killed recently. And these actions relate to patterns of violence left by decades of political fighting. If we are to address trauma, we have to address all these levels. And we have to address our own place in this: children's parents, friends, siblings, counselors, we have all been affected by the war and the violence spawned throughout communities.

I would also note the work of the Christian Children's Fund in Angola, which has led the way in conducting studies on the impact of war on children with attention to girls, and in implementing programs based on these studies.

Children today are much more profoundly muted in research than women, who are both well represented among researchers and an increasingly powerful and vocal constituency. Consider the impact if researchers were encouraged to investigate and document the international networks supporting child sexual and domestic labor, the (para)military networks that allow the strategic targeting of children, the community networks implicated in violating children's rights. One of the most common responses I hear is that "you'll be killed if you follow that line of research." Whether it is true or not (and I have been doing this work for over fifteen years without incident), this belief stops people from doing such research–and from publishing it.

Postscript

One consequence of more research of this sort would be to highlight the agency of children. Girls, even very young ones, often have a well-developed moral, political, and philosophical understanding of the events in their lives and worlds. Years of research on the frontlines of war have taught me that even very young children have profound experiences and opinions on conditions of justice and injustice, and think about both violence and peace in their lives.

Children fight and are fought against, but both sides of the equation are absent from public awareness. And yet UNICEF recently reported that in southeast Rwanda almost 56 percent of the children interviewed said they had seen children kill people, and 42 percent saw children kill other children (UNICEF 1995a: 28).

Silence also surrounds children's antiwar activities. Children worldwide have been involved in sophisticated peace-building efforts. From *Youth for Peace* in Northern Ireland to the peace-building work of the YWCA of Sri Lanka and the youth groups of South Africa, children have been working to forge viable platforms for peaceful coexistence.[10] Some countries have incorporated children into the peace process, providing models for other regions grappling with disruptive violence. For example, since 1992 all schools in Northern Ireland have been required to include conflict resolution activities designed to build cross-communal understanding in their core curriculum. Of the ninety-nine organizations listed as being involved with conflict resolution and reconciliation by the Community Relations Council of Northern Ireland, over half have a youth focus or are working to develop the youth sector (Abitbol and Louise n.d.).

These and other similar programs provide models for action across divisions of war and peace. The organizational and educational programs now dealing with conflict resolution in Northern Ireland could well be implemented in my hometown of Oakland, which had the debatable distinction a few years ago of being the most violent city in the United States. Of course, such an action would force Americans to confront the serious truth that, as victims and victimizers, children face violence that is for the most part domestic. Contrary to the persistent media representations of (predominately black) urban American teenagers with automatic weapons threatening the public at large, recent research shows that nearly 70 percent of all male youths who engage in violence do so against an adult man who is harming their mother.[11]

From the schools of Northern Ireland to youths trying to protect their mothers in Oakland, a pattern emerges showing children to be far more politically aware, morally developed, and actively involved in conflict and its resolution than most studies and media portrayals suggest. I am reminded of a drawing I recently received from the Nairobi journalist Miriam Kundu, whom I met when we served together as Election Observers in Mozambique. It was a child's drawing of a man, called Rwanda, hung by a rope from a tree. Standing by the hanging victim were two other men: one in indigenous African dress titled 'African Countries', the other in a suit with a UN insignia saying to the first, "Don't just stand there and stare at him, can't you do something?" Miriam's daughter Mzanza had seen a cartoon like this in a Kenyan local daily, redrew it, and gave it to her mother as "a surprise note." When her mother asked her why, Mzanza replied, "Please write about it, Mum." Mzanza is ten years old.

Because I am an anthropologist committed to fieldwork, I spend a great deal of time on the frontlines of wars. Many researchers do not get this opportunity, and thus do not have the chance to see how people actually act in the midst of violence. It has been my experience that in the midst of aggression, *most* people do not engage in violence, but work to stop or limit it. Violence, whether in war or in peacetime, is perpetrated by the minority. And it is only this minority that benefits from ideologies that characterize war as the bad side of human nature and as impossible to alienate. No fundamental evil is unleashed from the fonts of human nature in the heat of battle or greed for gain. These are actions people have learned, and have learned are possible. In many cases, they have been carefully taught, often through experience in abusive systems. If we accept that abuse and aggression are natural to human nature and society, we will not work as energetically or optimistically as we might to dismantle them. And simply believing that we can do so is as important an act as dismantling the systems that allow abuse.

Notes

1. Bruce Harris, a worker with an NGO dedicated to children's rights in Guatemala, notes in an interview with Richard Swift, "If that many people were in one country they'd have a seat at the UN" (Swift 1995: 31). Worldwide, many of these children "disappear, are beaten, illegally detained and confined, sexually exploited, tortured, and systematically killed by agents of the state" (Millett 1994: 294).

2. To give but a few examples of the incorporation of children or their specific study: Veena Das's (1991) inclusion of children's realities during the 1985 rioting in India; Ed Cairns's work (1987; 1995) on children and political violence in Northern Ireland; Marcelo Suárez-Orozco's study (1987) of the strategies of torture directed specifically at children; Neil Boothby's work with Ressler and Steinbock (1988) on unaccompanied children in conflict conditions; and R.W. Connell's book (1971) of children's voices describing their political identities. Dorothy Allison's recent novel *Bastard Out of Carolina* (1992), based on her own childhood of severe physical and sexual abuse, throws open the question of how much experiential separation really exists between what is called war and peace in terms of human rights violations and the suffering of children. See also Allison (1994) and Stephens (1995).

3. The following is an example of the politics of invisibility that I know of personally. It revolves around the larger issue of what happened to the 200,000 to 300,000 orphans of war in Mozambique. The answer for one child surfaced when she was unceremoniously dumped at a hospital. A group of men associated with a project under the auspices of a European embassy were making and marketing pornographic films. Their actions came to light when the dog they were forcing one girl to have sex with mauled her. The doctors at the hospital were unable to save the child. The hospital staff, and those they called in to witness the atrocity, were outraged. They petitioned the government to treat this as a formal crime, and the government representatives involved were equally outraged. Yet no media attention or formal court proceedings followed. Officials associated with the European embassy who counted the pornographers as countrymen stepped in to quiet the situation. The major offenders were escorted out of Mozambique without reprisal. The international network that exists to produce such films was neither exposed nor challenged.

4. See also United Nations Development Program (1992).

5. Poston writes that after the report was made some soldiers were quietly sent home. The report also stated that while the sexual trade in children did exist, it certainly was not restricted to UN soldiers. To many, this constituted a bit of a whitewash, but does point to a deeper injustice: trade in child sex that extends across societies and nationalities (French 1992: 30). Barnaby Phillips of BBC was in fact told by young prostitutes in Mozambique that there is no shortage of foreign clients. "They come from lots of different countries. But they are usually white. It is white men who like young girls best" (1994). These young prostitutes told Phillips that in accord with the preferences of their clients they use no condoms. The consequent impact of AIDS is already evident. A Community Aid Abroad report (1994) notes that just four months after arriving in Mozambique, a UNOMOZ major was sent home, and later died of AIDS. Tests subsequently confirmed that 90 percent of the troops from the same contingent were HIV positive. And yet etiquette dictates that sex tourists and contingents of aid, development, and diplomatic personnel are *not* routinely tested: the infection rates among these groups remains unknown.

6. For example, Marie Mies, professor of sociology at the Fachhochschule in Cologne and author of numerous books and articles on women's rights and issues worldwide, asserts that sex tourism was proposed as a development strategy by international aid agencies. She writes that this industry was first planned and supported by the World Bank, the International Monetary Fund (IMF), and the United States Agency for International Development (French 1992: 30).

7. Prevailing rhetoric implies the inherent naturalness of abuse and violence, rendering natural such clichés as 'war is inevitable', 'collateral damage (civilian casualties) is undesirable but inevitable', or 'rape is a consequence of male biology and inevitable'. As Cynthia Enloe (1993) stresses, much energy goes into perpetuating the notion that certain facets of social and political life are natural, the complete lack of rigorous supporting evidence for these 'truths' notwithstanding. What is defined as reprehensible but inevitable and practiced, like the abuse of children, represent sites of social and political silencing.

8. In truth, dirty war practices are ultimately ineffective in controlling a population. As Foucault has written, resistance starts the instant power is abused.

9. In spite of the difficulty, work is being done. New and sophisticated work on the plight of children in both wartime and peacetime is being undertaken by several NGOs. One is the Group for the Convention on the Rights of the Child, with a

Sub-Group on Refugee Children and Children in Armed Conflict. The UN has commissioned a study by Graca Machel (former Minister of Education in Mozambique) on Children in Armed Conflict in conjunction with UNICEF and the UN Center for Human Rights. The First World Congress on Commercial Sexual Exploitation of Children was held in Stockholm in August 1996, organized by the Swedish government in conjunction with UNICEF, ECPAT (End Child Prostitution, Child Pornography, and Trafficking in Children for Sexual Purposes), and the NGO Group for the Convention on the Rights of Children. The last is planning to undertake a study of the sexual exploitation of children in war. There are a number of other committed NGOs, including Save the Children, Defense for Children International, and International Children's Rights Monitor.

10. For an excellent resource on children and war, see Abitbol and Louise (n.d.) for a far-ranging and sensitive investigation of children in conflict situations. Even so, it is interesting to note that the book's sections looking at "women" deal with exactly that: "women." Women's experiences of physical and sexual violence and women's initiatives are discussed, *not* those of *girls*. Reflecting a common current in the literature and media, this enforces two dangerous tendencies: that women are interchangeable with children and are thus infantilized, and that girls drop out of public recognition altogether.

11. This statistic and many similar ones were available in the public show on Women and War, University of California Berkeley campus, May 1994, by Emily Graves, Dana Gerstein, and Monica Bereni.

5

Gendered Violence in War

Reflections on Transnationalist and Comparative
Frameworks in Militarized Conflict Zones

Wenona Giles

This chapter addresses issues of forced migration that surface in the gendered violations of women in homes and households in war.[1] I also explore the potential for comparative analysis of these issues across militarized conflict zones. From a comparative perspective, I argue that ideas and images of the home are often central to nationalist and protonationalist ideologies that inform these conflicts. In such cases, the home as an everyday, tangible and 'natural' conceptual unit is frequently mapped onto the intangible abstractions of nation and state. In this process, homes or households are then often rendered invisible in folk discourse. Nor are they considered relevant units of analysis in most studies of nationalism and war. One aim of this chapter, therefore, is to reveal key dimensions of the gendered nature of nationalism and war through an exploration of the violation of women, homes, and households in 'wartime' and the reflection or immanence of these practices in 'peacetime'. One of the most visible ongoing consequences of gendered violence in war is the massive movement of women and children from war zones. Gendered nationalist ideologies and the conflicts in which they are activated have direct implications for displacement and war, refugee-generating flight, and refugees' experiences thereafter.[2]

The chapter is organized in four sections. I begin by addressing the several concepts central to my analysis: household, home, and immanence. Second, I unpack the idea of comparative analysis, suggesting that transnational feminism at least partially addresses the potentially static essentialism of comparative approaches. In short, I argue for approaching the study of 'home' and households comparatively across conflict zones. In the third section, I assert that in order to understand nationalism(s), gendered ideas of home and household must be analytically addressed as dynamic structures. Finally, I consider the refugee camp-as-home, and examine some of the ways that normative definitions of home are reflected onto these sites, thus framing refugee women in particularly gendered ways.

Throughout this chapter I highlight connections between 'imagined' notions of home and household on the one hand, and nationalism, war, and gendered violence against women on the other. In conflict situations such as war, gendered images of home and household are part of group ideologies that have direct and sometimes predictable consequences for the forms and incidence of violence directed toward women and men in conflict zones. Moreover, gendered ideologies that characterize everyday peacetime significantly impact on gendered practices in everyday wartime; in this sense, peacetime is immanent in wartime and vice versa. In both the spaces of flight and resettlement, the definitions that prescribe the identity and thus the resources available to women refugees are directly related to the way that women have been historically defined in their homes and households. During flight and resettlement these sometimes complex definitions may become essentialized composites of the way women are defined in domestic spaces in their countries of origin.

Household, Home, and Immanence

Let me begin by clarifying several core concepts. Ideas of household and home are interwoven and difficult to define separately. Elsewhere (Giles 1997: 388) I have characterized households as small-scale forms of social organization supporting

> ... the survival of their members, across time and in the case of immigrants and migrants, across countries and continents. They are economic enterprises unto themselves, but linked to other households and always shaped by the larger economy and culture in which they are embedded. Their linkages to other households may be economic but are also affective, involving community and family associations.

The 'larger economy and culture' in which refugee and immigrant women experience the household is itself often shaped by the policies of international agencies and national state agencies in countries of resettlement. With regard to the latter, masculinist definitions of 'work' and 'skill' in Western immigration policies have resulted in most immigrant women being classified as householders on entering host countries (Fincher et al. 1994; Giles, 1997: 395).

Host countries may reinforce naturalized images of women by positing that it is the 'home [country of origin] culture' that prevents immigrant/migrant women from securing better jobs, more education, and fluency in the language of the host country. As a result, these kinds of policies may lead to a privatization of immigrant and refugee women's lives, isolating them from a sense of the broader community in which they may have resettled (Giles 1996; 1997).

For my purposes, a 'home' is something quite different. As I have discussed elsewhere (Giles 1997: 387), a home is a complex of ideas that may refer to a country of origin and an associated national identity; it may also correspond to a specific dwelling place, household, or family. The idea of home is a contradictory phenomenon: while it may confine women, it may also represent escape and freedom. For some it is a locus of resistance and struggle. Home is a gendered phenomenon and is the 'location' from which many immigrant women begin to describe, defend, or justify themselves and their acts (Giles 1997: 387). In short, gender relations in immigrant or refugee households are influenced by traditional ideologies that involve a 'remembering' on the part of immigrant or refugee women of attachments to ideas of home and thus also to households, as experienced and remembered (see Gómez, this volume).

Bhattacharjee's (1997: 313–4) recent work deepens this characterization of home. In research on South Asian immigrants in the US, she shows how homes are spoken of at three different levels: first, "the (conventional) domestic sphere of the heterosexual and patriarchal family"; second "as an extended ethnic community separate and distinct from other ethnic communities"; and third, in reference "to nations of origin, often shaped by nationalist movements and histories of colonialism." As in Bhattacharjee's example, women's overlapping and cross-cutting identities pertaining to these different homes often challenge the notion of sharp boundaries around women refugees' identities, as I discuss below. In addition, Bhattacharjee writes that, in this particular case as in many others, immigrant "women are in danger of being made invisible in all three homes." For example, women may experience silencing in heterosexist and patriarchal homes; suffer public invisibility due to illegal status and a lack of documentation; experience dependency on men in the immigration and resettlement process; and face essentialist gendered definitions of national culture in their own ethnic group or community, which sometimes validates or dismisses instances of abuse and violence against them (Bhattacharjee 1997: 322).

Contemporary analyses of immigrant and refugee women clearly necessitate a better understanding of households than that achieved through use of the traditional anthropological (and also state-defined) model of the household as a highly bounded, functional entity. When traditional household analysis either neglects gender relations entirely, or is associated with universalized gender relations, the result can be dangerously misleading. It may make it impossible to get beyond classical public-private characterizations of women's activities and commitments. The application of static, normative status and role constructions (for example, husband-father, wife-mother, and children) to studies of households are also profoundly limiting. If we accept the notion put forth by Indra (this volume) and others that households are dynamic structures that are always 'in process', can we not then go further to describe homes as the meaning structures attached to households by both those within and without "imagined communities" in the Andersonian sense? Approaching households as processual allows deeper comparison across communities, regions, or nations; such an approach also has implications for our understanding of transnational practices and gendered relations between war and peace.

At the beginning of this chapter I stated that peacetime is immanent in wartime and vice versa–a notion that is deeply considered by Nordstrom in this volume. Taking this a step further, some of the key social relations of war and militarism can be considered as being immanent in homes at three levels: in the (conventional) domestic sphere, in the community, and in remembrances of nations of origin.

By 'immanence', I refer to the concept developed by Brah (1996: 16, 181, 209) in her theory of "diaspora space." She uses the concepts of diaspora, border, and the politics of location to generate a "conceptual grid' for historically analyzing "trans/national movements of people, information, cultures, commodities and capital." For Brah, diaspora space is "the site of this immanence."

> Diaspora space is the intersectionality of diaspora, border and dis/location as a point of confluence of economic, political, cultural and psychic processes ... [and] is 'inhabited' not only by those who have migrated and their descendants but equally by those who are constructed and represented as indigenous. (1996: 181)

Brah's ideas have important implications for analyses of forced migration and gendered violence in war. The concept of diaspora space allows us to envisage the ways that some dimensions of war and its associated violence are part of what are conventionally referred to as everyday peacetime. In this perspective, the expulsion of women and children from their homes and into exile as refugees, the existence of gendered forms of violence against women in war, the promotion of cultures of "masculinized militarism" (Enloe 1993), and the production and trade in military weapons are not processes located 'elsewhere', namely in war zones. As Enloe notes, "masculinized militarism," as a distinctive set of beliefs and structures, is entrenched in everyday life by a wide range of everyday, 'normal' societal processes (1993: 246). Gendered violence in war in particular does not exist aberrantly, isolated in time or location. Rather, such acts are parts of much larger processes that can be linked back to gender relations in households and to ideologies of homes.

These processes do not affect everyone the same. Peoples, cultures, commodities, and the like may share the same time and space, but, as Brah points out, regimes of power situate them differently, so that in reference to forced migrants, "... the concept of diaspora centers on the *configurations of power which differentiate diasporas internally as well as situate them in relation to one another"* (Brah 1996: 183); some are empowered and others disempowered. In particular, racial, gender, and class discourses and practices deeply affect circumstances of leaving as well as arrival and resettlement (see Kosmarskaya, this volume).

Comparative Analysis

Comparative research, potentially an activist approach working toward the elimination of inequality and oppression, is often undertaken at such a high level of abstraction that it is sometimes difficult to see the link between research and social change. Comparative work of the traditional variety is, for example, likely to incorporate static essentialisms that mask critical differences and divergent histories of domination. Brah's treatment of diaspora space is one method of comparison that incorporates generalization and difference in a reasonable analytical balance. Bhattacharjee's work on the home in turn provides some guidance on how to better link comparative analysis and activisms. The three levels that she defines as cornerstones for diasporic definitions of home (the domestic sphere, the ethnic community, and the nation of origin) are all social sites of gendered struggle, and she further notes that feminist activism typically challenges the status quo of all three 'homes' (1997: 327). All three are, of course, linked by the construct 'woman' (Bhattacharjee 1997: 324).

Many forms of activism that articulate with these different notions of home can be envisaged: activisms, for example, that are rooted in local feminist politics and that inform and are connected to national and global feminist politics.[3] In considering these issues, Alexander and Mohanty (1997) argue for a retheorization of feminism, central to which is a comparative analysis of feminist organizing, criticism, and self-reflection. This is to be associated with a "comparative, relational feminist praxis that is transnational in its response to and engagement with global processes of colonization" (Alexander and Mohanty 1997: xx). J. Hyndman also argues for a comparative model of "transnational feminist practices: political action which conceives of differences as linked, if unequal, and which upsets commonplace markers of social, cultural and political identity" (1996: 17). She, along with Grewal and Kaplan (1994a), regard developing feminist transnational practices as challenging purely locational politics, and as engaging and connecting rather than distinguishing and distancing people of different locations. Viewing war zones in this way, she notes: "Women whose bodies, families and communities bear the violent inscriptions of war and hate are neither universal subjects, nor unrelated individual subjects in their different locations" (J. Hyndman 1996: 17–18).

'Transnational feminism' in this context evokes ideas of global alliance that many today view as arising from a critique of, and a response to, earlier models of 'global sisterhood' that were built on unequal, metropole-generated, 'center-periphery' or 'First World/ Third World' models (Alexander and Mohanty 1997: xxix). Such authors affirm the necessity for 'national democracy', but they also call for a more global 'feminist democracy': a "transborder participatory democracy" (xli). Although the articulation of the 'national' and the 'nation' in theories of the transnational requires much more analysis,[4] it is clear that the connections here will challenge the conceptions of borders and boundaries in feminist politics. Developing such an approach that is linked to "relational and historically based conceptions of feminisms" (Alexander and Mohanty 1997: xvi) will help reduce essentialism, and will perhaps provide a useful way of grounding theories of transnationalism (V. Preston, personal communication).

Gendering Homes and Women's Bodies in War

To discern why and how images of women take on a specific significance in war and to understand the relationships between this

gendering of their bodies to the violation of homes, it is first necessary to reconsider conventional gendered constructions of the private and public. War and its expression in militarization is, as Enloe
points out, part of a patriarchal structure of privilege and control,
and not simply the consequences of a capitalist military-industrial
complex and/or the prevalence of hierarchical states (1993: 69–70).
The way that patriarchy is constructed through social and ideological relations in homes is clearly reflected in militarization, and militarization does not only occur in so-called war zones; nor is it
associated with one specific site or static phenomenon. Militarization
is informed and informs gender relations in factories, police stations,
refugee camps, and bedrooms (Enloe 1993: 68).

Indra (this volume) describes gendered social relations in a household as often being represented in ways in which men 'fall from
view', and women in their reproductive and domestic roles become
'foregrounded'. This tendency surfaces strongly in ideologies of ethnic nationalism (in war), in which women and their bodies are constructed in particular ways. For example, Korac notes a distinction
between "patriotic women" and "disloyal women" that was commonly made in the former Yugoslavia (Korac 1996a: 28): the former
were those through whom the nation could "rebuild links with 'honorable' histories, religions and traditions," while the latter betrayed
the "ethnic-national collective" by seeking to initiate or maintain solidarity across ethnic-national boundaries (Korac 1996b: 254; Cammack, this volume). As Moore writes, a crucial issue concerning the
occurrence of gendered violence is whether, and the way in which,
the behavior of others threatens the self-representations and social
evaluations of the perpetrator of violence (1994:67). In this regard,
'disloyal women' in the former Yugoslavia were likely to be the targets of violence by those whose identities as Serbs, Bosnians, Croats,
and males were threatened. Ironically, the raping of women may
also inadvertently transform them into 'patriotic women' for the purposes of other nationalists, who may use such women's assaulted
bodies as easy metaphors for assaults meted upon imagined homes
and, thus, upon the nation. In this process, women's bodies are foregrounded as both the targets of violence and symbols of a violated
nation. Patrick Matlou (this volume) discusses this in relation to
recent ethnic conflicts in Africa.

As Moore notes, the social space of households and images of
home produce "specific sorts of persons with specific social identities
and particular rights and needs" (1994:93). These do so in combination with a myriad of experiences outside of this social and intellectual space, all of which tend to strongly circumscribe women's

responses to injustice in larger frames. This is, of course, one way in which the home is immanent in national spaces. For example, de Alwis's work on the Mother's Front in Sri Lanka demonstrates how the protests of women against state violence were "limited to tears and curses." Defined "primarily through familial subject positions such as wives and mothers," they were unable to transcend their gender and class stereotypes to make links with other women's groups in Sri Lanka and elsewhere (1996: 13). However limited these forms of resistance, they did "create the space … for [further] protest in a context of terror and violence" (ibid.). Similarly, the silent "Women in Black" demonstrations seen in several militarized war zones, including Belgrade, Israel/Palestine, and Spain under Franco have rendered more visible the connections between political opinion, gender relations, and war, and have opened space for new forms of protest and organization. In Belgrade, for example, such a group eventually generated other activities and programs, some specifically for refugee women.

The Refugee Camp-As-Home

One of the inevitable outcomes of the interplay between nationalist fantasies of power and ideologies of home and household is the contradictory construction of refugee camps as both places of refuge from the nationalist and gendered violence of war, as well as sites of gendered violence. Refugee camps are a deeply informative site for analysis of ways that naturalized images of home are mapped onto representations of the state, the nation, and international agencies. It also well illustrates the immanence of militarized violence, particularly because it is a site where strong attempts are often made to create everyday peacetime on the periphery of everyday wartime. There is, of course, a great deal of variation in the history, organization, and culture of camps that only case studies can ultimately capture. My aim here is to consider alternative ways of thinking about how women and homes are ideologized in refugee camps.

I believe that looking at the refugee camp-as-home through the various conceptual levels of home addressed by Bhattacharjee (1997) helps reveal why women have so often been privatized and rendered invisible in these sites (Camus-Jacques 1989: 141; Giles, Moussa, and Van Esterik 1996). Consider first the refugee camp-as-home conceptualized as the domestic sphere of the heterosexual, patriarchal family. We often find that when camps are thought of as private spaces, refugee homes within camps–pertaining to households composed mostly of women and children–are managed and controlled mainly by refugee men and foreigners (see Boelaert et al., this volume). Indeed, while some of the management 'gaze' of camp workers may incorporate basic values of gender equality based on international agency standards, much of what actually happens in camps reinforces unequal gender relations (see Matlou, this volume). This is either because watching/management practice is unequally gendered and gives gendered violence and discrimination little significance, or because what actually happens in refugee households is so powerfully informed by gendered, normative assumptions of the heterosexual and patriarchal home that no further inquiry is deemed necessary.

Considering the camp-as-home in the sense of being an imagined ethnic group or community calls into question many public/private camp distinctions. Camps are routinely organized along ethnic lines, often with the overt rationale that this provides aid more fairly and efficiently and diminishes tension and violence; in this way, individual refugees are supposedly able to operate primarily in terms of 'the group's' shared cultural values and practices. They may be in camps, but at least in some senses they are at 'home'–or so some think. In this way, the camp-as-home inevitably assumes an overly homogeneous appearance which conceals what can be profound gender, class, and other differences. From the perspective of refugees themselves, moreover, one's ethnic or natural culture and practice as manifest in everyday camp life are to be carefully guarded (see Cammack, this volume). As Bhattacharjee (1997: 318) describes in the case of South Asian immigrants in the US, ethnicity may be regarded as private space where women, in particular, are frequently regarded paternalistically by both women and men as the repositories of ethnic culture and heritage–not to mention family honor. They are therefore more likely to be carefully controlled, and to control themselves, in the 'private' space of the group or community. In these spaces, women are also more vulnerable to abuse and violence, which in turn are less visible and harder to address. At the same time, ethnic identities and identifications articulate with larger public arenas where they affect how states and international institutions determine who gets aid, who is destined for resettlement or for a prolonged future in a refugee camp, and who is repatriated. Again, these processes are gendered: women are given less consideration and are usually classified as either the protected dependents of men or as encumbered by children.

A third way of analyzing the camp-as-home evokes images of the nation of origin, shaped as it may be by nationalist movements and histories of colonialism and war. It has been well documented that the nation is often partly defined in relation to notions of womanhood and its protection. It would be naive to think that *regarding* refugee camps as havens from nationalist conflict *makes* them so. Often the first stop for people fleeing conflict, the refugee camp is likely to be a center of competing ethnic-nationalist ideology and activity. As Cammack (this volume) shows in her case study of Afghan refugees in Pakistan, refugee women in such situations can be extremely vulnerable to the gendered politics of nationalism when it characterizes them as 'mothers of the nation', or as symbolic of the 'other' nation or outsider cultural pollution.

Conclusion

Gendered distinctions in war/postwar situations are related to the way that women are ideologized by nationalism and nationalists: as mothers, wives, partners, workers, warriors, enemies, victims or heroines, located in highly political private and public spaces. One such space is the refugee camp. In this context, the refugee camp-as-home frequently becomes framed as a set of ambiguously defined, overlapping private spaces that contain women in an ideological as well as material and physical sense. By examining the ways that women are ideologized in these overlapping spaces, we can reach a better understanding of why and how women are gendered in war. Gendered militarized conflict zones are, in a sense, the backdrop to how women are constrained to operate in households and are characterized chiefly by their roles arising from the home. I also use the example of the refugee camp to point to some of the ways in which local gender relations reflect the global arena of gendered international refugee and aid politics and ethnic nationalist politics. Ideologies that frame and articulate with the refugee camp-as-home, that represent this site as a necessary haven for women, are suspect, as many case studies testify.

To develop an activist agenda, we need to incorporate theoretical and comparative analyses and involve local grassroots groups, researchers, and international agencies. In this chapter, I have presented some initial thoughts outlining an approach to do so. At the same time, I have suggested ways to challenge "purely locational politics," as J. Hyndman (1996) terms it, by comparatively addressing ideologies of the home, constructions of the household, and their immanence within ideologies of war, nation, and state.

Notes

1. I would like to thank the Social Sciences and Humanities Research Council of Canada for the financial support of the Women in Conflict Zones Network. The Center for Refugee Studies, the York Center for International and Security Studies, and the Center for Feminist Research at York University have all provided administrative support for the Network. In particular, I would also like to thank Maja Korac, Alison Crosby, Doreen Indra, and other members of the Women in Conflict Zones Network for their helpful comments.

2. This chapter arises out of ongoing reflections and discussions that have taken place over the course of the last year with an international network (The Women in Conflict Zones Network, originating at York University, Toronto) of individuals involved in research, activism, and policy concerning the situation of women in militarized conflict zones. One of the principal reasons for the existence of the network, as I understand it, has to do with developing comparisons across regions of conflict that can potentially support activist agendas and social change at both local and international levels.

3. Although it is beyond the scope of this chapter, in my view it is also crucial to understand how larger-scale processes, such as capitalism or nationalism, affect the local level community, household, or home, and to be able to compare these across regions involved in conflict. It is at this point that de Alwis's (1997) reflections on comparison are germane. De Alwis has commented that comparative analytical frameworks can occur either at the level of global structures of power, such as capital, imperialism, and international aid, or with reference to particular conceptual categories such as nationalism, ethnicity, motherhood, and home. The challenge is in combining these two levels of analysis to compare regions or class-specific social locations.

4. One such issue for further analysis pertains to the extent to which self-defined nations and/or women associated with these nations can in fact engage in a global alliance of transnational feminism. Women in Afghanistan who are now sequestered in purdah are but one example.

6

Gender Relief and Politics During the Afghan War

Diana Cammack

*Women no longer have the right to work or attend school.... We want
to set up a government based on the precepts of the holy Koran and the
Prophet's recommendations.... The Book stipulates that women should
not mix with men either at work or in school. If they want to study,
they can do so at home under their husbands' supervision.*

Sayed Abdul Malek, Herat, Afghanistan

It was with horror that many people read these words in the *Guardian Weekly* (29 October 1995), for observers had hoped that the
newest mujahedeen movement, the Taleban, then sweeping through
western Afghanistan, would bring enlightenment, unity, and, finally,
peace to the beleaguered country.[1] This was not to be, for the appearance of the Taleban simply added one more player to the
crowded field of warlords vying for power in Kabul, and initiated yet
another rearrangement of alliances between old and bitter rivals.

Readers should not have been surprised by the conservatism of
the Taleban, for it is guided by young Islamists whose convictions
were shaped by exile politics and in the extremist atmosphere of
*madrasah*s (Quranic schools) during a time when a severe form of
Islamic ideology held the moral high ground. But the Taleban's
social and gender policies are not that much different from those
established by other mujahedeen parties at home and in exile during

the last fifteen years. Indeed, in many respects the changes in policy evident in 1995 to 1996 were not so much a matter of substance than of degree.

Still, many foreigners were outraged by the Taleban's restrictions on Afghan women (and to a lesser extent on men) as these came to their attention in 1995. This appears partly because most outsiders were previously ignorant of the restrictive social policies of the mujahedeen. Their ignorance was, in turn, a result of more than a decade of biased news reporting and propaganda efforts that too often idealized and praised the Afghan 'freedom fighters' while ignoring some of their less admirable traits.[2] In that decade, Westerners typically were also uninformed about the role their own governments—and their aid dollars and ecu—played in supporting the mujahedeen's reactionary sociopolitical policies, and in creating the current situation.

War and Gender

It would be an exaggeration to say that the war in Afghanistan was fought over the status of women, but it would not be wholly untrue. In the two decades preceding the Saur Revolution of April 1978, Afghanistan had undergone rapid economic development and sociopolitical liberalization. Legal measures were enacted that gave women more power to choose and divorce partners, and 'bride price' and child marriage were legally abolished—measures that were important for urban women especially. The 1964 constitution enfranchised women when it outlawed discrimination; by 1977 the twenty-member Constitutional Advisory Committee had two women, and the nearly 400-member Loya Jirga, a dozen (Dupree 1991).

In these years, Afghanistan was being integrated into the world economy. For centuries it had remained isolated, successfully repelling colonial overlords. During this period, the domestic economy began to industrialize and differentiate, as technical assistance and funds flowed in. Women gained access to education and the workplace, while traditional restrictions on their mobility, political rights, and social behavior were relaxed. By the late 1970s, girls comprised about 10 percent of the Afghan student population, and urban women were becoming a significant sector of the paid work force. Some had become nurses and midwives, but many others had become technicians, administrators, doctors, teachers, and industrial and office workers. Many wore Western dress and lived relatively independent lives.

Things were different in the countryside, though, where the economic and social transformations had not taken root. There, the same forces that for centuries reinforced tribal and regional isolationism and kept integrative political and economic forces at bay ensured that rural women stayed on farms and in villages. Many remained illiterate, undernourished, and weakened by frequent pregnancies in youthful, polygynous, and arranged marriages. On the eve of the war, divisions between town and country were stark, and differing views about the role of women in Afghan society was only one of the many rural-urban contrasts. The Saur Revolution of April 1978 brought the Afghan communists to power. The following year the Soviet army entered from the north to bolster the factionalized and beleaguered leftist cause. These two events and the subsequent imposition of revolutionary reforms on the countryside together ended any hope of gradually transforming Afghan society and a woman's place within it.

The vanguard Afghan communists who came to power in 1978 aimed to revolutionize what they considered a backward and oppressive feudal regime. They did so in Soviet fashion by trying to impose central government control over the relatively autonomous and factionalized countryside, a move that generated as much opposition as their reforms. The harsh and uncompromising way the reforms were implemented by urban cadres caused additional resentment in the villages, as did the introduction of a mass rural literacy campaign.

In principle, the communists' reforms were quite sound, considering the overwhelming need to modernize and integrate Afghanistan's backward and impoverished political economy (Hyman 1992).[3] For instance, central to the reform process were three decrees: one enacted to break the cycle of peasant indebtedness to landlords, another to abolish 'unjust patriarchal and feudalistic relations' between husband and wife, and the third to undermine 'feudal and prefeudal relations' by redistributing land. Yet for a variety of reasons each of these gave great offense to the rural population. This attack on rural institutions, on the elite, and on aspects of religious and tribal ideals and behavior became identified in the minds of rural Afghans with the corrupting secularism of Westernized Kabul, central government interference in tribal affairs, the dangers of mass education (for schools were seen as un-Islamic and "breeding grounds for communistic ideas" [Dupree 1988]), and outsiders' attempts to alter the proper subordinate position of women. The Soviet intervention in late 1979 provided an additional dimension to the conflict: an attack on Afghans' right of national self-determination.

In assisting the mujahedeen to combat the Soviets, Western governments not only took on the role of Cold Warriors fighting communism,[4] but they and aid agencies often found themselves supporting reactionary personalities and organizations and repressive sociopolitical and gender policies. As a result some humanitarian aid was used in indefensible and unethical ways, including the ongoing suppression of Afghan women's human rights.

War, Factionalism, and Flight

By 1979 the countryside was in rebellion, and refugees were leaving for Pakistan and Iran. Where there had been 1,400 refugees in Pakistan in 1975, by the time the Soviets intervened there were some 400,000. During the following two years almost 100,000 a month crossed the border into Pakistan, and by mid-1981 their number had climbed to over 2 million. Thereafter, the exodus slowed, yet by 1988 Pakistan hosted about 3.5 million refugees, nearly three-fourths of whom lived in the North West Frontier Province (NWFP), including the tribal agencies, and the rest in Baluchistan and the Punjab. Just over one-half of them were children, and an estimated 26 percent were women. Nearly 3 million more refugees lived in Iran, where they were largely integrated into Iranian society and were allowed to work at menial jobs.

After a decade of war, in February 1989 the Soviets withdrew from Afghanistan, leaving as president the communist Dr. Mohammad Najibullah. Few expected Najibullah's government to remain in power for long. In the countryside, the warlords and mujahedeen parties continued to fight against government forces and each other. Najibullah's regime managed to remain in power until April 1992, when a coalition of mujahedeen parties took Kabul, forced the president to seek asylum in the local UN compound, and formed the Islamic Government of Afghanistan.

In the ensuing years, the mujahedeen were no closer to agreeing on a power-sharing arrangement than they had been in exile, though Burhanuddin Rabbani held on to the presidency, as coalitions came and went and factional fighting continued. Warlords maintained control of outlying areas. Especially important were: the Uzbek General Rashid Dostam in relatively peaceful Mazar-i-Sharif in the north; Ismail Khan in Herat in the far west; Gulbuddin Hekmatyar in the Pushtun east; and the Tajik General Ahmad Shah Masoud, based in the Panjsher Valley north of Kabul. International sponsors continued to meddle in Afghan affairs, with regional powers—Saudi Arabia,

Iran, Pakistan, and Uzbekistan mostly—and world powers less openly supporting particular parties against the others. When the communist government fell in 1992, refugees thought they could return home. Soon, though, they found that renewed factional fighting meant a continuation of instability and insecurity in the countryside. Land mines, infrastructural damage, a weak economy, lack of social services, and banditry also deterred many. On the other hand, people were induced to return by a fear that their land would be taken by other returnees; by the introduction of returnee aid packages and assistance, the UN-sponsored reconstruction program, and the elimination of rations in the Pakistani camps; and by various Pakistani decrees declaring that the refugees should repatriate. About one-half of the three million refugees left Pakistan in 1992, while a few hundred thousand returned from Iran (Marsden 1996a; UNHCR 1993).

In the ensuing years, fighting among the mujahedeen generated new refugees. For instance, a huge number of individuals fled Kabul for Jalalabad and Pakistan during faction fighting in January 1994 (British Agencies Afghanistan Group 1996f). Afghanistan's villages were repopulated by families that returned from Iran and Pakistan, and by people who never left the country but lived in caves and dugouts in the mountains during the war. Many refugee families returned in stages, with menfolk going ahead to find work and rebuild their homes before bringing their wives, children, and other dependents. In villages all over the country, families rebuilt their homes, sometimes bartering goods and services or doing manual labor to earn wages. They cleared the irrigation channels and began farming as soon as possible. Female-headed households and those headed by a disabled person remained the poorest, though extended families and charity eased their plight when possible (British Agencies Afghanistan Group 1996b).

While the mujahedeen parties fought for control of Kabul and the hinterland, a new force arose in exile. The Taleban first appeared in October 1994, protecting a trade convoy from Pakistan through Afghanistan. Building upon its rumored support from large traders and Pakistan's Inter-Services Intelligence, it cleared and pacified major routes and moved on to Kandahar in the south in November, where it was largely welcomed by locals longing for peace. Sweeping through the provinces of Logar, Paktika, Paktia, Nangarhar, and Ghazni in the east, it was also welcomed by the population because it brought a degree of security and peace. The Taleban occupied Nimroz, Farah, and finally Herat in the west in early September 1995. In Herat, Taleban rule was opposed because there had been peace there since 1992 and because the Dari-speaking multiethnic population did not want to be governed by a Pashtun Pashto-speaking force.

Despite minor insurrections in areas under its control, the Taleban then turned toward Kabul, controlled by Rabbani but already under attack by Hekmatyar's forces. Absorbing new towns and provinces on its way, the Taleban finally entered Kabul in late September 1996 and immediately executed ex-President Najibullah, who had remained in hiding in the UN compound. The forces of President Rabbani and Generals Masoud and Hekmatyar fled north, followed by the Taleban, who soon engaged them along with the forces of General Dostum. An alliance of several old mujahedeen parties and warlords was formed. This alliance became the basis of the new opposition against the Taleban, who refused to join a coalition government (*Guardian Weekly* 27 August 1996;[5] British Agencies Afghanistan Group 1996c, 1996e).

The stalemate in the north was broken at Mazar-i-Sharif when a member of the alliance, the Uzbek General Abdul Malik, staged a pro-Taleban mutiny against General Dostum at the end of May 1997. As Dostum fled for Turkey, the Taleban entered the city and, in spite of local sensitivities, swiftly imposed a strict Muslim code (for example, closing girls' schools, prohibiting women from working, and enacting dress codes for men and women). Most imprudently for them, the Taleban also began to disarm the men of Mazar-i-Sharif. Within four days, the mujahedeen had rebelled, killed, or captured large numbers of Taleban, and had halted the Taleban's roll through Afghanistan. This military shift favored General Masoud and his mujahedeen allies, who were closely watched by neighboring states and international oil companies. At midyear, there was no indication that the war would soon end (British Agencies Afghanistan Group 1997b, 1997c; *Economist* 17 May 1997, 31 May 1997).

As the new year arrived, bombardment of Kabul, the countryside nearby, and areas to the north created new waves of refugees; thousands of Afghans fled to quieter parts of the country and into neighboring states. For instance, some 15,000 crossed into Pakistan in October 1996, and about 7,000 fled to Turkmenistan in the first week of November. At the end of 1996 there were more than a million refugees still in Pakistan and 1.4 million in Iran (UNHCR Press Release, *Islamabad*, 11 November 1996, enclosed in British Agencies Afghanistan Group 1996d). And in the five months before 1 April 1997, another 250,000 Afghans were displaced by the interminable fighting (British Agencies Afghanistan Group 1997a).

Exile and Aid

In Pakistan, the Afghans settled in refugee villages (numbering 350 by the mid-1980s), where they were initially provided tents–though they soon built mud *katcha* houses enclosed by high 'purdah walls'– and food, water, clothing, bedding, medical care, and sometimes cash. Stabilizing the situation to prevent famine, exposure, and disease was the initial priority of the government and the United Nations High Commissioner for Refugees (UNHCR). Only in the mid-1980s did their thoughts turn to Afghan self-reliance and development, when a number of income-generating and training programs were started. Refugees in Pakistan were allowed to work, and many held jobs as laborers or traders.

Humanitarian aid provided to Afghans in the NWFP and Baluchistan was, with the possible exception of Central America, the most politicized in the world (Baitenmann 1990). During the final fifteen years of the Cold War, humanitarian aid was explicitly used by the American and Pakistani governments, and to a lesser extent by some Middle Eastern and European governments, to support not only the war effort generally, but specific factions of the mujahedeen (sometimes one against the other) and individual warlords 'cross border'. This was understood by UN agencies, which sometimes opposed the practice, but at other times acquiesced (National Security Archive, Washington DC).[6] NGOs were recipients and channels of much of the aid, the majority of which was used to feed, shelter, heal, and clothe refugees as well as internally displaced and war-affected peoples. Sometimes, though, humanitarian aid was used to gather military intelligence, enhance the power of specific commanders, keep people from leaving Afghanistan (where they had to abet the mujahedeen), increase control over refugees by certain political parties, and build the ever-illusory unity of the contentious Afghan factions.

During the period when the Soviets were still in Afghanistan and Western public support for the war was needed, little of this information–or details of mujahedeen corruption, gun running, and heroin trading–was disseminated. While many people are now well aware of the international and long-term implications of Western military assistance to the Afghan 'freedom fighters' (*New York Times* 28 March 1993; Weaver 1995),[7] few have more than a vague sense of what Western aid has done for or to Afghanistan and, more specifically, for and to Afghan women.

While aid workers the world over are motivated by a desire to 'do good', they do not always do so. For instance, agencies might provide material or logistical support to repressive regimes or factions and leaders that enables the latter to implement brutal policies. They might also convey legitimacy to unpopular authorities, empowering such authorities to manipulate and control populations and regions (de Waal and Omar 1994). Famous contexts in which questionable relief assistance was given include the Cambodian border camps, Ethiopia during the mid-1980s famine, the Hong Kong refugee detention centers, aid to the Somali factions, and, more recently, relief to the eastern Zaire camps.

Aid work on the Afghan border was sometimes as dubious, where a mixture of professional agencies, 'cowboy' operations, and 'solidarity' groups tried in their own particular ways to help the Afghan people, the mujahedeen, and their Pakistani hosts. Some organizations were thought to be fronts for intelligence operations (*The Progressive*, May 1990; *Columbia Journalism Review*, January–February 1990), while others (some unwittingly perhaps) channeled Western money to run humanitarian operations that provided intelligence and assisted with the military aims of specific factions 'cross border'. During this period, the overriding Western agenda on the Pakistan-Afghan border was military and political–to get the Soviets out of Afghanistan and to embarrass them in the process.[8] This greatly influenced the work of aid agencies, including the UN.

The relationship between the political-military agenda and the humanitarian program remains underexplored. It is difficult to pin down because it was sometimes hidden, and because it was often unacknowledged by diplomats and aid workers who shared the same vision. But the link is important because it affected the choice, design, and implementation of relief projects. It was particularly crucial to the creation and implementation of programs for Afghan women refugees.

Gender and Aid

To be fair, it was not easy to implement women's programs in the North West Frontier Province. It is the home of the Pushtun tribes and their sometimes cruel and always sexist code of ethics. Further, Pakistan, under Zia al Haq, was in the process of moving to a more fundamentalist interpretation of Islam. Next door, the *jihad* had become a leadership tool to rally the Afghan population. At the same time, the war was used by Islamic donors to "establish the 'perfect Islamic state'–a return to the seventh-century Caliphate" (*The New Yorker*, 6 December 1995), which further radicalized religious ideology in exile. As a result, the power of the Afghan religious elite, including the traditionally weak *mullahs*, was augmented, and a very conservative brand of Islamic practice and thought alien to the relatively tolerant Afghan religious tradition was imposed on Afghan exiles.

In addition, traditionalists and conservatives were adamantly opposed to any liberalization of the position of women because transforming women's role in Afghan society was one of the central aims of the communist regime in Kabul. By the late 1980s, with the flight of the Soviets and a diminished need for American firepower, the ideological enemy was no longer solely the communists, but any Western influence. For instance, the very presence of Western women, however decorously dressed, who worked, drove, taught, or simply went out shopping, was anathema to them.

Critically, the support provided by the Americans and other Westerners to the most fundamentalist elements of the mujahedeen such as Hezbi-Islami (Hekmatyar)—often because they were thought to be the most competent—strengthened their brand of Islam, which opposed the enfranchisement of women and 'bad' Muslim men. Moderate and Western-educated Afghans were underfinanced by donors and targeted by extremists. Many were forced to flee for their lives, and many who remained were murdered.

It is not as though Western donors were unaware of what was happening. While many (especially radical Islamists and Afghans) would like us to believe that the Americans were "duped" by people such as Hekmatyar, the US Agency for International Development (USAID) and probably other donors were "very aware" of the consequences of their helping the more "unsavory" mujahedeen. They knew the movement was a "monster in the making," but that was considered to be "a secondary concern" to their political agenda. As a result, any time USAID officials in Pakistan equivocated about the legitimacy of "their unprecedented and undiluted political support" for the mujahedeen, orders came down from "Pennsylvania Avenue to get on with it."[9]

The UN was also aware of what was happening. While UN staff might not agree that they were "a tool of Pakistan, the US and the Saudis," as one American official put it, certainly UNHCR and the UN's World Food Program (WFP) were in a relatively powerless position. Pakistan had not signed the 1951 UN Convention or the 1967 Protocol on the Status of Refugees, so this limited UNHCR's ability to set refugee policy in Pakistan. Though WFP and UNHCR appeared to have the power of the purse, it was the donors, Americans mostly, who had real control of the purse strings, and they wanted the UN, the Pakistanis, and NGOs to continue supporting the refugees and the mujahedeen.

As a result, UN officials sometimes acted naively, especially at the beginning of their relationship with the mujahedeen, when, for instance, refugees were aided only after they registered with one of the political parties. Later, they were mostly able only to complain about the Pakistani and American policies they disliked. As for their personal sympathies, which are harder to assess, it is likely that many UN officials, like many in the NGO community, were supportive of the mujahedeen cause, at least in the early years.[10] The overpowering military-political agenda, the conservatism of the host society, the arming of the Islamic parties, the weakness of moderate Afghan leaders, underlying Afghan traditions, the politicization of women's role in Afghan society, the international Islamists' agenda, and the *jihad* mentality all created a peculiar humanitarian environment, one that did little to foster the targeting of aid to women. In addition, the attitude of some Western relief workers contributed to the relative absence of women's programs. For instance, it has been argued that UNHCR's unwillingness to target women was the result of the organization's "stereotyping" of Muslim women and the fact that misogynists were "drawn" to its central Asian programs, and because the organization had a "weak development culture." The relative absence of Western women and the almost complete absence of Afghan women in senior positions in the UN and NGO aid programs also had an impact (Christensen 1990).[11]

Make no mistake, such factors affected program design and delivery, especially the agencies' decisions about how to assist (let alone empower) women. For instance, one experienced male field officer defended UNHCR's view that it was sufficient to aid Afghan "families" generally and male "heads of households" specifically in order to provide assistance to women. Not only did the aid reach women, but in this way, he said, there was no "distorting" of the Afghan social structure. It was not UNHCR's role to "set [a] priority ... to bring about that kind of cultur[al] change," he concluded, partly because that would undermine the "stable environment" needed to "manage" the overall refugee aid program.[12] Not aggravating their Cold War allies (Afghan males fighting the communists) was crucial to the Western diplomats' strategic agenda; for them, sacrificing women's rights was a small price to pay. Similarly, defending their unwillingness to aid women because of its 'cultural inappropriateness'—with cultural standards set by the extremist mujahedeen rather than educated Afghan women—was typical of many Western aid workers in the NWFP.

One result of this mixture of selective cultural relativism and sexism, politicized aid, and militarized Islam was the paucity of women's projects: some eighty-five in 1991, according to the Agency Coordinating Body for Afghan Relief (ACBAR), the NGO coordinator in the NWFP. In the field of girls' education, this had especially disastrous consequences. As mentioned, an estimated 10 percent of Afghan students were girls before the Saur Revolution. The illiteracy rate for women then was still upwards of 95 percent, little different than the roughly 92 percent for men nationwide. But by 1987, gender bias in educational programs resulted in a dramatic shift. As many as 60 percent of school-aged refugee boys could then claim to be literate, compared to 6 percent of girls aged six to eleven and 3 percent of girls aged twelve to seventeen. This reflected the amount of time boys and girls spent in school: some 50 percent of boys aged five to eleven were in schools in refugee camps, compared to 4 percent of girls. For girls reaching puberty, the figure was 1.4 percent (ACBAR 1990: 30; Christensen and Scott 1988: 27–30).

This is not to say that some sterling efforts to educate and train Afghan girls and women were not made. Indeed, some local and expatriate staff of NGOs risked their own lives to run women's projects (like sewing, tree planting, and education/training), most notably the International Rescue Committee, the Norwegian Refugee Council, the Danish Committee for Aid to Afghan Refugees (DACAAR), and Interchurch Aid. Indeed, getting "threats all the time ... [was] a normal part of life in Peshawar when you [were] running a girls' school," said one headmaster (Segal 1986: 23; Meijer and Weeda 1990: 37–38).[13]

Gender and Violence

For years Afghans in exile were targets of bombing campaigns by the Kabul communists. But those exiles opposing the mujahedeen, advocating dialogue or secular democracy, favoring the king, working for or with Western agencies, or supporting progressive causes were also victims of mujahedeen-inspired violence. This violence ranged from threats to actual bombings, shootings, and stabbings (Amnesty International 1995b). Also targeted for more than a decade were Afghans and Westerners who supported the education, training, economic independence, or empowerment of women. The extremes seen in Kabul under the Taleban today are only reiterations of misogynistic events that have gone on among Afghans in exile and at home for years.

Along the Afghan border, threats came to be a normal way of life for staff of Western agencies working for or with Afghan women, for Afghan women or women's groups working for Afghans, and for moderate Afghan men and women working for a Western NGO (Amnesty International 1995a). It remains difficult to say who exactly was responsible for these threats and acts of violence, for in their literature they only called themselves such things as the "Youth Secret Guerrilla Group" or the "Young Believers." Observers often blamed men loyal to Hekmatyar and the Arab-supported Abdurrab Rasul Sayyaf.[14]

Antagonism against women's programs and independent women was long-standing. For instance, in the mid-1980s even fully veiled Afghan women who went out of their houses in the NWFP were harassed by men who told them they had no right to be on the streets. Western women working in the camps were sometimes threatened as well. When the IRC opened its English Language Program for women, it became the target of threatening letters.

> The first step toward [the communist coup in Afghanistan] was the introduction of coeducation in Afghanistan, which is unlawful in Islam.... [It] is the obligation of every combatant Muslim to eliminate the centers of corruption.... The in-charge and responsible bodies of IRC are urgently asked to stop the girl[s'] classes as soon as possible, otherwise await a powerful explosion in your center. (Broadsheet cited in Segal 1986: 23)

Tension surrounding the aid program generally, and women's projects particularly, mounted in a period of a few months in 1989 to 1990. This was after the Soviets left Kabul, but at a time when the mujahedeen had as yet failed to unite their factions or oust Najibullah. Aid budgets came under threat from Western donors, and locals pressed to 'Afghanize' control of relief funds.

John Tarzell, a Canadian working with the Christian NGO, SERVE, was the first Western victim who was abducted in November 1989. Rumors spread that he had been preaching Christianity to the Afghans and that he was having an affair with an Afghan woman—claims his colleagues strenuously denied. His kidnapping was more likely the result of his helping a Pakistani widow whose Afghan in-laws were making 'unreasonable' demands on her. He was never seen again.

Two months later, there was a failed abduction of an American consulate worker walking alone at night. About the same time, the office/home of the Voice of America's representative was burgled, as were the premises of the Writers Union of Free Afghanistan, an organization of moderate Afghan intellectuals (*The Muslim* [Peshawar], 21

January 1990). Simultaneously, stories of Western women being stoned and spat on in public increased, as did those of aid workers being deliberately driven at and barely missed by vehicles. The Steering Committee of ACBAR tried to minimize the significance of the rising tension, announcing that there was an increase only because the "provisions for refugees in the camps are decreasing, people are rebelling against corruption, ... Shia-Sunni tensions are being played out, etc."[15] No link between the various incidents was made by ACBAR; neither was there mention of rising anti-Western sentiment, nor the increased targeting of women and women's projects.

Nonetheless, there were problems with implementing women's projects in the camps. For instance, in this period an American working in an international NGO reported that she and nine Afghan women visited a camp that a Pakistan government social welfare officer had targeted for assistance to widows and poor women. Their presence was cut short by a protest by the local *mullah* and men, who proceeded to announce seventeen new restrictions on women residents in the camp. Two of the rules were that refugee women would not be allowed to work with Western aid projects, nor would they be permitted to visit the health center (even in circumstances bordering death), unless there was a woman doctor in attendance.[16] Not long afterwards, a letter addressed to Afghan women working with Western NGOs surfaced. Its authors, the "Youth Secret Guerrilla Group," threatened to kill any Afghan woman who went "to foreign committees." Their doing so was a threat to the Group's "Islamic ideals, dignity and holy principles" by "non-Muslims and the enemies [who] want to destroy our morals, and principles under the shadows of Islam and Humanity."[17] Heeding the warning, many Afghan women stayed home from work.

In April 1990, a six-page printed pamphlet in Pushto from the "Islamic Youth Movement" appeared on the streets of Peshawar. It instructed Afghan women to remain at home because "Westerners want to teach you the way they live, which will spoil you, blocking your way to an Islamic life." Westerners would do this three ways. "[U]nder the name of education," Westerners would "make your life dependent on the evil ways of life. In this way they will hand your society over to the hands of the strangers." Introducing you to foreign ways, it continued, was being done in order to "place their sexual desires upon you." Secondly, by paying women for working, Westerners would be making such women rich by defiling their purity. Finally, "Westerners want to give you the way of life found in the twentieth century, and thereby take Islam from you." Concluding, it ordered women "...not to wander around [the streets]. Do not work for these so-called relief agencies.... Take care about observing *purdah* [seclusion]. " Finally came the threat: "You groups of women who do [not obey] will be terrorized and you all will be killed, and no one will be able to prevent this."[18]

On 26 April the situation deteriorated further when projects in Nasr Bagh refugee camp just outside Peshawar were looted and burned.[19] Opened in 1980 to house widows and their families, the camp and its NGOs offered Afghan women alternatives to the traditional custom of remarriage to the late husband's brother or another male relative. During the following decade, the camp had grown to include many other refugee families. During morning prayers at the mosque on 26 April, inflammatory statements were made. Soon afterwards the restive crowd, estimated to have grown to upwards of five thousand men, attempted to break into a clinic, where it was repulsed by gun-toting guards. It then turned its attention to the Shelter Now International (SNI) Community Center for Afghan widows and orphans and the SNI vehicle workshop. One hundred seventy-five tons of powdered milk was stolen from the Center (worth $300,000), the workshop was destroyed ($186,000), and nineteen vehicles were stolen or wrecked ($200,000). The SNI factory for the manufacture of building materials for refugee housing and Afghan reconstruction also suffered losses exceeding $200,000. A nearby Pakistani school for girls was destroyed as well.

For some months there had been complaints by Afghans about the SNI Community Center, with its kitchen gardens and sewing training center for women, and its playground equipment for children. Religious leaders were particularly incensed that the Center provided soap and a bathroom for women, which were seen as an attempt to "seduce" them to Western ways (*Newsweek,* 6 August 1990). They also objected when women were seen to sit on the children's swings, which was considered frivolous during a *jihad.* Claims were made that SNI distributed birth control pills and the New Testament—claims vehemently denied by the SNI. In March, the Pakistan Commissioner of Refugees had investigated these complaints and stated that "not a single issue ... was true." He concluded that "... these problems were created by a few people ... [and] if we now close this program for no valid reason, the next time they could come and try to close down another project of any other organization." After the Commissioner's report, tension continued to build. Women were verbally abused by the boys at the nearby school, who warned them that their cash allowances and food rations would be cut, and told them to stay away from the Center as it was going to be bombed. Within weeks the Center was in ashes.

The devastation at Nasr Bagh and the reaction by the aid community that followed highlighted several issues: the politicization of the Afghan aid program and women's projects, the disunity and weakness of the agencies, the general failure of the Western agencies to prioritize women's rights protection, and the destructive power of Afghan 'freedom fighters' and religious extremists. It also raised several questions: How can agencies and staff protect themselves against threats and violence in a highly politicized aid program? What is the most appropriate way for Westerners to aid Islamic women? Are human rights culturally relative or are there universal principles that cannot be compromised?

Two gossip-filled weeks after the riot, a full ACBAR meeting was held. There, SNI criticized UNHCR for its "slow and inadequate response" to the destruction of its projects, its lack of public support for SNI, and its "listening to rumor and allegations" rather than investigating the facts. The government of Pakistan was also criticized for pushing responsibility for lack of security onto the Afghans and demanding that they, not the government, pay compensation to SNI.

To be honest, it is not clear just what the government *could* do. At no time before had it taken a strong stance against mujahedeen excesses. Moreover, for years it had allowed its camps to be used as rear bases for the war, and by 1990 many of the 3.5 million refugees were well-armed and experienced fighters. Not surprisingly, the police had been unable to quell the riot, which lasted a full day and night. As one ACBAR member concluded: all the government can do now is "put up a show." While a few people at the ACBAR meeting tried to explain the anger of the crowd in terms of cultural issues like Westerners' insensitivity to tradition, the Afghan director of the Austrian Relief Committee (ARC) would have none of it. He very clearly placed the blame for the violence on unnamed political elements. The first stage, he said, was the killing of Afghan intellectuals. He himself had been the subject of threats to discourage other Afghans from working with foreign agencies. The second stage was now beginning. In response to intimidation and violence, he called for a week's closure of all NGO programs, though his proposal was reduced to a three-day work stoppage during which NGOs would explain to refugees their need for security in order to work. Also rising to address the ACBAR meeting was the representative of Médecins Sans Frontières (MSF) –France, who announced the death of a logistics officer in Badakshan, Afghanistan. This was the second attack on an MSF installation in as many months, he said, and the NGO had decided to "freeze" all its programs until investigations were complete.[20] In support of SNI and MSF, and to demonstrate the need for security to work, the strike plan was adopted.

Two other important issues were raised at the meeting, the first of which was proselytizing among Afghans. Shelter Now International denied it had been promoting Christianity, and as this issue was brought into the open, debated, and dismissed, it was no longer possible for the other agencies to claim immunity from future harassment on account of their secular nature. Secondly, the problem of the general hostility toward women's programs was discussed, and several agencies–including those known to be culturally sensitive–admitted that they, too, had problems in the camps. This discussion made it clear that Westerners' insensitivity was not the primary cause of Afghan hostility to the aid community.

The same week–the second in May–a new brochure was distributed in Peshawar. Like others before, it was intended to discourage Afghans from working with the international agencies. "Avoid catching AIDS," it began.

> The Christians brought you the most untreatable and deadly disease ... which will kill you right after you have been infected. This is AIDS.... This disease is spreadable and you may get it from sexual relations with people affected by this disease, and you may get [it] ... by sitting together and having close relations with Western Christians, those infected with the disease. Lately an Afghan was found to be suffering from AIDS and he was working for one of the Christian Committees. He claimed that he had sexual relations with a Christian woman, who worked with him for the same *committee*. The woman said after some investigation that fifty Western Christian women suffering from AIDS are working cross-border in Afghanistan with the mujahedeen and in the refugee camps in Pakistan. She also said that their main object was to spread widely this dangerous disease ... among the mujahedeen and the refugees ... to change their power to weakness and their victory to defeat ...[21]

Many expatriates laughed when they read the flyer. Afghans did not, partly because of widespread ignorance about AIDS, but also because it was reprinted in the mujahedeen press. The story was repeated for months by Afghans as though it were true, often inflating the number of AIDS-infected women circulating in Afghanistan. Such stories were used to legitimize mujahedeen threats and violence against the aid program and women's projects specifically.[22]

Soon it was announced in the English daily newspaper (*Frontier Post* [Peshawar], 12 May 1990) that "Afghan relief bodies may be asked to leave," giving substance to rumors that there was a list of NGOs that would shortly be asked by the government to halt operations. It also explained why some staff were having difficulty getting new work permits and reentry visas. Observers thought that since there was no sign of peace in Afghanistan, nor any indication that refugees were planning to leave soon, an expulsion of agencies was the government's indirect way of forcing Afghans to repatriate. A tiny retraction by an unnamed government official in the back pages of the next day's paper did little to relieve NGO concerns.

What the threat of expulsion did, though, was to undermine any action by ACBAR and the NGOs to demonstrate solidarity with SNI and MSF, defend women's rights, or demand an end to intimidation. Thus, the planned work stoppage never took place. Taking a much less forthright stance, the ACBAR Steering Committee warned that NGOs would "be forced to re-evaluate their future role" if the government and the UN "failed to respond adequately to the attacks and threats against relief agencies." This meant "concrete steps" needed to be taken by Afghan leaders as well.[23] Security concerns underlay ACBAR's announcement, but so did reactions to reports overseas about the violence against aid workers, mujahedeen factionalism and drug running, and the failings of the UN coordinating body. NGOs were also reiterating threats by donors to withdraw funding from the Afghan aid programs.

Anxious to wrest control of aid funding from Westerners who they wanted to leave, and in face of the moderate response by ACBAR and the UN, the mujahedeen continued their campaign. On 18 May, the ARC office was broken into, its guards held at gunpoint, and its telephone lines cut. The intruders demanded to know where the ARC's outspoken Afghan director was, and for an hour they grilled the guards about the organization. Papers were searched and taken, as were two vehicles. The director of the ARC asked that prompt action be taken by the UN and the government. On 20 May, ACBAR and UNHCR held a joint press conference, expressing their "serious concern" with the "deteriorating security situation." They also called on the government to ensure the safety of both refugees and aid workers, and asked Afghan leaders and political institutions to reaffirm their support for the work being done by the voluntary agencies and to improve the "operational climate" in which these agencies functioned.[24] At the same press conference SNI reported another incident directed against their organization. Its "cross border" building project had been attacked on 18 May by a group of about one hundred people, shouting "Down with foreigners. Down with Afghans that work with foreigners. Where are the people that work with foreigners?" The guard was beaten, the project looted, and two rockets shot inside the building.[25]

Soon the American ambassador to Pakistan, Robert Oakley, expressed donor concern with the violence. Specifically, he asked the

AIG (the Afghan Interim Government, a fragile coalition of Afghan parties in exile), the Pakistan government, and the Commissioner of Refugees to address the issue of security and provide protection to aid workers in the camps and 'cross border'. Undoubtedly motivated by strategic concerns as much as humanitarian ones, he warned of the possibility of a "sharp reduction in assistance" (*The Muslim* [Pakistan], 22 May 1990).

For some time, Afghan political leaders had wanted international donor funds to be given directly to them or Afghan NGOs, bypassing what they considered the unnecessary and dangerously international NGOs. Hezbi-Islami (Hekmatyar) explained the views of some: the Soviets were defeated in Afghanistan, leaving the US thinking that it was the "sole determiner of the fate of the world." The US is opposed to Islam and is doing its best to crush it. The Americans and especially the CIA are trying to weaken the mujahedeen through their "slanderous propaganda" (presumably meaning the increased number of articles on factional fighting and heroin smuggling). Prince Sadruddin Agha Khan, head of the UN operation, was appointed to "realize the nefarious American designs in Afghanistan under the guise of humanitarian assistance." Therefore, any assistance through the AIG, which Hekmatyar had broken with earlier in the year, through any non-Muslim organizations (including the UN coordinating body), or marked with American labels would be considered as "tools for the division of mujahedeen, penetration of foreign agents, and conspiracies against the *jihad.*" Those willing to help the Afghan people should instead send their goods through the "respected parties of the people of Afghanistan" (*Frontier Post* [Peshawar], 6 June 1990).

While indigenization of control of aid is to be supported in most refugee situations, in Peshawar it was clear that handing donor funds to the Afghan parties would lead to further politicization of humanitarian assistance, more factionalism, enhanced legitimization of and dependence by refugees on various leaders and parties, and additional restrictions on the use of aid for women. In response to the donors and agencies' request for security, the AIG reacted by attempting to extend its control over the NGOs. Specifically, the AIG asked agencies to register with it and said that if they did, the Pakistan government would take responsibility for the security of the agencies (*Frontier Post* [Peshawar], 24 May 1990). The fact that security was already the responsibility of the Pakistan government, and that there was a singular lack of information about the concrete steps that would be taken, did little to reassure the aid community.

Meanwhile, the simmering crisis continued. In May and June of 1990 several more agencies had their offices broken into, and money and equipment stolen. The threats against Afghan women also continued. For instance, in the third week of May a "last warning" was given. Afghan women "... must stop their erroneous ways–which destroy their Muslim morality–by working for [foreign] organizations under the name of training and education, which is hated by Holy Islam.... If not obeyed, the Young Believers will take action."[26] About the same time, a group of agencies doing women's projects met to assess the situation. Two rumors were laid to rest at this meeting: first, that Afghan women had been killed and, second, that it was no longer possible to do women's projects in the camps. Such optimism unfortunately did not stop the closure in the late spring of International Rescue Committee's (IRC's) English language program for women as a result of threats. Nor did it keep Afghan women from quitting their jobs in other agencies, nor from ceasing to attend training projects.

In mid-June the director of SNI and his six-year-old son were shot at while driving in a bazaar just west of Peshawar. Hurt by flying glass and after seven years of helping Afghans, he and his family fled the country. The "Afghan Jihad Group" claimed responsibility for the attempted murder and warned the American director of IRC, Tom Yates, that he would be the "next target." Yates left soon after (*Frontier Post* [Peshawar], 18 June 1990; *Newsweek*, 6 August 1990). About the same time, other agency offices in Peshawar were bombed and Afghan aid workers killed.

Tension jumped to a higher level in the late summer of 1990 when Western troops moved into the Gulf. In spite of the Pakistan government's formal support for the Allies, a number of American aid workers in Peshawar were threatened with death in retaliation for the US stance against Iraq's Saddam Hussain. Just before the Gulf War started, most Western agencies in Peshawar closed their doors and evacuated their foreign workers. After the war, threats and violence in the NWFP resumed.[27]

After Rabbani took power in 1992, Western agencies began moving their efforts increasingly 'cross border' into the relatively secure areas of Afghanistan. In Kabul, relief projects predominated because the city was often under attack from various faction leaders and then the Taleban, and because it hosted large and growing numbers of displaced persons. In other parts of the country, development projects were started. Seed distribution, veterinary, flood protection, irrigation, and demining projects were emphasized; schools, and vaccination and other health programs were opened.

Gender, Aid, and the Taleban

As should now be clear, the threats and actions since late 1995 by the Taleban against women, moderate Afghan men, and women's projects are a continuation of events begun in exile by similar groups of fanatical young men. In Peshawar, where Western agencies had their first experience of helping Afghans, threats and violence grew more common as time passed. Unfortunately, agencies there were unable to unite and take a strong stance in defense of political and religious tolerance, women, and human rights. Women's programs suffered, and Afghan radicals grew more confident.

The Taleban's reactionary social policies first came to the significant attention of the West when they moved into Kandahar and ordered women and girls to remain in their homes and avoid contact with men outside their families. Although women were allowed to work in the health sector, other females were not to work outside their homes or attend schools. Some local resentment of these restrictions was evident, though the people in Kandahar are also Pushtun and many accepted them as culturally appropriate. Agencies working there found some of the Taleban's policies difficult, including the "reluctance of the Taleban authorities to meet female expatriate staff from the international agencies" and their "requirement that they wear a *burqa*." With negotiation, it was agreed that expatriate women needed only to wear a head scarf, and that they could participate fully in meetings with Taleban representatives (British Agencies Afghan Group 1996e).

In relatively peaceful Herat, the Taleban were ethnically different than the local population and were considered by residents to be an occupation force. The population opposed the Taleban's decision to close all girls' schools and to prohibit women from working outside the health sector. As one-third of the teachers in *boys'* schools were women, sending women home resulted in the closure of some of these schools, which fueled resentment. Music, dancing, cinemas, and television were banned, and conservative rules on dress and behavior proclaimed. A climate of fear and intimidation resulted, which then reduced attendance of women and children at clinics and the hospital. Aid programs were affected when Afghan women trainers and officials left their jobs and when all women staff were forbidden to interact with administration officials (British Agencies Afghan Group 1996e; Kearney 1996). When the Taleban entered Kabul in September 1996, they decreed that

> all those sisters who are working in Government offices are hereby informed to stay home until further notice. Since *satar* ([a] requirement in

Islamic law for women to cover themselves) is of great importance in Islam, all sisters are seriously asked to observer the *satar* and to cover their faces and the whole of their body [*sic*] when they go out. (British Agencies Afghanistan Group 1996c)

Within the week the Taleban clarified its policy: education was not restricted for either men or women, but women should stay away from schools and offices until the administration decided how girls should be educated and until preparations were made for men and women to work in the same premises. Neither were men and women to travel to work together. Naturally, when local female staff of aid agencies were stopped from working, the relief program suffered. Especially hard hit were women's projects, for men were unable to interact with female beneficiaries, such as the thousands of war widows and disabled women in Kabul.[28]

The overzealous Taleban also threatened women who did not adequately conform to the new regulations regarding movement and dress. This spread fear among women, who then refused to leave their homes. Men were also subject to strong pressure to pray five times a day, to grow beards and wear *shalwar kameez.* Televisions were destroyed, films were burned, and football and other games were banned. Some adulterers were stoned to death (*Newsweek,* 11 November 1996, 30 December 1996, 6 January 1997; British Agencies Afghanistan Group 1996c, 1996d).

In provincial capitals and towns throughout Afghanistan, the Taleban inconsistently imposed differing levels of restrictions on women and men. In some places these were not considered onerous by the population because local culture dictated similar constraints or because women and men thought that restrictions on women were an acceptable price to pay for improved security and economic stability. In some areas outside Taleban-controlled towns, a range of constraints were imposed on women by local elders who wished them to conform. Complicating matters for aid agencies were regulations that varied from town to town, and fluctuated over time (British Agencies Afghanistan Group 1996e).

The reaction of the aid agencies to these constraints differed. In Kandahar, project staff continued to talk with the Taleban, eschewing confrontation as counterproductive. As a result, Afghan women were allowed to continue working in health programs and to attend clinics. Many families reportedly managed to adapt to the restrictions, as women opened girls' schools at home or as repatriated refugee families left their girls in Pakistan to complete their studies. It was not until the Taleban took Herat and imposed restrictions on women and girls there that agencies began to take stronger action.

UNICEF suspended its education programs in all Taleban-controlled areas where girls were denied access to education (Marsden 1996b). About the same time Save the Children Fund (SCF)–UK, which had worked with Afghans for more than fifteen years, decided to close its program. Angela Kearney (1996) explained its policy:

> Immediately after taking power in Herat, [the Taleban] closed all girls' schools and banned women teachers from work. In early January 1996, they issued a decree banning all women from working except in the health sector and refused to discuss the reopening of girls' schools…. If Afghan women continued to work they would be open to punishment as dictated by the Taleban in their interpretation of Islamic law. Collaboration between Save the Children and the Taleban-controlled government departments became impossible as the Taleban refused to meet any female staff from aid agencies…. In the two years of working in Herat, relationships had been established between SCF staff, communities and government authorities. Overnight this confidence was broken. It became impossible for SCF to talk to women in the community. SCF could not employ women translators to share ideas with international staff. Afghan men and women could not meet each other unless they were family members. Many vulnerable women who were participating in vocational training and income-generating schemes with NGOs and UN programs were denied employment and income.

In other words, SCF felt the Taleban policy undermined the functionality of the program, though it recognized the ethical issues involved as well.

> Humanitarian organizations are committed to the universal rights of children and women…. We need to listen to all voices—men, women and children—and value all opinions. From a perspective of justice and fairness it is critical that all actors are involved in decision-making at all levels…. (Kearney 1996)

Agencies familiar with the various personalities and parties, and their differing restrictions on men and women, felt there was an opportunity to reopen negotiations on these issues when the Taleban entered Kabul in September 1996. On 4 October, the UN Commissioner for Human Rights asked his local office to express his "strong concern for the situation of human rights in Afghanistan" and asked the Taleban "to ensure respect for such rights as the right of women to work and the rights of girls to education." Four days later, the UN secretary-general put the Taleban on notice that all UN assistance would be guided by the UN Charter, which affirmed equal rights for men and women.

That same day, a delegation of representatives of UN agencies and NGOs met with the Taleban foreign minister in Kabul, where they expressed their common concerns. Earlier that week the agencies had jointly produced a position statement, which they presented to the foreign minister. In it, they noted that the international agencies in Kabul share many common values and beliefs, including a belief in "humanitarian principles ... [that] underpin all our plans and programs ..." Secondly, they said they are "neutral in their provision of services ... [and] non-partisan." They also "believe in maintaining and promoting the inherent equality and dignity of all people, and do not discriminate between the sexes, races, ethnic groups or religions." Finally they said they "hold local customs and cultures in high respect."

They then asked the foreign minister to allow female staff in aid agencies to return to work. They also wanted women and children to be allowed to participate in programs and activities; women and girls to be given equal access to education and training opportunities; all agency staff to be assured of their personal safety; agencies to have the sole right to select and employ staff; agency staff of both genders to be given access to the authorities; and basic agreements regarding humanitarian assistance to be drawn up by the government and agencies.

The foreign minister agreed that aid was needed in Kabul, especially by widows and other women. But, he said, the Taleban's priorities were security and peace, the establishment of an administration, and gaining the recognition of the international community. As such, he was surprised by the international community's reaction and its concern for "the rights of a small portion of working women when the country faces such difficulties." The Taleban was prepared to continue paying women previously working with the government while the situation was reconsidered, and he assured the agencies that Islamic society and government would look after poor women.[29]

While the Taleban considered its course of action, at least one agency, OXFAM–UK, decided to suspend its operations until the Taleban allowed its eight local women staff members to return to work. While OXFAM took a principled stand–that women do matter–it also felt that the Taleban's restrictions had compromised the efficient functioning of its projects. In November, the OXFAM representative in Kabul, Sue Emmott, expressed her pessimism about the future in terms that reflected prewar antagonisms: "I don't have a lot of hope about our future under [the] Taleban, because I think they want an Islamic state where women are invisible, and the educated women of the city are reduced to the level of the illiterate in the village" (*Newsweek*, 11 November 1996). Divisions between town and country were evident to many foreigners and Afghans from

Kabul, who complained that the Taleban were ill-educated and backward peasants.

Toward the end of October, the European Parliament took a strong, principled stand and passed a resolution calling for a cease-fire and peace negotiations. This resolution condemned "discrimination practiced against Afghan women, the numerous violations of human rights [including the summary execution of Najibullah] and the forcible indoctrination of the Afghan people since Kabul was taken...." In doing so, it hoped that all assistance donors would "refrain from any new aid or cooperation programs, except emergency aid, until the human rights of men and women are respected by the administration."[30]

At the end of the month, the UN agencies in Kabul followed suit, reaffirming their "faith in fundamental human rights, in the dignity and worth of the human person and the equal rights of men and women." Arguing from a functional point of view, the UN agencies continued:

> ... access to all beneficiaries, regardless of gender, is essential for projects to succeed ... To ensure access ... the rights of female staff to work must be given due priority.... Equal access to education and training opportunities at all levels is also necessary to ensure the sustainability of assistance activities. Moreover, interference in the appointment or functioning of staff is not acceptable.... Staff of all UN agencies and their implementing partners should impress upon relevant Afghan authorities that the non-respect of the above gender principles will seriously limit, and even impede, the ability to deliver humanitarian assistance to the vulnerable population.... A Monitoring Committee ... has been empowered to review the compliance of assistance programs to these norms and standards.... [The Committee] will report to the Inter-Agency Task Force ... [and] based on the report the Task Force may decide to recommend that programs which consistently fail to meet these standards should be revised suspended [sic].[31]

The Taleban indicated that it intended to submit the question to a commission of Islamic theologians for consideration. It was unclear how soon the commission would meet or when its decision would be reached. In any event, the Taleban in Kabul, as elsewhere,[32] seemed unlikely to prioritize the issue, especially while fighting continued (British Agencies Afghanistan Group 1996e).

At year-end the UN agencies and NGOs were trying to determine which was the best way forward. Some counseled patience, while others advocated the withdrawal of development aid from Taleban-controlled areas, leaving only emergency relief projects. Others sought compromise by pressing the Taleban for consideration of the issues at every opportunity, and by redesigning offices so that agency men and women could work apart. The fact that some men within the governing *Shura* would be willing to see the aid program close and the international agencies depart weakened the resolve of agencies that wanted to continue providing humanitarian relief to the needy at all costs. Some agencies felt that it would be best to negotiate a series of small changes over a period of time, while hard-liners argued that this incremental approach would not work. These critics were constrained from speaking out by a fear that outsiders would use the issue to feed anti-Islamic views. Agencies' headquarters, some distance removed from the scene, took a less compromising stance than those dealing directly with the needy. While debates among the aid community continued, the UN and NGOs agreed to meet at the end of the year to consider conditionality, advocacy, and culturally appropriate implementation strategies (British Agencies Afghanistan Group 1996e).

The Way Forward

A number of important issues were raised by these events. First is the problem of articulating cultural relativism and rights. Whereas in Peshawar before 1992 staff in agencies were unlikely to claim that women's rights are universal and nonnegotiable, in Afghanistan today agencies now speak much more often about human rights and women in the same breath. In Kabul it is now less likely that Western staff will easily compromise women's rights. In some cases, this is because their home offices have been grappling with these issues for a while and now have well-considered human rights policies. Increasingly, the universality of basic human rights, including women's rights to education and employment, is accepted by aid professionals, who now consider it their duty to protect rights as well as to provide humanitarian relief. The cultural relativism of rights that was widely supported by workers in the NWFP and Afghanistan a decade and more ago is less acceptable in the Afghan program today.

In addition, aid professionals are now more aware that war and exile are transforming experiences and that few locals are unchanged by them. Access to decent health care, education, and employment, and exposure to new ideas and cultures have modified the views and activities of millions of refugees in the last decade. Even the comparatively conservative cultures of Iran and Pakistan were enlightening to the rural Afghan refugees, many of whom had known only their own villages, tribes, religion, and lifeways before.

No longer do aid workers typically see prewar Afghan society and a woman's place within it as static or unchangeable.

Another innovation since 1990 is that means have arisen to allow Afghan and other Islamic women to be heard more frequently. Many have spoken out very strongly against gender discrimination in aid programs. One such group met at Sharjah in the United Arab Emirates in 1994 (UAE 1994; see Elmadmad, this volume),[33] and called upon governments, NGOs, and UNHCR to "establish adequately equipped schools and training centers for women at appropriate locations nearby refugees camps and/or to provide transport facilities" and to "start effective education and training programs, targeting the most vulnerable groups, such as female heads of household."

As shown above, relief agencies have also come to realize that the lack of participation by women in relief programs is dysfunctional—a fact stressed by development workers for many years.[34] In fact, NGOs in Afghanistan may have some success over time in convincing the Taleban of their position by arguing, as they are, that in order to make their programs work, agencies must ensure that women have fully developed roles. That women may be empowered through greater self-reliance and economic independence is what the Taleban fear; if planned properly, this is exactly what the relief programs can promote.

There is another reason for this change in agency attitudes: in 1996 the political agenda of the donors was less central than it was five or ten years before. While the Americans continue to express concern about the war, their military involvement is much less and their interest is primarily confined to halting Iranian influence in the region, reducing the heroin trade,[35] stopping Afghan-generated international terrorism, and resecuring the Stinger missiles[36] they gave the mujahedeen in the 1980s. As the Cold War ended and the local strategic agenda became less compelling, donor support for the mujahedeen cause and its leaders have diminished. Also (as discussed below), in the last few years human rights protection has risen toward the top of the donors' agenda in aid-recipient countries. In combination, these factors have given the agencies in Kabul more 'space' to consider prioritizing women's rights than was available to them before.

Further, international pressure has been brought to bear on the Taleban because, unlike earlier in Peshawar, much media attention has recently been given to the situation inside Afghanistan. Lynching of televisions and the burning of films by the Taleban have made headlines in the Western press, while news magazines and talk shows have focused on women's issues. In years past, a media machine operated in tandem with Western intelligence agencies to generate stories in support of the 'war against communist aggression' and in favor of Afghan 'freedom fighters'. Control of news was especially easy in Peshawar, because it was difficult for journalists to 'go inside' unless they were in touch with certain suspect individuals, agencies, or information centers that facilitated it.[37] Moreover, while self-censorship was often the safer (and at the time more politically correct) option for journalists, certain stories—about the drug trade, for instance—went un- or underreported. As the Western political agenda was transformed by the end of the Cold War, media coverage diminished, then changed. As a result, outsiders are in many instances more accurately informed about what is going on now than when their televisions carried nightly news coverage of the war. This new knowledge contributed to the international pressure on the Taleban in 1996.

The role of aid conditionality is yet another issue emerging from the Afghan case. Conditionality came to prominence when Jimmy Carter began talking about human rights and foreign assistance in the mid-1970s.[38] Even so, prioritizing rights in aid was one of the first victims of the Soviet's incursion into Afghanistan, as Carter reacted by adopting a hard-line Cold Warrior's stance everywhere. With the end of the Cold War and the emergence of the 'New World Order', rights and conditionality have resurfaced. Many people now argue an even more assertive position: that the international community is obliged to actively intervene to protect the rights of individuals and peoples and to provide humanitarian assistance to communities in need, irrespective of national sovereignty. Such thinking links aid assistance to rights protection.

Once the principle is established that conditionality is a legitimate way to try to protect rights in general and women's rights in particular, the question arises: how effective is threatening to cut aid in molding another country's rights policy? This depends on several things: on how needy the country is, how much aid is at stake, how willing its government is to do without the aid, and whether there is another donor waiting to fill the gap left by the departing provider. In the Afghan case, the people are certainly in need of assistance, but it is not clear that the Taleban want the existing donors or agencies to remain. Perhaps others wait in the wings—say, wealthy Islamic states. Also, because democracy is not fully functional in Afghanistan, any local community's request that the aid agencies remain is likely to go unheeded by the Taleban. How effective such threats can be depends, too, on the strength and unity of purpose of the aid regime. The agencies in Kabul have a wide range of priorities and principles. How united they will be if the Taleban calls their bluff is the question. Weighing up the good they feel they can do, it is unlikely that all would be willing to close their doors to protest state discrimination against women.

Finally, the Afghan situation provides donors and agencies with the opportunity to reconsider how they can more effectively protect the rights of refugees and internally displaced persons, especially women, in highly charged environments. A number of strategies present themselves. For instance, agencies might consider using human rights lawyers to help write their relief and development policies, and employing specialist consultants to evaluate their own human rights records and the implications for empowerment of their work. Agencies can work closely with human rights and women's rights organizations when establishing their aid policies and when training their staff. They can foster local women's rights protection among displacees by funding and augmenting the training of indigenous lawyers and other human rights workers and by including rights training in their own educational and training programs. When rights challenges become severe, they can support the work of human rights groups by reporting abuse, working with journalists and the media, employing human rights monitors, and bringing international observers in to report, witness, and hopefully forestall further abuse. Withdrawal of aid should be viewed as a last resort by agencies.

Some of these measures have been adopted with varying degrees of success by agencies in other relief situations where a combination of politics, repression, and culture have combined to deny refugees and internally displaced persons their rights. The further implementation of these measures in the Afghan situation would do much to bring home the point to the Taleban and other mujahedeen that human rights and women do matter.

Notes

1. I would like to acknowledge the support of the SSRC-MacArthur Fellowship on Peace and Security in a Changing World, which made this research possible.
2. See reports on the 'Afghan Resistance' produced in the 1980s by the US Department of State, Bureau of Public Affairs, or on the 'Afghan mujahedeen freedom fighters' by the Washington-based Heritage Foundation.
3. Anthony Hyman (1992: 13, 87–88) notes that per capita gross domestic product (GDP) in the 1970s was approximately $160–$200, one out of two children did not live to the age of five, and life expectancy was approximately forty years.

4. *International Herald Tribune* (21 July 1992) cites Pakistan General Mohammed Yousaf as saying that 10,000 tons of arms and ammunition were sent by the CIA through Pakistan to the mujahedeen in 1983, a figure that rose to 65,000 tons annually by 1987.

5. Reprinting Frederic Bobin in *Le Monde*.

6. For example, American Embassy Islamabad to Secretary of State, confidential (2 September 1983), which reported that WFP's Trevor Page told US embassy officials that "WFP takes the lead from donor governments and if donors and the G[overnment] o[f] P[akistan] aren't worried about the working of the food distribution mechanisms, including possible diversion [of food aid to the mujahedeen], the WFP will not modify its own programme" (National Security Archive, Washington D.C.).

7. 'Freedom fighters' trained in Afghanistan are known to have been involved in the insurrections in Egypt and Algeria, as well as in terrorist activities in the US.

8. Cammack interview with senior USAID official, 11 March 1993, Washington D.C.

9. Cammack interview with senior USAID official, 11 March 1993, Washington D.C.

10. Cammack interviews with Ekber Memencuglo and Mark Ice, UNHCR, Geneva, 26 February 1993; Cammack interview with senior USAID official, 11 March 1993, Washington D.C.; see also American Embassy Islamabad to Secretary of State, confidential, 16 November 1981, 15 February 1982, 2 September 1983, and 9 December 1983 (National Security Archive, Washington D.C.).

11. Cammack interview with Ann Howarth, UNHCR, Geneva, 23 February 1993.

12. Cammack interview with UNHCR field officer, Geneva, 23 February 1993. See also Meijer and Weeda (1990: 74).

13. Cammack interview with Steve and Margaret Segal, previously of the International Rescue Committee, Peshawar, 12 January 1993, Lilongwe, Malawi.

14. While it is beyond the capacity of this author to analyze the emotions that motivated these men, looking at their literature it is clear that they include strongly held religious and philosophical beliefs as well as psychological needs with sexual undercurrents. The stress caused by war, flight, social disintegration, and culture shock surely contributed to their anxiety and their efforts to keep their society from unraveling and their power from dissipating further.

15. ACBAR Steering Committee Minutes, Peshawar, 31 January 1990.

16. Cammack, personal communication, Peshawar, 20 March 1990.

17. Mimeo letter, handwritten, in English, Peshawar, n.d. [April 1990].

18. Six-page pamphlet, Peshawar, n.d. [April 1990].

19. The best local coverage of the event was by John Jennings in *The Friday Times* (Pakistan), 17–28 May 1990. Further details are also available in the Shelter Now International Press Packet, distributed by ACBAR on 10 May 1990 in Peshawar.

20. ACBAR meeting, 10 May 1990; Médecins Sans Frontières (MSF) press release, dated 10 May 1990; and see *Newsweek*, 6 August 1990.

21. Rough translation of broadsheet distributed 6 May 1990, Peshawar.

22. For instance, one Afghan man was outraged when he claimed that refugees had found a box of artificial penises (perhaps speculum, for he described their function rather than named them) for the use of widows at the SNI facility at Nasr Bagh when it was ransacked in April. Cammack, personal communication, Peshawar, ca. 25 May 1990.

23. *The Muslim* (Pakistan), 16 May 1990 citing ACBAR Press Release, 15 May 1990.

24. Joint ACBAR and UN agencies meeting and press release, 20 May 1990; Austrian Relief Committee press release, 20 May 1990; and *The Muslim* (Pakistan), 21 May 1990.

25. Shelter Now International report of Bacha Saeb-Day Chowkidar Factory 2, Ghani Khel, Afghanistan, 18 May 1990, distributed at ACBAR, Peshawar, 20 May 1990.
26. Mimeo distributed the third week of May 1990, Peshawar.
27. For instance, in February 1995 Jamiatullah Jalal, an Afghan intellectual and head of a group of secular-minded Afghans, was abducted in Peshawar and never seen again. In December 1995 two female Afghan doctors were shot dead at a refugee camp near Peshawar (Amnesty International 1995b; British Agencies Afghan Group 1996a).
28. Kabul is home to an estimated 25,000 war widows (with children) in dire need of aid and employment. For instance, in January 1996 the UN's Emergency Winter Relief Programme aided fifteen bakeries hiring widows who supported 15,000 dependents, and 1,800 orphans and small children in institutions. The International Committee of the Red Cross targeted 3,000 widows and their families for relief aid, while CARE planned to provide emergency rations to 16,000 widows and their small children and to employ a thousand widows to produce quilts for sale to relief agencies for distribution to the poor (UN Office for the Coordination of Humanitarian Assistance to Afghanistan [UNOCHA] 1996). Programs such as these were impacted by restrictions on women working with the NGOs.
29. The Kabul Information Forum, "A Position Statement of International Agencies Working in Kabul," 5 October 1996 and its Press Statement dated 8 October 1996, enclosed in British Agencies Afghanistan Group 1996d.
30. European Parliament, "Resolution on Afghanistan," 24 October 1996, enclosed in British Agencies Afghanistan Group 1996d.
31. UN Department of Humanitarian Affairs and UN Office for the Coordination of Humanitarian Assistance to Afghanistan, "Policy Guidelines for Fieldwork on UN Agencies in Afghanistan," 31 October 1996, enclosed in British Agencies Afghanistan Group 1996d.
32. See Wickstead (1996) regarding MSF's decision to continue working in Taleban-controlled Uruzgan Province in spite of the fact that MSF believes "the majority of the [Taleban] movement seems opposed to prioritising women's health care or education."
33. Regarding Afghanistan particularly, see the report of the "Women in Development" seminar held in London on 25 April 1992 (ARIN 1992). Particularly outspoken in respect to Afghan women's rights have been Fatima Gailani, Safia Halim, Nor Seraj Safi, Hamayra Etimade, and Sima Wali.
34. See the discussion of women in development in Moser (1989:1799–1825) and Indra (this volume).
35. Estimates by the UN Drug Control Programme indicate that some three thousand metric tons of heroin were produced by opium poppies grown in Afghanistan in 1996, much of it destined for North America and Europe (International Centre for Humanitarian Reporting, 1996, 13).
36. *Weekly Mail and Guardian* (South Africa), 30 July–5 Aug 1993, which notes that about three-fourths of the one thousand Stingers supplied to the mujahedeen were not used, and that they are being sold on the black market for $100,000 each.
37. See especially, Mary Williams Walsh (1990), and *The International Herald Tribune* (18–19 May 1985, 25–26 October 1986) for early complaints about control of the media.
38. See, for instance, David Weissbrodt (1977: 231).

7

Response to Cammack

Peter Marsden

Dr. Cammack's chapter raises some very difficult issues relating to religious fundamentalism, identity politics, the role of humanitarian agencies in complex emergencies, and the interface between the West and the Islamic world.

Central to her thesis is the assertion that the West has been willing to openly condemn the gender policies of the Taleban whereas they ignored the very similar policies of the mujahedeen. Her argument that this is due to the greater strategic interest which the US had in continuing cooperation with the mujahedeen has considerable validity. Certainly, while the US is rumored to be backing the Taleban because of its concerns about drugs and terrorism, its wish to recover Stinger missiles given to the mujahedeen, and its interest in the development of a pipeline to transport Central Asian gas and oil to the Indian Ocean, these do not weigh as heavily as the previous ambition to bring the Soviet Union to its knees.

However, there are other factors which need to be taken into account. One is the strong response of the Western media to the very explicit statements of the Taleban regarding the denial of female access to education and employment. The fact that the Taleban were seeking international recognition as the government of Afghanistan and yet were still making such statements was highly newsworthy. By contrast, the Western media had less to latch onto in relation to mujahedeen gender policies; there was no consistent policy across the mujahedeen parties. There was little explicit denial of female access to education and employment, only the imposition of varying levels of constraint on that access. Unlike the Taleban, public statements by the mujahedeen on dress codes tended not to specify the *burqa*, a garment which, because it covers the face as well as the body, has a symbolic importance in Western eyes relating to female oppression; the headscarf does not have the same connotations. Thus, while the media coverage of the mujahedeen was highly negative after 1989, and focused as much on the gender issue as on the failure of the mujahedeen to unite, it provided little material for lobbyists to use to promote gender-related human rights. Western governments were therefore under little public pressure to take account of the gender policies of the mujahedeen. This was a very different situation from the present one, in which Western governments would find it very difficult to accord recognition to a Taleban government while basic gender-related rights continue to be disregarded–however much their interests might be advanced by a continuation of the Taleban in power.

It is also important to note the very different attitude of aid agencies to the present authorities in Afghanistan as compared with the mujahedeen period. As Dr. Cammack observes, the aid scene in the 1980s was very much part of the Cold War strategy. Aid workers felt genuine solidarity with a country that had been invaded by a superpower, and were influenced by the image created by the media of the mujahedeen as a heroic resistance movement taking on the mighty Goliath of the Soviet Union. The ranks of the aid workers included both liberals inspired by echoes of Hungary and Czechoslovakia, and rabid anti-communists. Many could be classified more as adventurers than experienced technocrats. However, as the years progressed following the 1989 Soviet withdrawal, the agencies became both more professional and less partisan. They set themselves clear objectives relating to the reconstruction of the country, and sought to wean themselves away from dependence on commanders and to work in support of village and neighborhood structures and of what remained of the government administration. To this end, they based themselves increasingly in Afghanistan, particularly after the 1992 fall of the Najibullah government. The Peshawar aid scene became, consequently, less important. It proved much easier to deal with the authorities in Afghanistan (including the Taleban) than with the Peshawar-based mujahedeen parties. Similarly, the agencies working in Afghanistan have not yet had to cope with a level of fear akin to that created by these parties during the late 1980s and early 1990s, to which Dr. Cammack so vividly refers.

The problems that agencies now face are ones encountered by all organizations attempting to deal with an ideologically driven or fundamentalist movement in which there is inevitably a spectrum of opinion ranging from hard-line to relatively moderate. Does one take a confrontational approach or seek to engage in dialogue? If one opts for dialogue, which benchmarks should be used as a basis for the dialogue? Should one draw on Western liberal and secular values? If so, how does one weigh and define these? Should the UN human rights conventions be the guide or are these, as the Taleban claim, based on Western value systems? Should Christian principles be drawn upon or is it more appropriate to look to scholars at Al-Azhar in Cairo for guidance? Alternatively, does liberal opinion in Afghanistan set a suitable standard or should the value systems of the rural areas provide the key? If so, does one look to the values of the more conservative Pushtun areas or those of the north of Afghanistan? One then has to take a view as to whether, in this case, the Taleban are a reflection of popular opinion or whether popular opinion is being used to further a pursuit of power. It is clear, in this regard, that the policies of the Taleban are consistent with rural values. What is less clear is the extent to which there may be an abuse of this reality to justify the creation of a movement which can be seen as meeting certain strategic interests. One could also argue that fundamentalist movements are a common product of conflict situations, a search for old certainties in response to societal crises. Should one be sympathetic to this response or remain critical of its manifestations?

Agencies operating in this kind of environment are very much at sea. They cannot be aware of more than a fraction of the many agendas involved, yet they are key players in the interactions which surround them. They have to be culturally sensitive, yet be conscious of how culture may be abused to justify the maintenance of power or of discriminatory practices. They have to take security very seriously and be ever mindful of how they might, inadvertently, fuel conflict through their programs. They need to take account of the fact that they may be legitimizing particular power holders vis-à-vis the populations they control, and that they may be indirectly resourcing such power holders by reducing their responsibilities to provide services to these populations. Agencies have to be guided by principles, yet take a view on how far they should compromise on these principles. They have to weigh the relative importance of keeping people alive through relief programs against the more intangible objective of relieving poverty by challenging restrictions on female employment. They also have to consider whether it is better to negotiate human rights improvements from a position of program suspension or from a position of continuing to operate programs.

To return to the central thesis, Dr. Cammack is right to note the differential response of the West to gender-related human rights abuses in Afghanistan now and during the mujahedeen period. There can be no doubt that humanitarian agencies are, to a degree, influenced by the strategic interests of their donors and that these can, under certain circumstances, lead them to ignore or not to have serious regard for human rights abuses. This was an important element in the early history of humanitarian aid to Afghanistan, but feelings of powerlessness and actual fear were also significant determinants of behavior in response to such abuses. However, the very explicit nature of the Taleban gender policies and the more neutral stance of the humanitarian agencies are important factors in the greater attention now being given to gender-related rights. In spite of these changed conditions, the task of seeking an improvement in the situation of women in Afghanistan remains far from easy.

8

Upsetting the Cart

Forced Migration and Gender Issues, the African Experience

Patrick Matlou

Introduction

This chapter covers the root causes of forced migration in Africa[1] and the related international refugee regime. It also touches on the participation of females and children in wars; the unraveling of the state, social institutions, and structures; assistance programs and their reinforcement of male domination; resettlement and voluntary repatriation. Although internal displacees are discussed, refugees are my main focus. In Africa as elsewhere, males have often been the instigators of violent conflict, yet they are not necessarily the ones who suffer the most. The vulnerable members of society—children, women, the elderly, and the infirm—usually come out worst in these conflicts. This chapter shows that the situation usually does not improve during the course of flight, while in exile, on returning home, or during resettlement. I also show that gender inequality is a significant cause of forced migration and vice versa. Without a fundamental restructuring of society, making it more equitable and reducing levels of violence, particularly those directed at the weakest members, forced migration will continue.

Root Causes of Forced Migration in Africa

There are now over eight million refugees and twenty-five million internally displaced persons in Africa. Almost every African country has been profoundly affected, with at least thirty such countries being either the producers or recipients of refugees. Women and girls comprise 80 percent of these displacees (Jack 1996: 11). In my view, there are four root causes of forced migration in contemporary Africa.[2] First, displacement and refugees are the legacy of the struggles for decolonization and majority rule in countries like Algeria, Angola, Guinea Bissau, Mozambique, Namibia, South Africa, and Zimbabwe. Secondly, there is the legacy of South Africa's purposeful destabilization of its surrounding region. Known as the "total strategy," the apartheid South African government curtailed regional support for the antiapartheid struggle by weakening its neighbors and forcing them to deport refugees elsewhere or to South Africa. Thirdly, post-independence conflicts have arisen involving political struggle, ethnicity, religious intolerance, East/West rivalries in Africa, and human rights violations in various countries like Algeria, Angola, Burundi, Lesotho, Liberia, Malawi, Mozambique, Nigeria, Rwanda, and Somalia. Conflicts in Sudan, the Horn of Africa, Uganda, and Zimbabwe have created millions of refugees and internally displaced persons. All of these conflicts have made Africa the most land mine infested continent–thirty-seven million mines in nineteen countries–Angola alone having ten million. Mines remain active for up to fifty years, a legacy of physical and socioeconomic destruction that will continue to take its toll on many African countries. Most infrastructure is destroyed, and large tracts of land will have to remain idle, thus stymieing economic production. Clearly, the human cost to pay is overwhelmingly high.[3] Fourthly, economic and environmental disasters creating poverty and starvation, including conflict over resources, droughts, famines, floods, and so on, fuel the displacement of populations in Angola, Mozambique, the Horn of Africa, and the Sahel. Often these disasters are exacerbated by ongoing wars and government policy.

The International Refugee Regime: Helpers or Spoilers?

Various role-players who deal with refugee issues together form what I call the 'international refugee regime'. They include the governments of countries of origin, host states, donors, intergovernmental organizations (INGOs), NGOs, researchers, and some elements of the general public (UNHCR 1979a: 3–27). Together, all these actors have institutionalized both normative and procedural expectations with regard to how refugee matters are addressed.[4] The record of the

international refugee regime in dealing with refugee matters is variable; in many cases it has achieved commendable results, while in
others it comes in for scathing criticism.

Western countries (especially the US), their personnel and agencies, dominate this state-centric international refugee regime in
Africa. The basis of this domination is simple: whoever pays the
piper chooses the music. Most people working in this industry are
males, so it is not surprising that policies toward refugees have not
often taken the interests of women or girl children into consideration. Moreover, the international refugee regime, of which the UN is
the hub, is now under severe strain. This is because of artificially limited organizational mandates,[5] outmoded international refugee conventions, dwindling resources, and the unwillingness of many states
to host refugees (Zarjevski 1988: 8–10).

UNHCR is of course the main intergovernmental refugee agency.
Established in 1951 to deal with about 1.5 million refugees from
post–World War II Europe (Crisp and Nettleton 1984: 7), UNHCR
now deals with many millions of refugees worldwide. In addition to
this daunting task, internally displaced persons have also been made
a special concern of UNHCR. Through material assistance,
UNHCR provides refugees with some economic security and protection. This aid is spread between emergency relief and durable
solutions. Distribution of monetary aid, however, is not always equitable: in every year from 1967 through to 1973, Africa received more
than half of all international aid, yet more than 60 percent of that aid
went to only six states (Pitterman 1987: 16). In 1981, the per capita
expenditure on an African refugee was $22 while that on non-
Africans was $50 (Alot 1981: 1).[6] Moreover, in order to achieve its
objectives, UNHCR depends upon UN members for the renewal of
its mandate every five years and for resources. This profoundly limits its capacity to adopt an overtly critical stance vis-à-vis its benefactors as that may damage relations with them.

Although refugees result chiefly from political events, the international refugee regime, oddly enough, conceptualizes and treats
refugees primarily as a humanitarian issue. The humanitarian industry that has arisen along with UNHCR has created a vast system of
organizations within the international community that now deal with
refugees. Presently a 'growing' industry, humanitarian-related spending went from 600 million dollars in 1985, to 3,467 million dollars in
1994. The proportion of disaster assistance provided by the North in
relation to their aid budgets leapt from 2 percent in 1990, to 7 percent in 1993 (Davies 1997: 28). While INGOs and NGOs vary considerably in size, philosophical orientation, operational styles, and

specialization, they both complement UNHCR's work. However, their need for governmental permission to operate and their dependence upon governments and the public for resources affects their respective relationships with these entities. Recent examples illustrate that relationships can range from the incongruent (such as in the Sudan during most of the 1980s) to the amicable (as in Kenya and Mozambique during the early 1980s). The nature of these relationships is significant given that, of the regions receiving UNHCR assistance, Africa has for many years ranked highest for local settlement and voluntary repatriation and lowest for third country resettlement.

Generally, though, NGOs are believed to operate much more efficiently than governmental and intergovernmental agencies because they are smaller and have less complex organizational structures. They also typically react more quickly to events, work more at the grassroots level, and operate mainly along humanitarian rather than politicoeconomic lines. However, NGOs now face criticisms similar to those made about other institutions. These include their tendency to provide inappropriate aid, to engage in intra- and interagency rivalries, and to not coordinate their activities (Harrell-Bond 1985, 1986; Mazur 1987, 1988; Pitterman 1985). Moreover, refugee work is mainly dominated by Northern agencies. For example, in early 1994 there were over 2,500 Northern NGOs compared to hundreds of Southern ones receiving large amounts of international assistance (Davies 1997: 28). This imbalance reinforces neocolonialism and undermines the authority of Southern states and indigenous agencies (Karadawi 1983; Rossiter and Palmer 1991; Shelley 1990).

In addition, numerous academic institutions and researchers are involved in refugee work. These mainly Northern Hemisphere actors—and the concepts, theories and methodological strategies they develop—greatly influence how refugees are perceived and treated. For example, for years they have portrayed refugees, particularly African ones, as weak, dependent people with little control over their lives.[7] They have typically depicted 'refugees' as undifferentiated and homogeneous, unconsciously equating them with adult males. Thus, neither women's perspectives nor gender issues receive much coverage in the body of work generated by these researchers and institutions. The negative consequences of treating or representing refugees as a homogeneous group informed primarily by male values are discussed throughout this chapter.

Every individual carries her or his own particular history and values into a research situation (Ben-Tovim 1987: 208–210; Thompson 1985; Wolpe 1989: 9), and historically this has profoundly affected the representation of gender in refugee studies. I myself am a well-traveled

South African refugee. While I thought I was open-minded regarding gender issues, the extent of my own myopia was revealed while conducting fieldwork for my doctoral dissertation in 1989 in Dukwe Reception Center for Refugees (DRCFR), Botswana. By this time, talk about gender issues had had an impact on every discourse in the social sciences, refugee studies included. Upon arriving in Dukwe, the Settlement Commandant introduced me to the Refugee Representative Council (RRC), comprising leaders of various refugee nationalities and organizations, mainly from eastern and southern Africa. He asked them to inform their 'constituents' of my presence and to arrange for my having access to their groups.

By going through the Commandant and RRC, I avoided a great deal of time and trouble I would have faced trying to gain access to the refugee population by other means. The representatives became my key informants and helped reframe my project to be more relevant to Dukwe. They enabled me to meet many refugees and respondents and to gain quickly their trust and cooperation. However, I later came to realize that my dependence upon these representatives to organize group interviews had profoundly limited my interaction with refugees (Matlou 1992). As a result of relying on male representatives to gain access to most groups, I interviewed mostly men, a practice I never questioned at the time.[8] Most women were involved in domestic chores and other activities for a great part of the day, leaving them fatigued thereafter; it would have been taxing for them and socially inappropriate for me to interview them at night. I now recognize, however, that with better planning and thoughtfulness, these obstacles could have been surmounted. Unfortunately, the Dukwe scenario in which women refugees lack representation, in both the camps and the research literature, replicates itself around the world.

The Increasing Impact of War on Women and Children: Great Losses, Few Gains

From the 1950s, the number and intensity of conflicts on the African continent has been on the rise, reaching a crescendo in the last decade. During this time, millions of people have been displaced, maimed, and psychologically abused. Meanwhile, the development of many states has been reversed or halted, and the roles that different groups perform in society have been greatly altered. Initially, during these conflicts women and children were mainly engaged in politico-cultural and socioeconomic activities—in at least noncombatant roles.

Over the course of time, the number who have been combatants has increased, as will be detailed below. Furthermore, civilians rather than soldiers are increasingly the main targets in war in Africa, as elsewhere. The proportion of civilian casualties in wars has risen from 5 percent at the beginning of the century to 15 percent in World War I, 65 percent in World War II and over 90 percent in the 1990s. Wars are now longer and more destructive. They are also different in character: they are now more chronic and episodic, and there are fewer clear battle lines. Institutionalized humanitarian activities are also no longer as safe in wars as they once were. Relief convoys, refugee camps, clinics, and feeding centers are now typically seen as military targets. As are women and children. Wars in this decade have killed more than two million children and injured more than four million; another million have been orphaned or separated from their families (Machel 1996). Women in particular have been victims of severe violence in civil wars across the continent.

During the processes of forced migration that so often result, ongoing social structures and institutions undergo significant changes. As the state disintegrates, its monopoly over the instruments of power and the allocation of resources disappears. Warlords, praetorian guards, religious zealots, and crime bosses take over the shattered shells of now weakened states and societies.[9] Development recedes, what progress had been made is lost, and violence becomes the order of the day as the weak are further subjugated. Institutions and infrastructure are destroyed, economic and social facilities are rendered useless, and thousands of human beings are killed, maimed, and made to suffer great deprivation. Every one of these processes is gendered and impacts differently on women and men even before they flee their homelands. Within countries of origin, family structures change, as the men often leave and become soldiers. The number of child- and female-headed households increases. The destruction of local level social and physical infrastructure leads to the differential deprivation, malnutrition, sickness and ill-treatment of women and children. For example, recently during the Somalian conflict, more than half of the (chiefly 'noncombatant') deaths in some places were the result of measles. A comparison of a peaceful Botswana with Mozambique highlights these effects—many of which do not initially appear to have anything directly to do with war and forced migration. In 1992, Botswana had a mortality rate for children under five of 80 per 1,000, and 89 percent of the population had access to health. In Mozambique, after fifteen years of war the equivalent mortality rate was 240 per 1,000, and 39 percent of the population had access to health services. By

1989, wars had led to the death of approximately 500,000 Mozam-bican and 350,000 Angolan children (Fair 1995: 213). It is also important to note that most of the African countries involved in wars have relatively low GNPs–less than $500 per capita in 1994. War-ravaged Mozambique then had a per capita GNP of only $80. In most such situations, war leads directly to accelerated underdevelopment and poverty and to consequent local level violence and social disorganization; often the line between nominally 'political' and 'economic' migrants blurs completely.

As communities unravel and families are stressed, the number of orphans, abandoned and unaccompanied children, widows, and abandoned wives also increases; it is estimated that about 95,000 children were separated from their families during the Rwandan war (Del Mundo 1995b: 14–15). Intense efforts by the international refugee regime has so far led to only 33,000 being reunited with their families by mid-1996. In Angola in 1995, UNICEF reported that over 20 percent of the children had been separated from their parents and relatives.[10]

Increasingly, forced cohabitation becomes the order of the day when local women are required to become 'wives' or unmarried partners of combatants and officials of the warring groups. They suffer various forms of physical, psychological, and sexual abuse. There are increasing reports from areas of conflict in Africa (including Mozambique, Uganda, Liberia, Sierra Leone, Somalia, Sudan, and Rwanda) of women and girl captives being sold as slaves or being kept in slave-like conditions. Reports are surfacing from refugee camps as well. In 1989, I gathered similar accounts during my research in Dukwe (DRCFR) in Botswana (Matlou 1992).

As another example, Serrill (1996: 28) notes the revival of slavery in southern Sudan, an outgrowth of a vicious, decade-old civil war between the Muslim north and the Christian and Animist south that has also killed hundreds of thousands. The regime in Khartoum allegedly encourages soldiers to compensate themselves through looting, the most valuable booty being women and children. Women are forced to become 'wives' who are in effect slaves. Meanwhile, the Sudanese People's Liberation Army (SPLA) is said to force captured youth to become soldiers (Serrill 1996: 28). There have also been reports of children being forcibly rounded up from buses and cars in order to participate in the war. Thousands of Sudanese youth, many younger than ten years old, undertook the arduous and lengthy journey from Sudan to Kenya in order to escape being captured.[11]

Indeed, gender-oriented violence is increasingly becoming one of the main weapons of war in Africa (see Nordstrom, this volume).

Psychologists have reported rape to be one of the most intrusive of traumatic events (UNICEF 1996b: 19). Rape has also become a potent symbol of conquest over others (see Giles, this volume). In Rwanda, rape was used extensively to destroy community ties: over 15,700 women and girls were raped between April 1994 to April 1995 (Machel 1996). A study by the Fondation de France found that almost all Rwandan women who had not been massacred in 1994 had been raped by the militias. It also found that between two and five thousand children could have been born of rape (Marshall 1995: 5). In RENAMO (Resistenca National Mocambicana) camps, young boys who were themselves victims of violence often inflicted sexual violence on girls (UNICEF 1996b: 19).

Forced migration often results in women- and children-headed households, the males either being at war, incarcerated, or killed. Female cross-border refugees have to fend for themselves in large camps where, sadly, they are too often the victims of violence and rape. Women are vulnerable in these situations and sometimes have to proffer sexual favors to fellow refugees and government officials in order to survive.

At a special hearing of the Truth and Reconciliation Commission in South Africa, Defense Minister Joe Modise reported that sexual harassment of women in African National Congress (ANC) exile camps in Angola had been a very serious problem. Some camp commanders were reported to have taken advantage of their position of authority to ask sexual favors of women in camps (*Sowetan* 13 May 1997: 2). A number of former high-ranking female Umkhonto weSizwe soldiers have confirmed the incidence of gender-specific violence in ANC camps. Though the ANC is supposed to have dealt with identified perpetrators, most of the victims have never had adequate counseling or rehabilitation. Furthermore, there are suspicions that some of the perpetrators are today top-level government officials (Sboros 1997: 15). During the Zimbabwean liberation war there were cases of male guerrillas raping young female colleagues or the latter having to offer sex for food and basic supplies; rape was used by Rhodesian soldiers as a weapon of war against women in the reserves (McCloy 1997: 28).

At this juncture it is important to link the discussion of rape with the transmission of sexual diseases, particularly AIDS. In Africa this disease is spreading rapidly in both normal societies and those at war. In war-torn areas it is believed that AIDS is spread mainly through women being made sex slaves (Nordstrom, this volume). The impact on these societies will be enormous. In this, we can look to Uganda where, as Buckley (1996: 5) shows, the social order has been turned on its head. The elderly now take on the full load of caring for young children, as the young adult population is decimated.

Many writers have reported being offered accommodation, food, and other valuables from the poorest and most deprived of refugees (Harrell-Bond 1986; Hitchcox 1989; Potten 1976) and I personally have had similar experiences in Botswana and Kenya. Even so, the deprivation and uncertainty that refugees often suffer sometimes lead them into conflict with each other over scarce rewards. In this regard, exile often serves as an arena for the continuation of conflicts begun at home and leads to the intensification of discriminatory practices that were already in place. This happens in refugee camps all over Africa. As a case in point, in Kenyan camps where I worked, Somali clans were usually led by men. Imposing themselves as leaders in the refugee camps, men from some clans that formed the ruling class in Somalia often effectively shut out other groups. Marginalized clans, women, and children were the greatest losers in this process. Islam was also often used to legitimate the marginalization of women and to keep them out of the decision-making process (see Elmadmad and Cammack, this volume). When women protested and sought direct contact with the aid agencies, men threatened them with violence. On top of this, Somali male elders also complained that young Somali women were acquiring foreign habits like wearing Western clothes, consuming alcohol, and mixing freely with men. Although young men also engaged in practices that their elders considered unbecoming, women endured stricter censure. These elders resented as well having to be told what to do by young refugee agency and host country officials, especially by women officers.

Assistance Programs and the Reinforcement of Male Domination

The international refugee regime has had to grapple with the challenge of assisting and protecting all refugees while simultaneously respecting their cultures. It does not come to this challenge without its own biases and expectations. As mentioned, the international refugee regime is male dominated, and certain associated biases are consequently replicated in its policies and assistance programs in Africa. This practice is buttressed by the fact that, while most refugees are women and children, men usually claim refugee leadership roles, are more educated and articulate, and are more likely to speak a European language. Their male colleagues in the aid agencies typically seem to see this situation as natural, and make heavy use of refugee men as culture brokers, translators, and facilitators. Far too often, the results are that ration allocations for men and women are different, that men receive more material assistance, and that most jobs in the camps go to men. When there are education programs in the camps, the female children and women are often discriminated against, either directly or because it is too unsafe for them to visit some parts of camps.

Moreover, it is remarkable how rarely women's needs are considered in the aid packages aimed at refugees in Africa. Where such programs do exist, they are often the first to be cut when there are funding problems (Marshall 1995: 8–9). These programs typically are not well institutionalized and rely mainly on the efforts of one or a few staff members; when these individuals leave, the programs die. Sometimes aid programs unintentionally increase women's work dramatically. As a case in point, in Malawi female refugees had to trek long distances in search of firewood to cook the beans they were provided. They also had to engage in the very laborious processing of the whole-grain maize provided by aid agencies (Wilson 1992: 36).

Poor site planning that fails to consider women's concerns also impacts negatively on women, particularly when camps are located deep in the rural hinterland. For example, the high incidence of rape in Somali refugee camps in Kenya in 1993 was attributed to the camps being located in isolated areas dominated by bandits and Somali militia. Many women were raped while out searching for firewood. In the Ivory Coast, women risked attack by going out into the bush in order to avoid using toilets located near those of male counterparts (Marshall 1995: 6). In Dukwe, the location of administrative and other facilities in the center of a large camp posed serious risks for women who needed to use these resources at night for education, recreation, and buying goods.

It is nevertheless encouraging that African women refugees are now playing increasingly important roles in developing refugee programs and administering camps and settlements, in spite of the continuing prevalence of male-dominated refugee policies. This shift reflects significant changes in international discourses on refugees. As Callaway (1987: 320) indicates, only in the last decade has the plight of this forgotten majority attracted global attention. A groundswell of opinion emerged within and without UNHCR about a decade ago that women refugees were not fully benefiting from its assistance and protection programs; in some cases women refugees were actually worse off because of it. Consequently, an internal working group comprising junior women employees was formed to analyze policy and suggest viable recommendations for improvements. Meanwhile,

NGOs were also in the process of examining women's issues in relation to their work. A major seminar held in 1988 resulted in the publication of a working guide pertaining to the specific needs of refugee women. In 1989, UNHCR's first Coordinator for Women was appointed, with a specific brief of apprising staff of the unique difficulties of refugee women and of measures to overcome them. In 1991, UNHCR issued its *Guidelines on the Protection of Women*[12] with the underlying principle of integrating the resources and needs of refugee women into all aspects of programming to ensure equitable protection and assistance activities (UNHCR EC 1991: 7). The guidelines cover legal protection and security, assessment and planning, addressing protection through assistance, and follow-up and reporting of protection problems.

In Africa, the progress made by UNHCR in implementing its own guidelines has been variable, as indicated earlier. Howarth-Wiles, the UNHCR Coordinator, sees lack of staff motivation as the major obstacle. Rather than incorporating the values of the guidelines in their daily activities, many see this as the work of the Coordinator and as peripheral to their main responsibility. Assistance programs are still being planned without sufficient consideration of women's needs. Some staff also believe that refugee cultural traditions should take precedence over respect for human rights, even if these cultural practices are profoundly misogynist. They have the perception 'that rape and sexual violence may be regrettable, but they remain essentially inevitable incidents in refugee life'; furthermore, they do not accept that UNHCR has any role in changing people's culture "and we should respect the traditions of refugees, whether this means the veil, forced marriage, failure to educate girls, genital mutilation, or lack [of] access to family planning" (Berthiaume 1995: 12–13). However, when staff are highly motivated, they have been able to make considerable progress regarding women's issues, as in the cases of Guatemalans in Mexico, Mozambicans in Malawi and Zimbabwe, Afghans in Pakistan, and returnees to Cambodia (Berthiaume 1995: 12–13).

Resettlement: Who Goes Where and Why

Like other humanitarian assistance, resettlement opportunities are supposed to be provided on a nonpolitical and ungendered basis. However, this is usually not the case in Africa. In southern Africa, from the 1960s until the early 1990s, resettlement was seen as a security issue. Asylum states often transported refugees farther north–

even outside the continent–to protect them from forces in their countries of origin. Removing refugees was also designed to deter attacks against the initial asylum states. Angola, Botswana, Lesotho, Malawi, Mozambique, Namibia, Swaziland, Tanzania, Zambia and Zimbabwe nevertheless did suffer such attacks, the main perpetrators being the Portuguese, Rhodesians, and South Africans. Agreements were thus reached to transfer many refugees to other countries; this explains why many countries of first asylum only established transit camps for refugees and chose not to integrate them. The UN in a Joint Inspection Unit (JIU) report criticized UNHCR for dealing inadequately with the security of South African refugees in southern Africa.[13] Almost all African refugees before 1980 nevertheless remained in Africa, as Western countries were very reluctant to accept them (Zolberg et al. 1989: 25). Programs in the West to resettle African refugees date only to 1980, when the US established a quota of 3,000 annually. Canada followed suit in 1981, with a quota of 500 that increased to 1,000 in 1983. Australia was the only other Western country to establish such a program, with a quota of 220 in 1984 (Rogge and Akol 1989: 187). Concern over the possibility of resettlement fueling racism, and spurious stereotypes of African refugees as rural, uneducated, and unskilled evidently conspire to keep Western resettlement minuscule (Rogge 1985: 72).

Voluntary Repatriation

So vast are the numbers of refugees and so few are the resources of asylum countries that voluntary repatriation is the most viable long-term solution for many refugees. This of course assumes that they will return to a homeland where the conditions that led them to flee have been eliminated and that they will be afforded opportunities to contribute to their own development and that of their country.[14] Some of the world's largest voluntary repatriation exercises have been undertaken on the African continent. These have so far pertained primarily to refugees who left their countries during the struggle against colonialism: particularly Angola, Guinea Bissau, Mozambique, Namibia, Zimbabwe, and South Africa. Most post-independence African refugees have fled from their own compatriots, and in many cases cycles of violence and oppression continue to persist. Thus, as one wave of refugees is returning, others are fleeing into exile. This happened in Zimbabwe during the 1980s (when Ndebeles in particular were persecuted), in Ethiopia in 1991, and presently in the Great Lakes region of Africa. In fact, the spontaneous return of thousands of refugees from Zaire to Rwanda was caused more by the fighting that broke out in the former country than for any other reason.

Since women and children form the majority of refugees, one might anticipate that they are the greatest benefactors of appropriate, truly voluntary repatriation. This is clearly not always so. The relevant conflicts may have ended, but a corresponding fundamental restructuring of society has rarely taken place. Women often return to homelands in which male domination is the order–domination that may have been exacerbated by war. In exile, some women do acquire new skills and education, and most have come to perform roles different from those their home society conventionally allocated to women. Many have internalized new values of democracy and equality. Upon return, women may be constrained in practicing these new values at home: opportunities for advancement are often blocked, and many are forced to accept roles subservient to men. Even women who took an active part in the liberation of numerous countries in Africa return home only to be marginalized; for them, the equality for which they fought is not entrenched in the new societies (Balch et al. 1996: 25).

This was the case in Zimbabwe, where for years after independence African women were still treated as minors or second-class citizens. This has been a theme of two recent, widely acclaimed Zimbabwean films: *Everyone's Child* by Tsitsi Dangarembga and *Flame* by Ingrid Sinclair. Throughout Africa, there remain significant inconsistencies between what is embodied in constitutions (which emphasize general equality) and traditional practices (which are male biased). Many countries continue to have gender discriminatory legislation on their books: laws concerning the ownership of property, citizenship, and access to jobs and occupations (Maluwa 1996; Smith, this volume).

Women comprise the majority of adults in most African countries, but this is not yet well reflected in public institutions, work places, politics, the economy, sports, media, or educational institutions (Afkhami 1997: 160).[15] In part, this reflects profound legitimations emphasizing the role of women as mothers and homemakers. Women typically are expected to play a subservient role in the family as wives, mothers, daughters, and sisters. In spite of this, recent initiatives have given increasing recognition to another traditional role of African women–that of peacemaker.

Women in Africa have developed several moves toward promoting peace on the continent. Recently, some progress was registered at the Pan African Conference on Peace, Gender and Development, held from 1–3 March 1997, in Kigali, Rwanda, where the Federation of Women's Networks (FWN) was formed. Presently it represents women from thirteen warring or conflict-ridden countries: Angola, Burundi, Congo-Brazzaville, Liberia, Mali, Mozambique, Rwanda, Sierra Leone, Somalia, South Africa, Sudan, Tanzania, and Zambia. Identifying the lack of involvement of women–traditional peacemakers–as one of the reasons for the failure of most African peace initiatives, the conference participants decried this type of marginalization of women and called for their greater involvement. The FWN accordingly called upon the Organization of African Unity (OAU) and UN to take appropriate follow-up action (Kayigamba 1997: 6). The FWN is also broadly mandated to evaluate conflict-resolution mechanisms established by the OAU and other organizations, to send fact-finding missions to conflict regions, and to organize conferences and workshops on conflict, peace, and related matters.

It must be noted that implementation of such directives is difficult. The Regional Conference on Women, Peace, and Development in November 1993 noted various preconditions for peace in Africa: the promotion of equality of the sexes, economic equality, the universal enjoyment of basic rights and fundamental freedoms, and the involvement of women in resolving conflicts on the continent. As a precondition to the last, women would have to be empowered both politically and economically through knowledge and education to render them operational as equal partners with men (Jack 1996: 11). The conference developed an Action Plan, which, among other things, recommended establishing a Committee of African Ministers and/or Plenipotentiaries that would be part of any new conflict prevention/management/resolution institutions and mechanisms created by the OAU. This committee would also be a part of all other policy and sectoral organs of the Economic Commission for Africa and the OAU. While the OAU Heads of States summits in 1994 and 1995 endorsed these recommendations, this plan has yet to be implemented. Unfortunately, this is the fate of many worthy ventures in Africa.

Conclusion

In this chapter, I have argued that African societies, which by and large are male dominated, typically make the lot of females worse during conflicts and forced migration. A distinction does have to be made here between African struggles for independence and the latter-day conflicts that have mainly been against indigenous oppression and disregard for human rights. During the former situation, women were often given opportunities to partake in the liberation struggles as comparative equals and have thereafter been involved in establishing new structures in their countries. The history of liberation in Algeria, Angola, Eritrea, Guinea Bissau, Mozambique, South Africa, Namibia, and Zimbabwe is filled with examples of this sort. However, post-independence war and political conflict have generated forced migration often resulting in a loss of whatever socioeconomic and politicocultural gains women had made earlier. They face significant oppression, inequity, and risk, both before and during flight, and when they reach exile. The few gains that women refugees may sometimes secure through forced migration can hardly compensate for the greater scale of loss.

In certain respects, African states have some of the most open and liberal refugee policies in the world. At the same time, they impose many restrictions upon refugees and typically treat them as a temporary phenomenon. These (usually poor) countries generally seek to reduce the costs of hosting refugees, while trying to gain as much economic and political mileage from the refugees' presence as possible. Refugees are usually treated as a significant security matter affecting the law and order situation, the host population, culture and socioeconomic resources, and relations with neighboring states and the international community. The rights of refugees in general are therefore often constrained in the name of security, and host states care little about the rights of women refugees. The poverty of many host states also leads to the domination of refugee work by foreign agencies and personnel, mainly from the North. This arrangement transfers most administrative, financial, and material responsibilities of assisting refugees to foreign organizations, which typically do not have gender issues high on their agendas.

I reiterate that forced migration in Africa usually reinforces male-dominated values and structures, not all of which originate primarily in Africa. The international refugee regime imports many. Others are a gendered consequence of war. A survey of conflicts around the world indicate a clear positive correlation between increased societal violence and the abuse of women. A pattern is developing in which attacks on women, such as rape, are becoming part of accepted military strategy. Amnesty International (1995c: 1) highlights the wide range of inequities visited upon women by armed men across 151 countries; as in the case of women refugees in Africa, their plight is often hidden by the sheer scale of the tragedies. These atrocities continue despite most governments having declared that women's rights *are* human rights at the 1993 World Conference on Human Rights. The international community pays lip service to "equality by the year 2000," the UN's slogan for the present decade (Amnesty International 1995c: 6). The African evidence suggests that the dawn of a new millennium will arrive with stark gender inequalities still firmly entrenched in a conflict-ridden world. Concerning refugees in Africa, we are a long way from fulfilling the goals of the Platform of Action of the Fourth World Conference on Women held in Beijing in 1995, which states:

> Equality between women and men is a matter of human rights and a condition for social justice and is a necessary and fundamental prerequisite for equality development and peace. A transformed partnership based on equality between women and men is a condition for people-centered sustainable development. A sustained and long-term commitment is essential, so that women and men can work together for themselves, for their children and for society to meet the challenges of the twenty-first century. (Afkhami 1997: 160)

Notes

1. Africa in this chapter comprises member states of the OAU including Morocco, which withdrew from the organization in the 1980s.
2. Although I concentrate on the period from 1945, the displacement of people in Africa can be traced back for centuries. Millions of people were displaced during the Islamization of Egypt and northern Africa, during the largely indigenous empire-building in Benin, Dahomey, Ghana, Songhai, Mali, Zimbabwe, and by the Zulus. The slave trade displaced millions more. European colonization of most of the continent generated its own displacees.
3. The Vietnam Veterans of America Foundation in a recent report, *The Enduring Legacy of Landmines*, found that girls and women are most vulnerable to mine injuries because of their roles in meeting the food needs of their families (Umoren 1995: 6).
4. Apart from international law pertaining to refugees, states develop municipal laws and structures to handle refugee matters. Note that in some states refugee matters are covered only by national legislation. Numerous African countries, in the process of ratifying international refugee conventions, have placed reservations on certain sections. Thus, they are able to impose restrictions on the movement, residence, education, naturalization, property rights, and welfare benefits available to refugees. Whereas these countries may openly admit refugees, through such legislation they are able to restrict considerably the freedom of those who come.
5. A classic example of this arose in the 1960s when the UNHCR attempted to initiate zonal development in Congo-Kinshasa and Burundi. The aim of this program was to enhance local development through refugee aid (Cuenod 1967: 51).

However, it was prematurely abandoned because UNHCR was not mandated to perform development work.

6. One of the reasons for the fall in Africa's per capita share of refugee aid and the increase in Asia's share was America's guilt for its role in Asia's numerous conflicts. Other factors included East/West rivalries, donor fatigue with African refugees, and Africa's low strategic value in international affairs.

7. The provision of 'aid' reinforces these stereotypes as well. Aid workers frame refugees as helpless victims requiring compassion and care (see Boelaert et al., this volume). At the same time, their exclusion from the policy process, particularly in organized settlements, makes them highly dependent on aid. Refugees then act in stereotypical patterns simply to survive, further reinforcing the stereotype.

8. Before 1980, females comprised the majority in Dukwe, according to the Lutheran World Federation (LWF 1978: 10). After that, they remained a large minority (LWF 1980–1989). The opposite pertains for most other refugee settlements, especially in Africa (Adepoju 1982: 31; Callaway 1987: 320).

9. In such situations, a woman sometimes rises to become a 'warlord' in her own right. For example, Alice Lakwena was a very powerful woman in 1980s Uganda, controlling thousands of supporters who blindly and faithfully obeyed her commands. She often convinced her followers to go into war armed only with rudimentary weapons, telling them that magic charms and belief in the holy spirit would protect them. Consequently, thousands of them died. Lakwena later fled into exile in Kenya where, in 1994, she was resident at the Ruiru Transit Center (RTC). At that time, I oversaw the RTC as a UNHCR field officer and dealt with many reports of incidents where Lakwena clearly continued to have a magical hold over her followers.

10. The increased use of children and women as combatants has exacerbated this situation in another way. In Rwanda, for example, there are hundreds of women and children in jail awaiting trail for genocide (Brittain 1996: 23; *The Citizen* 9 September 1995: 6; Turnbridge 1995: 10). Government and international agencies are now in a quandary as to how to deal with them given the inconsistencies in law, their young age (some are as young as seven), and the likelihood that they were coerced by adults into combat in the first place.

11. Despite the total contravention of international agreements (like the Geneva Convention and the UN Convention on the Rights of the Child) prohibiting the use of children under fifteen as combatants, child soldiers are found in virtually every large conflict in Africa. For example, in Liberia, where Charles Taylor's National Patriotic Front has a special child regiment (the Small Boy Unit) it is estimated that there are over six thousand child soldiers. The Ugandan National Resistance Army in 1986 had about three thousand children (including five hundred girls) in its ranks (UNICEF 1996a: 17). For the duration of their military service, these children are removed from everyday family life, receive no formal education, learn few civilian skills, and observe or participate in violent acts and atrocities. Following the conflict, they are released and expected to return to family and community groups to help rebuild their society. Disregarding recommendations such as those of the Machel Commission that urge the immediate demobilization (and UNICEF protection) of all units under eighteen years of age (Molefe 1996: 11), there are only a few NGOs with limited resources that are attempting to treat the physical and psychological trauma suffered by these children. One such program specifically designed for boy soldiers, the Children's Assistance Program (CAP), was established in Monrovia in 1992. While its early efforts were positive and several hundred boys were reintegrated into Liberia's

recovering society (Fair 1995: 214; UNICEF 1996a: 16), renewed fighting in Monrovia abruptly ended the program. All CAP property was seized or stolen, and the children were scattered or coerced back into combat (Hammer and Mabry 1996: 16). More recently in Rwanda, UNICEF has started a broader program to provide psychological counseling to Rwandans, especially children (Brittain 1996: 23).

12. This policy framework is grounded in various international conventions protecting women, especially the Convention on the Elimination of All Forms of Discrimination Against Women.

13. The report further noted "that this is regrettable considering that most South African refugees cannot be effectively protected by countries of first asylum and ... represent perhaps the single most large-scale refugee group in the region falling squarely within the mandate of UNHCR, in comparison with people displaced by drought, who are the concern of other agencies beside UNHCR" (Zolberg et al. 1989: 125).

14. Although most African governments often declare their intention to eliminate barriers to refugee integration in their respective countries, they nevertheless continue to practice the local settlement option. Very simply, placing refugees in holding camps allows governments to treat refugees as transients who will eventually either repatriate or resettle. Since refugees are commonly seen as a security risk by host governments, they are usually restricted in their movement and choice of residence. Contravening the many international conventions that these governments have ratified, they also place restrictions on the ability of refugees to fend for themselves. The practices of the international refugee regime also impede integration through the policy of aiding and assisting (or controlling) refugees in organized refugee settlements.

15. Some countries are changing more quickly than others. In South Africa much effort is presently being invested in creating a new, nonracial and democratic society. These goals are now entrenched in the constitution. The number of women in public life has increased dramatically since the demise of apartheid. The African National Congress specified a quota of 30 percent for the list of its parliamentary candidates, and women overall now hold 24 percent of parliamentary seats. Furthermore, the drive to create gender equality and to eliminate the inequities of apartheid is enhanced by the constitutional provisions for the Gender and Human Rights Commissions, the Public Protector, and the Constitutional Court. The sterling test of South African democracy, however, will be the challenge of giving substance to these constitutional guarantees.

9

Women Migrants of Kagera Region, Tanzania

The Need for Empowerment

Charles David Smith

The women who contributed to this study[1] were not refugees from political, religious, ethnic, or other persecution; they were forced to flee poverty and patriarchal custom.[2] They migrated to accumulate the capital needed to set up independent households. Haya women are the most productive members of their society but paradoxically are the poorest. This study of four villages in Hayaland, the Kagera region of Tanzania, confirms a common tendency in rural Africa: women carry out approximately two-thirds of all work but earn only one-third of the aggregate cash income. Most of women's meager incomes are used to care for children, leaving little savings or capital accumulation. Women have, out of necessity, developed a work ethic and the skills to manage their meager resources. This chapter explores the main reasons why Haya women are disadvantaged and forced to migrate. The tenacity of these women when confronting such conditions illustrates their resourcefulness as decision-makers and underscores their potential in promoting regional development.

Kagera region is located in the extreme northwest corner of Tanzania bordering Rwanda, Burundi, and Uganda: the Kagera River lies to the north and west, Lake Victoria to the south and east. Its rainy microclimate, horticulture, and dense population are a constant reminder that, unlike most of the semiarid East African savanna, this area is ecologically part of the Great Lakes Region of Central Africa. Haya culture and language are similar to those of the Hutu and Tutsi; however, for the Haya the divisions between 'royal' and 'commoner' clans have peacefully eroded since independence in 1961, unlike the ethnic cleavages in Rwanda and Burundi. President Nyerere achieved this by taking away the royal Hinda clan's privileges and abolishing the office of chief, breaking with the (British) colonial policy of 'indirect rule'. This environment of legal, political, and cultural equality has preempted ethnic tensions, and there has not been any ethnic violence in the last forty years. In 1995, Tanzania held multiparty elections and continued to liberalize its economy. Despite multipartyism and their geographical and cultural distinctiveness, the Haya have not developed an ethnically based civil society (associational life interacting with and influencing the state).

Since the pioneering work of Esther Boserup (1970), a body of literature has developed that details the contribution of women farmers and the particular constraints under which they operate (see, for example, Fortmann 1982; Guyer 1986a). Despite these important initiatives, there is a striking shortage of documentation on women farmers as decision-makers. There is likewise little empirical data on the type of independent women farmers who make up 30 percent of the surveyed heads of households in this study.[3] To help fill in this gap I interviewed people in seventy-six female-headed households and 113 wives, inquiring about landholdings, crops and yields, tools, inputs and methods of cultivation, division of labor, sources of income, household expenses, health, and nutrition.[4]

Forced Migration and Gender Constraints

Kagera's population tripled in the last forty years. Haya sons and daughters were often forced to set up new farms on marginal lands: soils needed to be upgraded, bush had to be cleared, and tree crops planted. Frequently, the location was far from markets. Along with expansion onto marginal lands came another major adaptation to population pressure and gender inequity—out-migration. The two processes were in some senses complementary, since the most common Haya method to accumulate savings for the purchase and development of arable land was to work off the farm for several years. Marginal land *can* be made profitable and productive, but this requires an injection of capital.

A large proportion of women migrate to accumulate capital.[5] The essential problem Haya female out-migrants face is their relative lack of education and marketable skills compared to men. At the same time, they desperately need to accumulate capital because of the gender constraints to be outlined here. Sampled households reported that 60 percent of sons and daughters between the ages of twenty-five and forty-five migrated to urban areas or to full-time non-farm employment. This is the same proportion as among interviewees who had themselves resided outside their villages. Sampled female and male migrants spent seven to nineteen years outside the region. Seventy percent of women (53 out of 76) were returned migrants, whereas only 53 percent of male-headed households had migrated (96 out of 174). Ironically, women and *richer* men exhibited a similar pattern (Smith 1994): nine out of ten of the richest male farmers had migrated in order to earn and save. The critical difference is that most women migrate and return in order to survive, while rich farmers return to prosperity. It is not clear what proportion of current out-migrants will return. The complexity of little understood pull factors (jobs, relationships, careers, business opportunities) and push factors (overpopulation, land scarcity, environmental degradation, fewer gendered options) makes this an open question for now.

Out- and In-Migration

Out-migration from heavily settled areas of Kagera, such as the Bukoba and Muleba districts, will continue unless alternatives, which include population control, rural industries, or intensive farming programs, are provided. Since over 50 percent of residents are under twenty-five years of age (the average sampled household consists of 5.2 persons), the population could double every fifteen to twenty years, faster than the projection of twenty-five years for Africa as a whole. The existing farming system cannot produce enough food to sustain its population, and in the future out-migration may take place under increasingly desperate circumstances. Already, village poverty increases the number of female-headed households, because there is a shortage of men able to pay bride price and start a family farm. Divorce is also common, generally increasing the number of female out-migrants. Some men who divorce their wives permit ex-wives to remain on the farm to grow food and provide subsistence for their children, but most divorced women are required to leave. In either case, if women are to survive on their own, they will need enough cash to buy a small plot.

Unlike the migrants of western and southern Africa who tend to move permanently to urban centers, the Haya more often migrate for a period of years and then return. Out-migrants are of two types:

(1) those with the best education and training who are able to find good jobs in the public sector or start successful private businesses–the most successful of these (primarily male) migrants go to commercial centers like Dar es Salaam, Arusha, and Mwanza; and (2) those who are landless, poor, and usually poorly educated, who migrate simply to survive. A greater proportion of women out-migrants fall into the latter category. Unskilled migrants face a difficult and sometimes desperate situation, although the challenge is not always hopeless or impossible. Some do manage to find jobs or business opportunities and accumulate capital for their return. One-half of female out-migrants in this study were government employees, teachers, nurses, and similar white-collar workers. The remainder were homemakers, service workers, or students.

Yet another economic factor has arisen very recently. Around ten thousand Tutsi from Rwanda quietly established themselves in the area as self-settled refugees in the 1960s, 1970s, and 1980s. However, after the civil war in Rwanda in 1994, a cataclysmic migration of Hutus took place. About one-half million Rwandan Hutus fled into the Kagera region, the equivalent of one-half the local population. This time, Rwandan settlement was restricted to refugee camps administered by the UNHCR. Even though these refugee camps were located in low population border regions, they generated a great deal of resentment and opposition at the national level. In 1995, I monitored the major East African newspapers and did not see a single positive statement about Rwandan refugees by any Tanzanian politicians, leaders of national associations, or other opinion-makers. The consensus reported in the press was that Hutu refugees were an economic burden, a security threat, and an environmental disaster. By 1997, the government had closed down all the camps and repatriated these refugees back to Rwanda and Burundi. Some refugees nevertheless went underground and joined the swelling local population.

Some village residents (primarily men) profited from the Rwandan crisis. The relief effort provided a boom market for local food surpluses, and as male-headed households were larger, they sold more food and reaped more benefits from the Rwandan crisis and relief efforts than did female-headed households. Both the need to employ large numbers of local drivers, construction workers, and security personnel, and security problems for women aspirants for employment tended to reinforce existing gender biases in employment and income; those who either worked in the camps or were able to take advantage of trading opportunities were predominantly men. The end result of the Rwandan refugee influx seems to be an intensification of existing gender inequalities.

In overview, the situation reported by Tibaijuka (1984: 77) persists today. Men predominate in "wage employment, building, handicrafts and skills, [and] trading...." While women's responsibilities represent two-thirds of the "total labor utilized," men enjoy two and one-quarter times more leisure time. Besides their agricultural work, women are responsible for close to 90 percent of domestic labor (Tibaijuka 1984: 77). Women clean house, collect most of the firewood (a job shared by children), draw and carry water from the nearest spring or stream, and cook the meals over open fires.[6]

Female Out-Migrant/Returnee Households

Wives typically do more farm and domestic work than their husbands but do not get a proportional share of the proceeds. Critically, if a wife divorces or her husband dies, her situation usually deteriorates, as she is unlikely to own land or other productive property.[7] This will be discussed further in the next section. Aspiring women farmers must often migrate to the towns in order to accumulate capital to buy and develop land; then they can eke out an independent living, even if most make do with far fewer resources than their male counterparts. Independent women farmers here follow the classic model proposed by Esther Boserup (1970) and adopt a range of innovations in order to survive. Most women who head households in Kagera region are indeed widowed or divorced and have lived independently outside their villages in order to accumulate capital. They are not women with absent migrant husbands, as was the case in Staudt's (1982) study in neighboring Western Kenya.

While male- and female-headed households grow identical staple food and cash crops (plantain bananas and coffee, respectively) and employ similar methods of hand hoe cultivation, they differ in many ways. Indeed, aggregate data provide a very distorted picture of the material conditions of women and men; gender differences are so great that it makes little sense to talk about the 'average villager'. Households headed by divorced or widowed women display characteristics distinct from those of male-headed households, whether poor, middle-class, or rich. This provides an important caution, to both refugee and development studies in Africa. A majority of adult refugees are women, and, even when accompanied by male family members, their personal goals, resources, and experiences are very different from those of men. Female-headed households are becoming more common all over sub-Saharan Africa, and studies that fail to disaggregate both male- and female-headed households risk misrepresenting both.

When we consider the gender-specific traits of Haya households, a clear pattern emerges. Female-headed households have smaller plots and more insecure tenure. Very few can afford regular or part-time labor or can afford agricultural inputs. Most have no access to extension services. They have far fewer opportunities to generate capital through nonfarm employment, and their education levels are much lower (see Table 9.1). Therefore, the economic imperatives that force men to migrate are even more imperative for women.

Independent women farmers typically practice a more labor-intensive and subsistence-oriented type of farming, supplemented by petty trading activities and the production and sale of beer and distilled liquor. Female household heads today are increasing production of beer bananas in order to generate a constant cash flow for essential goods and services, including food supplements such as maize flour. In the longer term, beer bananas take land away from

Table 9.1 Selected Variables Comparing Male- and Female-Headed Households

Item	Male-Headed (n=174)	Female-Headed (n=76)
Age of household head (mean)	54 years	44 years
Number of permanent household residents	5 persons	3 persons
Educational level of household head	5–8 years, primary school	no formal education
Reported acreage per household	5 acres	1 acre
Number of coffee trees per household	585 trees	176 trees
Estimated banana harvest (mean number)	228 bunches	184 bunches
Cows per household (mean)	3.9 cows	0.1 cows
Number of goats per household (mean)	3.5 goats	0.9 goats
Percentage of households with income from nonfarm salaried employment	37%	7%
Percentage of households receiving agricultural extension services	46%	7%

food crops and may threaten food security. Female household heads should be recognized not only as having a distinctive profile as smallholder farmers, but also as having distinctive needs in terms of future development of their capacity for food production and income generation. They experience distinct, social structural pressures that necessitate, or at least encourage, migration.

Unlike some areas of West Africa and the Caribbean, Kagera has comparatively few successful women traders and therefore few female networks of mutual assistance, finance, and technical aid. In my study, women-headed households comprised about one-third of the sample, but controlled only about one-tenth of trading incomes. The strongest local role models for girls are the women who both become independent and produce a surplus. Such women must accumulate capital from urban migration and then invest it in a sustainable, revenue-generating enterprise. They must effectively manage their primary enterprise as well as additional sources of revenue that provide insurance against hard times or natural catastrophes.

Guyer (1986b: 403) notes with reference to Africa as a whole that "while women provide the main agricultural labor force, their rights to the land are insecure." Certainly in the Kagera region of Tanzania, as Swantz (1985) and Bader (1975) have asserted, customary land tenure arrangements perpetuate the unequal position of both married and unmarried women farmers. The Villages and Ujamaa Act (1975, revised in 1983) formally provided for democratic allocation of land to all village members, but in actuality the customary land tenure practices were not displaced. By 1980, Kagera region had fewer official Ujamaa villages than any other region (Bader 1975; Raikes 1978; McCall 1987).

Women have few opportunities to acquire ownership of land under customary law (Swantz 1985: 67–68). Even in the absence of a direct male heir, the land will remain in the control of male relatives rather than passing to a wife or daughter. Many contemporary female household heads are therefore merely custodians of clan land and will never be granted a title deed. They must live in apprehension of eviction by male relatives or in-laws. The other avenue to women's land ownership is the purchase of alienated land. In 1918, the British established a system by which land could be converted to estate property with no customary restrictions. The Mrema government elected in 1995 is enthusiastic about further liberalizing land sales and transfers, but in densely populated Kagera, land held under title deed remains very scarce and expensive. Generally, land is available for sale only when the owner is deeply indebted or has no relatives who will inherit the land. As Weiss (1993: 30) puts it, "land that is inherited ... is a semi-alienable property."

Consequently, the female-headed households in this study had only two acres of land versus four acres for male-headed households. Only 17 percent of the female interviewees had purchased all or part of their holdings, in most cases from relatives. In contrast, 85 percent of the male household heads in the sample owned their principal plot, and 34 percent had added land through purchase. The majority of women household heads occupied land under the ownership and jurisdiction of male relatives, most often without any assurance that the house and land would not be taken over at any time by a male heir (see Table 9.2). Land tenure conditions for female-headed households are thus generally insecure and far less conducive to food and cash crop production than the conditions typical for land owned by male-headed households.

Table 9.2 Source and Type of Land Tenure for Female-Headed Households

Source and Type of Land	Percentage
Landless	24
Freehold title by purchase	13
Inherited occupancy rights, husband/husband's clan	28
Inherited occupancy rights, father/father's clan	17
Combination purchase/inheritance	4
Ujamaa tenure	13

Note: n=76.

Bride Price, Women's Marginality, and Migration

Male smallholders are privileged members of their patriarchal culture in other key ways. They usually benefit from the hard work and resourcefulness of wives and mothers. Out-migrating males exploit women's labor to develop and maintain family plots while they are away earning money. Marriage norms require payment of bride price, the acceptance of which locks a wife and her family into a restrictive set of social obligations (Cory and Hartnoll 1971). Bride price is now paid in cash and costs about a full year's income: $4,000 to $1,200 in the 1990s.

A bride thereafter becomes the primary domestic worker and childbearer. A husband expects a wife to be submissive and obedient;

he may divorce her for being otherwise or for many other reasons, including childlessness, laziness, and failure to satisfy him sexually. After a divorce or a woman's flight, *her* family is liable to repay the bride price.[8] Because of this, a woman seeking a divorce cannot usually expect help from her family of origin.

Production in Female-Headed Households

A woman out-migrant who does acquire land faces another set of challenges. The land tenure system forces female-headed households into more labor-intensive food production than cultivation by women farmers in male-headed households. All households studied grow the staple food crops of plantain bananas and beans. In addition, women in all female-headed households and one-half of male-headed households cultivate *omusiri,* supplementary crops grown on communal land outside the banana and coffee plantation: principally maize, cassava, sweet potatoes, and ground nuts. The range of crops grown is identical, yet female-headed households generally cultivate bananas more intensively and have lower production. The reason is clear: the average male-headed household has one acre of cultivated land per person, while the female-headed households average one-third of an acre. Both produce an average of eighty to one hundred banana bunches per acre, but the independent women farmers do it without access to hired or wife labor, manure, or agricultural extension services.

Coffee Production

Coffee is the long-standing regional cash crop: during the boom periods of the 1920s and the 1950s, Haya farmers planted millions of coffee trees to provide money for housing, school fees, and farm improvement. Despite record prices in the 1990s, the present system does not favor coffee production by women migrants and returnees. Women are excluded from extensive coffee cultivation due in part to its customary association as traditional men's work. Women therefore have rarely been formally trained and often lack hands-on experience in grafting, pruning, preparing seed beds, and correct transplanting. The small size of women's farms relative to the number of persons they support also restricts this option. On average, female-headed households had only one-third the number of coffee trees that male-headed households had (see Table 9.1), and only 18 percent of female-headed households were planting new coffee trees to expand production, compared to 42 percent of male-headed households.

Divorced female household heads (two-thirds of the total) also have little incentive to farm coffee if they occupy land owned by their ex-husband or his clan, as ex-husbands and their male relatives can and do exercise the right to claim the proceeds. Since independent female farmers use most of their available time to produce women's food crops, they must obtain hired or voluntary help (from male relatives) to cultivate coffee. However, 30 percent of female household heads were able to afford occasional help in farming, and most were not engaged in coffee production.

Cooperative Women's Work Groups

Out of necessity, women bolster farm production by forming cooperative associations, or *kyama*. These associations are modeled on the traditional male cattle owners guilds described by Cory and Hartnoll (1971). The *kyama* (Swantz 1985: 63; Boesen 1973) is an association of women who cooperate as fieldworkers and provide a social support network. It is the only viable form of cooperative work group I observed anywhere in the region. Four-fifths of the 189 women interviewed belonged to a *kyama*, typically with members of the same congregation or at least the same religion (as found earlier by Bader 1975). Those who contributed more land to the *kyama* got a larger share of both produce and cash (Margaret Bishubi, personal communication).

Gendered Access to Hired Labor, Agricultural Inputs, and Agricultural Extension Services

As mentioned, female migrant/returnees have little or no access to the major inputs used by male farmers to intensify cash crop production: wife-labor, permanent workers, cow manure as fertilizer, and agricultural extension services. Wives are responsible for the lion's share of subsistence food production, which reduces their cash-cropping capacity. Only one-third of the women interviewed could obtain fertilizer—cow manure—which is a significant handicap as manure can triple yields of coffee and bananas. Although 15 percent of householders used insecticide and sprayers, none of these were female-headed.

Indeed, the effective use of insecticides, improved farming techniques, and pruning virtually requires formal instruction. Female household heads here are often disadvantaged from the start by lack of education and a poor grasp of Swahili, the national language of education and government communications. Two-thirds of female household heads received less than two years of formal education, compared to only 10 percent of male household heads. While more women household heads than men attended adult education classes, none of the women's programs featured agricultural education. It is hardly surprising, therefore, that only 7 percent of independent women farmers (see Table 9.1) make use of available agricultural extension services, and only 19 percent reported receiving any form of extension assistance (see Staudt 1982 for parallels in Western Kenya).

Access to Capital: The Pattern of Income-Generation

Off-Farm Employment for Men and Women

The migration cycle is the principal route to accumulation of capital from trading or salaried employment and to subsequent success as a village smallholder (Smith 1994). However, patterns and strategies of capital accumulation vary greatly for men and women. Sixty percent of the male household-heads surveyed used capital from salaried employment and trade to expand or improve their farms, contrasted with 22 percent for women. Men are less often *compelled* to migrate, but they tend to derive greater benefits if they do. Since wives and children can be left behind to operate their farms, male farmers have been able to take long absences (of up to twenty years) from the village. They frequently return with sufficient capital to purchase additional land, hire permanent laborers, build better houses, buy cattle, and, occasionally, to invest in transport vehicles or other nonfarm business ventures. The most successful Haya farms have long been integrated enterprises involving both farm and capitalized business activities such as shops, transport, watch repair, tailoring, butchery, and furniture-making. Beyond farming, women farmers of necessity specialize in craft industries that require very small inputs of capital: brewing, distilling, collecting herbal medicines for sale, midwifery, and weaving mats and baskets. Overall, the male farmers and household heads interviewed reported an annual (mean) cash income of $760 compared to the $370 for women household heads.[9]

Migrant Women, Wealth, and Commercial Sex Work

Haya women are well known as commercial sex workers in major East African cities such as Dar es Salaam, Mwanza, Kampala, Nairobi and Mombasa (Hyden 1969; Southall and Gutkind 1957; Stevens 1995; Swantz 1985; Weiss 1993; White 1990). Luise White's (1990) impressive study of the history of prostitution in the regional metropole depicts Haya women as the innovators of a more entrepreneurial type of prostitution that entirely changed the trade. Previously, sex workers rented huts in Pumwani (a Nairobi neighborhood) and waited discreetly for customers to find their homes. Haya women, in contrast, sat outside, called out prices, and even banded together to beat up customers who would not pay. As White also points out, Haya sex workers typically returned home to set up independent households: "In the time I interviewed in Pumwani I could not find one Haya woman who had been a prostitute between 1936 and 1946. All had gone home" (White 1990: 110).

Because they had money to buy farms, returned sex workers gained status and became female role models. Bader (1975), Stevens (1995), Swantz (1985), and Weiss (1993) all present cases of Haya women who returned to purchase farms with capital saved from urban prostitution. So prevalent was this practice that, as Bader (1975) points out, many women returnees who set up farms were classified by their neighbors as returned commercial sex workers even if they had been white- or blue-collar workers or business people. Prostitution continues to be a significant means of capital accumulation and land acquisition for Haya women, especially the divorced.

Even so, only four women in this study admitted to being returned commercial sex workers, and data on recent out-migration from the 250 households indicates that many women now leave to take up white-collar employment. Interviewed parents reported that 58 percent of their female migrant children were students or employed in white- or pink-collar jobs such as government employees, teachers, nurses, or secretaries. Paradoxically, successful independent women today are more likely to have been brought up in male-headed households willing and able to send children (especially sons) to private secondary school.[10]

Beer and Liquor Production in the Economy of Male- and Female-Headed Households

In the sample as a whole, brewing represents only one-ninth of aggregate income. In the female out-migrant/returnee households, beer-related income accounts for about two-fifths of the total.[11] Beer and liquor are sold commercially in innumerable household sitting rooms and at kiosks scattered around the villages, each of which attracts a mainly male clientele of twenty to thirty people each evening. Value-added profit increases at each stage of the operation, beginning with beer bananas and ending up with the commercial sale of liquor. Most households in the villages engage in some facet of the enterprise. Household interviews, informal participant observation, and interviews of bar owners and workers all indicate a pattern of gender inequality or, to use McCall's (1987) terminology, of "male hijacking" of the illegal but more profitable large-scale public sale of hard liquor. Men dominate the "*konyagi* revolution" (Tibaijuka 1984), the use of petrol drums as boilers and submerged pots as collectors. This method, which quadruples production, is dominated by men because of the need to establish hidden stills and evade or bribe the police and local vigilantes (the *sungu sungu*).

Even so, the small-scale production and sale of beer and liquor is the single most important source of cash for women. In the five sampled villages, two-thirds of women farmers reported selling beer or liquor, and in one village, all but one woman derived the largest share of her income from this source (see Cecelski 1984 for parallels). As with the banana food-crop, male-headed households produce a larger overall volume, but independent women farmers produce 50 percent more beer per acre of land.

Patterns of Expenditure in Male- and Female-Headed Households

The female migrant/returnee households in our sample were under more pressure to use the available cash for foods and essential services (see Bryceson 1990 for parallels elsewhere). They were less likely to have houses made of fired brick or cement. Fourteen percent of female-headed households had no furniture at all, and 21 percent had only a single bed. Two-thirds of female-headed households had fewer consumer items than the median rank for the sample. No female-headed household had a car, and only 11 percent possessed a bicycle, all of which were inherited. Female-headed households in this study were using one-third of their cash income to feed themselves and their family, giving special priority to improving the diet of their children, while male-headed households spent but one-sixth of their cash income on food. Indeed, children were more likely to get breakfast (maize porridge, milk, and sugar) in female-headed households than male-headed households despite their lower income.

The cash flow problem of female-headed households is aggravated in times of severe food shortage due to banana crop failure. Four-fifths of household heads recalled at least one "wakati wa njaa" (season of hunger) during the preceding decade. Most frequently mentioned were the countrywide shortages of the mid-1970s, the 1979 war with Uganda, and banana crop shortfalls in 1982, 1985, and 1986. At each period, many households were forced to buy maize flour and cassava at black market prices. For the average female-headed household, cash expenditure on food supplements (including staples like processed maize flour) is becoming a chronic necessity. The situation may be aggravated by the conversion from food banana to beer banana cultivation, the only available income-generating activity that is culturally acceptable for women and brings a fast and constant cash return.

Routes to the Good Life: Case Studies of Rich Women

Those few who eventually transcend patriarchal restrictions and become rich through migration must have drive, intelligence, and good luck. Only five women among the sixty sampled female householders could be considered rich by local standards. If gender were a neutral factor in becoming well off, there should have been seventeen such cases. The following cases illustrate the ingenuity and tenacity necessary to confront the structures of gender inequality at work in the Kagera region of Tanzania.[12]

Broadly speaking, these successful role models–Subira, Neema, Susanna, Maria, Anna, and Zipporah–followed two career patterns. Three finished four years of high school (termed Form Four Leavers), obtained high-status jobs, and then accumulated capital. The other three, with only an elementary school education, accumulated capital through trading and invested it in highly profitable but also high-risk, illicit enterprises.

Subira migrated to work in Bukoba after completing high school. She was hired as an accounts clerk and later became the common-law wife of her employer, an elderly European businessman. She inherited her capital from a former consort, who left her a plot, an improved cement house, a cow shed, and seven purebred dairy cows. This was the source of her start-up capital. She rented out rooms in her house and sold milk: the dairy operation provided the lion's share of her income (about $1,000 per year). In 1994, when I last saw Subira, she was trying to diversify her interests by taking a training course to become a magistrate.

Neema, who was also an out-migrant, completed high school and a course at an agricultural college. To acquire start-up and operating capital for a profitable sideline, she worked as a *bibi shamba* or an agricultural extension officer. Profits from a catering business supplemented her $600 a year salary. In fact, she derived the major share of her annual income of $1,450 from this catering business, which she built up over ten years. She awoke at 4:00 A.M. to prepare fried cakes (*mandazi*) and meat squares (*samosa*) before her salaried work. Her houseworker, a fifteen-year-old migrant girl from an outlying district, delivered the cakes and *samosas* to local restaurants, and then spent the rest of the day selling the remaining stock from a stand near the house. Although this extension worker's income depends greatly on hard work, her salary and her initial savings were made possible because her family sent her to high school: her education was a type of inheritance.

Susanna is a former commercial sex worker who lived for six years at an important tourism center on the Kenyan coast. After saving enough money, she returned to buy a small farm near Bukoba. She derives an annual cash income of about $300 from coffee and poultry production. Making and selling yogurt brings her an additional profit of about $800. She also owns and hires out a bicycle that earns another $100 a year, and receives a $200 to $300 remittance from her migrant daughter in Dar es Salaam in return for taking care of three grandchildren.

Maria completed primary school and obtained employment in Bukoba town. She quit her job when she realized she could earn more money in business. She began as a seamstress (using her own sewing machine paid for by her own wages) and supplemented her sewing revenue by brewing and selling maize meal beer. She used her profits to purchase a nearby farm. After divorcing her husband for suspected adultery, she launched into a highly profitable but risky trade. She purchased a motorbike and began buying black market gold nuggets from the mines near Geita, reselling them to goldsmiths in Mwanza. This trade earned her about $3,000 a year, and she wisely invested her disposable surplus in a second farm; the bottom fell out of the black market in gold in 1996 when a Canadian company began a multimillion dollar commercial gold mining operation in the area.

Anna was formerly a commercial sex worker who runs an illegal bar in a rented house in the Bukoba area. She started her money-making career as a market trader, buying wholesale quantities of tomatoes and reselling them in small portions; she also grew and sold her own maize, potatoes, and yams. She gave up vegetable trading in favor of selling illegal home-brewed banana liquor. Her bar provides her with about $1,500 a year in cash income. As an only child, she inherited a farm in an outlying village where she is building a big cement house.

Zipporah's case is slightly different since she does not plan to return to her place of birth. Like Subira, she married a wealthy businessman and became a widow in the mid-1980s. Her two sons are in university in India. Two of her four daughters are married in Dar es Salaam and live close to their mother, while she owns a flat in a fashionable neighborhood. One of the two younger daughters is a fashion designer in Nigeria, and the youngest daughter is a hairdressing student in Nairobi. Zipporah supports her family by renting out seven houses in the Dar es Salaam residential areas and by importing and reselling used and reconditioned cars from Japan, United Arab Emirates, and Europe. Her family and import business keep her tied to Dar es Salaam, but there is another reason she has not returned to her village. After her husband's death she was living on his large coffee estate west of Bukoba town. Her husband's two surviving brothers claimed that the farm was their property as custodians of the deceased husband's clan. This claim was upheld in High Court, and Zipporah and her family were evicted (see Colson, this volume, for other gendered consequences of traditional patterns of land tenure in Africa).

The final case in point illustrates the reasons discussed above why women household heads want to be independent of men. Constance, a local police woman, is already caught up in the out-migration/return cycle and plans to have children with her male partner. At the same time, she wants to avoid the constraints of official marriage and the bride price system. Her ambition is to save enough money to buy a small parcel of land and set up an independent farm. If she succeeds, Constance will face the daunting prospect of growing enough food on a small plot of land to feed her family. Unlike typical men who inherit land, she will have little capital for farm inputs, trading, or small scale industry as more of her accumulated capital through migration will go to pay for land. If she does marry, she will not own this land, even if she paid for all or part of it.

These rich women share important characteristics: all are younger than their male counterparts; all live in close proximity to Bukoba town where there are more profitable opportunities for enterprise;[13] all are independent of men. In contrast, none of the 113 wives I interviewed have personal incomes above the $1,250 yearly cash minimum used to demarcate 'rich' farmers (Smith 1994). The basis for their primary accumulation of capital is either inheritance or illegal activity. In short, women who follow the culturally prescribed system of marriage and child-rearing cannot expect to accumulate wealth.

Conclusion

This study suggests the need for further investigation of female-headed smallholder households and the gendered dynamics of migration as a survival mechanism and strategy for advancement. Women out-migrant/returnees in this region of Tanzania have distinctive characteristics that dramatically affect their contribution to aggregate food and cash crop production. In many ways, their profile resembles that of poor, male-headed smallholder households. Nevertheless, female household heads in Kagera face constraints that virtually necessitate migration and in some cases push them to engage in commercial sex work–despite the enormous risk of HIV infection. Their children undoubtedly will face many of the same constraints and be forced to migrate in even greater numbers.

No one officially categorizes Haya women as political refugees. Rather, they are seen chiefly as 'economic' migrants. And yet the major factors forcing them out *are* political: their educational disadvantage, their inability to inherit land under customary law, and their exclusion from serious involvement in coffee production. That marriage is no guarantee of material security and may even make life more difficult for women is also political. Women who out-migrate and return need improved access to land and inputs as well as income-generating alternatives to the beer trade, which sheer enterprise and will alone will not provide. In the midst of these constraints, it is encouraging that women farmers support themselves as well as they do by being well organized and hard working, despite economic disadvantages perpetuated by a patriarchal culture. They set a heroic example of enterprise and reliability. During part of my fieldwork in the 'ridge top village', I stayed in a mission hospital guest house. Mary, who lived next door, was an obstetrics nurse with seven children. She put in long hours to do her job at the hospital and care for a farm in the adjacent village and tended a garden at her hospital residence. Her thirteen-year-old daughter has already started her working life; she has taken charge of her one-year-old brother. With great determination, Mary refuses to succumb to the gender inequities around her.

Notes

1. This research was supported by a postdoctoral fellowship and research grant from The Social Sciences and Humanities Research Council of Canada and a travel grant from the Center for Refugee Studies, York University, Canada. My fieldwork for this research was carried out between 1986 and 1996. I used a sample of 250 households drawn from four villages, and was resident in a village of

1,200 people for a period of ten months. I subsequently returned six times to the region for varying periods totaling a year.

2. Some scholars argue that predominantly patrilineal sub-Saharan Africa was not patriarchal, at least not in the sense of society exerting strict control over women's sexuality—a cultural context that Goody terms "Eurasian." However, even those who reject the term patriarchy (for example, Caldwell, Caldwell, and Quiggin 1989) define patriarchy in terms of "an obsession with controlling women's morals and mobility" and not the ability to exert control. As Weiss (1993) points out, women's mobility is an evasion of the Haya's androcentric, agnatic clan-centered patriarchal norms. He shows, in fact, how clan leaders *are* obsessed with this situation that they cannot control.

3. An annotated bibliography on women and development in Tanzania (Mascarenhas and Mbilinyi 1983) cites only two works which deal to some extent with female household heads as farmers, and both of these studies (Bader 1975; Swantz 1985) are concerned with the Kagera region, formerly colonial Bukoba.

4. My operational definition of the household is: a group of people who presently and normally eat and sleep on the same *kibanja* plot year-round. The sample was arrived at by choosing one household from each of the fifty "cells" of ten households organized by the ruling Revolutionary Party (Chama Cha Mapinduzi). Since each cell of ten households is a geographical cluster, this method ensured representative coverage of the village. We interviewed male and female household heads (and the spouses of the former) and carried out a census of household members and migrants. Interviews were carried out in Swahili, using an interpreter in cases where the interviewer preferred to use Luhaya. The average interview lasted two hours, though we made repeated informal visits to many households.

5. For women, a main alternative to out-migration is marriage. Women who marry and stay in the region gain social status, but they work very hard and are seldom able to claim land or other wealth should their husbands die or divorce them.

6. I once followed four women to their nearest water supply. In each case the return trip took over one hour. These women carried a twenty-five liter gerry can (more than fifty pounds when full), which had to be filled twice a day. Each woman spent at least two hours a day drawing water and about an hour gathering wood. A few local households own small kerosene stoves, but no women in my sample used one on a regular basis, making the search for firewood a daily necessity.

7. Swantz (1985: 72), citing the 1978 Tanzanian census, reports that this region has one of the country's highest divorce rates, double that in Kilimanjaro, the nation's other densely populated banana/coffee growing zone.

8. White (1990) notes that Haya prostitutes send money back to parents to help them repay bride price obligations. Despite growing awareness of the risk of HIV infection (which doubles for divorced or separated partners), marital instability remains a pervasive social problem (Nabaity et al. 1994).

9. We arrived at estimations of household income by extrapolating from known quantities. For example, coffee incomes were based on the number of kilos sold to the cooperative and the fixed price cited by farmers and the coop staff. For income from other cash-generating activities including the sale of banana beer, bananas, food crops, dairy products, livestock, firewood, handicrafts, and traditional medicines, we carefully obtained average quantities sold per week, verified local market prices, and probed to discover seasonal or monthly variations. Salaries were checked against government wage scales.

10. In the sample, there were 107 secondary students, of whom 80 percent were males. Only 10 percent of high school students came from women-headed

families. Female-headed households were more egalitarian, and while proportionately fewer children could be sent to high school, boys and girls went in equal numbers.

11. Coffee accounts for 14 percent, salaried employment for 12 percent, and small trade and crafts for 54 percent of the aggregate income.

12. As a resident of Dar es Salaam, Zipporah was not a member of the sample. Her case nonetheless presents a good example.

13. Both widows, Subira and Zipporah, had been much younger *second* wives.

10

The Relevance of Gendered Approaches to Refugee Health

A Case Study in Hagadera, Kenya

*Marleen Boelaert, Fabienne Vautier,
Tine Dusauchoit, Wim Van Damme,
and Monique Van Dormael*

Gender is increasingly recognized by social scientists as a significant vulnerability criterion in forced migration (Sapir 1993), and several international aid agencies have recently developed a gender policy (UNHCR 1995a). Before rushing blindly to establish a parallel fashion trend in refugee public health, it seems sensible for health professionals to reflect carefully on the relevance of gender as a public health risk factor in crisis situations. What *is* the evidence for gendered differences in health in crisis situations? *Do* women have specific health needs in these situations? Are the health staff of relief programs aware of gender issues and do they implement specific health interventions targeting women? What is the rationale for such differential intervention? What is the impact of such specific interventions? To shed some light on these questions, we did a review of a refugee health program in Kenya.

Introduction

A gendered approach to health and illness first of all examines differences in disease manifestations between men and women, and their perceptions of, and meanings given to, these events (Feldmeier, Poggensee, and Krantz 1993). It also looks into the gendered aspects of health care delivery (be it curative or preventive), and the consequences of intentionally and unintentionally gendered care. As health programs in emergencies focus greatly on facilitating survival, on the surface they seem only legitimately concerned with the biological question of vulnerability differentials: who is most at risk of dying? Aiming to decrease overall mortality in a more efficient and equitable way, they often target specific groups within a refugee population. The labeling of such a population subgroup as 'vulnerable' is linked to the perception of their increased mortality and morbidity (Davis 1996). In this regard, the particular vulnerability of under-five children and pregnant women in emergency situations caused by forced migration has been well established. However, gender morbidity differences are not solely biologically related. They are strongly influenced by social context, for example, by the position women and men occupy in society, the access each gets to services, and the kind of medical care each receives.

The assumption underlying this study is that the particular social context of a refugee camp will affect the health needs of all refugee women in it, not only those of pregnant and lactating women. The way that women's health needs in general are affected by forced migration and camp life needs to be clarified. Our case study of a refugee health program in Kenya addresses two related questions. First, is there any evidence for general gender differences in health needs in emergencies in this situation? Second, to what extent are health professionals aware of such gender differences (real or anticipated), and do they undertake specific action to address them?

Background

Because of civil war and famine in southern Somalia, more than two hundred thousand people crossed the Kenyan-Somali border in 1991–2. In 1997, an estimated one hundred twenty thousand of them were still living in three camps around the northeastern town of Dadaab: Ifo, Dagahaley, and Hagadera. This is a very arid area in which the local population are mainly cattle farmers who suffered losses in the droughts of 1992 and 1996. This study focuses mainly on the Hagadera camp. A nongovernmental organization (NGO), Médecins Sans Frontières (MSF), has been in charge of health care delivery to refugees in this camp since May 1992. Health services in Hagadera are organized according to an agreement with the Ministry of Health (MOH) that reflects Kenyan national health policies. These services and programs are based on a model of refugee health care that was empirically developed within the MSF over the years to target health priorities in refugee camps (MSF 1997). The health service in this camp is organized on a classic two-tier basis: a first line, where basic curative and preventive care is given, and a referral hospital for the cases needing higher level technical care. In Hagadera camp, male auxiliary nurses of Kenyan nationality are in charge at the three first-line health posts (HP). They finished secondary school and received limited training during the early phase of the refugee program. The HP offers a complete package of preventive services, including immunization, antenatal care, and family planning (FP). However, the package of curative care available is limited. The auxiliary nurse prescribes from a limited list of eight essential drugs, and no direct access to the hospital is allowed except for emergency cases. On average, between 20 and 30 percent of HP patients are referred to the hospital. In the hospital, a medical doctor is in charge, supervising a team of clinical officers. Paramedical and medical certified staff in the hospital are Kenyan nationals, seconded by MOH. Most of them are male, except for midwives. Only some of the Kenyan staff speak the language of the Somali refugees.

Very early on in the emergency, relief workers also established a network of community health workers (CHWs) from within the refugee community to actively bridge the gap between the organized health service and the community. Almost all of them are male, as prior CHW training in Somalia and the ability to read and write are criteria for their selection. CHWs are responsible for vital event surveillance and health promotion activities. Traditional birth attendants (TBAs), selected from the refugee community, have been involved in antenatal and delivery care activities from the beginning of the refugee program. At the time of the study, MSF employed two European expatriates in the camp: a male medical doctor and a female nurse.

Methods

To examine the available evidence for gender differences, we tried to identify and assess the specific health problems of refugee women in Hagadera. We reviewed the data from the health information and surveillance system for the period September 1992 to November 1996. This quantitative information (Centers for Disease Control 1992)[1] was coupled with qualitative data from six focus group discussions held with women in Hagadera camp in November 1996. We used qualitative methods to address the second question of the extent to which health professionals working in this program were aware of gender issues and undertook specific action. Interviews with traditional birth attendants, community health workers, auxiliary nurses, midwives, doctors, and medical coordinators provided information on their awareness of the specific health needs of women refugees and of the services provided.

Refugee Women in Hagadera: Are Their Health Needs Different?

War, famine, and forced migration do not affect women and men in the same way. Often men lose more of their previous public sphere status than women when they seek asylum in refugee camps. Also, the demographic structure of the population in a refugee camp is often profoundly altered, which cannot but affect the role and position of both men and women in the refugee community. Hagadera's population statistics show that the overall sex ratio (M/F) in 1994 was 0.99 (UNHCR 1994). Even so, within the age classes, sex ratios were not homogeneous, as shown in Table 10.1.

Table 10.1 Sex Ratio (M/F) by Age Group in the Dadaab Camps, 1994

Age (years)	Ifo	Dagahaley	Hagadera	Total
0–4	1.15	1.07	1.06	1.08
5–18	1.18	1.10	1.03	1.07
19–44	0.93	0.95	0.89	0.92
>45	1.31	1.33	1.19	1.26
Total	**1.09**	**1.06**	**0.99**	**1.05**

In each of the camps there seems to be a 10 percent surplus of women in the nineteen to forty-four age group, and a striking 30 percent deficit of women in the age group over forty-five years. Selective in- and out-migration seems the most plausible explanation. Adult men were/are probably more involved in military and/or economic activities outside the camp. As a consequence, female-headed households are probably more frequent in the camp than they were in the home country. Elderly women might have stayed behind in Somalia more often than elderly men when families migrated, or might have experienced higher mortality during the crisis. The forced migration from Somalia clearly does not affect both sexes in the same way.

Notwithstanding a lack of sex-specific morbidity surveillance data, there is other evidence that life in the refugee camp has been more unhealthy for women than for men. Maternal mortality ratios in Hagadera camp were very high (above 1,000 per 100,000 live births), despite a well-functioning and accessible operating theater located inside the camp, where cesarean sections were of a good standard. Most maternal deaths were attributed to anemia in pregnancy and eclampsia. An outbreak of hepatitis E at the end of 1992 also resulted in high mortality among pregnant women.

Gender inequities in food distribution also were apparent, and nutritional problems were common. Indeed, the food situation had worsened dramatically since August 1995, when the WFP individual ration was gradually decreased from 2,100 kcal. to 1,700 kcal. a day (Boelaert et al. 1997). Over a sixteen-month period, the average quantity of food received on distribution days reached the minimum requirements of 1,900 kcal. a day *only two times*, as indicated by data from food basket monitoring. This was clearly a particular problem for poor and destitute households, estimated to make up 50 to 60 percent of the camp, who relied on the WFP ration for 85 to 100 percent of their food. Using the global acute malnutrition rate as an indicator, we found a significant increase in the prevalence of acute malnutrition rates: 28 percent of six- to fifty-nine-month-olds[2] had a weight/height index below minus two z-scores or else had edema (95 percent CHI 24.0–32.0 percent).[3] Under such circumstances, pregnant women are differentially at risk of nutritional deficiency diseases such as scurvy and anemia because of their increased dietary needs. Scurvy had been a constant problem in the camp, and during the latest outbreak (July–October 1996), 508 cases were recorded.[4]

A food assessment mission by a joint SCF/WFP/UNHCR team in October 1996 noted that women were not involved in any way in pre– or post–food distribution discussions and planning, and that they received unequal treatment during food distribution. As the UNHCR report notes, "Women are treated particularly badly when they question the size of their ration, to the point where they no longer feel it is worth inquiring and often do not have the time to waste arguing" (UNHCR 1996).

But health differences stretch beyond the mere physiological consequences of childbearing. Access to health care more generally seems to be different for men and women. For example, detection of tuberculosis (TB) showed striking gender differentials in Hagadera. As elsewhere, the incidence of TB here is, in all probability, equal among men and women (Hudelson 1996). However, only 20 percent of enrolled patients were female at the start of the TB program in 1993, according to the medical coordinator. As the result of an information distribution effort by health workers, case detection in females increased, and the proportion of females enrolled in the TB program rose to approximately 40 percent in 1996. The medical coordinator attributed the low case detection rate for women at the start of the TB program to the perception that the social stigma attached to a TB diagnosis is more important for a Somali woman than for a man, and stigmatization prevented women from seeking care. It was believed that a woman with a known TB diagnosis faced expulsion from her family or lost her chance to get married.

Compliance with treatment also shows gender difference. One pertinent study looked specifically at gender with regard to the nutritional programs in Ifo and Dagahaley. Although the nutritional survey found no difference in malnutrition prevalence between boys and girls at the time, there were striking differences in the outcome parameters of the supplementary feeding (SF) program (Quillet 1994). A feeding program was organized in which malnourished children received high-energy milk twice daily, plus a take-home ration of biscuits. This provided a total of 1,585 to 1,770 kcal. a child per day. Mean weight gain in girls nevertheless was significantly lower (3g/kg/day vs. 3.6g/kg/day), and girls were more likely to stop participating in the program and less likely to be discharged than boys. Higher defaulting in girls was believed to be partially the result of mothers relying on daughters to help them with the household tasks.

These gender differences in weight gain were also attributed to possible gender preferences in intrahousehold food allocation in an overall situation of food shortage. Substitution and sharing are commonly observed phenomena in food emergencies. Substitution occurs when enrollment of a child in a feeding program has the unfortunate consequence that the child in question will not get any more food at home. Sharing occurs when the supplement given to a malnourished child as a dry or take-home ration is shared by the other family members. It is possible that these phenomena of substitution and sharing among refugees might be gender-specific, as gender-unequal food distribution within poor or food-short households is a commonly observed phenomenon around the world (see Nordstrom, this volume).

In November 1996 women refugees were asked about their health problems and their opinion about health services. They quite consistently pointed to the low level of care they were receiving at the first-line health posts. They lacked confidence in the skills of the auxiliary nurse and in the potency of the essential drugs they received. Their satisfaction seemed higher with the hospital service. Overall, it was their view that the main problem was not health care, but rather the very precarious food situation in the camp. Completely dependent on food rations that were insufficient both in quantity and quality, women expressed their anxiety about physical weakness, about anemia in pregnancy, and about the dangers of multiple pregnancies under such precarious conditions. They said they were going to the health service chiefly to look for substitutes for food: vitamins, iron tablets, and drugs. They consistently expressed their distress about the overall state of dependency in which they were living.

Are Health Workers Aware of Gender Issues in Health, and Do They Act on Them?

The particular vulnerability of women and girls in complex emergencies is now recognized among social scientists (Slim 1995). As a result, generalized poverty can no longer be the exclusive key social determinant of vulnerability. Moreover, epidemiological evidence confirms that women face a higher mortality risk than men in both natural and man-made disasters (Sapir 1993). This higher risk cannot be explained by biological factors alone. Field-based health professionals dealing with complex emergencies may not be aware of the significance of gender-specific vulnerability. To them, purely biological factors may seem more straightforward and important to address, resulting in targeted programs such as antenatal care. It is not clear to what extent health professionals themselves unconsciously offer gender-unequal care. Although relief organizations recently have produced a number of gender policy papers, it seems important to investigate what is going on in the field.

At Hagadera, both NGO and MOH staff are confronted daily with undernourished and anemic pregnant women. Nevertheless, no specific effort has been made so far to document these anecdotal observations with the kind of gender-specific epidemiological data that could be used for policy and program development advocacy in the current food shortage crisis. An analysis of the monthly medical reports from the Hagadera camp showed that no gender-specific morbidity data is routinely collected, with the exception of hospital admission data. If differences exist, they will go by unrecorded. Even the demographic structure of the refugee population is only roughly known, and there is no accurate gender breakdown. Indeed, the standard method for monitoring malnutrition in refugee populations worldwide does not include gender-specific analysis of collected data (UNHCR 1991). It is thus not surprising to find that out of the eight nutritional surveys performed in Hagadera since 1992, only two give gender-specific results. They show no significant difference in the malnutrition prevalence rate between boys and girls. A global malnutrition figure can, however, mask important and significant sex-specific differences, such as those shown in our reanalysis of the most recent survey done in August 1996. The global acute malnutrition rate was then 18.2 percent, 14.4 percent for girls and 21.8 percent for boys (p=0.004). This is a striking and unexpected difference against a background of a deteriorating nutritional situation for the whole population.

As mentioned earlier in the case of the tuberculosis and malnutrition (SF) program, gender differences in health are sometimes noticed by health professionals, and sociocultural hypotheses are often put forward to explain them. The accuracy of these hypotheses is difficult to assess, as they remain plausible but speculative. For example, gender preference in intra-household food allocation in times of overall food shortage sounds plausible, but has not been verified.

Summarizing, we can say that while the literature suggests that refugee women and girls will be more vulnerable, in the field health data is not always analyzed in a gender-specific way, and differences can go unnoticed or untreated. When differences are observed, they are often attributed by health workers to sociocultural factors—attributions that rarely stem from careful observation of the social organization of the camp.

Gender-Specific Interventions and Programs

Specific health programs directed at camp women exist, but they exclusively address only problems related to the physiological differences between men and women. During the emergency phase, for example, specific food supplements were distributed to pregnant and lactating women. Another major health problem for women in the camp has been sexual violence (Wilkes 1993). The security in and around the camp has not been good: killings and rapes by bandits have very frequently occurred when refugees go out to fetch firewood. This problem has been linked to the precarious, unprotected conditions women face, and to clan rivalries in the area (Hoerz 1995; see also Matlou, this volume).

A policy of care for victims of rape has been established by camp authorities and is strictly followed by camp agencies, including the health services. If a raped woman reports to the health service, she is examined by a medical doctor in the maternity premises. Emergency contraception is offered and usually accepted. A confidential medicolegal report is drafted. Counseling is offered, and women are referred for psychosocial assistance. It is acknowledged, however, that only the most courageous women come forward to say they have been raped, and that focusing only on self-reporting rape victims ignores the root problem.

In early 1994, health professionals started exploring the demand for family planning (FP) services. In discussions with camp leaders, traditional birth attendants, and community health workers, refugee women and men showed great reservations about FP. Although the negative outcomes on women's health of multiple pregnancies under camp conditions were acknowledged by refugees themselves, the community focus appeared to be on having as many babies as possible. A Kenyan Somali nurse-midwife who is well accepted by refugees is now in charge of the program. The success of the FP program is higher in the health posts than in the hospital. An explanation given by the midwives was that women apparently prefer the easy access and the polyvalence of the first-line health posts. Moreover, as many women try to hide their practice of FP from their husbands, they find it easier to go to the HP rather than to have to explain why they went to the hospital. However, FP is far from universally accepted, as shown during focus group research in November 1996. As one person put it, the "UN wants to kill our children, they want us to have family planning."

The health service thus offers specific services directed to women. Given the above programs (antenatal care, care for rape victims, and family planning), the question might be raised as to whether the male, non–Somali speaking health workers are able to establish effective communication with women refugees, and to what extent women's health problems are in fact effectively dealt with. From the limited evidence provided by the focus groups, there seems to be a significant problem with the health posts. In particular, women did not have confidence in the auxiliary nurses. Their medical skills were questioned. As one person stated, "In the health post they always give the same drugs to everyone, and they don't ask for the complaints. Everybody receives already prepared, old drugs in envelopes…. They give drugs like UN gives the food. Drug distribution." Male refugees expressed similar concerns.

Are Health Emergency Programs for Refugees in Need of a More Gendered Approach?

Women and children in crisis situations are often spoken of as innocent victims by relief agencies, and they are given close media attention in the never-ceasing pursuit of private donor generosity. The innocent victim image pertains to a certain mythology cultivated by Western relief organizations—a mythology that suggests that societies in violent conflict could be easily divided into active (male) fighters and passive (female) victims. This is of course rarely true. Data about the part women took in the genocide in Rwanda are but an extreme example of the active role women play in societies in conflict (Summerfield 1996; see Nordstrom and Matlou, this volume). To engage in more gender-related health programs exclusively because of the 'ideological' (if not commercial) image of the innocent victim would be the worst service to render to refugee women.

Moreover, the current biomedically oriented criteria for the identification of 'vulnerable groups' need to be reexamined from an epidemiological perspective. In a recent paper, Davis (1996) identified the disproportionately higher mortality risk adults and children over five years of age faced in emergencies when compared to children under five. This evidence contrasts with the current practice among relief workers, which is to aim health and nutrition interventions at children under five years of age. As Toole (1996) points out, the historical focus on under-five children can be explained by three elements: (1) an objective analysis of mortality patterns in previous emergencies; (2) the availability of affordable measures to prevent the most common causes of childhood deaths; and (3) an emotional concern for the plight of children on the part of the public who form the donor base of most relief agencies. One lesson to be drawn from this study is that health professionals cannot avoid independent, on-site assessment of specific emergency situations, as each emergency is different. Relief workers today tend to stick too closely to standardized intervention schedules and, in doing so, can miss major gender-specific risk differences within their target population. In the Hagadera case study, there has been almost no gender-specific analysis of the health problems of refugees. This is partly explained by lack of data, but this lack is rather poorly rationalized by standard epidemiological surveillance practice, which collects only data relevant for action. This practice in turn implies that gender-specific information was at some point judged to be irrelevant to what health professionals did, apart from the biologically determined events associated with childbirth. Nevertheless, we found indications that overall health risks for women are disproportionally increased in the camps and therefore warrant specific attention.

A gender-sensitive approach to health care in refugee emergencies, however, might instead be a matter of better, rather than more, care. The demands women express today are hardly taken into account. It is a general and understandable observation that, in acute emergencies, health professionals spend very little time discussing health issues with the community; in addition, they are hindered by significant language and cultural barriers. This pattern unfortunately tends to persist long after the initial emergency is over. Moreover, there is often a strong gender bias in communication between officials, workers, and refugees, as shown very clearly by Sommers (1995). The representatives of refugees who can most effectively transmit their demands to relief officials are mainly men with a university education. Only a small percentage of women typically speak the language of the relief officials (Sommers 1995). It can be assumed that the demands of women are rarely heard or taken into account, either at the policy or at the field implementation level.

Is a gendered approach relevant to emergency health programs? The relief workers we interviewed feared that the glossy gender policy papers so far produced by international agencies might constitute a dead end for those in the field, as they seem to focus almost exclusively on reproductive health. In the field, it was observed that recently introduced 'specific programs' directed at women still address the issue from a biological perspective only, and as such seem to ignore the fact that gender cannot be reduced to sex. As documented previously, women's specific health needs are not limited to the reproductive domain only. Women's increased health risk is linked to their social positions and statuses within their societies, which in some cases will limit their access to food and other resources in the refugee camp, as it did at home. An exclusively technical and selective intervention will probably not address this key issue.

Gender *is* an important determinant of health status in refugee situations. However, the causal pathway is as yet far from understood. Although there is growing awareness in international agencies and NGOs about the role of gender in forced migration, strategies to address the issue in the provision of health care are still immature. The first priority today seems to be to better understand and document a variety of field situations. Much gender-specific epidemiological data is needed, complemented with qualitative studies of health promotion and health services. The most urgent intervention needed, however, is to effectively improve communication between health workers and women in refugee camps.

Notes

1. Epidemiological surveillance was done in the camp since September 1992, according to standard methodology, described by CDC (1992). All data from the surveillance data base were reviewed over the period 1992–96.

2. In emergencies, general malnutrition rates are estimated using data from the under-five children, for this population is the most sensitive to acute food shortages that translate into an immediate and important weight loss. The use of this measure does not imply that responses are targeted only to this age group.

3. The global acute malnutrition rate is an indicator used to estimate the severity of malnutrition in a population. It is measured by the proportion of children from six to fifty-nine months with a weight/height index below minus two Z-scores and/or with edema (NCHS/CDC/WHO reference curves).

4. No gender-specific anthropometric data for adults were available.

11

Post-Soviet Russian Migration from the New Independent States

Experiences of Women Migrants

———

Natalya Kosmarskaya

Introduction

Issues related to post-Soviet migrations and to their gender dimensions are seriously underexplored in Russia.[1] It is true that there are many signs that research on migration is on the upswing and that this new work will derive much strength from established academic traditions. Concerning migration studies, the major thing needed now is sufficient time for scholars to comprehend and digest those new migration patterns brought about by the collapse of the former Soviet Union. In contrast, research on gender relations remains in its infancy. To extend the metaphor, the study of the intersection of gender and ethnicity (including migration as an ethnically based issue) is at best embryonic (Kosmarskaya 1995: 153). In fact, I am unaware of any academic book or paper especially focused upon women migrants, save for a small one by Galina Vitkovskaya (1995). Official migration statistics collected by the Federal Migration Service (FMS) and other state bodies provide nothing more than the number of migrating males and females according to age groups.

This mirrors a slightly earlier phase of Western scholarly developments, as Western investigators have also been far from satisfied with how female migration is represented and interpreted in research and policymaking. Referring to the work of the mid-1970s, Gina Buijs

(1993: 1) wrote that "women were invisible in studies of migration and, when they did emerge, tended to do so within the category of dependents of men." Mirjana Morokvasic (1984: 899–900), who reviewed the state of the field in the late 1970s and early 1980s, was also far from enthusiastic, noting that an increase in the number of migration studies had not changed the representation of migrant women. As she noted, "… many questions of relevance to the theory of migration remained unanswered simply because they were never asked." Almost ten years of subsequent progress did not prevent the authors of one migration-related report from declaring in 1993 that "black and migrant women's concerns are largely ignored in policy, in campaigns and in research" (European Forum of Left Feminists 1993: 3).

Even so, considerable progress has been made in the West in building an empirical base of gender and migration studies and in theoretically engendering migration. Looked at in the light of the paucity of work in Russia, claimed analytical shortcomings are often just an extension of evolving virtues. To my mind, though, there is one central weakness of this work: the tendency to universalize certain approaches and perceived practices in the Western academic debate. Working from a Russian standpoint, this is particularly true of behavioral and attitudinal models used to explain women migrants in the realities of modern Europe. Should we take these Western-informed models as normal and universal? I think not. Morokvasic advocates a "much needed exchange of knowledge … in the field which has, far too often, remained confined to national or regional boundaries" (1984: 900), and this view is highly consonant with what I see as my goal in this chapter.

I shall endeavor to examine the marked geopolitical, ethnosocial, and cultural differences between the migration patterns prevailing on the Western European scene and in the former Soviet Union, the inevitably contrasting realities migrant women and men face, and their varied responses to these different realities. I will argue that many gender characteristics of the societies under consideration may in fact show more differences than commonalties. Henrietta Moore (1988: 9) has observed that

> while women in a variety of societies share similar experiences and problems, these similarities have to be set against the widely differing experiences of women worldwide, especially with regard to race, colonialism and the rise of industrial capitalism.

This also holds in regard to the breakup of the huge empire that was the Soviet Union. In spite of these differences and a lack of theoretical and empirical maturity, incorporation of a Russia-specific agenda into the European debate on the gendered aspects of migration, and developing a mutually fruitful dialogue with European scholars, is now very timely, given my country's slow but hopefully steady move toward becoming an integral part of a new Europe.

In this light, my chapter analyzes the experiences of Russian women who have moved from the New Independent States (NIS) to Russia contrasted with the experiences of female migrants to Western European countries. The idea here, therefore, is not just to present an isolated case study based on field observations, but rather to use such data to begin to develop a comparative model combining macrolevel factors (migration patterns, legislation, policies) with microlevel ones (people's attitudes, perceptions, and behavioral modes), as these have manifested themselves during my fieldwork in different parts of Russia and Central Asia from 1994 to 1996. My primary focus will be on postmigration shifts in family dynamics and women's social statuses as part of their integration into the receiving society. What follows is the first attempt of this kind in Russia, and while the chapter raises more questions than it answers, I hope that some significant implications for further research are identified.

Two Migration Patterns: A Comparative Overview

Since World War II and especially after 1970, Europe has been a continent of immigration and migration. The prevailing direction of peoples' movement since the 1960s has been north from southern Europe, Turkey, the Middle East, South Asia, the Maghreb, sub-Saharan Africa, and the Caribbean. This movement is mainly driven by a wide diversity of economic conditions and choices. In the case of states that formerly had colonial empires, a large share of immigrants came from former colonies. Ironically, once-colonized peoples are now rapidly colonizing the centers of their colonial overlords. Another significant group of migrants are asylum seekers and recognized refugees (Mÿnz 1996: 202–7).

Migration typical of the post-Soviet period in the East looks very different—so much so that it largely explains why there is a problem with the "lack of relevant comparative experience in world history as a basis for understanding changing migration patterns in Russia" (Mitchneck and Plane 1995: 17). To highlight these differences in a limited space, I am obliged to address some complicated and dynamic issues in a somewhat simplistic way. After the collapse of the USSR, a change has gradually taken place from the so-called 'normal' migration patterns of the past that were motivated by economic and personal considerations (such as moving from village to town, seeking work, marriage, studying) to that characterized by stress and felt compulsion. 'Normality' is certainly a very loose concept to apply to people's resettlement earlier, both as purely voluntary migration in a proper sense, and as a set of actions resulting in positive benefit to the migrant, which was often the exception.

While a classic push-pull combination of factors did typically inform migration decisions during the Soviet period, recent migration patterns have been motivated mainly by the push end, with people often having very weak, if any, destination attractions. Their migration experiences are characteristically more stressful than were those of earlier generations. In this regard, the term *forced migrants* has now appeared in both the academic and political lexicon to identify those ethnic Russians and Russian-speakers in the NIS who, having found themselves in an environment no longer protective, comfortable, or friendly, decided that they have little option but to move to Russia. This is an outflow of Russian-speakers who feel helpless in the face of new ethnopolitical and social realities and who are disturbed by the rise of what they perceive as discrimination against them on the part of the titular nationalities of the NIS. In some cases, the stronger term *forcible* migration could be aptly applied to people's displacement provoked by the ethnomilitary conflicts and pogroms in different parts of the NIS and Russia such as Tajikistan, Nagorny Karabakh, Azerbaijan, and Chechnya. It is quite clear that ethnicity and nationalism are now key factors underlying Russian population mobility, its roots and its consequences.

In addition to Russian-speaking forced migrants, there are other examples of ethnically based population movements in the former Soviet Union (FSU): ethnic groups that had undergone deportation under Stalinist rule (like the Crimean Tatars) are now returning to what they view as their ethnohistoric Motherlands. A range of rural-urban migrants in the major cities of Central Asia and the Transcaucasian states may also contribute an additional factor forcing the Russian-speaking population to leave: so called 'trade minorities', or people engaged in 'shuttle' petty trade of a criminal or semicriminal nature (such as the Chinese in the Far East and Siberia, ethnic groups from the Caucasus and Transcaucasia in the cities of the European part of Russia).

Nevertheless, if we turn to Russia itself, it is the forced migration of Russian-speakers from the NIS that numerically dominates. According to the latest official estimates, over 6.8 million of such people resettled in Russia between 1989 and 1996 (Center of Demography and Human Ecology 1995: 4; State Statistical Committee of the

Russian Federation 1996: 23; 1997: 32). This migrant flow also has the most potential sociopolitical importance for Russia's development. While the inflow is still large, the number of Russian-speakers entering Russia from the former republics peaked in 1993/94; 1.1 million arrived in 1994, as compared with 800,000 in 1995 and roughly 600,000 in 1996. For better or worse, those Russians who remain in the NIS have been slowly adapting to their new roles as ethnic minorities, in no small degree due to a marked decline in nationalist fervor of titular NIS ethnic groups. At the same time, potential migrants are getting increasingly discouraged by what they hear of the hardships of resettlement experienced by their country folk in the historical Motherland. In my view, however, the ethnic variable will continue to define the nature of the post-Soviet migration (Panarin 1997). What is taking place, I believe, is the natural result of the collapse of the empire: the repatriation or return to the metropolis of the empire's dominant ethnic group (or groups) through the exertion of the same energy by which the empire functioned, developed, and sustained itself for several centuries.

European and Russian Migration Flows

The European-based migration patterns do not strongly predetermine or preselect the main 'moving object' involved, that is to say, whether it is primarily males, females, or families. While it is well known that women with children predominate in flows of refugees and environmentally forced migrants (as in Africa or in the former Yugoslavia), 'normal' European-based migration patterns looked at in overview are not gender skewed.

However, it is true that labor migration patterns in the postwar period often showed men to be more mobile than women. While I cannot go deeply into the roots of this phenomenon, it is worth mentioning the historical constraints on women's 'independent' mobility imposed by sending societies and the specific employment demands and immigration policies of the receiving countries (Morokvasic 1984: 888; van Amersfoort 1996: 248–250). Even so, the predominant 'migrating unit' on the European scene has long been–or at least has been characterized as–the nuclear family, or, as it is sometimes called in relation to women's participation, "accompanying migration" (Brochmann 1991: 113), following the admittance of a family-based man.

With the passing of time, evidence of women's independent migratory activities has of course been growing, evidence that demonstrates that this independence varies substantially, from women's migration and commitment being an integral part of a household survival strategy, to more or less autonomous steps undertaken by particular types of women "who seem to be more migratory than others (barren, widowed, separated, divorced) and those who, as single, have limited access to resources in the local area and are obliged to leave" (Morokvasic 1984: 896). Women migrants have sometimes been considered by their husbands and menfolk as an important source of remittances sent back home–a widely described situation of which one of the most recent examples is a Somali migrant community in Naples consisting of 80 percent women (Decimo 1997). Escriva (1996) writes about this with respect to Peruvian women in Barcelona. Abadan-Unat (1977: 33) outlines a Turkish example.

In contrast to this variety of migration patterns, the stream of forced migrants from the NIS to Russia is much more homogeneous. Repatriation in this case involves permanent resettlement from the former colonial periphery to a historical Motherland. This apparently causes migration to be a family venture and a family-based responsibility. What are referred to as 'investigation trips' to Russia are done primarily by men in search of appropriate jobs and housing, and it is not uncommon for some family members to stay behind for a period of time to settle up family matters (such as selling a flat or a house). Nevertheless, family separation is usually only a temporary measure, and families primarily move together.

Among these migrants, nuclear families consisting of a married couple with or without children strongly predominate, according to the last All-Union Population Census of 1989 (Vishnevsky 1994: 57). Moreover, there are indications that migrants maintaining this form of household, with both spouses of working age and with a minimal number of dependents, has most easily overcome the hardships of resettlement, especially in the initial stages. Migrating together with older family members (chiefly parents) has also been rather common, especially if they shared accommodations in the country of origin.

What about independent female migrants in this context? The migration options of women migrating alone are very limited. This is so even though there are no 'social acceptability' restraints imposed here on women's 'post-colonial' mobility by cultural tradition, unlike the case in many sending countries supplying migrants to Europe. In fact, a large proportion of Russian-speaking families are headed by women. This is due in part to the high rate of divorce typical in the USSR, combined with poor chances for women to marry again. Large numbers of children are also born to unmarried mothers, and the approximately twelve-year difference between the life expectancy of women and that of men leaves many women widows. Nevertheless, unlike the situation described by Morokvasic (1984: 897–8), there are few factors other than economic hardship that preferentially 'select out' those Russian-speaking women in the NIS for migration who are single or heads of families.[2] In fact, single women and women family heads are the least likely to be able to afford resettlement migration to Russia, unless they can rely on the solid support of someone in the host community. While doing my research on the adaptation of migrants, I heard many variations on the theme that "Russia receiving us as a stepmother is not a place for a single woman to survive!" The few exceptions to this that I found only confirm the rule.[3]

It is of course useful to compare Russian and Western European migration. I am concerned, however, that facile comparison based on established assumptions about Western migration may predetermine researchers' expectations of post-Soviet migration. In particular, a historical experience of higher migration mobility among men and stereotypical perceptions of migrating women as men's passive dependents have contributed to a male bias in research on Western European migration, and to the inadequate visibility of women migrants, especially given their active participation in migration on an accompanying or independent basis. In Russia, we have very different historical gender roles and migration concerns, and migrants face uniquely post-Soviet problems and challenges. Because of the prevalence of family-based migration and a general lack of awareness of gender and gender relations, migration surveys, statistical reports, and research papers continue to represent migrants as a sexless, undifferentiated mass of 'forced migrants', 'migrant populations', or 'resettlers'. As a result, women migrants' perceptions and behavior have been almost completely overlooked in the main canon of literature on migration.

A Comparative Look at Relevant Legislation and Policies

The specific needs of women forced migrants have also been virtually invisible to legislators, policymakers and social workers in Russia. To properly cover the topic of European immigration legislation and state-based policies toward migrants would, however, require many volumes, so I will limit myself here to a few points simply to provide a comparative background for addressing the Russian situation. One characteristic of great comparative significance is that European legislation is unambiguously restrictive when it comes to establishing permanent residence in the receiving country, and due to women's ideologically generated invisibility in 'official' migration, they inevitably bear the brunt of these restrictive measures. On the other hand, European states have been pursuing consistent policies concerning immigrants possessing legal status, usually providing programs with a solid financial base aimed at facilitating migrant integration into their new surroundings. It is also worth noting that some European governments have developed special programs to tackle the problems of migrant/minority women (Saharso 1996).

Russian immigration laws and policies dealing with the Russian-speakers repatriation from the NIS contrast strongly on each of these points. Let me start with the legal basis for entry and residence within Russian territory. In short, there are no restrictions on the entry of ethnic 'repatriates', nor, for that matter, on the entry of Soviet passport holders irrespective of their ethnic origin or former place of residence. This openness of the country's frontiers is to a large extent a consequence of political sensitivity to the 'Russian question': the position of more than thirty million ethnic Russians and Russian-speakers in the former Soviet republics has been one of the trump cards of the nationalist wing of the political opposition. From here, however, we go to the political and social dark side of the moon—Russia's legal system in general. In the initial stages of building a civil society, we are now increasingly appreciating that a large gap exists between many very informed and responsibly written laws, and the mechanisms for their implementation. It is rather the rule than the exception that the state's laws as they appear on the books generally do not work: regional authorities, state institutions, and even individual representatives of the bureaucracy are instead pursuing their own interests with impunity. Furthermore, the bureaucratic system itself is unreliable: rapidly changing regulations do not reach the authorities in time; disorganization is accompanied by low discipline and morale.

A good illustration of the powerful regional interests now at work within the Russian legal system directly concerns migration. More than twenty territories of the Russian Federation, including Moscow, St. Petersburg, and Stavropol, have imposed their own restrictions on forced migrants and the residence of refugees, even though the Constitution proclaims the right of every person staying legally in the country to move freely and to choose his or her place of temporary or permanent habitat. Another persistent problem in the system is poor organization and coordination of efforts to help migrants and potential migrants: forced migrants in the village where I conducted fieldwork were unable to secure Russian citizenship (which should be automatic) for more than six months simply because the necessary forms were not delivered. In the area of policy and programming, the contrast between the two immigration systems is very stark. Policies aimed at the material and social support of forced migrants in Russia are administered in such a cavalier and ineffective manner that, putting it succinctly, refugees are practically left to the mercy of fate. It is true that the Law on Forced Migrants was adopted in 1993 and that the Federal Migration Service (FMS) with its developed network of territorial branches has been in operation since July 1992. Nevertheless, the material support granted by the law was very limited, and the revised version of December 1995 actually reduced the responsibilities of local authorities to provide assistance to forced migrants in the spheres of housing and employment. Reflecting the severe and lingering financial crisis the country has been experiencing, state funding of FMS activities was never very generous. Worse still, funds allocated in the state's budget in 1995 are not always available in reality. For instance, the FMS received only 40 percent of the sum specified in the budget (Komarova 1997: 30). The last three years have been disastrous for programs of forced migrants' support, as the bulk of money that has been made available has been channeled to help refugees from Chechnya. In the end, despite the existence of a massive bureaucratic machine to deal with the forced migrants' problems and many welcoming political declarations, I would have to say that the state's attitude toward these people is, putting it mildly, indifferent. This is widely recognized by refugees and explains why only 27 to 30 percent of resettlers (of these, 53 percent were women) went through the official FMS registration process granting formal forced migrant's status between 1 July 1992 and 1 January 1997 (State Statistical Committee of the Russian Federation 1997: 73).

Moreover, all these new laws and regulations that have appeared in response to recent changes of the political map have little coherence, and almost never overtly articulate with gender-related categories, objects, or processes. Rather, they reflect their originators' intentions to ground new laws on a formal commitment to the equality of all citizens irrespective of gender, race, and ethnicity. Some characterize this set of laws as gender-neutral, a term that, in my mind, carries a positive meaning. I prefer the term 'gender-blind', because these laws and their implementation reflect the customary lack of gender recognition of social policy in Russia. Formally, women are on an equal footing with men, but when it comes to the law's practical implementation, women's rights are rarely considered.

Despite the above-mentioned 'family-based' pattern of repatriation, there are also certain categories of women migrants that are in need of special support, such as single mothers and women of retirement age. There are, for example, twice as many women pensioners arriving as men, who receive little support. Indeed, while the law specifies that a certificate of a forced migrant be issued to adult migrants to prove their status–so that they might receive whatever miserable material aid and privileges *are* available–in practice, no such certificates were issued to the migrant adults I studied during their first years of resettlement. Instead, people were registered as families, with a certificate issued only to the 'family head'. All my women and men respondents registered from 1993 to 1995 depended on this kind of a 'family' document. There is also a large gap between legislation and practice concerning the parenthood rights and responsibilities of women and men that has significant implications for women. Quite in line with international legal norms, the sexist terms 'single mother' and 'working mother' were replaced in law by 'single parent', 'parent with family obligations', or analogous terms. This was, of course, intended to imply gender equality in this sphere. In practice, however, in the majority of cases these labels are used exclusively to describe women. Moreover, migrant children from 'families with one parent' (in practice, the children of divorced or separated mothers) face barriers to Russian citizenship. According to legislation, Russian Federation citizenship cannot be granted to children without the agreement of both parents. This is very problematic for the migrant mothers of such children, who may possibly have to obtain the permission of a former spouse living in another state or 'lost' during ethnomilitary conflicts. Women who separated without a legal divorce face even greater difficulties.

An equally significant reason for the current lack of consistency between legislation and its implementation is the prevalence of gender stereotypes concerning family and social roles of men and women. Representations of women migrants have been, as one might imagine, primarily as subordinate wives and mothers. Let me use an excerpt from an interview to demonstrate how this form of stereotyping excludes women from full consideration under the law. This example depicts one of the key episodes of the migration process for Russian forced migrants: negotiation with local officers over the terms and prospects of resettlement. The conversation is between my female respondent, who had covered five thousand kilometers to come to the village in question from Uzbekistan, and the local farm manager.

Respondent (V): He [the farm manager] told me that he would talk to my husband only, because he was a family head.

Researcher (N): How did he explain this?

V: Well, he said there were many strange people around, who could be swindlers benefiting from migrants' privileges and then disappearing.

N: So, in his mind, only women can be swindlers, but not men?

V: Well, I didn't think about that at that moment. I just went to Moscow to stay with my relatives for two weeks until my husband arrived and settled everything.

Another woman described similar situations in more general terms. Before coming to the village where we met, her family had settled several times in Central Russia.

Respondent (T): If I were without a husband, nobody would take me here.

Researcher (N): Why do you think so?

T: Because wherever I arrived before, I was asked immediately about my husband. Why just my husband? Their first words were, "Is your husband coming or not?" It offends me.

Reefs of Post-Soviet Repatriation: A Case Study of Central Russia

Under the migration patterns prevailing in Europe, a newcomers' integration often takes place under conditions marked by social and cultural divisions between the immigrant and host community. Race, ethnicity, language, and religion may all be different. In the repatriation of Russian-speakers from the NIS, there are typically few sizable ethnic, linguistic, or sociocultural barriers between the repatriates and the host society of the imperial center. This widely observed characteristic of repatriation led researchers in my country not to anticipate that any serious ethnocultural or sociopsychological complications would arise in migrants' adaptations. Rather, great attention has been paid to the material side of migrants' lives, issues of accommodation, jobs, and social security taking center stage.

In reality, however, considerable sociopsychological distance does exist between newcomers and host communities with specific gender implications. In my opinion, the diversity of sociocultural settings both in the NIS and in Russia itself is so vast that what must be brought to the forefront of the analysis is the intricate combination of what is, in each migrant context, left by migrants 'there' and what is faced 'here'. In this light, three points deserve special attention as characteristic of forced migrants moving to Russia.

First, judging by the statistics of the FMS as of 1 January 1997, the lion's share of registered forced migrants are emigrants from

Central Asia and Kazakhstan (60 percent) and from Transcaucasia (22 percent) (SSCRF 1997: 62). Despite many differences between Central Asia and Kazakhstan on the one hand, and Transcaucasia on the other, the social position and psychological challenges of Russian-speakers in these regions during the Soviet regime were broadly similar. This distinguishes them from their former compatriots living in such places as, say, the Ukraine or the Baltic states. These 'Russians in the Orient', have maintained a great deal of cultural distance between themselves and their respective titular ethnic groups. In Soviet times they also maintained a strong sense of ethnosocial superiority and a paternalistic 'senior brother' ideology of domination over local people. Furthermore, these migrants' heightened sense of their belonging to what might be called 'Central Asian Russians', is a significant factor in the internal cohesion of the group, and at times makes their entry into host communities more difficult. These points will be further developed below in relation to women's responses to resettlement.

Central European Russians also were characterized by their concentration in large towns and industrial centers at the time of the collapse of the USSR. According to the last All-Union Population Census of 1989 (as reported in Arutyunyan 1992: 25), 70 percent of the Russian inhabitants of Kirghizia were urban; in Kazakhstan the figure was 77 percent; in Armenia, Georgia, and Azerbaijan, 85 to 95 percent; and in Tajikistan, Uzbekistan, and Turkmenia, 94 to 97 percent. Moreover, as the same census shows, around half of the Russian-speaking population of Central Asia and Transcaucasia were born in those locales, and many more had lived there for more than ten years (Arutyunyan 1992: 52).

Those who arrive in Russia from these source areas are mainly people who left behind rather 'oriental', albeit sovieticized, sociocultural and ethnic milieus. They came from societies where, as a ruling ethnosocial group, many had enjoyed a privileged urban existence. As repatriated migrants, many have been obliged to settle in rural areas where they definitely do not comprise the local elite.[4] Officially, rural resettlement is voluntary, but in practice migrants have no choice, because of the housing crisis and growing unemployment in the towns.

Besides this basic urban/rural division, migrants in Russia must also contend with a regional dimension: life in the twelve rural *oblasts* (the main administrative divisions in Russia) of the Central region and of the adjoining North-West and Central Black-Heath regions. This is a vast zone of socioeconomic depression with poor soils and a very low level of agricultural production. For decades the region was in need of state funding in order to keep afloat unprofitable collective and state farms. Predictably, for many years the flow of able-bodied inhabitants out of the countryside into urban areas has been considerable. Things became so bad that the phenomenon of 'dying villages' became prevalent: villages whose only inhabitants were a few elderly women. Today, this territory is characterized by inadequate systems of communication, transportation, and social infrastructure. The income of the predominantly agricultural population is extremely low and housing conditions are squalid: homes might have a stove and a well, but no inside plumbing, baths, or bathhouses.

This local experience is a harsh contrast to the former everyday environment of most migrants; even villages in those parts of Central Asia with a reasonable number of Russians have better public services and utilities than does rural Russia. This disparity is the result of the contradictory and inconsistent imperial policies of Moscow: colonization of the peripheries of the USSR necessitated a provision of reasonable living conditions, especially to Russian colonial foot soldiers. In 1994–95, I was able to do fieldwork in just such a typical Central Russia rural setting. The migrant community centrally under study was located about 450 kilometers from Moscow, in Oryol *oblast,* and comprised two villages where the newcomer and resident population lived and worked intermixed on a collective farm (the main sample). To verify the results, data were also collected in three other migrant communities scattered around the *oblast* (the second sample). This research was based mainly on qualitative methodology, so it makes no claim of being representative in the strict sense of the word. However, the sample did not deviate far from the general profile of the migrant populations registered both in Oryol *oblast* and Russia as a whole: their ethnic compositions, birthplaces, and regions of exodus were very similar.

In these five villages, 106 respondents of working age (65 women and 41 men) were surveyed using a detailed questionnaire containing both open- and closed-ended questions. In most cases, interviews evolved into a semistructured discussion, producing a great deal of nonformalized, qualitative information. An on-the-spot analysis of the questionnaire data was used to establish the basic reference points for in-depth, unstructured interviews. These discussions with women (twenty in number) were basically oral histories describing migration and resettlement through time, space, events, and shifts of attitude.

The general tone of the interviews reflected refugee disappointment with their new surroundings. However, the difficulties of rural life in a more severe climate, and of the necessity (especially for women) to master unaccustomed and unpleasant domestic labor (tending kitchen gardens, pig and poultry breeding, milking cows), did not seem to be the main reason. Most respondents had picked this place themselves on the advice of friends and relatives, and most had the opportunity of visiting these places and even living there for some time before making a commitment. What turned out to be a very discouraging surprise lay not in the conditions of material life but rather in relations with the host community.[5]

As my more detailed findings show (Kosmarskaya 1996; 1997), the following are the main lines along which tensions arise between the two groups of the population:

- The feudal character of Soviet agricultural social relations, which had remained practically intact, with its arbitrary rule and patronage.
- Soviet envy of other people's material wealth, which was fueled by a perceived gap in living standards. Local people feared that there would be fewer goods available due to the migrant influx.
- Perceived competition for jobs between the newcomers and the resident population, as well as differences in labor ethics.
- Differences in sociocultural traditions and norms of community life heightened by the migrants' expectation that they were joining communities of the 'same' ethnic affiliation. Indeed, migrants to Central Russia were sometimes blatantly labeled by their host communities as 'nye russye' (a derogatory expression deriving from the ancient name of the country), meaning 'non-Russianness'. In other cases, they were called 'Kirghiz' or 'Kazakhs', or otherwise labeled as distinct from the host community.

In short, repatriates who thought they had returned to their historic Motherland found themselves living in what they saw as another world.

Russian Women: The Impact of Migration on Family Life

At first sight, the general situation faced by women migrating to Europe and by Russian women repatriates is broadly similar: they enter a new world, attempt to overcome its barriers and meet its demands, perhaps taking advantage of its opportunities; at the same time they are bearers of the sending societies' ideological heritage. However, this broad resemblance falls apart when considered in greater detail. To see why, let me look more closely at some effects of migration on women's lives popular in Western research.

Many Western scholars exploring the effect of migration on women's status in family and society share a number of common ideas:

- The impact of migration on the family has been treated mainly as a struggle for power between household women and men.
- The form and degree of women's access to the labor market has been taken as a critical determinant of their economic independence and family-based power.
- The assumption is made that there is a chance for new (better) opportunities for women migrants entering Western societies than they had before migrating.
- When confrontation arises involving women migrants, it is most often between themselves and their husbands, less often between themselves and their male relatives, followed by instances of confrontation between themselves and the native male population, then finally native women.

This perspective, however, does not adequately address the particular situation of repatriated Russian women and the effect migration has had on their status within the family and society.

In post-Soviet migration from the NIS, women's family roles and social status are quite parallel in the host and receiving societies. Russian-speaking women in the NIS have long been bearers of a widespread universal, sovieticized, gendered culture. Moreover, even in Central Asia, where there is great ethnocultural distance between Russian-speakers and indigenous people, gender culture among Russians derives from the metropole and exerts a strong influence on local traditions. The overwhelming majority of Russian women in Central Asia with whom I talked about ethnic issues there characterized native women as having become more 'modernized' and 'emancipated' due to the Russian presence. Moreover, given Russian women's typically high level of economic activity, including those in the NIS, the mere fact of employment in a new place of residence does not, by itself, cause marked changes in the family balance of power.[6] So similar are these pan-Soviet sociocultural norms regulating gender relations, if changes in family gender relations do emerge when women migrate, they are not easy to trace. For the same reason, this issue is not very migration specific, and is probably best addressed within the more general framework of family change in the Russian transitional society, an area of research greatly needing attention by Russian social scientists. Women's unemployment and downward social mobility adversely affect almost the entire female population of Russia.

Another aspect of the 'family and migration' problem that is perhaps more pertinent to the study of post-Soviet realities than power relations is family stability. This seems to be downplayed within the Western European debate, save for when considering a few specific forms of migration in the West that entail long separation of spouses. Gaining a better understanding of migration-specific family instability was one of my primary reasons for collecting women's life histories in the Oryol *oblast*. Out of fourteen married women who would discuss this topic, three said they did not see any changes in their family dynamics due to resettlement, and three others claimed that relations with their husbands improved because they no longer lived with their husband's parents, as they had prior to migration. The other eight women reported that relations with their husbands had seriously worsened—as a direct result of migration. Men's drinking, unemployment, and lack of money figured significantly.[7] My respondents believed that these family problems were brought about by resettlement in Russia. From a sociological point of view, however, this may not be quite accurate because these are primary factors foremost in undermining family stability all across contemporary Russia.

Another important clue to understanding the migration-specific roots of family instability among returning Russians lies in the sphere of women's and men's migration decisions. This topic does not command much attention in Western scholarship. It is perhaps too quickly taken for granted that decisions to leave or not to leave are the prerogative of men only, or that 'families' make these decisions. In some situations it can appear this way: when a survey of South Asian women in Britain were asked about their aspirations at the time of migration, "… the women found this question very hard to answer and would often laugh in response. They found it difficult to express their own aspirations separately from concerns about their families" (West and Pilgrim 1995: 366). In the case of post-Soviet repatriation, people often experience great pressure to leave and considerable postmigration loss of status, with greatly reduced prospects of restoring it. Unanimity among family members in deciding whether to stay or move could hardly be expected. My findings in Kirghizia and in the Oryol *oblast* support this point. In the autumn of 1996, 350 Russian-speakers in Bishkek were asked, "Who initiated migration in the families of your friends and relatives that have already moved to Russia?" and "Who pushed the matter forward, who was the most insistent?" Forty-three percent thought it was a joint decision, 8 percent thought it a decision of parents, 21 percent refused to answer, and 28 percent identified either a "wife" or "husband" as the main decision-maker.

In the Oryol *oblast,* married couples were asked a similar question about their own prehistory of migration. According to 27 percent of wives, it was a joint decision, 12 percent said it was their parents' decision, 34 percent named a husband as the main initiator, and 27 percent of wives presented themselves as the key decision-makers. Corresponding answers by husbands were very different: 20 percent, 7 percent, 53 percent, and 20 percent respectively. These data suggest that premigration, intrafamily disagreements might be a serious threat to family stability upon resettlement. The situation in the family with whom I stayed during my field visits to the village is illustrative: contrary to her husband, she was very reluctant to leave Uzbekistan, and three years of hardship in Russia had not reconciled her to his decision. "Why on earth did you bring me here?" was her leitmotif in their everyday squabbles and disputes.

Russian Women Forced Migrants: Identity, Social Status, and Societal Access

Turning again to Western interpretations of the shifts in women migrants' social status as a contrasting background for conceptualizing Russian women's experiences, we encounter a theoretical concentration on opening opportunities for women and men-women oppositions as key causal factors in shaping status trajectories. Thus, Fereshteh Ahmadi (1997: 3) constructs status differences between Iranian migrant men and women in Sweden as in some ways the reverse of those in Iran:

> In Iran ... men are ... perceived as having higher status and power in society. The refugee/immigrant situation is, however, likely to reverse that perception since the situation in the host country often means that men have lost many of the social attributes that gave them a higher status. Women, on the other hand, did not, as a result of their relatively lower original status, suffer a comparable loss in societal power and status ... Having greater possibilities to find jobs ... and having a better psychological status than the male Iranian immigrant ... provides the Iranian immigrant and refugee woman with the feeling of Self and ... helps her ... to adapt herself to the new society.

A similar conclusion is made by Hollands (1996: 11–12) in reference to refugee integration into Dutch society:

> Refugee men tend to refer longer to a past in which they *were* somebody [italics in the original]. Due to male dominance in most societies, they

more often than women had positions of power and status, in the field of work, in the field of politics and also as men ... Refugee women on the other hand seem to refer sooner to the present and to a future in which they hope to *become* somebody ... For women this might create some space to escape from oppressive social codes concerning female roles, female behavior and female identity. Their position as women has not been that self-evident as it had been for men ... This can be also a basis for solidarity, with other refugee women, migrant women, but also Dutch women.

Russian women migrants also demonstrate a different trajectory here as both Russian women *and* men *were* somebody in the past: members of a conspicuously privileged ethnosocial group supported by the imperial center. These women had strong self-identification along ethnosocial rather than gender lines. During my last visit to Kirghizia in October 1996, the marginalized position of women of different ethnic groups in the labor market was already a concern of the progressive journalists and scholars. Nevertheless, the Russian women I talked to viewed their problems as a complex seesaw of values within the dialectic of Russian and Kirghiz life, and not simply as a result of their gender. Interestingly enough, there are some parallels between the primarily ethnic commitment of Russian-speaking women in the former Soviet peripheries and British women who emigrated to South Africa a century ago. Many of the latter were from lower social groups at home, but in South Africa they enjoyed the advantages of white skin and imperial support. As a result, "Although white women are discriminated against as women, their membership of a privileged racial group softens the impact of gender discrimination and works against their identification with black women as women, with shared problems" (Walker, cited by Buijs 1993: 14). In general terms, moreover, the gender component in Russian women's identities and, correspondingly, their sensitivity to being discriminated against as women, was substantially weakened under the Soviet regime. Rather, one typically saw "... pronounced women's identification with a class, professional group, [or] labor collective together with a very low personalized identification ..." (Malysheva 1996: 279). This combined with a potent, state-supported myth of gender equality to greatly reduce women's affiliation along gender lines.

I should perhaps also note that the move to Russia itself represented a loss of social status both for women and men. Their personal statuses in the NIS had been seriously undermined by the collapse of empire, and their inability to reconcile this made many of them emigrate. The psychological baggage of empire, though, could not be so easily left behind; we could hardly expect either their superiority complex or their 'missionary' ambitions to be repudiated or restructured by migration alone. Female and male respondents' reactions to the question: "Do local Russians differ from those who live in Central Asia, and how?" is illustrative. All of the 104 respondents save one, answered "yes" to the first part of the question. People then talked about what they saw as a wide variety of contrasts between the local Russians around them and themselves. It is striking that every person who responded depicted local people's 'otherness' in negative terms only.

These very polar views have significant implications for women, in particular because of their specific 'public' obligations and roles in community life. In both Soviet and post-Soviet society, women often find themselves in the demanding role of mediator and contact person, at the intercommunity, interfamily, and interpersonal levels. This is in part because of the very high rate of economic activity typical of Soviet women. However, the prevailing pattern of family roles still prevalent in the post-Soviet families is also consequential. Child care, childbearing, housekeeping, and the like are primarily in women's hands. Women also are extensively involved in everyday contacts outside the home, such as standing in queues, visiting shops, hospitals, marketplaces, and schools. As a result, they are more visible and more involved in certain public spheres than men. This is even more so in villages.

Besides enlarging women's everyday responsibilities and psychological burdens, the particular demands of these public obligations contribute significantly to their comparatively ungendered identity construction. Only two women out of the twenty interviewed through an oral history approach said that they preferred contact with women in their new locale, and in each case this was only because of men's drunkenness and rudeness. Three other women showed no preference. The majority of interviewees (fifteen) expressed a strong preference for dealing with *men* in various everyday, social, and professional activities. Highly stereotypic ideas about 'women's nature' based on past unhappy experiences were presented as grounds for this bias. Moreover, it appears to me that a strong sense of being 'migrants', 'newcomers', and another (superior) kind of Russian blinded women to existing gender discriminatory practices and prevented them from creating a 'basis for solidarity' with local women.[8] Not surprisingly, there are hardly any women migrants' self-help groups or organizations, as are frequently noted in the European context.

Let me leave the psychological dimension of migrant women's experience to briefly consider the more sociological side of things.

Given the paucity of effective supportive state policies and the poor state of the Russian economy, economic opportunities for migrants in general are few and far between. This may be even more the case for Russians from the NIS, as post-Soviet repatriation was largely stimulated by 'push' rather than 'pull' factors. Clearly, the previously noted fall in social status that the majority of migrants experienced after resettlement cannot therefore be treated entirely in social-psychological terms: concurrent with migration they experienced a dramatic worsening of living standards, accompanied by a loss of what I will call a professional-based social status.

While no specific research has been done on migrants' job-seeking strategies, problems, and effectiveness, my research indicates that migrants are disadvantaged in many ways when compared with others of similar class background. Migrants lack necessary personal and professional ties to get good jobs, and are severely limited in their job search by where they can find housing. Ever-growing competition in the labor market also appears to have weakened the negotiating positions of migrants. A large-scale survey conducted by the Federal Migration Service found that 81 percent of the working-age population of Russia had paid employment in mid-1993, as compared with only 69 percent of comparatively better skilled working-age forced migrants (Komarova 1997: 29; Federal Migration Service 1995). As usual in Russian studies, no gender-disaggregated findings were presented. In fact, no countrywide or regional-level data comparing the employment prospects of migrant women and men is available. Neither do we have any data that compares gender-specific populations of migrants with long-term residents.

Proceeding tentatively from my own survey results, I suggest that among those who resettle in rural areas, women migrants have fewer occupational and educational opportunities than do comparable men. The problem here appears to me to be, in part, the result of the glaring discrepancy between the pattern of these women's employment in cities of the NIS, and that typical of the small towns and rural areas of this economically depressed part of Russia. This gap is exacerbated by the striking underdevelopment of infrastructure, services, and communication in the Russian hinterland; by the poor state of trade, educational, and medical service networks; and by a comparative lack of recreational and leisure facilities. This has a strong impact on women migrants whose occupations are concentrated in the service sector. Women teachers, doctors, nurses, sales assistants, hairdressers, secretaries, typists, and the like have few chances to find a job in their field. Moreover, local authorities are unwilling or unable to further develop these employment areas. For example, I once heard a farm manager very proudly tell a hair-dresser, "We, the locals, do not cut hair!"

As a result, I would predict that in the future women migrants' unemployment rates will probably be much higher than those of men. Locally, I found that around half the women did not have a permanent job, and that in general women doctors, teachers, and other 'white-' and 'pink-collar' workers were being encouraged to take on low-status and low-paying agricultural work as milkmaids, pig and calf tenders, and the like. Migrant men also face difficulties in finding jobs that match their qualifications and experience. Predominantly engineers and industrial workers in the NIS, many do have to accept work on farms. There is, however, considerable engineering and mechanical work on collective and state farms, and many secure work that is at least somewhat analogous to what they did before. Furthermore, the felt degree of downward mobility experienced by men may also be less because men are, on the whole, less educated than women. This is the pattern across the former USSR, and my own observations in the Oryol migrant communities are similar: out of sixty-five women interviewed, 39 percent had the same education as their husbands, 3 percent had less, and a striking 58 percent had more. In addition, gender stereotypes prevalent in mass consciousness that characterize men as the main economic supporters of the family also have to be taken into consideration. As a case in point, in the migration histories I collected from women, the key topic discussed in relation to employment was securing appropriate jobs for their *men*. Women's employment prospects were usually considered secondary.

Conclusion

In conclusion, I would like to address the problem of women forced migrants in a broad socioeconomic context as one related to human rights and people's legal consciousness in present-day Russia.

Beyond the serious economic and social issues in question here, my research strongly indicates that many of the problems faced by women migrants arise from the human rights situation in present-day Russia. Human rights legislation and its enforcement diminish in salience as distance from urban centers increases. Given this, alternative mechanisms have developed in more isolated rural areas to mediate economic and political relationships; they are based on patronage, local chauvinism, personal and kinship connections, and membership in illicit networks–all of which affect access to money, resources, and mass media.

Effective access to human rights protections and economic conditions are, of course, strongly linked. From autumn 1996, when I first drafted this paper, to the present (spring 1998), severe economic and financial crises have been accompanied by great delays in payments of wages, salaries, pensions, allowances, etc., by the state. According to sociological surveys, the majority of the Russian population (72 to 77 percent) has been affected by these disturbances (Oslon 1997: 4). Physical survival has become the highest priority for millions of people. This has pushed their concerns (if any) about 'abstract' rights and freedoms, including gender equality, to the periphery of their consciousness.

Returning to women migrants, they are exposed to discrimination and prejudice as women, and in this, to a large extent, they share many experiences with the general female population of Russia. They are also discriminated against as migrants, irrespective of gender. The gender component of their disabilities as migrants tends to be backstaged and muted because of the great economic and social turmoil in Russia today, limiting women's awareness of their problems as specifically women's problems. I should note that women migrants share hardships with other marginalized social groups highly dependent on state support and consisting not only of women: pensioners; people with disabilities; unemployed, single mothers; families with many children; and others. I hope my Western feminist colleagues will appreciate that women as such are not, and have never been, the most discriminated against part of the population.

At the same time, these particular women migrants belong to Russian-speaking repatriate communities that are not only deprived of state material and financial support, but also, because of shallow rootedness into the local 'networking of favors' (a system well analyzed by Ledeneva 1998), have very limited access to power and resources.

This 'dissolution' of women migrants' interests and concerns into a wide range of those experienced by many other people in Russia adds, to my mind, to the distinctiveness of Russian women migrants' situations in comparison with migrants in the Western European context. Making these women migrants more sensitive to violations of their rights and more visible to the political powers that be certainly should remain part of the political, academic, and feminist agenda. Alongside this, from a humanitarian point of view, any loosening of Russia's painful economic and social constraints will make these women's lives much easier.

Notes

1. This chapter was written as part of the Moscow Center for Gender Studies research project *Gender-Based Expert Analysis of Russia's Legal Reforms*, funded by the Promoting Women in Development (PROWID) grants program. An earlier version was presented at the Third European Feminist Research Conference, University of Coimbra, Portugal, 8–12 July 1997. I would also like to thank Doreen Indra for her infinite patience in understanding my circumstances and for her very helpful comments on the manuscript.

2. In regard to this, a random sample of 305 Russian-speakers of working age were interviewed in 1996, in Bishkek (Kirghizia). Seventy-five percent of women were married; 4 percent, unmarried; 18 percent, divorced; and 3 percent, widowed. Men's marital status was: 89 percent, married; 2 percent, unmarried; 7 percent, divorced; and 2 percent, widowed.

3. Because of the lack of microlevel research and gender-specific migration statistics (for example, the first official survey on the marital status of forced migrants to Russia published in 1997 is completely gender-blind), my reflections in this section are based on more than two hundred in-depth interviews with Russian-speakers in Kirghizia and Tajikistan, and with repatriates in Central Russia. The number of individuals polled was in fact much larger than this, if the respondents' references to the experiences of their friends and relatives are included.

4. The latest FMS data at my disposal suggest that 38 percent of those in Russia as a whole settle in rural areas. (FMS 1995: 35–36).

5. The majority of forced migrants migrate as individual families, not as professional or kinship communities, or as a group from one locality. Homogeneous communities stemming from chain migration are quite rare.

6. According to the last All-Union Population Census of 1989, more than 80 percent of women had paid employment, compared with 87 percent of men.

7. A correlation between growing family strain and sociopsychological relations between newcomers and the host population was found by Elena Filippova (1997: 146–51), who framed these linkages in terms of "cultural distance." This extensive survey of 350 forced migrants in five *oblasts* of the European part of Russia did not disaggregate its findings by gender. Reporting the views of 'respondents', no distinctions between female and male attitudes were made.

8. Women much more strongly identified themselves with "other similar migrants" than did men: 55 percent of women compared with 20 percent of men in the main sample, and 55 percent and 24 percent respectively in the second sample.

These Afghan refugee girls in Khorasan Province receive free primary education from the host government of Iran. Few refugee girls worldwide are so fortunate. [UNHCR/A. Hollmann/1993]

Women usually continue to carry the primary responsibility for providing children with care in exile. Rwandan women and children queue for supplementary food rations in Zaire. [UNHCR/R. Chalasani/1997]

Personal security is often threatened in and around refugee camps, which can be the size of cities. This one at Ngara, Tanzania, is the temporary home to hundreds of thousands of people. [UNHCR/C. Sattlberger/1995]

The violent forces that displace people are often gendered. Internally displaced people at Yuai, southern Sudan. [UNHCR/S. Greene/1993]

Women in camps have few ways to make money, and economic development projects rarely target them. These women meet to submit business proposals to camp administrators in Ethiopia. [UNHCR/W. Stone/1996]

Fall of empire produces many refugees. Ethnic Russians in Tajikistan meet to hear about immigrating to Russia. [UNHCR/A. Hollmann/1995]

Millions of people become environmentally forced migrants each year. This whole village in Sirajganj District, Bangladesh, was soon destroyed by the shifting Jamuna River. [N. Buchignani/1990]

Refugees returning from Bangladesh reunite with family members who stayed in Maungdaw township, Rakhine State, Myanmar. [UNHCR/A. Hollmann/1997]

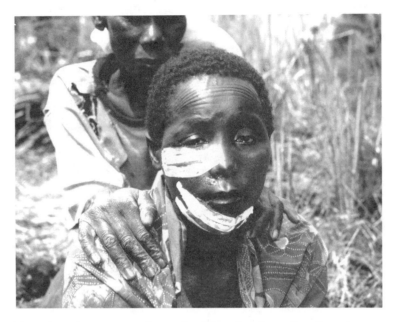

The violence that generates refugees often follows them into asylum. Rwandan woman in Mugumga camp injured in an attack. [UNHCR/B. Press/1994]

Flight profoundly disrupts family and community life, often in unanticipated ways. Rwandan refugees arrive in Goma in 1994. [UNHCR/J. Stjerneklar/1997]

Refugee aid work is also gendered. Teferi Ber Camp, Hararghe Region, Ethiopia. [UNHCR/W. Stone/1996]

Flight often leads to family separation. The daughter of this Muslim refugee in Zenica, Bosnia, was kept in Banja Luka by his Serb in-laws. [UNHCR/A. Hollmann/1994]

12

A Space for Remembering

Home-Pedagogy and Exilic Latina Women's Identities

Inés Gómez

Why is it that in Chile we know more about the United States than this country knows about us?

Alicia, high school student[1]

It is a shame—since our North American cousins have unspeakable interests in this regard—that we continue to live in Latin America without knowing each other.

Paulo Freire (1994)

Language is the main signifier of the historical self. We constantly name our autobiographical search that witnesses what is inscribed, remembered, or appears to make sense: the 'here' and 'there' in the space configuration of our positionality. Our utterances trace the ambiguities of a past. To remember anything nostalgically is to do so through the lens of one's present, at the same time projecting it as a sign into the future. The dilemma of exilic memories is that language is caught between the language that names what is already known and the language of 'difference', which tries to articulate experiences. In this way, the past often becomes woven in a poetic reencoding of metaphorical and metonymic logic of multiple representations, which acts "at the very edge of semantic availability" (Williams, cited in Rutherford 1990: 22). Likewise, the diasporic and displacement process of 'interpreting' and 'reading' identities is far from immune from the forces of conflict and tension in the dialectical operations that bring women's experiences to the frontline of displacement as a subject's history, to where "language is the site of history's enactment" (Scott 1992: 34).

Often enough, the partial, biased records of refugee women's accounts and activities presently available have limited our understanding of their contributions to the host society. Notably, social science constructions of gender have left unexamined the complexity of the conditions of transnational feminist practices in the postmodern era of diaspora and displacement. In the process of building an essentialist and historically reductive discourse about refugees in general and women refugees in particular, Western scholarship has ignored "the complex interconnection between First and Third World economies and the profound effect of this on the lives of women in all countries" (Mohanty 1997: 257). Within this general representation of refugee women as 'an oppressed group', they have been "constituted through and judged by a Western standard" (Mohanty 1997: 272). Moreover, Western scholarship has typically treated gender simply as an additive category to the general image, backstaging the historical specificities of culture, ethnicity, language, race, age, gender, and religion.

And yet, within the reflexive modality of home-pedagogy as a space for teaching and remembering is much evidence for the prevalence among refugees of an interplay of cultural signs from a distant past and from a present "entangled in other powerful global histories" (Clifford 1997: 244). To better represent this process, we urgently need to problematize and take more serious notice of gender, class, race, and age diversity among the cultures of displacement and to work to eliminate unilinear concepts of refugeeism (Gupta 1992; Malkki 1992). We must also seek an alternative conceptual approach that acknowledges refugee 'identity' as a contested site of interstitiality and hybridity caught between centers and peripheries of the cosmopolitan host society. The historic and social positionality of refugee women and their families must be addressed within such a framework, emphasizing deterritorialization and specificity (Indra, this volume).

In this study, I focus my attention on the multiplicity of refugee women's stories localized in their specific sites of transnational feminist practices, and on the hybrid character of their narrations, which varies according to their national positioning. Viewed in this way, the spatial-temporal tension of their accounts can be examined as sites both of marginality and of resistance. Motivated by their social-cultural milieu and socioeconomic constraints, the participants of this study project a diasporic conscience that has forced me to reconceptualize the politics of remembering, selfhood, and cultural identities operating through their narratives of displacement. Moreover, deeply addressing the histories of refugee women in this way may also transform ethnographic practice. My focus is drawn from ongoing research with a specific Latino refugee family group comprised of women and young adolescents from Chile, Guatemala, and El Salvador who live in several communities in northern California. After many conversations with women in family settings, it became clear that despite the many constraints on their lives, centrally relating to family instability and racial exclusion (Suárez-Orozco 1996; Ong 1996), these women perceive themselves as "cultural holders" (Moussa 1994: 3; Ferris 1992: 91), able to hold their families together.

I then sought ways to adequately characterize their perceptions and their narratives. As stressed throughout *The Anthropology of Experience* (Turner and Bruner 1986), I found it essential to capture how these individuals experience their culture, feelings, and expectations; experiences that often expressed themselves in stories or dramas, or in impressions and nostalgic images that form the fabric of meaning in reflection. As Victor Turner (1986: 36) explains: "What happens [in such contexts where we try to put past and present together] ... is an anxious need to find meaning in what has disconcerted us, whether by pain or pleasure, and convert mere experience into *an* experience." A number of works outside refugee studies such as Luisa Passerini's *Fascism in Popular Memory: The Cultural Experience of the Turin Working Class* (1987) now center on understanding such subjective experiences, exploring the historical circumstances within which people articulate their passions, their unconsciousness, and the dissonances in their everyday social relationships in talk about the past. In this study, I want to highlight such processes among refugees and account for how language takes on multiple meanings through popular memory, when concealing or expressing a historical conscience. For the participants in this study, *contar* (to tell) is a reenacted drama. It is the actualization of past events rooted in a given historical moment about which "no one can tell" (Gómez 1993a: 12), events that involve overwhelming experiences of human loss. How are these occurrences realities of a sort that cannot be expressed in words?

The paradoxes of feeling, remembering, and telling extend further, into the realm of epistemology and experience. These participants have come to know and have acted to change their predicament by using, adapting, and mediating the social and cultural resources at their disposal. When their experience is articulated through *contar*, their language use determines, at least in part, how to make sense of symbols, social practices, and cultural forms (Myerhoff 1986). It also challenges the common separation of their children's school knowledge from home knowledge, as I demonstrate below.

This chapter is woven around a series of narratives that highlight particular dynamics and questions. My intention is to open, rather than conclude, discussion and to experiment with new methods to better represent refugee understandings. This chapter is therefore divided into two sections: first, a set of (counter)narratives of young adult refugee students about school and home knowledge are presented to set the stage; the second section contains a more contextualized discussion of the (counter)narratives of women.

At the outset, I should stress that I also came to this study from many social positions: as a university professor (an educator), as an active participant in refugee support groups, and as an exile from Chile who, as a single parent, has lived in the US for many years. These identities and positions obviously shape the way I understand and represent the experiences of refugee others (Gómez 1993a, 1993b; Lather 1991; Patai 1987).

The School Curriculum As a Site of Amnesia

The absoluteness of geographical space is never questioned, and the political ramifications filter back to infect the map of the social: social location, inherently fluid, is inadvertently mapped as absolute. So–mundi, is a blank space on to which social locations are projected–a New World of sorts, ready for colonization; identities are located, positioned,elbowed into an already existing social mosaic.

Smith and Katz (1993: 77)

Because classrooms are not isolated or insulated from the outside world, teachers and students often construct school knowledge based on contradictory and conflicting assumptions about race, gender, and class. These typically fashion a leveling "discourse of amnesia" (Frisch 1981) in the curriculum and in everyday school dynamics. Even so, students often resist in significant ways and their interpretations and meanings are a text that contributes in important ways, to understanding curriculum as a "discursive formation of identity and difference" (Pinar 1993: 61).

The following refugee students' narratives are examples of contingency, marginality, and 'talking back' to the school curriculum that, often enough, is deformed by absences and denials. As other researchers have found earlier among immigrant children (Igoa 1995), these students' inner dialogue of past/present experiences brings forward their silences and formulates (counter)narratives of their own. Francisca, a high school student, remarked:

> After the military coup we left Chile with my parents. We went to Peru, from there to Venezuela, Panama and then to the United States. I was constantly changing schools, friends, neighborhoods and so on.... When I arrived in this American school, I already knew so much about geography, history, politics and what it is like to be a refugee, but ... I could not use it ... in my classroom. Nobody was interested, least of all the teacher. It was not part of the school program.

School classrooms are social, political, and cultural spaces where identity and popular memory intersect. For some refugee students I interviewed, the classroom is a differentiated cultural map that becomes a metaphor for other social realities in their own experiences. Consider the words of Alicia, a high school student:

> I told one of my teachers that the US was totally implicated in the overthrow of the government of my country, and that was the reason my family and I are here as exiles ... I asked her why we do not study these issues in my history class ... She thought it was too complex a topic to be taught to the rest of the class ... I felt more alienated because I thought it is in the classroom where this type of thing should be taught and learned about ...

Luis, a high school student, noted:

> ... I am interested to learn how the school history books hide the stories ... how they do not ... always tell the truth.
> ... probably the United States is the most powerful country in the world, but they cause many problems in other countries, and ... I have problems with students at the school because they think their country is the best in the entire world and they think that it cannot do anything wrong ... I have discussed this with one of my teachers.... Some of them think I am right ... others think that these are Marxist statements. She is right. These are Marxist statements [he laughs].

The narratives above mark a struggle over popular memory. This is a fight against pedagogical control that sets up practices that obstruct the flow of "subjected knowledges" (Giroux 1988: 99) and where curricula, as symbolic representations of a "space of enclosure" (Lankshear, Peters, and Knobel 1996: 54), profoundly fail to address questions of history, geography, collective memory, and social structural inequality as constitutive of the everyday social practices of refugee students, who are displaced subjects from other lands.

According to these and many other students' narratives, they are to learn only what is deemed legitimate by teachers and textbooks. The students' language and their refugee perspectives are often over-looked, or are generalized as sporadic comments or interested inter-ventions. The violations of normative boundaries by these students positions them in the 'in-between' zones of marginality. In this vein, Juan, a junior high student, bemoans the fact that he is somehow now "missing" from the US curriculum: "Here the only thing they teach is America, America and America.... Nobody knows where is Chile. Some think Chile is in Europe and that I speak Portuguese!" María, an ESL student in middle school echoes Juan:

> In class I would like to talk ... to talk different about my experiences.... I would like to teach my peers and my teacher about El Salvador, our struggle back home ... but nobody cares.... I sit there totally bored with these words almost coming out of my mouth ... and the stupid sentences that do not have any meaning to my life.

These student sentiments appear anchored in a deep awareness that power and other social forces profoundly shape educational practices and institutions. Despite commitments to the cultures of the "diversified student population" on the part of those who devise instructional goals for the class as a whole, and despite a genuine interest on the part of refugee students to learn and participate in the schooling process, school remains an alien place for many of these students. Teachers and administrators have so far found it virtually impossible to incorporate into school discourse the diversity of stu-dent values, cultures, and languages (Delgado-Gaitán and Trueba 1991). And yet, as the US approaches the twenty-first century, it is increasingly marked by insistent signs of difference, polyvocality, plurality, and multiple diasporic counternarratives "produced in spheres generally ignored by schools" (Britzman et al. 1993).[2]

Students' questioning back of approved knowledge in the classroom in turn sets in motion a desire to understand how one's life as a refugee has been constructed within school texts and what the historical forces are that have so constructed that life. As Sylvia, a high school student, observed: "I never chose to go into exile. Nobody chooses to go any-where like that. My family discussed how refugees are 'made' by big political powers.... I think the 'making' still has not ended."

Currently, the monologic classroom attempts to suppress the choice of some students to speak up, or to try to speak in a language that resists the arguments of the curriculum or the teacher. In this instance, the subjected knowledges of their own identities as students and as refugees resist their being passive recipients of 'approved' lessons. These students bring into the classroom a cultural competence that yearns to move forward their exilic experience. Furthermore, these students' counterhegemonic feelings help them construct their own identities within a text that is diasporic, contingent, and historical. As William Pinar asserts (1993: 61): "Identity becomes a central concept in the effort to understand curriculum as a racial text. Identity is not a static term either, reflective of a timeless, unchanging inner self. Rather, identity is a gendered, racialized and historical construct." This tension between the official discourse and counterhegemonic narrative practice, moreover, has implications for the students' home life, as Alma Flor Ada (Igoa 1995: 46) asserts: "Schools can never be neutral in this regard ... the conscious or unconscious practices of the school, including its approach to literacy, serve to either validate or invalidate the home cultures, thus helping or hindering family relationships."

The Significance of Nostalgic Women's Accounts in the Configuration of Home-Pedagogy

"So what if it's nostalgic; it's OUR nostalgia. They expect us to be satisfied with THEIR NOSTALGIA."

in Kondo (1996: 97)

I must stress that the language of longing has a dual practice: oppositional or counterhegemonic, as well as pedagogical. Both are part of the same feminist alternative in the discourse of refugee mother-child talk. Here, gender becomes informed by a discourse of power relations, within the articulation of the multiple semantics confronted by the transnational cultural flows of the politics of the host society (Grewal and Kaplan 1994b: 17). The notion of 'otherness' becomes transformed through speech into a cartography of 'naming', poetically reencoding the archive of the imagined according to its own logic. Through speech, private memory enacts its "hidden transcripts" (Scott 1985), transforming memory into public stories (Gómez 1993a). As Benjamin (1973: 257) notes: "To articulate the past historically does not mean to recognize it 'the way it really was'. It means to seize hold of a memory as it flashes up at a moment of danger...."

What is in question, therefore, are not longings for a lost, idealized nationhood or romantic, uncontaminated origins, but refugee women's understanding of the historical location of the present. The present articulates with the very conditions of existence of women refugees, within which they are able to achieve a quality of what Kobena Mercer terms a "critical reverie" (1988: 54). "Critical reverie" acts upon the spatiotemporal intersection of everyday existence in ways that are not always linear. Each personal story becomes disrupted, uprooted from the quotidian, eliciting a critical instant that 'takes note' of the manner in which memory works contextually and involves the sensitive prism that filters and selects elements from the world that is evoked (Alegria and Epple 1987). In claiming their past memories, refugee women may devise gendered spaces as a way to confront their multiple realities; while separated from their homes, extended families, network of friends, and societal roles (Freire 1995). As such, these women devise ways of expressing their subject position within diverse modalities based on their own situational, cultural, national, class, and geographical specificities. The language of nostalgia in these women's narratives mediates experience and the contingencies of their positionality.

Extending arguments made in the opening section of this chapter and by several other authors (Ganguly 1992; Naficy 1991; Stewart 1988), the discursive language of nostalgic narratives may generate a critical sociosymbolic terrain that allows self-relevant modes of representation and cultural practices to be validated in the everyday life of people in the diaspora. As Naficy (1991: 289) observes:

> ... the 'real' past threatens to reproduce itself as a lack or loss: it is against the threat of such a loss that the nostalgic past must be turned into a series of nostalgic objects, into fetish-souvenirs that can be displayed and consumed repeatedly ... these are the recurring micronarratives of nostalgic return.

María expresses this more poignantly: "El pasado se mete por donde quiera, y yo le dejo entrar ... es mi historial y tengo que darselo a mis hijos" (The past comes from everywhere, and I let it in. It is my history, and I have to give it to my children). She added: "Ahora vivimos aqui, y tenemos que saber vivir con lo que trajimos y hacerlo de nuevo" (Now we live here, and we must know how to live with what we brought and make it anew).

Nostalgia, as Stewart (1988: 277) points out, can bridge the present with the past in such a way as to ameliorate tensions arising from a spatially and temporally fragmented terrain of new experiences. More importantly, he observes:

> Nostalgia is an *essential, narrative, function* of language that orders events temporally and dramatizes them.... By resurrecting time and place, and

a subject *in* time and place, it shatters the surface of an atemporal order and a prefab cultural landscape. To narrate is to place oneself in an event and a scene–to make an interpretive space relational and [one] in which meanings have direct social referents. (Emphasis added.)

Nostalgic talk constitutes a form of practice mediating differences, shaping a context in which these women represent themselves to themselves and others. An extension of this insight has been put forth by Keya Ganguly (1992: 29–30), who suggests that the past becomes a special place for those whose present is "unstable or unpredictable." Indeed, as he observes:

> … the present acquires its meaning only with references to a disjointed and conflicted narrative of the past–in which references to official narratives about colonization and a historical memory are tangled up with personal memories and private recollections of past experience. The authority of the past depends on people's present subjectivity and vice versa.

In a process shaped by gender, the act of 'interpreting' and 'reading' women's new identities as exiles is an act of 'reworking the past' with the present. Such events of remembering are not immune to the forces of conflict and tension, which are apparent when one tries to bring women back into their own histories (Minh-ha 1989: 95). The results are interpretations that inform us about a special kind of gendered exile knowledge–the "authority of the past," in Ganguly's words–that is in opposition to what is usually perceived about such people as refugees and as women. These evocations, these "structure of feelings" (Williams 1977) are not simply factual, logical, and national. They evoke voices, smells, sights, tastes, desires, and secrets (Abu-Lughod and Lutz 1991; Lutz 1982: 113). Feelings and emotions play a central role in the nostalgic imaginary–in what Ruth Kruefeld (1992: 5) describes as refugee and immigrant "cognitive mapping."

In my earlier analysis of Chilean refugee women's discourses (Gómez 1993a), I found that a rhetorical content of feelings was of particular relevance in understanding the content of the local desires and the way feelings help exile women make self-grounded sense of their individual experiences in relation to others. These women wove their experiences in powerful, impetuous, emotional language steeped in loss, rootlessness, alienation, and resistance. These profoundly narrated experiences were much more than mere essentialist psychological readjustment to traumatic social events (Kleinman and Kleinman 1991).

Emotions also help define the signs, codes, and strategies designated to accommodate and capture women's encounters with their exile landscape. Yet the search for an appropriate language to adequately capture refugee women's imaginations is also an encounter with problematic and contradictory sites of disruptions and violence that "can elicit a nostalgia for a past golden age that never was, a nostalgia that eludes exclusion, power relations and differences" (Kondo 1996: 97). Images intercept remembrances and reveries, constructing identity at the margins in a borderland terrain of mixed stories, images, and languages: the shifting centers and peripheries of the topography of the self (Kondo 1996: 41). Reflecting on her experiences, Alicia felt that she was still, "con un pié aquí y otro allá ... entre la pena y la alegría" (with one foot here and the other there ... between sorrow and happiness). She simultaneously felt an urgent need to maintain memories of the homeland to hold her family together with "the inevitability of a desire for a home in an inhospitable world."

Like individual identity, cultural identity is, as Stuart Hall (1990: 225) explains, constantly transformed. Articulating with but never *fixed to* an essentialized past, cultural identity transcends temporal and spatial boundaries. For Alicia, as for many other refugee women, cultural and individual identities are

> ... a matter of "becoming" as well as of "being"... Far from being grounded in a mere "recovery" of the past, which is waiting to be found, and which when found, will secure our sense of ourselves into eternity, identities are the names we give to the different ways we are positioned by, and position ourselves within, the narratives of the past. (Hall 1990)

Home-Pedagogy and the Sense of Space

> It wasn't our fault that
> we were born in times of need.
> Times to take to the seas and set sail.
> Anchor down in boats and in whirlpools
> Flee from tyrants and the wars
> to the swing of the pendulum
> to the rhythm of the sea.
> The one who bore the letter took
> refuge first.
> The letter was wet, it was dawn.
> From somewhere, we saw the ocean
> come.
>
> *Cristina Peri Rossi (1988)*

One thing that was very clear throughout my conversations with refugee women about the schooling of their children was their view that there existed a profound contradiction between the formal content of school learning and how their children saw themselves. They felt that teachers, despite a lack of clear intent to discriminate or exclude, held and used the hegemonic values of the dominant society. Their teaching was believed to be impersonal, detached, and remote from the cultural experiences of the children who made up their classes. Participants in the study felt that the schools created cultural and categorical boundaries that unfairly made their children outsiders. They also felt that both teachers' attitudes and the general atmosphere of the schools limited the teachers' understanding of the educational experiences of their children. In the words of Marianela, "I have participated in everything we could if the child needed something ... but the Principal never calls you ... it isn't personal, it's just whoever goes, goes." Another participant commented: "Here they do not prepare [the students] to see the world as it is. Here only America exists. My son knows these things [about his own heritage] because he has learned at home and not at the school."

These women believed that the educational system had failed to develop teaching materials and techniques grounded in themes, values, and words that were meaningful to the lives of their children.[3] Embodied also in participants' reflections on the educational system were fears of school-based promiscuity and drugs–specific elements in a more general concern over the 'Americanization' of their children. As Alicia said:

> Because we see things day to day, the contradictions that present themselves.... I tried to keep the culture, I try to keep the language ... but I live in a constant struggle. American culture penetrates everything: music, friends, everything ... but we live here. That is a reality that we have to accommodate.

For Gonzalo, Alicia's teenage son, the result was a diasporic conscience and a divided self. He was in a liminal zone, where his homeland had become a free floating abstraction in language enunciating marginality as "location" at the edge (Smith and Katz 1993: 78): "Life for me has been very difficult.... I do not know if I want to go back to Chile ... a country that I barely know, but also I do not know if remaining here is the answer, a country where I feel I do not belong.... It's a real mess."

Because of similar concerns, a number of 'corrective' schools and programs have been created on the initiative of refugee parents (Eastmond 1993; Gómez 1993a; Habte-Mariam 1989; Parada 1990). Most of these schools have stressed maintaining refugee cultural values, facilitating communication, reducing intercultural conflicts, and building effective bilingualism. Lacking access to such opportunities for her own children, Eloiza bemoaned their lack of knowledge about her homeland: "My only hope is that these children will be able to learn at home what is not given to them elsewhere.... I never thought before that I would have to teach them like this.... I always thought that was the role of teachers–at least it is in El Salvador." Most women expressed to me topics that they would like to see included more often in the schooling of their children: more of the geography, history, and literature of their source countries and others; a more international school curriculum; and teacher knowledge of Spanish.

Many women have compensated for the lack of such school programs with what I have termed home-pedagogy (following Clifford 1997). The Russian psychologist Lev Vygostky recognized long ago the strong role of "situated knowledge" in the development of children's value systems and culture–knowledge arising from those "spontaneous concepts acquired by the child outside of the explicit instruction" (cited in John-Steiner and Mahn 1996: 201). In this sense, home-pedagogy is not formal instruction at home. Rather, it refers to situated spaces that spontaneously open up in women's nostalgic recollections–spaces that create possibilities for their children to enhance their learning beyond the normal constraints of school. As Diega said, "I talk to my daughter anywhere possible.... I always teach her about things from home, especially when we go out for a walk, to the market or other places." Similarly, Luisa added:

We arrived without anything. The only thing we had was our history.... I said to my husband, "We have to give this history to our children. They ought to know why we had to leave Chile.... I will teach them anywhere–talking to other parents, organizing ourselves for teaching them ... we must not forget."

Moreover, as many writers (Agosin 1987; Ferris 1992; Freire 1995; Gómez 1993a; Radcliffe 1993) have noted, the political practice of refugee women has also taken many 'public sphere' forms when the lives of their children and the groups they represent are at stake. Such observations challenge traditional Latina images that are related only to the 'interior' of their homes. For politically active women refugees, 'mothering' becomes difficult to categorize and identify as distinct from other roles (Jetter, Orleck, and Taylor 1997). As Sarah Radcliffe (1993: 103) notes, one must deeply reconsider the largely unexamined "relationship between spaces (public-private/spatial-metaphorical) of women's roles in their construction of subjecthood and identity in the multiple enunciations and different forms of social practices."

In this regard, Patricia commented on her more formal and public attempts to compensate for school deficiencies:

> How did we all do in that small community of refugees? ... We organized a place for teaching geography, literature, history, music and dances to our children. We wanted to keep our memories alive here. In the American school's map, we do not exist.... We women had to contribute very much with our efforts–organization and knowledge.

For Brunilda, the term 'community' had come to mean a kind of homeland, being with a diversity of local people: "I like to live in a multicultural environment, in a neighborhood with different groups of people. To learn from them. That is what I understand by my 'community' ... " These are only a few of many examples of how extra-school pedagogy is also tied to public places and practices. As refugee women who had been forced to 'travel' with their children, the context of teaching or remembering has become public as well as private, and their nostalgic language may be shaped by a wide range of modes and sites of performance, according to circumstance.

The task identified here, therefore, requires that necessary space be available for women (many of them single parents) to teach their text alone, between shifts of uncertain jobs. Even so, for most, transmitting one's history and culture has been a priority, and clearly mediates women's feelings of uprootedness and loss. The evocation of nostalgic language acts as mediator or 'cultural carrier', incorporating words, drawings, songs, proverbs, and imagery that confers meaning and value in the representational system of 'knowing' or wanting to know. In this regard, de Certeau's (1988: 117) notion of space "in language" is highly relevant:

> Space is like the word when it is spoken, that is, when it is caught in the ambiguity of an actualization, transformed into a term dependent upon many different conventions, situated as the act of a present (or of a time), and modified by the transformations caused by successive contexts.... In short, *space is a practiced place.*

Refugee Latina women compose a social text that informs and shapes subjectivity, using nostalgic accounts to facilitate learning among young listeners. The significance of their texts is always relative–never linear, organized according to a particular set of circumstances, with overlapping chronological times and cultural elements. Lucia and Maria talk about these challenges:

> *Lucia:* And as I was telling them one day ... when we were children, like them today, we used to go all the time with our parents to the Guatemala

mountains to participate with my family in the Indian ceremonies of the villages ... but what was important for my children now to know is that we were always together as family and community ... to keep alive our rights. That is what counts most for them to know now ... My children ask me many questions and I always answer them with even more details if I can. *Maria:* Ours is not a simple story, nor a fairy tale. I tell them that never in their school will they learn what it is like to fight for your rights, for poor people like us, for social justice.... What it is like to live under a dictatorship.... Yes, they do understand ... in their ways, but it is important that somebody teach these things. Despite that, I yearn to return and live again where I was born ... in Atitlan.

Marianela spoke about the importance of passing on information about culture and history:

Eudocia Quilpan was an old Mapuche Indian[4] woman from the south of Chile. She lived with us, and all of her stories were from her native region.... I remember seeing her sitting near the fire at the dusk of the day ... it was from her mouth that I learned from an early age what it was like to be an exile when she told us about her sufferings.... Eudocia had to leave her tribe in order to go to work in the capital. She suffered many, many problems, including racism, but most of all solitude, because she too, like us, was yearning for her land and her people. I tell this and more about Eudocia to my children in order for us to get the strength necessary, when living far away, and for them to understand better their present situation.

It is in such 'remembering what is remembered' that spontaneous home education takes place. Poetic and evocative images are often employed, which in fact do not obstruct the historicity of the accounts or the ability of the pedagogical event to work as performative documentary. As "critical narratory," these personal narratives are read 'against' the school curriculum's "treasure stock" (McLaren 1995: 91), bringing to the forefront key personal remembrances–remembrances presented, as women stated, so "that the child will understand in his/her own ways," and so that "the children will have a sense of belonging and history." This discursive reproduction aimed at creating personalized, contextualized, familiar knowledge and a grounded sense of self is aimed at generating what Bourdieu (1977) refers to as "habitus." In the construction of the pedagogical event, then, a 'remembered' habitus itself becomes a social component, expanding the notion of 'nostalgia'. While North American popular constructions of 'nostalgia' often connote negative notions of staticism and 'past glories', 'nostalgia' for these women is more of a meaningful signpost where its discursive space supports ongoing struggles.

The arpillerista,[5]
artisan of remains
burns with rage and cold
as she tenderly
picks through the remnants of her dead,
salvages the shroud of her husband
the trousers left after the absences
submerges herself in cloth of foaming, silent blood
and though she is fragile she grows large,
sovereign over her adobe hut,
her ragged scraps
and determined to tell her story
truer than the tale woven by her
sister Philomena.

Marjorie Agosin (1987/88).

Un Espacio para Recordar (A Space for Remembering)

For Maria and her mother, space became a metaphorical device for recalling the past and foreshadowing the future. While exploring and fixing temporal and spatial distance to events and practices, they appropriate the latter as nearby.

When my mother started to compile stories from El Salvador ... we thought it was necessary, since my son was born here.... So we thought it would give us some time to build a space for remembering ... to be able to teach my son what we remember back home, the good and the bad, the difficulties, the civil war, the sufferings, and the endurance of our families [and] ... how we arrived in the United States. We just talk and talk, looking at the photos, maps, pictures, crafts, the "recuerdos de la patria" [homeland remembering]. Always talking in Spanish ... we are very much aware of the need among the youth today to understand these things, to give them a sense of belonging.

Metaphorically, these "Women piece together quilts from scraps of clothing, and in every scrap a memory and so a story" (Stewart 1988: 236). In this way, a meaningfully engendered narrative is pieced together, as Ignacia's words illustrate:

I tell my daughters the story of Dona Chon, a rebel woman from Ixcan ... how she was brave and fearless, whether she was at the barricades or cooking tortillas for the soldiers or leading marches against social injustice. She was inspired by our history of injustice and discrimination ... and like her, [the stories of] so many other anonymous peasant women that fought and died in Guatemala. I tell my children this for them to learn what is real women's history for us.

Once in a while, nostalgia even bridges the distance between official curriculum and home-pedagogy. In this sense, the following narrative is doubly nostalgic: "el jardin de mi abuela" (my grandmother's garden), or a botany lesson by Norma, an elementary teacher:

> When I teach my daughter and my students ... what comes to my memory are the names of flowers, wild plants, vegetables, trees, birds.... Everything I can remember from that beautiful garden of my grandmother, with whom I planted and took care every season of my childhood.... It is those images that I most miss from my homeland: my grandmother's garden, that started to fade away little by little after she was dead. I began to miss that garden even before we had to leave San Miguel as refugees. And now I think about it even more.... But, when I teach botany, I recreate that garden for others and myself ... in that way, I bring the image of my homeland and its nature into my teachings, and in the way we name it in our own language.

And Finally

> *Diasporas always leave a trail of collective memory about another place and time and create new maps of desire and of attachment.*

Breckenridge and Appadurai (1989: 1)

The domestic space of these, and I suspect many other refugee women is the locus of memories, a site where the act of remembering transforms a contested terrain of affirmations, struggle, and longing. In the porous space of home, the teller's imagination 'travels' and renders many things possible, despite the risks, challenges, and limitations of the host world. As reconstructed, the homeland is both a distant and present location–a blurred boundary of stories that enter the imaginations of those who listen and those who tell. Both mother and child are equally subject to the meaning-making of what has been spoken and heard. Both depart on different *and* same paths of understanding, further transforming themselves in counternarratives of "circulation" (Bhabha 1991). Both appropriate each other's words, as Bakhtin explains (1981: 293–4), turning them to their individual intentions and thereby making them their own.

Memories as embodied knowledge construct a text of impressions and emotions, as Alicia intuits: "I feel one foot [is] here and another *there.* I feel divided in my thoughts and in my memories ... memories hit me ... in my body." In memories, real knowledge is not restricted to a single organized structure, but intertwines with history and desire. The resulting texts build a symbolic pedagogical language of the home that "relies on the ability to withhold information as well as to let go of knowledge and intention" (Minh-ha 1992: 146; Giles, this volume).

In this study, I see women's folk notions of pedagogy and remembering as a site of historicized struggles, in which the teaching of their children is much more than a litany of nostalgic, romantic homeland visions. This teaching reflects active longing, a paradigm of remembering and a pedagogical journey of resistance to uprootedness and identity in flux. These are diasporic experiences that inscribe in these refugee women's imagination a deep-rooted understanding of their historical imagined community (Deleuze and Guattari 1987). Woven in domestic spaces, these exilic accounts mark spaces in language that contain voids and evoke some of the most profound experiences of liminality (Turner 1967).

These women refugees' discourses on homeland are positioned with respect to their own understanding of "what it is like to be here." In particular, many ambiguities and contradictions exist between their versions of local and global historical encounters, and their children's significant experiences, identities, and ongoing formal schooling. In this sense, women's counternarratives resist Eurocentric, essentialized representations of women refugees as a "silent majority" (De Vos 1993) and act as voices of dissent against the school curriculum's geopolitical and historical amnesia.

Notes

1. To assure anonymity, the names of all participants have been changed. All participants spoke in Spanish, their native language. All translations are my own unless otherwise noted.

2. More generally, Roger Simon (1994: 131) notes that "... the complexity of this assumed educative relation between present and past is important to those of us who—as cultural workers and teachers—create, organize, distribute, and structure ... [such engagements]." In this regard, my pedagogical concern is how to rearticulate memories that inform the social imagination of refugee students in a manner that current naturalized, taken-for-granted curriculum becomes problematized.

3. Although it is beyond the scope of this chapter, this refugee mothers' critique again raises the question of diversity in American schooling: to what extent does the system meet the needs of children from different cultures? As Hoffman (1996) asserts, the rhetoric of multicultural education as 'defined' by American cultural assumptions lacks a deep understanding of the complexity of cultures

and languages in the society at large and in everyday classroom practices. In this situation, the educational experiences of refugees, exiles, and immigrant children will continue to challenge the school system.

4. The Araucanian-speaking Mapuche people, the largest indigenous population in Chile, have had a long history of anticolonial struggle since the time of the Spanish Conquest (Gómez 1974).

5. *Arpilleras* (burlap) are embroidered appliqués that were first created in 1974 by Chilean women artisans to denounce the Pinochet regime (Agosin 1987).

13

Eritrean Canadian Refugee Households As Sites of Gender Renegotiation

Atsuko Matsuoka and John Sorenson

Introduction

Forced migration and processes of resettlement and adaptation to new environments require exiles and refugees to come to terms with unfamiliar circumstances and demands, often by assuming new roles and renegotiating expectations, behaviors, and relationships that have operated in the past. Many of these new circumstances are lived most intensely within the context of the household and are frequently enacted along the lines of gender. Household and gender relations, therefore, offer important sites for understanding how exiles and refugees come to terms with their new situations. This chapter discusses some of these renegotiations by setting them in the case of the Eritrean-Canadian diaspora population. We consider such renegotiations in the context of altered situations for employment and education, of encounters with North American culture and the influence of nationalist ideologies. Our observations are based on over a decade of participant-observation with communities in several Canadian cities, as well as data from interviews, focus group discussions, written questionnaires, and discourse analysis of various written texts and public meetings.[1]

The Eritrean Diaspora

The Eritrean diaspora was generated in the context of Eritrea's thirty-year war of independence from Ethiopia. In 1962 Ethiopia annexed the former Italian colony a decade after a federation of the two entities was implemented by the United Nations, despite opposition from much of the Eritrean population (Bereket 1980, 1989; Okbazghi 1994; Tekie 1983; Trevaskis 1960). Prior to its outright incorporation of Eritrea as a province, Ethiopia had steadily undermined the terms of the federation, thus channeling discontent into armed struggle, which broke out in 1961 under the direction of the Eritrean Liberation Front (ELF) (Firebrace 1985; Jordan 1989; Markakis 1987; Pateman 1990; Permanent Peoples' Tribunal 1984; Pool 1980, 1982, 1983; Sherman 1980). After one of the century's longest wars, Eritrea emerged as an independent state in 1993. Following an internationally supervised referendum, Ethiopia's government was deposed and replaced by the Ethiopian People's Revolutionary Democratic Front (EPRDF), a coalition dominated by the Tigrayan People's Liberation Front (TPLF) (Sorenson 1993, 1995; Amare 1994). The war was conducted mainly on Eritrean territory and turned much of the civilian population into a target for repression, terror, and violence. Hundreds of thousands of Eritreans (and Ethiopians) were forced to flee their homes; the majority went to neighboring countries such as Sudan and Somalia, but thousands were scattered throughout the Middle East, Europe, and North America (Adelman and Sorenson 1994; Kibreab 1987, 1990; Kuhlman 1990). This population comprised part of one of the twentieth century's largest refugee situations: in 1990 there were approximately two million refugees in the four states that then comprised the Horn of Africa (Djibouti, Ethiopia, Somalia, Sudan). Some estimated that a million Eritreans were refugees; according to Berhane Woldemichael (1992: 172), this constituted a quarter of Eritrea's population, while others have suggested that a third of the population was displaced. Such estimates may be somewhat inflated, but it is clear that a very substantial portion of the population had been internally displaced or had crossed an international border.

In 1997, the Eritrean-Canadian diaspora numbered roughly five thousand people, most of whom arrived in the mid-1980s and now live in Toronto. The population was at first disproportionately male, but this changed noticeably by 1990. The majority come from urban backgrounds and have at least a high school education; many have university degrees or diplomas from technical training institutes. Reflecting the severely gender-imbalanced educational system in

Eritrea, women in general face more problems than men in developing language facility and securing employment in Canada. Nevertheless, the diaspora population includes a number of well-educated professional women. Although most of the Eritrean population is rural, illiterate, and poor, few such people migrated to Canada but instead fled to Sudan or to rugged mountainous areas held by Eritrean nationalist troops, where they endured extremely grim conditions. Eritrea's population is divided almost equally between Christians and Muslims, as is the Canadian diaspora population. Processes of settlement and adjustment to life in Canada, including gender-related issues, were affected by people's class and religious background, but commitment to nationalist goals and to specific political ideologies has also played an important role in shaping the diaspora experience.

Diaspora communities were greatly influenced by the ongoing nationalist struggle in Eritrea. Virtually all of the people we interviewed believe that they had been forced to leave their homes because of war or political repression, even though not all of them are officially recognized as refugees.

> People think we want to come to Canada. Why would we want to come here? To this weather? To work like a donkey all your life? I have to tell people, "No I'm not an economic refugee." They don't have any idea why people come here to save their lives. Why would we want to leave our homes? We were forced to go out. We didn't want to go to Canada or any other country.

Another informant expressed the position succinctly: "Every Eritrean is a refugee."

To assert one's status as an Eritrean and as a refugee (regardless of the refusal of the Canadian state to officially recognize these categories at the time) was a political statement, an expression of commitment to the nationalist cause. Many in the diaspora kept close links with the Eritrean People's Liberation Front (EPLF), which emerged from the ELF's internal civil war as the major nationalist movement in the late 1970s. It later came to form the government of the independent state. Although sharp divisions from the civil war persist among supporters of rival nationalist movements that had splintered from the ELF and been defeated by the EPLF, much of the diaspora population depended on the EPLF for regular information and contact with Eritrea throughout the war. People also broadly subscribed to its goals, contributed to it financially, and supported its actions. For most individuals, the nationalist struggle constituted an overdetermining influence, a frame of reference for appropriate behavior, and it often served to determine the boundaries of significant social relationships. Although some Eritreans in the diaspora did oppose the EPLF, the majority of them voted for independence during the 1993 referendum. Most individuals migrated to Canada with the stated intention of returning to Eritrea once independence had been achieved, but the effects of prolonged conflict on an already-impoverished region have severely restricted this option. Independent Eritrea faced serious challenges in terms of food and water supply, housing, sanitation, education, employment, rehabilitation, and military demobilization, while relations with the Islamic fundamentalist regime in neighboring Sudan posed a threat to peace and security. In addition, over the course of several years, many had established themselves abroad and realized that it would be extremely difficult to relocate once more. For those in the Eritrean diaspora, the end of the war brought a sense of relief and pride that independence had been achieved; it also required them to reassess their own position in relation to their 'homes'–both those they had left and those they currently inhabited.

Feminist Approaches to Refugee and Diaspora Studies

To understand the particular reassessments made among Eritrean-Canadians and processes of identity renegotiation in general, we may turn to Doreen Indra's (1989a: 22) proposal that feminist theory can make major contributions to the field of refugee studies. By extension, we may apply this to the study of diaspora populations, not all of whose members may be legally identified as refugees. Indra notes in this volume that before 1980 little attention was given to gender issues and that refugees were viewed in terms of a "genderless stereotype." While an emphasis on participation in development has now been extended to refugee studies and there are repeated calls for more participation by refugees in decision-making processes, Indra argues that this has not been matched in practice and that the omission remains particularly glaring in terms of women. There has been a considerable increase in research into the situation of refugee women over the last decade (for example, Ager, Ager, and Long 1995; Kibreab 1995), but women are often still considered peripheral except in regard to conventional 'women's issues'. Such a situation is in itself unacceptable, and is particularly problematic given that women comprise over half the world's adult refugee population (Forbes-Martin 1991).

Feminism, of course, is an extremely diverse and internally divided analytical field, incorporating numerous perspectives and areas of concern (Bordo 1990; di Leonardo 1991; Landry and Maclean 1993). Clearly, it has offered major innovations in social analysis, providing important new empirical data and conceptual approaches applicable to refugee diasporas.[2] This chapter seeks to apply some insights of gender analysis to one of the major forced migrations of this century: the movement of refugees and displaced people from their homes in the Horn of Africa.

Effects of Forced Migration on Households

One of the most immediately apparent effects of forced migration is the splitting and scattering of Eritrean households. In the process of flight, virtually all Eritrean families have been separated; as extended family units are very common in Eritrea, this applies even to those apparently preserved nuclear families who migrated together to Canada. Particularly during the early period of Eritrean settlement in Canada, much of the diaspora population consisted of men who had arrived alone. This included both unmarried men and men separated from their wives and children. Many couples were separated for years by the war and circumstances of forced migration. Often wives were left with their in-laws and some women talked about difficulties they experienced in such situations. The words of one woman in her thirties show a glimpse of this:

> We were married only a few months. Please don't think that they [in-laws] are bad people or mean people. After all, I did not know their ways of doing things at home. You know, each family has different ways of making spices.... I felt that I was always watched ... [by] his parents and also his siblings. I wanted to do well and to be liked.... Later, I found out that I was pregnant with my son. They were very happy because it was a boy. It was good. But it was not easy.... I got a lot of help, but I was told this and that about how I was doing with my son.... I did not fit quite well. I really longed to join my husband soon.

In this case, the household consisted not of husband, wife, their children, and their relatives but a wife, her child and her husband's relatives. Some wives who had stayed longer in Eritrea felt that they were missing an essential connection to their in-laws because their husbands were refugees in other countries.

While some married women were left with in-laws in their home country, others were forced to survive with children as single mothers in foreign lands before they could join their husbands. These women described experiences filled with uncertainty, anxiety, and stress. In a number of cases, couples did not see each other for many years. This meant both partners had to live as married adults, but alone or as single mothers with in-laws. When women rejoined their husbands, conjugal relationships were never the same:

> I am one of the very first women who came here then. No women were here to show us how to do things here. It was my husband who took me to stores and showed me where I could find things and how things work when I came here. I cooked for men who were living here alone. All other women who were here earlier did the same. A lot of people came throughout a day. Nobody had a 9 to 5 job.... Whenever they came, I served meals or tea ... often both. I was in the kitchen almost all day, most of the time by myself. That was different from home and I felt very lonesome. No women to have tea and chat.... So I talked to my husband probably more than if we had stayed in Eritrea. I guess I am lucky because he helps me. He had to. I had children to look after and all these men who visit. Later I started to work. I had to [as they had sponsored their younger siblings, and later, their cousins]. So he helped me to cook a little, or do laundry. I did not drive, so often he shopped. But not all the men are like him. Many men expect the same as back home, even when they know things are not the same here. If we were in Eritrea, I wouldn't have worked. I would have had a lot of help. He wouldn't have needed to discuss so many things with me. Now we have more relatives in Canada and America, but at that time we were it.

In Canada, wives and husbands typically had to negotiate new relationships to meet needs of their immediate community as well as to meet expectations of their families back home. After several years of separation, reencounters, and adjustments to a new country, relationships were not always easy. In some cases, men and women made rather untraditional decisions regarding separation and divorce. One professional woman going through the process of divorce (after more than ten years of marriage in Canada following several years in Eritrea separated from her husband) recalled the time when she came to Canada:

> I worked back home, so it was very natural for me to look for a job right away. My child was still young. Back home I could have hired someone to take care of my child and house. But it was not possible here, so my husband wanted me to stay home to take care of her. Then a job opportunity came up for me and I took the job, although I had to start from the bottom and had to take many courses later. We needed jobs to sponsor our relatives. Now I think he was jealous. He could not get a job in his area. His degree was not recognized here in Canada, but he did not have money to go back to school.... There were very few women from my country at the time I came. So when men came to our house, they expected to have good meals, traditional meals. My husband did not

help me. He believed in EPLF but could not bring himself to help me in the kitchen or change diapers.... He could not take more responsibilities at home. I found that Eritrean women accepted new responsibilities and adjusted better than men. Many husbands do not help their wives. They do not help enough.

Some men whose wives were employed outside the home or who attended classes found themselves taking on additional domestic duties, mainly related to child care and food preparation; these are tasks traditionally seen as 'women's work'. Nevertheless, in the majority of cases, primary responsibility for household matters was left to women, regardless of extra demands placed on them by employment and education upgrading. This expansion of roles and responsibilities (Crosby and Jasker 1993) of those working outside the home led many female informants to express considerable dissatisfaction toward Eritrean men. It also often put them in a bind: changes in personal demands and household responsibilities seem to have led many couples to build new relationships for themselves, but expectations from the community toward such married couples did not change very much. Wives, in particular, desired more flexible sharing of household tasks, rather than maintaining the sharply divided 'traditional' domestic division of labor.

The splitting of families affected other gendered relationships, beyond those between husbands and wives. Parents and children were also often separated. In the case of exiles who left elderly parents behind in Eritrea, this generated anxiety associated with having left vulnerable family members behind in a war zone. It also made it difficult for them to meet culturally prescribed responsibilities. This anxiety was especially acute for eldest sons, who normally would be expected to assist both parents and younger siblings, and also entailed anxieties about the appropriate performance of culturally specific masculine roles. Some male exiles worried constantly about family members with whom they were able to have only sporadic contact. Adults of both sexes, particularly older ones, felt a duty to care for their parents overseas, and most provided assistance in the form of financial remittances and through sponsoring their siblings and other relatives. As much of Eritrea was under military occupation for many years, these remittances were often uncertain and irregular, sometimes smuggled in from Sudan in the form of cash. Many men consequently felt they were not meeting their family responsibilities as material provider.

Life in Canada occasioned a new sense of responsibility for female exiles. As one can observe in the quotations above, women also provided significant financial support for family members left behind. A woman in her late twenties who had been unemployed and on welfare conveyed her urge to fulfill the new responsibility:

> I send money to home and my sister in Greece whenever I can … it is not easy…. If it weren't for the war, I would have been married now and I wouldn't have thought about it or needed to send money…. It is almost expected to send money to support our efforts and family back home. I feel I have to. If I had a job I could send money to my father and sponsor my sisters and brothers….

Many siblings left Eritrea at different times and went in different directions. Those who settled in Canada often provided financial support to siblings and cousins who were stranded in other countries without work permits or good opportunities, as felt responsibilities extended to a wider network of relatives than those typically recognized by North Americans.

Many married male exiles also had been forced to leave their own children behind. Thus, some men were prevented from fulfilling their duties both as sons and as fathers. Coming from a social context in which family values are valorized, this splitting and scattering frequently led to a deeply felt sense of personal loss and regret, entailed a strong sense of unmet duties and failed responsibilities, and provoked further tensions and stress. At the same time, similar circumstances obliged many Eritrean women in the diaspora to assume a greater range of responsibilities in households.

The absence of family members constituted a source of worry even among families in which a married couple migrated together with all their children. In the absence of additional personnel from the extended family, many couples found themselves the sole supporters and supervisors of their children; at home, a broader group would normally share such duties, operating within a system of familiar values, customs, and behavior. Furthermore, extended family members in Eritrea would have provided assistance with other material tasks and would sometimes have acted to resolve marital discord. Exiled couples often found themselves burdened with many new responsibilities in the context of greater intimacy-in-isolation.

Forced Migration and Constructions of Gender

Following Indra's approach, viewing the concept of 'gender' not as a substitute for 'women' but as a relational process, we consider the effect of forced migration and resettlement on men as well as women. The analysis in this chapter, therefore, is not an attempt to return to a more traditional approach to refugee studies after having paid ritual obeisance to current trends. Women do not live in gender isolation, and their situations cannot be adequately analyzed as if they were. Rather, this approach requires us to recognize that masculinity is also socially constructed. Furthermore, discussions with Eritrean women refugees clearly show that they do not analyze their own situations as being separate from that of men, nor do they wish to see themselves in such a way. Although they recognize that women face specific problems, women view their lives as being affected by the same social, political, and historical forces as men. They also see their lives as being inextricably interwoven with those of men.

Gender-based research on refugees and forced migration has necessarily emphasized the need to understand the special problems faced by women in processes of flight, resettlement, and exile. Facing many of the same risks and dangers in the processes as men, they are also subject to the additional dangers of sexual assault, exploitation, and neglect because of patriarchal ideologies that construct them as less valuable human beings (McSpadden and Moussa 1993; Moussa 1993). Forced migration frequently leads to situations in which women must confront a variety of new, gendered demands in order to survive and support their dependents. A gender-cognizant problematic and research strategies that fully take into account the special circumstances of women are therefore essential to develop policies that more effectively assist displaced and resettled people. While endorsing this approach, it is also important that gender-based analyses address the situation of men. Masculinity is no more a natural category than femininity, and an adequate understanding of forced migration must also take into account how both men and women represent and negotiate masculinity in the changed circumstances of forced migration.

Cultures of the Horn have quite clearly delineated male and female spaces that, broadly speaking, are common to many other cultures: men have primary access to 'public' space while women chiefly inhabit 'private' domestic spaces. However, neither this dichotomy nor actual practice are as distinct as they may seem. Lamphere (1993) and many contributors to this volume reject this public-private opposition as a conceptual trap, arguing that activities in the public sphere have an impact on domestic matters. Lamphere cites Reiter's (1975) observations of how men and women use public space differently in a French village and takes up Yanagisako's (1987) point that the dichotomy relies on a mixed metaphor of spatial and functional divisions.

One may also note that in Eritrea, the use of public space was circumscribed for both men and women by years of military occupation, curfews, repression, and the constant threat of violence. 'Traditional' behavior, already modified by urbanization and colonization, was greatly constrained by this situation. Within that context, women were not entirely absent from Eritrean public spaces but they did not always use them in the same way as men, and these traditional gendered divisions of space were strongly mediated by class, ethnicity, and geography. In urban areas, higher-class, educated women held administrative, teaching, and nursing positions, while those from lower classes either worked as maids, or in bars and restaurants, or sold agricultural products or alcohol in the markets. Rural women, in addition to tasks within the home, performed agricultural labor in the fields. While most of those who comprise the Eritrean diaspora in Canada come from urban areas, are educated, and have experience in white-collar occupations, links to rural communities and more traditional values remain strong. It is not surprising, therefore, that it is now considered acceptable for women to engage in certain forms of waged labor despite the persistence of broad gender divisions in the use of space: just as respectable women are expected not to frequent bars for social reasons or the community drop-in center, men do not often enter women's primary domain–the kitchen.

Forced migration did nevertheless alter the sense of gendered space. Many work outside the home to support themselves, their families and relatives. In some cases, this has required an extreme transgression of both space and morals, as some women have been forced into activities considered disreputable, such as prostitution (Kibreab 1995). Even elite, cosmopolitan women found their use of space transformed by forced migration, as they were often required to work for wages and to perform domestic tasks that in Eritrea had been done by servants. A few young women stated that they regarded waged employment as an opportunity that would allow them to live independently, with less supervision from relatives. In general, the use of public space by diaspora women continues to be circumscribed by the direct exertion of control by men and through rumor, gossip, and innuendo. One young university-educated woman described how her reputation suffered because she went alone to coffee shops and bars to discuss politics with Eritrean men. This indicates the disjuncture between formal expressions of support for policies of gender equality promoted by the nationalist movement and the continuing influence of cultural expectations about appropriate use of space–one of many such contradictions faced by both women and men.

As is true in many other societies, the various cultures of the Horn of Africa encode notions that essential differences exist between males and females, and it is commonly accepted that boys and girls should be raised differently. Most cultures of the region have a strong patriarchal orientation that relates power to biological sex and usually ensures that males have a higher status than females. The birth of a daughter is not celebrated to the same extent as that of a son. Women are widely regarded as less significant, less intelligent, and less deserving of equal rights. This is readily demonstrated by some of the common proverbs of the highland cultures of Eritrea and Ethiopia: "Just as there is no donkey with horns, so there is no woman with a brain"; "Women and donkeys need the stick." Before independence, women in Eritrea were excluded from inheritance of land and had fewer rights in marriage than men. Divorce was the prerogative of men, and remarriage was difficult in some groups, ultimately creating economic hardship for divorced women. While women do much of the domestic and subsistence labor, they are in many cases denied its fruits, eating last and least in times of food shortages. While women from some groups participated fully in agricultural production tasks, other groups restricted women almost entirely to the household sphere and circumscribed their movements within narrow limits.

The EPLF endorsed the emancipation of women and sought to implement measures that would increase their social and political participation. In the liberated areas held by the EPLF during the war, reforms were applied to practices involving land tenure, inheritance, and legal rights, and the EPLF encouraged development of a broadly based women's organization, the National Union of Eritrean Women (NUEW). NUEW operated chiefly within the liberated areas, but also made links with women in the diaspora, soliciting their support for development work, such as the construction of a small underground factory for sanitary towels. Following independence, NUEW became the first recognized NGO in the new state. NUEW activities and the participation of women as soldiers and technicians in the EPLF clearly validated key dimensions of women's participation in the diaspora—even if persistent gender divisions prevailed. Women, for example, actively participated in community social events to raise funds for the liberation movement, yet they prepared food in the kitchen while men organized the functions. Both men and women were equally welcome at most such community events, yet women often did not participate because of child care responsibilities; seating tended to be gender segregated, although not exclusively so. Women performed as singers while most musicians were male, with the exception of all-female EPLF bands visiting from Eritrea. Most political speeches at public events were delivered by men.

McSpadden and Moussa (1993) have commented on ways in which male and female Eritrean and Ethiopian refugees had different experiences of life in North America. Our research also indicates that for women (particularly those of a higher social class), forced migration sometimes offered opportunities for further education and for satisfying employment that enhanced their sense of personal capability and autonomy. New situations also encouraged new divisions of tasks and responsibilities within households: "At home, the father managed all the household money. Here, the man gives money to his wife for household management." Such new-found autonomy was not an automatic result of life in the diaspora, however, and some women lived a severely restricted existence in the home, with few friends or contacts.

In contrast to what were sometimes expanded opportunities and responsibilities for women, forced migration often meant that men's space was reduced. A lack of employment possibilities left them more often at home; men also entered unfamiliar domestic areas, learning to do laundry and to cook for themselves. In terms of both class and gender, men and women thus faced redefinitions of their roles. Some men found this difficult to take: "I really can't stand to see that" said one, referring to men in kitchens. Others reacted with more equanimity:

> I got laid off so my wife started to work. I couldn't get a certificate to work [in my field]. I had no papers from Ethiopia but I was allowed to take a qualifying exam. So I had to study while the kids were sleeping. I listened to a cassette when I was cooking. That was trial and error cooking, you can say....

Still other men were quite proud of their newly acquired domestic abilities and promoted more equitable relationships as desirable:

> Back home, men don't even know where the kitchen is. Here I cook and I look after the kids. Marriage is team-work; I think that's the best. You have to be open-minded. Some may like to sit and order people around because they grew up that way, but even the children criticize you if you do that here. My wife went on vacation to Las Vegas and I stayed here with the kids. I made the house clean for her when she came home. Some people may criticize me because as a husband I have become too Western. But later those same people may say it was a better way, [that] I was right.

At least publicly, Eritrean masculinity is categorized as exclusively heterosexual, and the topic of homosexuality is seldom discussed within the diaspora. It is apparently assumed (or at least, publicly argued) that this is an entirely Western phenomenon and that homosexuals do not exist among the population of the Horn. Homophobia is extensive, and no homosexual households were observed. We came across no individuals who were openly homosexual, and the majority of informants either denied that any Eritrean homosexuals existed or rejected this condition as unthinkable or shameful. Unfortunately, the circumstances of forced migration have led to a fusion of the homophobia that exists as an ideological component of various cultures from the Horn with North American homophobia (and certain related attitudes toward the body). This now circumscribes some of the cultural forms of expressiveness and physicality that had once existed as markers of closeness among male friends. Whereas it is common in some societies of the Horn for men to express friendship by hugging and holding hands, members of the diaspora communities were shocked to learn that Canadians might interpret these as homosexual overtures and warned friends not to engage in such behavior. In part, it is through the imposition of such restrictions on, and reconceptualizations of, what constitutes appropriate gender behavior that Canadian identities are grafted onto Eritrean ones.

Not surprisingly, double standards for sexuality exist for heterosexual women and men. In most cultures in the Horn, it is considered inappropriate for women to express sexual desires. A bride's virginity before marriage is expected and enforced through family supervision and control. Failure to meet this standard is grounds for divorce and a cause of dishonor to the family. These controls over women's sexuality both mark and sustain the powerlessness of young females. In various societies of the Horn, genital mutilation remains widespread as a means of controlling female sexuality and is seen as a method of ensuring family respectability and creating 'good women'. Both clitoridectomy and infibulation are widely practiced. Although the EPLF discouraged these procedures and banned them among its own troops, it did not attempt to outlaw the practice, arguing that such traditional behaviors were deeply rooted in the cultures of the region and could not be abolished by decree. Possibly, EPLF leaders also reasoned that such a ban would create animosity toward the organization. Some in the diaspora charged the new government with caving in to traditional values in order to avoid conflict over this and other issues of particular concern to women. The EPLF was not the only national liberation movement to have promoted the emancipation of women. In the eyes of many commentators, however, it was the most progressive of African or, indeed, Third World liberation movements.[3]

Women throughout the Horn also have been differentiated by class and ethnicity. In Ethiopia, the ruling elite of the highland Amhara and Tigrayan cultures dominated ethnically similar peasants, and also exerted hegemony over the Oromo majority and many other smaller cultural groups. Some argue that gender inequalities in other groups were the consequence of conquests carried out by highland groups and the imposition of their cultural forms. Others argue that the Oromos and other groups had equally hierarchical systems of gender stratification. It is noteworthy that some cultural groups in Eritrea, such as the matrilineal Kunama, have been organized on a different gender basis, with women enjoying more social rights. It is also noteworthy that these cultures have been among the most marginalized in Eritrea.

In contrast to the general circumstances of women throughout the Horn, the people who have enjoyed dominant positions in social life and have controlled both economic and political decision-making have been men, although obviously not all men have had equal shares in such power. While it is true that some women have exercised political power, this has typically been through and on behalf of their male relatives. The style and model of control of the state has been patriarchal, hierarchical, and rigid, with authority achieved in part through violence. This has also characterized family organization, with the male head exerting domination over both women and children. Because these forms of hierarchical power also flowed along the lines of class, ethnicity, and generation, not all women were or are natural allies.

Nevertheless, this provisional model of hierarchical gender relations identifies some of the significant dimensions of the experience of diaspora men and women—dimensions and experiences that varied according to the geographical and the social distances traveled. The variety of such experiences has significant implications for repatriation and resettlement, for both the original generation of migrants and their offspring. As noted, the majority of refugees from Eritrea and Ethiopia fled to the neighboring states of Djibouti, Somalia, and Sudan, with these states also producing their own outflows of refugees. While a few refugees in these countries were able to establish themselves in businesses such as transportation and to live in relative comfort, the majority of refugees faced impoverishment and an uncertain future, whether in camps or independently settled. Women in particular suffered from the loss of family-based economic support and from the imposition of local cultural norms. For example, some women from Christian cultures of the highlands who fled to primarily Islamic Sudan and Somalia, were forced to adopt forms of veiling and to abstain from productive activities they had undertaken in the past (Kibreab 1995).

For those who settled in North America, traditional, patriarchal gender ideologies that had been a convention of social organization faced significant challenges. In general, North American systems of gender relations offered greater liberality in employment, education, use of public space, and so on; and Western feminism offered a much different analysis of gender relations than many had previously seen. Of course, there was no neat dichotomy to be made here between Eritrean and North American societies. As noted, most diaspora individuals came from urban areas, where they had already partially abandoned rigidly patriarchal gender relations. Furthermore, the EPLF's political ideology, including its expressed support for women's emancipation and social participation, was a key structural feature of the distinct cultural system (the *mieda* culture of the *tegadelti*, the EPLF fighters) that evolved in 'the field'. This system also evolved in diaspora communities, so these developments were not necessarily more 'advanced' in North America. For example, when female EPLF fighters visited North America to solicit diaspora support, they expressed disappointment at the extent of sexism they encountered there and at women's lack of power. This is but one illustration of the ways in which the nationalist movement exerted a major influence on the diaspora communities through its propaganda efforts and 'mass organizations' abroad. These communities contributed financially to the EPLF and regularly attended public events organized under its auspices. Although people undoubtedly enjoyed the purely social aspects of these events, they also paid diligent attention to speeches and reports on military and political developments. These events typically included silent commemoration of 'martyrs' who had been killed in battle, and the *tegadelti* were publicly honored as heroes and moral exemplars. Activists in the diaspora described their efforts to emulate the spirit of service, sacrifice, and self-reliance of the *tegadelti*, including a more egalitarian conceptualization of appropriate gender relationships.

In this respect, the progressive ideology of the EPLF may have had a much more structured, sustained, and significant impact on diaspora gender relationships than did North American feminists, who were often described as intrusive, frivolous, and irrelevant to the practical concerns of Eritrean women. One recurrent criticism was that North American feminism is not adequately sensitive to racism, which informants found to be a new and disturbing experience. While noting the severely repressive gender bias in Eritrean cultures, other women objected to feminists who presented men one-dimensionally as enemies. The experiences of the younger generation of Eritrean-Canadians raised in Canada are, of course, somewhat different. For them, community events are now less often structured around crises such as war and starvation, which mobilized the older diaspora population over the last three decades. For them also, gender more deeply reflects North American attitudes, popular culture, and mass media. Obviously, their attitudes frequently clash with their parents' values.

In overview, refugee men and women were caught up in both the immediate material demands of exile and the clash of various conceptions of appropriate gender relations. Men whose self-images had been shaped by patriarchal gender ideologies in the Horn found these images challenged both by the EPLF's political ideology and by images of North American male behavior (from personal experience and media images). This led to a variety of responses, with some men asserting the superiority of their own cultural values and others finding reason for their modification. Some men found their identities (emphasizing authority and the desirability of economic autonomy and control) profoundly threatened by new conditions of life in exile. Many men experienced a sharp loss of status, especially relating to employment: some who had occupied highly prestigious government, bureaucratic, and professional positions now faced unemployment and dependence on welfare. Both conditions were regarded as demeaning and degrading, and conflicted with prevailing Eritrean constructions of masculinity. They also contradicted the strong work ethic that pervaded the Eritrean-Canadian community, which was based both on traditional precepts and the EPLF's ideology of self-reliance. Other men found that their previous skills and credentials were not recognized and were thus forced to take jobs they considered beneath their dignity. In this regard, McSpadden (1989a; this volume) notes that Ethiopian refugees in the US believed that they were entitled to 'good' jobs, and highlights the stress resulting from demands placed on them to take available jobs that did not meet these expectations.

Many Eritrean men in Canada also faced the loss of status attendant to unemployment or underemployment. However, unlike those in McSpadden's study, many professional class exiles assumed menial positions, hoping that such arrangements would be temporary. Likewise, many Eritrean women in Canada grudgingly took on work as cleaners regardless of their educational qualifications. Many such men and women consoled themselves with the idea that they would return to Eritrea (and to their prior statuses) once independence had been achieved. After liberation, these individuals faced extremely difficult decisions. Eritrea was devastated by war, and many people faced shortages in housing and other vital services. Some men felt they nevertheless would have more personal options if they were to return, but realized that their families would suffer. One woman, whose husband wanted to return to Eritrea, worried about the educational opportunities for her children there: "I'm killing my husband for the sake of my children."

Women's transition to exile was also affected by their class position in Eritrea. Some women had servants and nannies to do domestic work there, and others were actively in business. Like their male counterparts, most of the female informants who had attended college or university abroad found that their achievements received little recognition in Canada. Consequently, they felt compelled to enroll in the Canadian education system at levels they had already surpassed, or to accept menial jobs as cleaners, custodians, or laundry workers–jobs which some women (and men) perceived as unsuitable and degrading. Many women today are angry, although often quietly so. Education for both males and females has been emphasized strongly in the Eritrean diaspora beyond its use to gain better, higher status jobs for themselves and their immediate households. Informants frequently claimed that relatives in Eritrea and scattered abroad depended on them for financial support, providing both an incentive to achieve more in terms of education and employment, and an obstacle to such achievement, as many directed their energy to work that presented the greatest and most immediate flow of cash.

Another important pressure on exiles in Canada was the expectations of relatives and others that they would improve themselves by taking advantage of the (sometimes imaginary) opportunities. The EPLF, too, strongly encouraged those in the diaspora to educate themselves so that they could eventually return with skills and knowledge useful to the reconstruction of Eritrea. This complex of expectations sometimes led exiles into conflict with Canadian government officials and counselors, who emphasized immediate employment of any type. Such insistence was shaped by both bureaucratic agendas and stereotyped expectations of refugee gender and 'race'. Such confrontations created a sense of crisis for many, in which gender, 'race', and class intersected in complex ways, and in which individuals' sense of personal power and control over the future was threatened.

The outcome of these negotiations also had serious economic implications. In some cases, economic uncertainty, lack of (even unsuitable) employment, recourse to welfare (often accompanied by a sense of failure, inadequacy, and shame), and the psychological stress associated with exile, adaptation to a new culture, and loss of status led to attempts by men to strengthen traditional forms of hierarchy and dominance within the family. This sometimes erupted into violence directed against women and children. Indeed, some men experienced status loss and marginality explicitly related to changes in family-based gender roles. Women in the diaspora often worked outside the home for wages, sometimes earning more than their husbands or providing the family's sole source of income. To some men, this presented a threat to the traditional image of the male as provider. In other cases, this contributed to a greater sense of women's autonomy and to increased participation by women in family decision-making. While some husbands adjusted to this with relative equanimity and a sense of common purpose, others were deeply resentful and strongly criticized the growing independence of Eritrean women in North America. What they saw as a lack of appropriate submission to male authority often was attributed to the negative influence of Western feminism, conceived of in its most radical, oversimplified, and caricatured forms:

> The main problem is with the women. The women get educated and now they aren't following our culture. Now they want to be equal to the man. Some of them can't even write their name but they want to be equal. This has happened since they came to Canada. They don't want to follow our culture anymore. It's because of the feminists and because of the way of life here in Canada.

Men who maintained this position and often also supported nationalist movements that espoused policies of female emancipation and social equality found themselves facing (or rather, attempting to evade) an uncomfortable paradox: publicly endorsing politically based ideologies of gender equality while enforcing male authority in their own homes and personal relationships. Such paradoxes were not the sole preserve of the rural and ill-educated. For example, one university-educated Eritrean informant employed in a high-status profession in Canada epitomized reactionary Eritrean views of coercive male sexuality by stating that a man should not believe a woman who said "no" to sex because her protestations would merely be culturally standard mechanisms of guaranteeing her status as a 'good' woman—not genuine indications of lack of consent.

Moreover, it seems that a number of men did not regard diaspora women as suitable marriage-mates: they were too emancipated, too North American. Several women also believed that some men viewed diaspora women as 'damaged goods' due to the exigencies of refugee flight (namely rape and other forms of coerced sexual activity). While no male informant ever directly stated such a view, these ideas did circulate among men. During most of the 1980s, women were in short supply in the Eritrean and Ethiopian diaspora communities. Even so, most men preferred to date (and certainly to marry) someone of the same ethnic origin. This was both a personal choice, based on the ease of communication and sense of comfort that comes with shared understandings of the world, and an explicitly stated commitment to group maintenance. Only a few men married outside their specific ethnic communities, and they found that their marriages met with disapproval by others in the group. Regardless of whether their wives were from other parts of the world, from other ethnic groups of the Horn, or Canadian born, some men found themselves ostracized and alienated from their peers.

As we have seen earlier, many men fled Eritrea on their own and, separated from their old social relationships, endured prolonged social isolation in Canada. Particularly during the early days of resettlement in Canada, a large number of young, single Eritrean men experienced profound loneliness and anxiety about their inability to fulfill cultural expectations about marriage; and yet, marriage outside the group was widely regarded as undesirable. Even after the number of diaspora women had increased in the late 1980s, some men looked only to the Horn for suitable mates rather than to those who might be available in North America. Indeed, after independence a number of men returned to Eritrea or to Ethiopia specifically to search for suitable wives: those who would more closely conform to the ideal of the traditional, submissive woman. Some men also took advantage of their proclaimed higher status (not always accurately represented) as Canadian residents to obtain younger, attractive brides; others sought to use their Canadian status to marry into wealthier or more prestigious families in Eritrea.

And yet there was much disapproving comment about this practice. Some informants cited these efforts as illustrative of the persistence of 'backward' gender attitudes. Some also said that a number of men who undertook such bride-hunting expeditions did so with the expectation that they would gain in status within the Eritrean-Canadian community by obtaining a traditional, younger, wealthier, or higher status 'trophy' bride in Eritrea. It was suggested that some men sought young, attractive 'ornamental' women with little education in the expectation that they would act as subservient wives and bestow higher status on their husbands; the same informants indicated that what many of these men actually received was not increased status and prestige, but ridicule. Some diaspora women saw these bride-hunting expeditions as direct personal criticism, perceiving themselves as having been consciously rejected for being less traditional or authentic. Both female and male informants complained that this practice was a disrespectful rejection of women who lived outside Eritrea and who were seen as too old, Westernized, or liberated. A number of men in Eritrea in search of traditional brides acted in irresponsible and selfish ways that were widely reported in Canada and that offended community sensibilities. The EPLF itself criticized such men for their actions, and in various Eritrean-Canadian communities they were widely regarded as fools. In fact, when some of these marriages subsequently failed, reactions did not follow tradition. Separation and divorce are usually regarded as an extremely unfortunate last resort in Eritrea. Even so, these men received little sympathy when their marriages dissolved; they were thought to have deserved what they got.

Some diaspora women also considered returning to Eritrea to find appropriate mates, where the response to their inquiries was strongly gendered. Although their permanent resident status in Canada must have had some appeal to prospective husbands who sought to maximize their own chances of emigration, these women also faced a number of constraints not encountered by men. Since the active pursuit of a husband would be a violation of cultural expectations, marriages would have to be arranged for these women by others. Sometimes, there were negative connotations attached to women living abroad, including notions that they were sexually promiscuous or too independent and uncontrollable. Furthermore, many women faced contradictory and impossible demands from relatives: to marry and perform the traditional family roles that followed, while also continuing to support relatives around the world.

Reconceptualizing Household Gender Relations: Masculinity and Power

Largely under the impact of feminist analyses, there has been a reconsideration of the conventional image of the household as a site of unity and harmonious interests and objectives (Moore 1988). Overall, this has provided a useful corrective to a wide range of oversimplifications. In abandoning consensus for conflicting models of the household, there is a danger of substituting one stereotype for another and of overlooking the greater complexity and contradictions that exist in everyday family life. In the conflict model of the household, family relationships sometimes seem to resemble zones of hostility, dominance, and power relations, while mutual support and companionship disappear. Acknowledging the existence of patriarchal ideologies of source and host social contexts and appreciating that these ideologies can be exacerbated by forced migration, we should also be aware of exceptions to these tendencies. It is important to point out that the maintenance or amplification of some of these patterns are only *some* of the possible outcomes of the social forces and ideological operations involved; analysis should neither pathologize nor homogenize this population, which is as varied as any other. Many gendered family relationships are not characterized simply by force and domination but rather present many instances of cooperation, mutual respect, support, and friendship. Redefinitions of gender roles among the diaspora population most certainly were shaped by practical constraints that led to the loss of economic control over the household by some men, more financial independence for some women, legal prohibitions against formerly accepted practices, the absence of other family members, and the pervasiveness of alternative media images.

It is equally true that ideologies of female emancipation and women's equality promoted by liberation movements were taken seriously by many individuals, and some men made determined efforts to adapt them to their own personal lives. In the opinion of some Eritrean women, though, the proportion of such men is too small and their efforts are still woefully inadequate. Nevertheless, it is significant to note the steps that these men have taken to reject patriarchal images and to recreate themselves anew. Modern, progressive attitudes are not held exclusively by North Americans, and it is equally important to stress that these men are not mechanically emulating North American ideas about 'liberated masculinity'; this reconception of masculinity is also a product of intellectual and political engagement with philosophies of national liberation and with the concrete and sometimes mundane circumstances of life in exile. At the same time, attempts to reconceptualize masculinity are trivialized and opposed by more traditional men who are perhaps threatened by the suggestion that they might have to change also.

There is a parallel here among diaspora women, many of whom are concerned about emancipating themselves but are also suspicious of solutions offered by North American feminism. They seem particularly critical of what they see as the antagonistic models constructed by some Western feminists. Diasporic Eritrean women are actively trying to construct emancipatory models that derive from their own experience; models that are inclusive of men and do not characterize them as an essential Other. These women quite remarkably downplay the extremely oppressive situations that they faced as women in Eritrea. Here, too, liberation ideologies have been significant. It is therefore necessary to reject Western gender ideologies as progressive, modern exemplars to be emulated by the more undeveloped people of the Third World.

Conclusion

For female and male Eritrean-Canadians, refugee flight and life in exile present many new role requirements and demands. Reactions to these new roles and responsibilities vary. Just as feminist theory now stresses that the generalized category of 'women' is not unproblematic, so we may recognize that the category 'men' is also internally divided, both generally and in this case. For example, some men found themselves facing a contradiction between traditional ideologies of male superiority and dominance, and the EPLF's ideology of gender equality. Not all of these conflicted men have resolved this challenge in the same way. Other men felt no such contradiction in the first place. In this regard, it is important to contest the common assumption that Eritrean (or all 'Third World') men are embedded in patriarchal ideologies to a much greater extent and more uniformly than supposedly liberated, enlightened, and variable North Americans. This reproduces a highly political narrative of a 'civilizing mission' under Western tutelage in which Third World women will be rescued from the oppressive traditions imposed by Third World men. Rejecting this narrative does not require one to overlook the actual subordination of women where this does occur or, as in this case, to deny that patriarchal attitudes and structures remain extremely strong in the communities under discussion. Neither does it require one to exaggerate the degree of diaspora support for women's emancipation and equality. What it does oblige one to do is to reject a number of unhelpful essentialisms and binary oppositions, to recognize the actual diversity of male attitudes and actions, and to acknowledge the existence of profound relationships of solidarity and mutual support forged in refugee and exile conditions of almost unspeakable intensity. In fact, male attitudes and actions varied considerably within these communities, and sometimes changed over time, as noted throughout this chapter.

Forced migration and exile in Canada also led to the renegotiation of women's gender roles and beliefs. It has been increasingly recognized that female refugees endure the usual hardships associated with flight compounded by threats of rape and other forms of sexual victimization. In addition, as Colson (this volume) amply demonstrates in her longitudinal analysis of Gwembe Tonga developmentally forced migrants, women refugees may be more disadvantaged due to a lack of resources, skills, and experiences, or because gendered constraints do not let them maximize these things to the same extent as men. In Sudan, for example, a number of desperately impoverished Eritrean women refugees had little option but to enter into prostitution. Many of the Eritrean women who have migrated to Canada possess a greater number of skills and found a broader range of opportunities for education or employment than the typical Eritrean refugee in Africa–male or female. In assessing their situation in exile, many younger women have concluded that life in Canada could offer them greater opportunities in these areas and more personal freedom. Although this was most immediately apparent for those urbanized, educated women who were able to pursue their careers in Canada, we found that those women who obtained employment in menial positions such as cleaners typically perceived themselves as having a broader range of options as a result of immigration. Even so, this was not the only view expressed, nor was this position experienced in an unambiguous way when it was held. Many women, particularly single mothers, relied on welfare or meager incomes as menial laborers while shouldering an unrealistic range of domestic responsibilities. These women, like others who emigrated under more fortunate circumstances, were also cut off from the social support system of relatives, friends, and neighbors who could have assisted them in Eritrea.

To conclude, 'the' exile household offers a rich site for investigating the renegotiation of gendered relationships. However, investigators cannot hope to proceed far if they rely on stereotypical models of the household. In the past, analyses rendered key gender relations invisible by characterizing the household as fully integrated when its members have common interests and goals (see Indra, this volume). The same danger exists in using a model which imagines the household as a site of conflicting interests and objectives. In the case of the Eritrean-Canadian diaspora, the latter approach also conflicts with the self-perceptions of informants. Almost uniformly, informants saw the household in an essentially positive manner, and violence and serious conflicts of interest were not viewed as inevitable. They likewise objected to Western feminists' adversarial models of gender relations. Discomfort with such an oppositional model is apparent even as women comment on their unequal status:

> We don't necessarily want to be like the feminists in the West. Many times, we have different concerns and a different struggle. We don't see

men as the enemy. It's true that women are not treated as equals and we want to change that. But it is a process of educating the men. They will also benefit from our liberation.

Notes

1. This research has been supported by three grants from the Social Sciences and Humanities Research Council of Canada, whose assistance we gratefully acknowledge.
2. It has also been subject to constructive criticism. Among the important criticisms that have been raised include essentialism, the tendency for some women (variously identified as white, First World, Northern, middle-class) to define and manage the agenda for other women (variously defined as black, Third World, Southern, working-class), and the propensity for feminism to duplicate the ethnocentric operations of earlier colonial discourse (Ong 1988; Chakravorty Spivak 1987; Young 1990).
3. In other countries, women gained or were promised much during decolonization and national liberation struggles only to see their progress rolled back after independence was achieved at the state level (see also Matlou, this volume). It is too soon to know to what degree the EPLF's ideology of women's emancipation and gender equality was a fundamental component of its social revolution and to what degree it was merely instrumental or opportunistic.

14

Negotiating Masculinity in the Reconstruction of Social Place

Eritrean and Ethiopian Refugees in the United States and Sweden

Lucia Ann McSpadden

Introduction

This chapter explores the challenges to masculine identity experienced by a selected group of Ethiopian and Eritrean men in the United States and Sweden by virtue of being refugees.[1] Their varied and situational responses provide a view of efforts to reconstruct a coherent identity as men, an identity that may provide positive meaning and dignity within a harsh reality of usually forced choices. As such, this chapter is a point of departure for understanding the gendered nature of these men's particular experience, of the refugee experience itself, and of the multiple layers and sites of relationships that shape the social reconstruction of masculine identity of these persons as men and as refugees. Longitudinal data highlight the long-term significance to these men of resisting perceived subordination and loss of respect, of exerting control, and of having experiences of power and choice when faced with the often confusing and risk-filled situations inherent in developing a sense of belonging in a new sociocultural context.

Moussa (1993) and I have elsewhere argued that the refugee experience in all its phases is importantly gendered. As Indra asserts (this volume):

... that neither in talk, research, analysis, policy, nor programming can 'gender' be equated solely with women, nor solely with women's activities, beliefs, goals, or needs ... 'gender' is instead a key *relational* dimension of human activity and thought–activity and thought informed by cultural and individual notions of men and women–having consequences for their social or cultural positioning and the ways in which they experience and live their lives.

My earlier research explored the effect of US government resettlement policy on the psychological well-being of Ethiopian and Eritrean male refugees (McSpadden 1989a, 1991). During this research, I became increasingly aware of the effect of these policies upon refugees *as men*, and I began to explore linkages between 'refugeeness', identity, and gender. Collaborative, comparative analysis with Moussa, who has worked closely with Eritrean and Ethiopian women in Canada, illuminated further the diverse gendered experiences of these refugees as women and as men (1993, 1996).[2]

And yet I continue to have questions about the gendered nature of men's refugee experience. If the "relational dimension" of gender is understood to be based centrally upon relations between women and men, then what of the majority of Ethiopian and Eritrean refugees in North America who are young men, alone, without close family or other kin, without many female countrypersons?[3] For example, would relationships with, or images of, non-Ethiopian or -Eritrean women and/or men become more salient? What elements of the host culture would come to be important in gendered identity? How does gendered identity involve types of relationships other than male-female? Are we stuck theoretically in essentialist dichotomies which mask more complex social realities, as Cornwall and Lindisfarne (1994a: 2–3) assert?

Individual-level gendered phenomena must be understood contextually. The immediate experiences of refugees must therefore be a primary field of analysis. Here, issues of power and differential access to societal resources come immediately to the fore. In fact, much of the social complexity of how gender and the refugee experience are intertwined relate to power and control. Being male is often associated with having power to dominate others (cf. Carrigan et al. 1985)–and the strongly patriarchal cultures of the Horn of Africa are consistent in their higher valuation of men. There, this commonly translates into social, economic, and political benefits. As refugees involved in resettlement, both men and women are often inserted into the society in subordinate, dependent, and relatively powerless socioeconomic positions.

This is not to suggest that refugees do not actively shape salient aspects of their lives. Indeed, the choices which they make can be life

determining. At the same time, few can determine the overall context in which they operate. Their resettlement experience is powerfully shaped by governmental policies and programs and informed
by the cultural values and norms of the receiving society. Refugee
choices are typically very constrained; their options are constructed
and shaped by systems over which they have little control or influence. An important research challenge is, consequently, to clarify the
nature of the choices available, the outcomes desired by refugees
themselves, and the limitations they experience, and to determine
how choices might be exercised (cf. Bach 1993).

In linking gender with struggles to reconstruct social identity or
with experiences of unequal power relationships, one must continually ask which context is relevant to refugees: the native country, the
country of resettlement, the broader society, the home? The attachment of migrants and others to places, and of cultures to bounded
territories is often assumed. It should not be, for both are outcomes
to be explained in terms of the gendered politics of space. Since
refugees are by definition forced migrants who have been physically, socially, and culturally displaced, the foci of the analysis must
also be transnational *and* gendered. To put the question simply: In
what ways might a man's identity become transnational?

In my previous work (McSpadden and Moussa 1993, 1996), it was
stated that "two interrelated issues critical to a gender analysis of the
development of social place emerged: power and belonging" (1996:
9). What are salient sites of belonging and of power? Given that gender is a context-specific sociocultural construction, how does being
an Ethiopian or Eritrean particularize the gendered experience of
these men? Additionally, the first groups of male refugees were often
highly educated, which conferred high social status in the Horn of
Africa. Such achieved statuses are problematized in flight and resettlement. Being 'black' in a racially sensitive host society, which is
socially constructed to reward being 'white', raises further issues of
power and belonging.

'Refugeeness' is an experience characterized by flight, force, fear,
struggle for control over basic life issues, and especially ambiguity.
In contrast to some analysts who posit a linear progression (cf. Berry
1991), I suggest that in this instance 'the' refugee experience is
processual, composed of multiple and sometimes overlapping phases.
As Roger Zetter notes, the refugee experience is a continuing, evolving process, which "may simultaneously create a parallel structure of
'new' and powerful agendas ..." (1988: 102). Such new or emerging
agendas become part of the experience itself and are important to
the understanding of refugees' gendered struggles to develop a

meaningful social place. Gendered issues and constructions that are salient during one phase–for example, during flight–are replaced in subsequent phases by others as people face new challenges, such as the attainment of economic self-sufficiency. Yet these very basic life issues must be addressed in a cultural and social milieu that is essentially unfamiliar: it is uncharted territory. Some analysts have characterized this experience as a forced and rapid desocialization requiring the individual to learn to perform 'new' social roles and to grapple with rebuilding one's cognitive map in order to make effective sense of an unfamiliar social and cultural context (Eisenstadt 1954; Hansen 1981; Rumbaut 1985). The alternative is to play badly a role in a drama which one does not comprehend, predictably resulting in an assault on mental health.

Gender is embedded everywhere in the social relationships of community for Eritreans at home and in the US. But for the latter, 'community' is deeply compromised and must be redeveloped. A loss of power and control is intertwined with this loss of community and social support, so rebuilding social statuses, relationships, and community is problematic. It is nevertheless an intentional process, available to individual reflection, that restructures power differences. Central to these objectives is the concept of 'social place', the place of the individual in the sociocultural system and the urgent need of refugees to develop or gain a sense of belonging, a sense of 'home' (see Gómez and Giles, this volume).

In my previous research (McSpadden and Moussa 1993), North American refugees spoke insistently about the need to rebuild and reshape what they had lost. Grounded in their cultural identities, actively contesting the roles assigned to them in resettlement, they were at the same time forging new identities in North America. Subsequent interviews with Eritreans and Ethiopians in Sweden reveal the same struggle to build meaningful identities and relationships within the new society–relationships that 'work' in their land of resettlement and yet are congruent with their extant values and beliefs (cf. Glick-Schiller, Basch, and Blanc-Szanton 1992; Sutton 1992).

As Bennett (1993: 39) notes, "One's self is both a cultural product and a producer of the meanings that constitute cultural patterns ... people consciously select and integrate culturally disparate aspects of their identities." The individual is being challenged to integrate multiple frames of reference in which (s)he is "always in the process of becoming *a part of* and *apart from* a given cultural context" (emphasis in the original). Bennett asserts that in order to be able to make choices in such a confusing context an individual must be able to make effective contextual evaluations leading to intentionally chosen behaviors (1993: 42–43). The ability to make effective contextual evaluations is especially important for refugees who perceive themselves as having been oppressed and constrained, possibly in both their country of origin and their host country. Such evaluations may enable the individual to recognize, reject, and resist oppressive elements in society without rejecting it wholesale.[4] Refugees, as women and as men, experience and attempt to shape their realities in accord with cultural and subcultural frames of meaning, previous socialization, and expectations for the future. They do so within the constraints of their immediate context. All of these factors, of course, are gendered.

Implicit in developing identities and social places that link the country of origin and the country of resettlement is the question of social differentiation: How has the resettlement experience reinforced, elaborated, or changed the social-structural relationships of these men? Do they feel that they are fully members of the same social groups or class as they were in their country of origin? How do they renegotiate group membership and form new bases for social associations. As Cornwall and Lindisfarne (1994b: 15) note:

> ... each episode [in life] is part of a continuing process whereby people negotiate relative positions of power as individuals and as representatives of social categories such as those based on gender, age, class or ethnicity ... at different stages in the process of negotiating masculinities ... attributions of masculinity can and do change radically.[5]

As Gilmore (1990: 3–6) claims, "Every social situation is an occasion for identity work" in which individuals negotiate masculinity.

In summary, the processual and shifting nature of the refugee experience is dialectically related to the situational and relational construction of gender. My research focus contextualized choice-making and power, which leads me to address the following here:

1. Do these refugee men have clear priorities regarding power, and, if so, do these priorities change over time?
2. What does power symbolize to these men who are, as refugees, typically powerless? How do they experience subordination and how do they resist it? Is perceived subordination related to social class or other factors within the Ethiopian and Eritrean culture?
3. How do relations with women enter into the dynamics of power for these men? Are these affected by their ascribed or achieved status within the Ethiopian and Eritrean contexts?

4. What does it mean to be a 'successful man'? Which groups are salient in understanding oneself as a success or as a failure? How do factors such as family, economic or political status, education, religious affiliation, age, and urban/rural differences affect these assessments?
5. If power implies the ability to control significant aspects of one's life, what factors are salient?
6. How does being perceived as 'black' in various contexts affect these men?

Eritrean and Ethiopian Cultural Themes: Masculinity and Power

Ethiopian history, including the forcible annexation of Eritrea in 1962, has been characterized by struggles of various emperors to establish hegemony over diverse and scattered peoples. These struggles, often enacted along linguistic, ethnic, religious, and regional lines, have been exacerbated by a rugged terrain that separates peoples and regions (cf. Levine 1974). The societies that are now encompassed by the Ethiopian and Eritrean states are linguistically and ethnically complex. Considering both, approximately equal percentages of Muslims and Christians (slightly less than 49 percent each) live together with groups of traditional African animists. The more powerful settled agriculturalists of the highlands live a markedly different life from the agropastoralists and nomadic-pastoralists of the lowlands. Eritrea is much smaller than Ethiopia but has similar religious and ethnolinguistic diversity, although it is not as strongly coupled to political agendas as in Ethiopia. There, the success of the liberation struggle, which united the Eritrean people in a common cause (albeit through internal armed conflict between the ELF and the EPLF), generated a pervasive commitment to national identity and unity that has continued six years after liberation.

Social power and access to societal resources in Eritrea and Ethiopia have historically followed ethnic, religious, and regional lines, both for women and men. For centuries, highland Amhara and Tigrayan cultures prevailed over other cultural groups, and key privileges like education and governmental employment were unequally held by these highland peoples. Likewise, Coptic Christians typically had had significantly more access to such privileges than Muslims and animists. Overlaid on this structure was profound class inequality within most groups and populations. Even today, within specific ethnic, religious, and class contexts, the highest social value in Ethiopian and Eritrean society (especially among Amharic and Tigrayan groups) is assigned to men.[6] Ideas of masculinity draw their strength from a high valuation of respect, honor, and authority (Giorgis 1984; Pankhurst 1990) and emphasize aggression, a type of competitive social 'merit system', and community judgment of personal failure and consequent shame (Levine 1974: 47, 203). With some exceptions, this is a pan-Ethiopian value system that, broadly speaking, cuts across ethnic, religious, class, linguistic, and regional categories (Levine 1965, 1974).

Ethiopian and Eritrean societies traditionally strongly ascribe key statuses on the basis of gender and family. These dimensions transcend ethnic, class, and religious differentiations. There is consequently a male preoccupation with fine gradations of power, authority, and honor, and with the maintenance and improvement of one's position. Gilmore goes so far as to describe this as a "win-lose" contest (1990:13–14) in which men fear public failure and loss of honor and power. For Ethiopians and Eritreans: "... [achieving] the male gender ideals of personal autonomy, masculine honor, and prestige–all available for public scrutiny and evaluation–protects both respect for the individual man as well as the family's and group's reputation" (McSpadden and Moussa 1993: 211). In this way, masculinity is intricately linked to the social well-being of the family. Community acknowledgement of a 'successful male', both validates a man's identity and accords him and his family a higher social status (Levine 1965: 104–5; Giorgis 1984).

Many have noted (Cichon et al. 1986; Center for Applied Linguistics 1981; Giorgis 1984; Levine 1965; Tebeje 1989) the exceptionally high cultural value given to education in Ethiopia and Eritrea. Education is now seen as a pathway to high-status employment and community respect; it is a contemporary sought-after means to personal and family *achievement* in a chiefly status-by-ascription society. Education-based social mobility is gendered. Statistics from Ethiopia and Eritrea consistently show that men of all groups and regions have significantly greater access to education (see Almaz Eshete 1991a, 1991b; Gennet Zewdie 1991; Levine 1974). It also is much more often accessed by those with means in towns and cities. The 'typical' educated young person from Eritrea or Ethiopia would likely be an urban, Christian male from a family of high social status and economic class.

My original research focused on single male refugees from Ethiopia and Eritrea, and was carried out in the western US during 1982 to 1989 (McSpadden 1987, 1989a, 1989b).[7] At that time I was employed by a national voluntary agency contracted by the US Department of

State to resettle refugees. As refugee concerns coordinator, part of my responsibility was to develop refugee sponsorships within US voluntary associations. I was initially motivated to undertake this research by the greater difficulty–in the judgment of agency staff and volunteers–that Eritrean and Ethiopian men were having in their resettlement experience, as compared with other refugee populations in the US. Agency staff and volunteers consistently discussed Eritrean men's depression and apparent mental illness, their resistance to employment training and to low-status work, their complaints about the difficulty of low-level tasks, their anger and suicide (West 1987a, 1987b; Van Prang 1986; Giorgis 1984).

My work eventually revealed significant variations in both the perceived and actual behaviors of these men. At times they were reported as being angry, hostile, volatile, threatening, stubborn, and difficult. By way of contrast, they were also reported to be shy, soft-spoken, diffident, hesitant to be assertive on their own behalf, and dependent upon Americans for help. I found that these perceptual differences were related to substantive differences in their resettlement experience, differences related to unequal access to social resources for economic self-sufficiency, and to their perceived and real potential for status mobility. Building upon this work, Moussa and I then did a comparative gender analysis of our separately derived US and Canadian data followed by another comparative study of the decision-making of Eritrean women and men regarding the issue of returning to Eritrea after independence. Subsequently, as part of a separate study for the Life and Peace Institute, Uppsala, Sweden, I traveled to Eritrea, where I met with returnees from the West. Long-term refugee residents in Sweden were interviewed about their current connections with Eritrea as well as the possibilities of their return to their native land.

A Profile of Migrant Men

Approximately 1.25 million Ethiopians/Eritreans were refugees in 1991, just prior to the liberation of Eritrea. Of these, 23,500 had been granted resettlement in the US since 1980 (US Committee for Refugees 1991: 10–11). Ethiopians represented but 2.7 percent of refugee admissions to the US during 1983–92 (US Office of Refugee Resettlement 1993: 18).[8] By the standards of Ethiopian and Eritrean society, the men first interviewed in the US represented for the most part an educated elite. They were also young, ranging from nineteen to thirty-six years of age, and predominately urban; 84 percent had completed at least seventh grade (on a scale that ranged from "no education" to "postuniversity"), while less than one percent of their age cohort in Ethiopia and Eritrea had done so (Levine 1974). Fifty-three percent had been students before fleeing Ethiopia/Eritrea; and 7 percent were professionals. The occupation of their fathers indicated a comparatively high social status in Ethiopia and Eritrea: 64 percent were sons of government officials, judges, professors, teachers, lawyers, large landowners, or military officers. The remainder were sons of farmers or small businessmen. Almost two-thirds of the men were functional in English. Given that they had been in the US for less than two years, a remarkable 78 percent were employed at least part-time.

They also faced a number of disabilities. These new immigrants were without close families. Small and scattered across the US, Eritrean communities were also fragmented by political, ethnic, and linguistic differences: Amhara, Tigrinya speakers (Ethiopian and Eritrean), Sidamo, Tigre, Beni Amir, Oromo, Muslim and Christian (including Jehovah's Witnesses), highlanders and lowlanders. Those who had been students had little work experience. The skills they did have were not easily transferable to the US work environment. Their employment in the US was so marginal financially that only 8 percent could afford to live alone. Additionally, these men often faced racial discrimination. Subsequent interviewing years later, when the men had been in the US from two to eleven years, showed considerable improvement. All were working at least part-time, and most were combining work with school. One had recently completed a university course in hotel management; another had just finished medical training and was working at two professional jobs. Some men had brothers and sisters with them or lived with wives and children who had joined them from either Sudan or Ethiopia/Eritrea. One had traveled back to Ethiopia, married, and returned with his wife.

The general situation of Ethiopians and Eritreans interviewed in Sweden was quite similar. Although these men were somewhat older than their American counterparts (ranging from twenty-eight to fifty-one years of age), all had completed at least high school; some were university graduates. Their backgrounds were similar to the men in the US. All were functional in Swedish having been in Sweden for a minimum of nine years. Most could also speak English. All were employed in some capacity. Of the small number of Eritrean returnees interviewed in Eritrea (seven men and one woman) all but one had postsecondary education and had been employed in the US, Germany, or Sweden prior to their return. They had all been in

Eritrea less than two years, yet five had secured professional or government work, two (including the woman) had opened businesses, while the other was continuing his schooling.

Migrant Priorities

Sartot Mablat *(Having Worked, to Eat): Independence and Self-Reliance*

Men's responses to Cantril's Self-Anchoring Scale were very consistent. Almost all of the men identified issues related to becoming self-sufficient, noting: "I have a good job" or "I can support myself." Others commented that they were "Being independent: not being a burden," or "Going to school" as they wanted "To succeed by my own efforts." The consistency of the men's responses here may reveal values that transcend group and class differences and that appear to be deeply embedded in Ethiopian and Eritrean cultures. Interview data showed that men were intensely focused upon getting an education that would, in turn, produce good jobs, status, money, and respect. Then they could "truly be an adult man." For most, an ideal 'good job' was one that conferred high status in Ethiopia and Eritrea.

These men also reported high stress (on the Goldberg questionnaire), and they strongly indicated that they currently had a "bad life" exemplified by being underemployed, unemployed, or on welfare. There was much concern expressed over working at low-status and/or manual labor jobs. Men also indicated concern with being dependent, and appearing "to be a beggar."[9] Here, the comparatively high status or class of the men in their homeland, both in terms of education achieved and of their fathers' occupations, appeared to dramatically affect the men's perception of a good or bad life as well as their judgment of how to achieve a good life—thus reflecting class as well as culture. These once-privileged men clearly favored class-congruent life trajectories and at least verbally rejected what they judged to be class inappropriate.

However, what they actually did was more complex. Several highly sophisticated and internationally experienced men tolerated low-status situations as part of long-term plans for the future. A few men with little or no education were exercising an opportunity that in the Horn of Africa had been denied them—a formal education—and saw their experience as extremely positive, even if they had menial jobs. Those men who had completed their university education in Ethiopia or Eritrea and had gained professional positions there seemed to be the most negatively affected by resettlement in the sense that they remained focused upon regaining their previous status through professional employment in the US–an unrealistic goal in the short term. Those who had been students before flight emphasized the goal of becoming students again and resisted menial employment in the absence of an opportunity to attend school.

The emphasis in the US upon rapid self-sufficiency for refugees, while on the surface apparently congruent with Ethiopian and Eritrean values, utilized very different values and tactics. Bureaucrats pushed refugees into immediate employment, usually low-paying, dead-end jobs without any prospects for upgrading. Independence, in terms of this bureaucratic mindset, was equated with narrowly defined economic self-sufficiency, rather than with acquiring the necessary means to facilitate upward social and class mobility and the acquisition of high status employment. The psychological effects on men pushed into such situations were sharply revealed by their high levels of stress as compared with those men who were able to combine working with further education.

When pressured to take low-paying, dead-end jobs that they experienced as demeaning, men often resisted by 'stubbornly' refusing employment, quitting after a short time, or becoming hostile to those they judged responsible. An illustrative example was that of Tekle,[10] who quit a job at a gas station, refused to take a job in a convenience store, and insisted upon going to school. Removed from institutional refugee support because of this behavior, Tekle was 'rescued' by an American who provided Tekle with free room and board in her home, enabling him to attend the local community college. A year and a half later he was working part-time as a janitor and going to college full-time. His apparent change of attitude hinged on his ability to define himself as a student, rather than as a janitor: to place himself into a community-recognized track leading to the educated class: "This is the perfect job for me! I can do this on my own time schedule and it gives me enough money to live. I can go to college full-time. Other jobs wouldn't let me do that. This is a perfect job!"

Fissaha, a teacher in Eritrea, was in an even more challenging situation. Already a trained professional, he did not seek out schooling or upgrading, and insisted that he should be able to reestablish himself as a recognized professional based purely on his prior experience and training. He was nevertheless placed in a menial, less-than-minimum-wage job. His response was anger, rage, and, ultimately, gendered violence: "They are all dumb, dumb, dumb. When they suggest a dishwasher's job, they look at me as if I were an animal. They see a dishwasher. I am not a dishwasher. *I am a good man. I must have a good job.*" Fissaha quit that job, was forced by the resettlement system into a job doing yard work, and walked off that job asserting that his supervisor (a second-generation Greek immigrant) did not like Eritreans. He became sullen and depressed. His wife and daughters, for whom he had struggled with great tenacity to bring from Sudan, eventually left him, saying that he had begun beating them.

Negussie also resisted bureaucratic expectations by defining himself as a student and through some creative time-juggling. Needing to support himself but wanting to go to school, he moved into a one-room apartment in a rundown, low-income neighborhood. Taking an evening job as a parking lot attendant, a job which allowed him to study, he attended the local community college during the day. In many conversations, Negussie repeatedly described himself as a college student and only talked about his job as being instrumental to his study.

Some young men creatively combined responsibility for their families with obtaining higher education, thereby circumventing the US resettlement pressures for quick employment in different ways. Berhane lived with two younger brothers whom he had brought with great effort from refugee camps in Sudan. These brothers, of high school age, were granted monthly stipends by the US since they were expected to be in school. By living together in a one room, low-income apartment, this money was sufficient for Berhane to attend college full-time while his brothers completed high school. Another man, Bereket, worked hard to bring his female cousin from Sudan. When she arrived, she moved into Bereket's one-room apartment. As soon as she was able to find employment, Bereket cut back on his work hours and increased his time at the college, highlighting the greater importance Ethiopian society places upon men getting an education.

For those who found themselves in a low-status job without being able to connect to being a student, highlighting their identity as refugees often became a way to resist loss of self-esteem. Said one, "I would not be working at this job if I were not a refugee. I am a university-educated person!" Such an emphasis was, at the same time one of many ways in which elite men distanced themselves from immigrant groups they viewed as being predominately less educated and lower class. Mulatu, working in a convalescent home, was deeply pained and angered when his supervisor, a Filipina nurse's aide, gave him orders. She, a woman, had less education than he, and she treated him as a subordinate! Perhaps to compensate, he frequently gave her lectures about the situation in Ethiopia and why he, a highly respected, well-educated person, had to flee his country.

Although not well off financially, those Ethiopians and Eritreans living in the US who had reasonably well-paying jobs, were receiving schooling, and/or had jobs with some recognizably hopeful future have worked extraordinarily hard since arriving to achieve their class and status goals. To accomplish their gendered goals in this new context, they have renegotiated their cultural notions of appropriate use of time and energy as men, and were now doing things which would have been unthinkable in their home countries. As Habtegabriel said:

> I never tell my parents what I am doing! My mother would be so shamed…. These jobs we have–never in Ethiopia–never! It is a shame. Only if you are poor do you do what we do here. To work in a restaurant–oh! But here it is what we have to do so we can live, so we can go to school. But we never tell our mothers.

Such effort comes at a cost. Yohannes Haile came to dinner to my house one afternoon and fell asleep at the table. He was attending a community college in the day and working the graveyard shift at a warehouse at night. He said he had never been so tired nor worked so hard in his life, but that he had to get his education. For those who are unable to renegotiate cultural notions and personal identity, the consequences can be tragic, as in the case of Dawit who consistently refused to take 'inappropriate jobs'. He was subsequently sanctioned by having his public welfare payments cut off. In despair, Dawit killed himself (West 1987a, 1987b).

The situation for the Ethiopians and Eritreans in Sweden when they were first resettled–a time parallel to that of the men in the US referred to above–is instructive in its difference. The government resettlement policies stressed that newcomers needed time and specific education to be able to integrate themselves effectively into Swedish society. The resettlement process was formally structured into stages. In the initial stage, refugees were considered to have particularized needs that made it unrealistic to expect that they could then enter into Swedish society successfully. Newly arrived refugees at that time were housed in special refugee settlements and were provided with money adequate to live, Swedish language instruction for an extended period, and job-searching support. They were allowed to be dependent for a minimum of a year to gain the skills for long-term independence. This was congruent with Ethiopian and Eritrean cultural values for young men in training, who would typically remain dependent on family until they finished their education. These men talked about being welcomed, and being prepared for entry into the Swedish labor market at a "good level."[11] Although this historical Swedish information is anecdotal, these men today definitely do not present a history of anger, depression, or suicide. As noted, the men have now completed high school or better, are fluent in Swedish, and are working.

Racism and Resistance

Although Ethiopians and Eritreans were somewhat aware of racism in the US before moving there, it came as a shock when Americans classified Ethiopians and Eritreans in the same social category as African-Americans. One might assume that such experiences would strengthen links between African refugees and African-Americans. However, every Ethiopian and Eritrean I initially interviewed rejected this association. African-Americans were sometimes characterized as 'not working for their future'—a perception, no doubt, reinforced by their experiences living in low-income neighborhoods. Several men were fearful that associating with a group they perceived as being an underclass would cause them to risk 'losing their future'.[12] This position had not changed significantly in subsequent interviews.

A Longitudinal View: Education, Work, and Status

After eight to ten years, my interview data indicated that the general goals and priorities of these men had not changed, at least for those who got onto a track which gave them some hope in the early years. Negussie, after nine years in the US, graduated from university with a degree in hotel management. Teklemariam took twelve years to complete a university program in pharmacy while working part-time jobs to support a wife and several children. His wife has indicated her interest in going to school, but so far "it hasn't been possible."

All of the men I interviewed who had been able to combine part-time or menial work with going to school when they first arrived or eventually entered what they considered hopeful employment have continued along this path after eight to eleven years. Some chose to continue their university education; others left university for a financially rewarding or high-status job. Some approached their goals in ways that contravened the refugee resettlement guidelines, and many resisted the US government expectations, while renegotiating Ethiopian and Eritrean ones. Many have depended on younger siblings, lived in crowded conditions to share expenses, applied for special programs, taken out student loans, or worked part-time—all to avoid being stuck in full-time, dead-end, low-status jobs. The gendered goals of an elite man inculcated in Ethiopia and Eritrea have not greatly changed, but the strategies and tactics employed to reach these goals have.

A significant minority nevertheless held on to the Eritrean and Ethiopian notions of appropriate male success but could not find ways to achieve these goals. Defining themselves as caught in a 'bad life', these men face the dilemma articulated by Merton (1957) in his classic analysis of anomie. Anger, depression, and, for some, mental illness and suicide appear to be common personal responses among these men.[13]

The personal goals of Eritreans were brought into question again with the possibility of returning to Eritrea after liberation in 1991.[14] When those in the US were initially interviewed (1982–88), all declared that as soon as Eritrea was free they would return. Today, however, priorities are different. Most men continue to see education as their highest priority—as a route to a desired job and as something more easily secured in the US. They also link education with their need to help their families in the US and in Eritrea:

> [There is] ... a lot of opportunity here.... Most people [are] thinking about school to get education here. Besides education we have to work or have financial aid ... so the government [helps us] to go to school.
>
> My kids are going to school. That is the first thing. Our kids will have more opportunity for education here.... My wife is thinking about going to [———] College.... I hope she will ... [she] really wants to go do something.

One man's comments clearly revealed perceived connections between education and power:

> It is a hard decision [whether to return]. [One has to] have something in hand—education or money.... I must go to my country as "a refreshment." I have money, and I can invite people for tea. People are very poor. Money has power. Also, education has power.

One man, now with professional employment that had taken him twelve years to obtain, asserted:

> Part of my life is here, my family. Especially my work is here.... It is a very young country.... *Your home is where you work....* I don't even know what kind of job I could look for over there. I don't think I would take *any* kind of job. I would work in a hospital or own my own business. That takes a lot of money. *I have to take a job according to my experience or my training.*

The Eritreans I interviewed in Sweden about returning to Eritrea spoke of social and economic security that the Swedish state provided. Their jobs were secure; their families were comfortable. Their primary goal with reference to Eritrea was to cooperate financially to buy land there for themselves or for their families currently living in Eritrea.

Private Lives: Choices and Negotiations

Marriage

The life trajectory of which men spoke early in their US resettlement was an Ethiopian and Eritrean ideal. They would get an education leading to a well-paying job. Then they would become independent of their families, get married, and establish their own households. For most, the exigencies of resettlement stalled the implementation of such a life agenda. One man said, "I can't think about getting married. I have to go to school; I have to build my future." Moreover, there were few single Eritrean/Ethiopian women then resident in the US.

After a few years, several men I initially interviewed had traveled to Sudan or even secretly to Ethiopia, married, returned to the US, and petitioned to bring their wives to join them. One man had a short-lived relationship with an American woman by whom he had a child. None, however, had married American women. Several men commented that it was best to marry 'traditional women' (which they said meant not Westernized), who came directly from their country. In this context, some men discussed the tension which Ethiopian/Eritrean men experienced because of the relative freedom and resultant power which many Eritrean/Ethiopian women obtained through resettlement in Western countries; in this volume Matsuoka and Sorenson elaborate on this theme in the Canadian context.

The comments of one young man, who had lived in the US for six years (and who was contemplating the comparative benefits of returning to Eritrea after liberation), clarify the social power differentials in male/female relationships that he continued to maintain:

> It is not hard to find a woman if I return as an educated person from America. That is why it is easy there.... Some say it is like buying a woman.... The best way is to go there and choose a wife and take a risk. You have to be sure the woman is a virgin, especially if she is young. When you have some education and money, the women [in Eritrea] approach you. If you go from here, you know they want your money. But the man is doing the selecting, so you know what the situation is.... I should have to bring her here or send money to her.

Relations Within the Home and Within Families in Africa

Most men in the US initially lived together. In this situation they learned to cook, clean, and entertain. Although their behavior necessarily changed, and they now appear to be more flexible in their understanding of acceptable roles for men, their core values related to masculinity and the use of home reference groups to judge these values do not seem to have changed. Indeed, the need to be seen as adult men by home reference groups may be a catalyst in the emergence of parallel agendas (discussed above). One man stated openly and unequivocally that "I would never do this in Ethiopia/ Eritrea. Here I have no choice; I must do this to survive. I will not do this when I return; I would be shamed!" Visiting the homes of the few men who were married, quite traditional gendered patterns seemed evident. The women prepared and served the food; I sat and talked with the men. Sometimes the men and I ate while the women stayed in the kitchen. Over a period of five years in which I visited these families, observable patterns did not seem to change appreciably, even when women were employed outside the home.

When we first interviewed, many men expressed conflicting emotions about having left their mothers, sisters, and/or wives behind in Ethiopia and Eritrea. Often mothers, who knew the risks that their sons would be killed, had insisted that the young men flee. One deeply depressed young man talked of his sense of guilt at having left his mother alone in Ethiopia; even though every one of the men in his family—twenty people—had been killed! Many men sent small remittances to their mothers, money which grew over the years. When possible, many men worked diligently to bring brothers, sisters, and cousins from Sudan or Djibouti to the US. Overall, the men articulated a painful sense of masculine responsibility, a responsibility that they were unable to fulfill given their own reality as refugees.

On the whole, the social benefits enjoyed by diaspora men in Sweden provided more economic security, and therefore a greater ability to contribute financially to their families in Ethiopia/Eritrea. A group of Eritrean men in Sweden have also developed a financial pool with which they intend to purchase or lease property in Eritrea, if this becomes legally possible. The object is to provide economic security for their families in Eritrea as well as a place to which they might eventually return upon retirement.

Conclusion

The central challenges to masculine identity among Ethiopian and Eritrean refugee men in the US and Sweden center around education, work, marriage, and family responsibilities. Their priorities naturally are informed by the cultural and social values of certain classes in Eritrea and Ethiopia. These priorities are consistent and clear: get an education and find an 'appropriate' job to regain or to attain honorable status among the educated class of Ethiopia and Eritrea. This mindset reconstructs the gendered class inequalities characteristic of its society of origin; men understand themselves as more enabled than women to care for their families in Ethiopia and Eritrea, as well as in resettlement, and seek ways to increase their ability to do so. These priorities have not markedly changed over a period of a dozen years. The many forms of resistance to perceived subordination–economic, racial, social–amply illustrate that these priorities are deeply embedded and of high salience. The specifics of their resistance also underscore the importance of their community-based status as men and the need to enhance and validate their masculinity.

The persistence of these masculine values underlies the transnational reality of the men's social places–both in US/Sweden and in Ethiopia/Eritrea. Their desire to live up to Eritrean ideals of masculinity links them to Eritrean social places; to be an adult Eritrean man is to assume responsibility for the status and well-being of oneself and one's family. These men feel responsible for constructing a social place in both the refugee diaspora and their society of origin. This is clearly expressed in their focus in all three locales upon education and employment, in the privileging of men's access to these desired social resources, in their efforts to assume responsibility for their families in Ethiopia and Eritrea, and in their desire to maintain traditional power and status differentials between men and women. It would also appear that many of these men have not developed the social, cultural, and psychological flexibility to easily address situations in which their plans do not materialize or their goals are not realized. There remains much ambiguity and tension in these men's lives as they reconstruct a social place in the refugee diaspora. These ambiguities cluster around the shifting economic realities in the West; racism; isolation from family, friends, and communities in Africa and the US/Sweden, making it difficult to see family; and the shifting social relations between women and men, both in the diaspora and in Ethiopia/Eritrea. These ambiguities are expressed poignantly by one young man: "I will want to go back to Eritrea in ten years. There is no psychological happiness here. We don't belong to blacks or to the whites.... Everyone will apply for citizenship here.... *I can get American citizenship, and I will always say, 'I am an Eritrean.'*"

Notes

1. See Matsuoka and Sorenson, this volume, for an overview of the large refugee movements from the Horn of Africa.

2. I am indebted to Helene Moussa as a valued colleague who combines analytical rigor with a sensitivity to the real human issues of individuals. She challenged me years ago to revisit my research with a more gendered gaze.

3. In two studies of 'Ethiopian' refugees resettled in the US, approximately 80 percent were single men; the US and Canada do not distinguish between Ethiopian and Eritrean refugees in earlier government statistics (Cichon et al. 1986; McSpadden 1989). In the US in 1992, approximately 67 percent were men with a median age of 23.8 years. In Canada, 67 percent of the "Ethiopian" refugee admissions for 1983–92 were male. Between 1982 and 1990 the predominant age range at the time of landing was 20–29 years (McSpadden and Moussa 1993: 208).

4. Latin American researchers and therapists in Europe have also noted the importance of "critical integration," which includes the ability to critique one's country of origin and of asylum and/or resettlement, and to find spaces and relationships in resettlement that are congruent with one's values and ideology (see CIMADE 1981; Vasquez 1981).

5. See also Cornwall and Lindisfarne (1994b: 23) for a Foucouldian discussion of masculinity, power, and resistance.

6. Some observers assert that the Oromo (who comprise more than 50 percent of Ethiopia) are less patriarchal, a position that is refuted by other analysts.

7. The following methods were used in my initial research: interviews/life histories of fifty-nine single men who had been in the US between six and twenty-four months; interviews/life histories with a further one hundred Ethiopian and Eritrean men and women; the short version of Goldberg's (1972) self-administered questionnaire for the detection of nonpsychotic mental illness, available in English, Amharic, and Tigrinya; Cantril's (Cantril and Roll, Jr. 1971) Self-Anchoring Striving Scale ("The Ladder of Hope"), which explores refugee perceptions of their current life situation and their hope for the future; interviews with resettlement agency staff and volunteers; participant observation within resettlement agencies and Ethiopian and Eritrean organizations/events.

8. Ethiopians/Eritreans who fled after the fall of the Mengistu regime in Ethiopia and the liberation of Eritrea in 1991 were not considered admissible to the US as refugees.

9. This concept is discussed more fully in McSpadden and Moussa (1993).

10. All names presented in the case studies have been changed.

11. The situation for new refugees in Sweden today is markedly more restrictive and less welcoming.

12. Levine and Campbell (1972) stress that groups striving for upward mobility typically do not use a group at the bottom of the socioeconomic ladder as a reference group.

13. Over the long run, those who were less well educated appeared to be more flexible or opportunistic in dealing with entry-level, menial labor employment. Some also believed that resettlement provided them with opportunities they would not have had in Eritrea or Ethiopia.

14. See McSpadden and Moussa (1996) for a full discussion of the comparative responses of women and men.

15

The Human Rights of Refugees with Special Reference to Muslim Refugee Women

Khadija Elmadmad

Introduction

The situation facing refugees and other forced migrants is one of the most serious of this century of displacement. Today, we speak of 20 to 23 million refugees and of 24 to 25 million internally displaced persons. It is well known that women and children now represent 80 to 90 percent of these numbers (Jack 1996: 11). Few, however, appreciate that the majority of these migrant women and children are Muslim. Not only are the human rights of most of these female Muslim refugees *not* guaranteed, the very violation of their rights has become a well-institutionalized dimension of war. All four main terms in the title of this chapter ("human rights," "refugees," "women," and "Muslim") have something in common: their conceptual ambiguity and inconsistent usage. This can lead to much practical confusion and to inadequate legal and physical protection for members of this large population. It is important to reflect on this association of terms and to analyze each one individually.

Firstly, international declarations notwithstanding, notions of human rights vary according to ideology, geography, and culture. They can also differ according to which legal instrument has precedence in any given jurisdiction. Indeed, the concept 'human rights' reveals all the problems we face in balancing universality and specificity. Promising an end to the dominance of overarching 'master' ideologies from the West and East, the fall of the Berlin Wall signaled a new era in which human rights could be conceptualized and used in increasingly different ways, as we have seen. This reflects the resurfacing of local and regional interests and beliefs previously muted. Even so, I think it can be said that there is a universal thread running through this diversity. Human rights in a universal sense pertain to the rights that guarantee respect for human life and dignity. These rights are, in turn, grounded in notions of justice, liberty, and equality.

The word 'refugee' also has several different meanings: legal, linguistic, sociological, religious, and so forth. There are even several major international definitions that are not consistent with each other: the 1951 United Nations Convention and its 1967 Protocol Relating to the Status of Refugees, the 1969 Organization of African Unity (OAU) Convention, and the 1984 American Cartagena Declaration. Western Europeans monopolized the definitional origins of the concept. Concerned as they were with keeping others out and with making statements about the lack of freedom under communism, the framers of the 1951 Convention used a much more restrictive definition of who is a refugee than, say, the OAU. Again, there is a universal thread running through the legal language: a refugee can be simply defined as someone fleeing persecution and in need of protection because his or her human rights have been, or are at risk of being, violated.

The dangerously global term 'woman' has an even wider range of contextual meanings and connotations. It varies dramatically according to national and international law, social group, culture, religion, and situational practice. Generally, a 'woman' is, of course, someone of the female sex who has attained majority: one who is no longer a girl-child. However, there is no internationally agreed upon definition of a child, and no international consensus on the age of majority or on when maturity is reached (see Nordstrom, this volume). The 1989 International Convention on the Rights of the Child does not give a fixed age for the end of childhood.[1] Based upon masculinist ideas of individual responsibility within civil society, inter- and intranationally there are differing standards and different ages for majority: civil (commonly 18), penal (often 16), and military (informally accepted as 15). Therefore, a woman in one place could be a girl elsewhere, and vice versa.

Difference-leveling Western stereotypes notwithstanding, the meaning of 'Muslim' varies with the type of Islam adopted. Theologically, Islam is one faith; it is the religion of all Muslims. It is based on five pillars: belief in the Prophet Mohammed, praying in the Islamic way, fasting for one month, giving alms (*azzakat*), and going on pilgrimage to Mecca when possible. However, there are socially and politically different 'Islams', and various kinds of Muslims have different interpretations of the Islamic sources and form different sects (Shia and Sunni), schools (Hanafi, Hanbali, Maliki, or Shafii), and political states (secular or nonsecular). Sometimes ethnic and national cultural differences strongly affect Muslim belief and practice even among those practicing what is nominally the same form of Islam. Hence, what is allowed in one Muslim state can be forbidden in another, as in the case of polygyny. We could perhaps stereotypically distinguish these cultural differences in yet another way as 'liberal' or Westernized, 'conservative', and 'fundamentalist' Islam.

Why Pay Greater Attention to the Protection of Muslim Refugee Women?

Today more than ever before, women have become the specific victims of refugee-generating cruelty and injustice. Muslim refugee women, in particular, often face specific persecutions because they are both Muslim and women. Their persecution arises from a range of factors, including the resolve of certain non-Muslim groups and states to destroy or distort Muslim religion, cultures, and traditions. Recall that, as noted above, when we speak of the violation of the human rights of 'refugees', the majority of the adult people to whom we refer are Muslim women.

Their Specificity As Women Refugees

Talking about 'the' special situation of refugee women, the United Nations High Commissioner for Refugees, Sadako Ogata, has noted that "Refugee women and children bear a disproportional share of the suffering" (Marshall 1995: 4) involved in forced displacement. In fact, refugee women are likely to face gendered violence before, during, and after fleeing their countries of origin. Tragically high numbers of women are victims of 'men's wars', and they are the ones who often suffer the most from armed conflicts, even when they take little active part in them. A potent symbol of 'our' superiority over 'them' (see Giles and Matlou, this volume), rape is a prevalent and persistent threat.[2] As is the case for other refugee women, many Muslim refugee women are forced to flee their places of origin because of fear of reprisal by the state or its agents for the actions or beliefs of a father, brother, or husband. This is yet another way in which violence against women is often used as a means to punish either a particular man or a whole community. After exile, women often still face violence. While Islam condemns all sexual relations outside of marriage, rape and forced prostitution in refugee camps have become common practice. In addition, the employment opportunities for men and women in asylum countries are often profoundly unequal, both inside and outside camps. Discrimination against refugee women in the type and allotment of most services and development programs is also a common practice in refugee camps. Critically, women also face problems of access to food and services; when men are in charge of distributing assistance, they often forget the weakest people.

Their Specificity As Muslims and Women

Homayra Etemadi, from the Geneva-based international NGO Working Group on Refugee Women, declared in her address to the November 1994 Sharjah Conference on Uprooted Muslim Women that

> Muslim women were facing persecution, massive human rights violations and armed conflicts in different parts of the world. Those affected were not only Afghans, Azeri, Bosnians, Palestinians and Somalis, but also the Muslim communities in Cambodia, Kashmir, Mozambique and the Philippines. (*Gulf News* 13 November 1994: 3)

Millions of women from as diverse places as Bosnia, Burma, Azerbaijan, and Palestine have been targeted by non-Muslims for violence. At the same time, Muslims themselves use violence against women and push them, their families, and their communities to flee their countries and to look for security and protection outside their place of origin. Here, different Islamic ways of thinking and behaving have important consequences, as women are often a focal point of pan-Islamic and local controversy. Violence against women is a common way of effectively asserting one faction's perception of the Islamic religion over others. Such struggles can be found in Afghanistan (see Cammack, this volume), in Algeria, and even in Egypt.

Such strategies are not unique to Muslim factions, but the prevalence of patriarchy and the rise of Islamic fundamentalism certainly make discrimination against Muslim refugee women more obvious than that against others. Persecution against 'deviant' women by fundamentalist groups is, for example, a common means employed to stop the spread of liberal Islam. To illustrate, in Algeria the present civil war is, in part, a war against women. As reported in the Moroccan newspaper *Libération* (16 May 1997), women are killed daily in Morocco if they do not wear the 'Islamic veil' or if they do not stay at home. Others are victimized to punish their male relatives. In Iran, the work of the Islamic revolution has, at least in symbolic terms, turned into a "veiling revolution." In Sudan, many refugees are displaced non-Muslims from the south; women among them are unfamiliar with Islamic codes of conduct and yet nevertheless persecuted for their non-respect of Islam (see Matsuoka and Sorenson, this volume). Even though these forms of persecution constitute well-founded reason to be granted asylum, Muslim women are frequently refused asylum. Perhaps it is because of persistent stereotypes of Islam and Muslims. It is my impression that when seeking asylum, Muslim refugee women receive less help and are less often welcomed by their hosts than Muslim men or other refugee women. In some cases, Muslim refugee women are clearly thought to represent a danger to non-Muslim communities and are not granted asylum for fear of Islamic contamination. The case of Bosnian refugee women is one example of this.

In refugee camps, discrimination against Muslim women by Muslim men is obvious everywhere. They suffer particularly from discrimination in education, food distribution, and employment opportunities. During the November 1994 International Conference on Uprooted Muslim Women, the representative of UNHCR, Mustapha Al Jamali, said:

> In refugee camps Muslim women are subject to violence from their husbands and family members, because men have nothing else to do but fight against their wives and children. This doubles the volume of pain for women particularly. (*Gulf News* 13 November 1994: 3)

Access to education is particularly problematic. Ideally, education is an obligation for all Muslims, men and women, but practice can be quite different. As a case in point, many Afghan refugee women in Pakistani camps were denied an education.[3] Moreover, those who try to educate girls there often find themselves at risk (Colville 1995: 24; see also Cammack, this volume).

Inequalities in the distribution of assistance is exacerbated by patriarchy and fundamentalism. Neither of these are unique to Muslims, but both are prevalent among them. To illustrate, during the Kurdish crisis of 1991, refugees fled to the northern mountains of Iraq, and an internationally organized food distribution program was put in place. UNHCR eventually realized that little food was going to families headed by women, the key reason being that most of the appointed food distributors were men. Much malnutrition, exploitation, and suffering were the result (Marshall 1995: 3). Unfortunately, I could provide a number of examples of this (see Matlou, this volume). In this particular instance, UNHCR representatives were obliged to change their method of distributing food to achieve greater equity and to keep women and children from starving. In other contexts, UNHCR operates differently. Many humanitarian organizations avoid dealing with this problem, arguing that to act decisively would be to impute their values on what they perceive to be the 'cultural traditions of Muslims'. For them, direct distribution of food or giving a greater voice to women in assistance programming may also violate Muslim men's sense of what is moral and right, and weaken their self-esteem.

Displaced Muslim women, of course, have specific needs beyond the distribution of assistance. Those who have undergone rape or other sexual violence need specialized care, too. The nature of many source cultures at least nominally associated with Islam is such that Muslim women are generally viewed as being responsible for what happened to them. They may be punished, humiliated, and eventually rejected by their families. Children conceived in rape are usually not recognized by their community. Very often, violated women receive little formal or informal assistance and either flee their communities, commit suicide, or keep their secret to themselves out of a sense of shame. The scope of this particular problem and its consequences is enormous. In Bosnia, for example, more than fifty thousand women are thought to have been victims of rape.

The Limited Protection of Muslim Refugee Women

Muslim refugee women are not adequately protected either under international law or according to Islamic law and traditions pertaining to asylum and refugees. With reference to international law, no specific mention is made concerning women in any of the international instruments relating to refugees, including the foundational 1951 UN Convention Relating to the Status of Refugees and its 1967 Protocol, and the 1969 OAU Convention governing the specific aspects of refugee problems in Africa. Moreover, all such universal and regional international instruments dealing with refugee protection focus on what are primarily men's activities or else frame 'human rights' largely in the image of men's public sphere rights.

The consequent neglect of the protection of refugee women has been characteristic of the international community for a long time. A prime example of this is the legal framing of rape. Until recently, rape was not considered an international crime against humanity, and no international treaties deal specifically with this crime. Nor is it clearly stated in the Geneva definition that the threat or acts of sexual violence constitute forms of persecution or specific reasons for claiming asylum, despite some national efforts toward their inclusion as a Convention reason for granting asylum (see Macklin, Crawley, and Gilad, this volume). It is only in the late 1980s that UNHCR became sensitive to this oversight and began campaigning for the more effective protection of refugee women. There has as yet been almost no movement to make international law more gender inclusive.

With Reference to the Present Islamic Practice and Laws on Asylum

According to Islam, *aman*, or the sacred act of granting asylum, is a form of protection that should be extended to any asylum seeker (*muhajir*) fleeing injustice and violence and looking for protection–whatever his or her origin, religion, race, or sex. Asylum in Islam, or *hijra,* is a right of all seekers and a duty for all hosts, both on an individual and societal level; no political leader should refuse a request for asylum (Arnaout 1986; Elmadmad 1991: 461–81; Elmadmad 1993).[4] Many verses and an entire chapter of the Koran deal with *hijra.*[5] Asylum is also a duty for oppressed Muslims, who should vigorously resist oppression and violation of their rights but should flee and seek refuge elsewhere when it is impossible to resist further. Moreover, asylum plays an important role in Islamic history. The Islamic era, for example, starts in A.D. 622–not with Prophet Mohammed's birth, but with his flight from Mecca to Yathrib, which was later renamed Medina, the town of the Prophet. This history is also replete with examples of influxes of refugees and of cases of forced migration, such as the flight from Mecca to Christian Abyssinia (now Ethiopia) five years after Mohammed received the message.

At the same time, throughout the Islamic world there has been little reference in today's laws to Islamic prescriptions and principles on refugees and asylum in general, or to any specific Muslim rights of refuge for women in particular. At present, most Islamic states refer in their laws and practices only to 'modern' international legal instruments relating to refugees. They are mute to the progressive and humanitarian characteristics of the concept of *aman* and *hijra* in Islam, and to the obligation to protect those in danger.

How to Better Protect Refugee Muslim Women

To secure better protection for Muslim refugee women, three complementary routes seem possible: further developing the kinds of protective initiatives already taken; reviewing the laws and regulations relating to refugee women in general; and ensuring respect for the human rights of women everywhere, particularly in the Muslim world. Until the stories of sexual violence against Southeast Asian women became widely known in the media in the early 1980s, there was no sustained international effort to specifically protect refugee women. The first recommendation on refugee women taken by the Executive Committee (EXCOM) of UNHCR was issued in 1985 (UNHCR EXCOM 1990). Various actions and much discussion of the question followed. Thus, in 1988 a roundtable on refugee women and an International Consultation on Refugee Women were held. In 1991, UNHCR issued its *Guidelines on the Protection of Refugee Women*, which have subsequently been used by Australia, Canada, and the US to develop more gender-inclusive policies and practices in granting asylum (see Macklin, this volume). In 1995, UNHCR (UNHCR EC 1995) produced a document entitled *Sexual Violence Against Refugees: Guidelines on Prevention and Response.* These guidelines state that refugee women share the protection problems experienced by all refugees, and that

> ... refugee women and girls have special protection needs that reflect their gender: they need, for example, protection against manipulation, sexual and physical abuse and exploitation and protection against sexual discrimination in the delivery of goods and services. (1995: 7)

The UNHCR has an official policy to extend gender-specific protection to refugee women. However, these UNHCR guidelines are far from being fully implemented. With reference to refugee women, Ann Howarth-Wiles, UNHCR coordinator for refugee women, summarized the past five years of policy and program evolution: "The problems of refugee women are too often relegated to second rank priority. There is always something more pressing to do than to deal with the difficulties that women, in particular, encounter in refugee situations" (Del Mundo 1995a: 10–13).

Recent Measures Taken by the International Red Cross and Red Crescent, and Others

The definition of a refugee given in international humanitarian law is more comprehensive than that given by refugee law. International humanitarian law considers refugee women primarily under the category 'civilians in need of protection', a category that includes both refugees and internally displaced persons. Concerning women, it therefore broadens the scope of their protection by incorporating those who have remained within their countries of origin. It also expands the criteria for protection from the narrowly political to include economic, health, and environmental catastrophes. Furthermore, under this mandate the International Committee of the Red Cross (ICRC) has long been very active in protecting refugee women, often taking significant risks and being a significant innovator. The ICRC, for instance, was the first international organization to denounce sexual violence against women in the former Yugoslavia and in Rwanda. As stipulated in its 1994 Code of Conduct (Refugee Studies Programme 1995: 16–19), the new policy of the International Red Cross and Red Crescent Movement is to seek greater coordination with other international NGOs and agencies.

Other international bodies, most notably a range of international Islamic NGOs, are also beginning to promote and protect the rights of Muslim refugee women. Thus, for the first time an international conference was organized on the theme of uprooted Muslim women in Sharjah, United Arab Emirates, in November 1994. It was organized by the International NGO Working Group on Refugee Women (based in Geneva), the International Islamic Relief Organization (based in Jeddah, with a branch in Sharjah), and UNHCR. Other international organizations present at this conference included the ICRC and the International Organization of Migration.

The Sharjah Conference was an opportunity to discuss the problems specific to Muslim refugee women. Diverse themes were discussed by a diverse group composed of Muslims, non-Muslims, and Muslim refugee women. Papers were presented on Muslim refugee women from Kashmir, Lebanon, Palestine, Afghanistan, Iraq, Somalia, Bosnia, Sudan, and Azerbaijan (RPN 1995: 37) that addressed the issues of violence against women, the limited protection of refugee women, and the problems of seeking assistance and education. Concluding the Conference, a declaration was issued underlining the need for, and ways of, protecting Muslim refugee women.[6] Not legally binding, the Declaration text is nevertheless a good starting point to better address the problems of uprooted Muslim women.

In overview, better protection could be achieved by enforcing existing international stipulations relating to the protection of refugees, especially by taking into greater consideration the varying gender-specific situations of women when granting them asylum, and by promoting an awareness that women's rights are to be considered in a disaggregated way. There are many means that could lead to this end:

1. Implement more thoroughly the UNHCR guidelines. The new UNHCR policy stipulates that representatives and field officers *should* be attentive to women's needs in issues as fundamental as

site planning, distribution of food and other supplies, as well as obvious specific questions involving health care, skills training, and education (Marshall 1995: 4). To this end, the attitudes of male staff members toward women should be changed. It is obvious, however, that these goals are very far from being realized (see Boelaert, Matlou, and Cammack, this volume).

2. Make assistance and specific avenues to asylum for uprooted women more widely available. While some countries have already enacted specific guidelines granting asylum to refugee women–notably Canada, Australia, and the US (Macklin, this volume)–many others such as Britain have not (Crawley, this volume). Generally, leaders should be made more aware of the importance of securing human rights for *women* (as well as men) in times of both peace and war.

3. Coordinate more closely the efforts of the various humanitarian organizations now in the field. Joint action by both Muslim and non-Muslim NGOs should be encouraged as NGOs are rapidly becoming the primary means by which refugee assistance is provided.

4. Use Islamic rules and principles on asylum and *aman* more extensively in law and practice. This is critical in those Islamic countries that are now closing their borders to refugees on the basis of their secular sovereign right to grant or refuse asylum.

5. Issue *binding* instruments that specifically address refugee women and their situation. Following on the Sharjah Declaration (November 1994) and the OAU Declaration (July 1995), more international conferences and meetings on women's rights should be held where these matters can be discussed openly.

6. Punish those responsible for crimes against women. An international tribunal for judging crimes against women could be created, as has been done in the Hague and in Arusha.

7. Empower women. Women should have a greater part in decision-making, especially those decisions which concern the start and end of wars. More to the point of this volume, refugee women must participate in decisions that directly concern them as refugees, such as repatriation and food distribution.

Conclusion

Despite its early promise, the 'New International Order' heralded by the fall of the Berlin Wall seems to have been characterized by the further uprooting of millions of people as well as the dislocation of previously dominant ideologies. Today, much more than ever, there is a pressing need to respect women's rights in normal situations to achieve this respect in exceptional ones. In this chapter, I have outlined some ideas on how to do so, as well as how to address the specific and unique needs of Muslim refugee women. If we listen to them, perhaps we will also find solutions for other problems.

Notes

1. In fact, Article I of this Convention declares: "For the purpose of the present Convention, a Child means every human being below the age of eighteen years *unless, under the law applicable to the child, majority is attained earlier.*"

2. Vietnamese women being raped in front of other refugees was a very common sight for 'boat people'. Somali women also experienced the same horrific treatment. During interviews I conducted with refugee and displaced women in Sudan in 1992, I observed that some of them could not enter the country without granting sexual favors to the border officers.

3. In Iran, the situation was quite different. There Afghan women refugees could enroll in vocational and training courses.

4. For more information on asylum in Islam, see Ghassan Maârouf Arnaout (1986) and Khadija Elmadmad (1991, 1993).

5. For example: Chapter 2 (Al-Baqara), verse 125; Chapter 3 (Al-Imran), verse 97; Chapter 4 (An-Nissaa), verses 97, 98, 100, and 101; Chapter 9 (At-Tawba), verses 6 and 57; Chapter 14 (Ibrahim), verses 35, 36, and 37, etc. Chapter 59 (Al-Hashr) deals with the exile of the Jewish people.

6. The full text of this Declaration can be obtained from UNHCR, the International Working Group on Refugee Women (IWGRW) in Geneva, or the International Islamic Relief Organization in Jeddah (Saudi Arabia).

16

A Comparative Analysis of the Canadian, US, and Australian Directives on Gender Persecution and Refugee Status

Audrey Macklin

Introduction

Like migrants themselves, ideas about migration diffuse across national borders. More often than not, these ideas concern how to keep migrants out–witness the European Community's *Dublin Convention* and the draft *Memorandum of Understanding* between Canada and the United States.[1] A refreshing exception to this trend has been occurring of late, however. In March 1993, the Chair of Canada's Immigration and Refugee Board (IRB) released *Guidelines on Women Refugee Claimants Fearing Gender-Related Persecution* (Canada IRB 1993). In May 1995, the United States' Immigration and Naturalization Service (INS) issued *Considerations for Asylum Officers Adjudicating Asylum Claims from Women* (US INS 1995, hereafter "US Considerations"). A year later, in July 1996, the Australian Department of Immigration and Multicultural Affairs (DIMA) followed suit with "Guidelines on Gender Issues for Decision-makers" (Australia DIMA 1996, hereafter "Australian Guidelines"). In response to evolving jurisprudence from higher courts, the IRB revised the Canadian Guidelines (Canada IRB, hereafter "Canadian Guidelines") in November 1996, but the additions to the text were not major.

The Canadian, American, and Australian directives can be usefully compared with one another. Their impact can also be contrasted with the situation in England where, as Heaven Crawley explains (this volume), state authorities do not consider guidelines necessary or desirable. Notable differences exist between the legal environment of Canada, the US, and Australia in matters of process and, to some extent, the substance of refugee determination. My objective is not to compare the merits of each system in the abstract. Rather, I explore how the directives formulated in Canada, the US, and Australia respond to the issues raised in gender-related claims within their respective legal, political, and administrative milieus. I have elsewhere described and critiqued the Canadian Guidelines (Macklin 1995: 213). My present goal is to comment on the common and distinctive features of the US and Australian initiatives in comparison to the Canadian precedent. I will also review some of the outstanding issues that either remain, or have arisen, in the wake of the various directives. In so doing, I consider jurisprudence from the three jurisdictions that preceded or followed the directives.

Like the Canadian Guidelines, the US Considerations and Australian Guidelines take the form of administrative directives, not law. They are intended to give decision-makers a method of interpreting and applying the international refugee definition in a gender-sensitive manner, and to provide practical instructions on rendering the hearing process less intimidating and more respectful of women. My analysis and hypotheses regarding the impact of directives about gender persecution is informed by my own experience as a member of the IRB for two and a half years (1994–96).

Canada, Australia, and the United States are parties to the *1951 Convention Relating to the Status of Refugees* (hereafter, the "Convention"), and each country incorporates the international refugee definition into domestic law. A refugee is defined in the Convention as, inter alia, a person who:

(a) by reason of a well-founded fear of persecution for reasons of race, religion, nationality, membership in a particular social group or political opinion

(i) is outside the country of the person's nationality and is unable or, by reason of that fear, unwilling to avail [her/him]self of the protection of that country

All three countries apply this definition of a refugee in their determination of refugee status.

Over the years, policy and decision-makers erected many obstacles to recognizing the validity of gender-related refugee claims. Such barriers did not inhere in the definition. Rather, they seemed to arise almost despite the definition and the jurisprudence. For example, beating a man was usually deemed an obvious form of persecution; raping a woman was not. Ethnically motivated attacks by thugs in the face of state indifference constituted persecution; systematic domestic abuse of women in the face of state indifference did not. Torture of political dissidents in the name of social control was not protected qua legitimate cultural practice; excising a girl's genitalia to control women's sexuality was. 'Women' was too large and amorphous a group to warrant refugee protection; 'Christians', 'Sikhs', and 'Blacks' were not.

The Canadian and Australian Guidelines and the US Considerations each offer gender-sensitive interpretations of the refugee definition. Their approaches are very similar, though each must abide by the jurisprudence of their respective higher courts. Broadly speaking, all three delineate forms of persecution unique to, or predominantly inflicted on, women (e.g., sexual violence, genital mutilation, forced abortion, domestic violence, etc.). Each considers whether 'women' (or a subgroup thereof) may constitute "a particular social group" to be included in the Convention definition. Finally, they all address state protection, asserting that a refugee claim may be established both when a state persecutes directly or when the persecutor is a private actor and the state is either unable or unwilling to intervene. The recognition that harms inflicted in the so-called 'private sphere' may constitute persecution under the Convention is particularly significant. In virtually all countries of the world, women are brutalized by their male partners, fathers, and kin in an atmosphere of state indifference, impotence, or condonation. When challenged, representatives of the state often express the inappropriateness or inefficacy of intervention in a so-called 'private' matter.

Sources of Inspiration

In 1985, well before the IRB issued its Guidelines, the Executive Committee of the United Nations High Commissioner for Refugees (UNHCR) adopted *Conclusion No. 39 (XXXVI)* concerning international protection of refugee women:

> (k) States, in the exercise of their sovereignty, are free to adopt the interpretation that women asylum-seekers who face harsh or inhuman treatment due to their having transgressed the social mores of the society in which they live may be considered as a "particular social group" within the meaning of Article 1 A(2) of the 1951 United Nations Refugee Convention. (UNHCR EXCOM 1985)

Five years later, the UNHCR Executive Committee issued *Guidelines on the Protection of Refugee Women* (UNHCR EXCOM 1991). The document discusses various issues of relevance to women refugees, including protection from physical, sexual, and other forms of violence in refugee camps; legal aspects of status determination; access to food, shelter, and other services; and repatriation. These UNHCR Guidelines also elaborate on *Conclusion No. 39* by recommending that women

> fearing persecution or severe discrimination on the basis of their gender should be considered a member of a social group for the purposes of determining refugee status. Others may be seen as having made a religious or political statement in transgressing the social norms of their society. (UNHCR EC 1991, 40 par. 71)[2]

While the Canadian, US, and Australian directives acknowledge the UNHCR precedent in formulating guidelines and recommendations with respect to women refugees, each national initiative goes much further and offers much more sophisticated substantive analysis. Both the US and Canada also recognize the contribution of nongovernmental organizations (NGOs), scholars, and activists. Indeed, the US Considerations describe the product as a "collaborative effort" (US Considerations 1995: 703). In the Canadian case, a Working Group on Women Refugee Claimants had been active within the IRB since 1991, building relations with NGOs and gathering documentation relating to women refugees.

The US Considerations and the Australian Guidelines bear striking resemblance to the Canadian Guidelines; indeed, the Considerations explicitly acknowledge the latter's influence, stating that "[m]ore than two years after their release, the Canadian Guidelines remain a model for gender-based asylum adjudications" (US Considerations 1995: 702). All deal with the process by which women's claims are heard, as well as the substance of the refugee definition as it applies to women making gender-based claims. Beyond this, the content of the directive is also very similar, although the distinctive administrative, legal, and jurisprudential landscape of each jurisdiction affects the interpretive space available to the drafters of the directives.

Structure of the Decision-Making Bodies

Although the Convention obliges states to adopt the same refugee definition, asylum/refugee determination remains within the exclusive purview of each State Party. It is thus useful at the outset to outline the different administrative and legal contexts in which the Canadian, US, and Australian directives operate. The Canadian IRB is an administrative tribunal which is independent from the federal Department of Citizenship and Immigration. The Members of the IRB are appointed by the Cabinet, and their independence from the government is a key feature of the Canadian system. Members hear and determine claims from all refugee claimants who make port of entry or inland claims in Canada, regardless of when or how they arrived.

The Canadian Guidelines were promulgated by the Chair of the IRB, Nurjehan Mawani, and apply only to its Members. They do not apply to visa officers abroad, and women who apply for refugee status outside Canada do not benefit from the Guidelines. About three-quarters of all refugees admitted into Canada annually are selected from overseas. The IRB operates as a full administrative tribunal with relatively formal procedural protections. A panel typically consists of two Members.[3] Claimants are usually represented by counsel, and are entitled to legal aid in most provinces.[4] A Refugee Hearing Officer (RHO) assists the panel by presenting documentary evidence relating to the case, and by questioning the claimant. The panel may also question the claimant. The IRB supplies professional interpreters for the hearing, and proceedings are tape recorded. Transcripts may be ordered by those seeking leave to apply for judicial review to the Federal Court of Canada (Trial Division).

In the United States, first level asylum adjudication is performed by officers of the Immigration and Naturalization Service (INS) Asylum Corps, unless the asylum applicant has been arrested by the INS, in which case his or her immigration status (including a possible asylum claim) is determined in the first instance by an Immigration Judge. The Asylum Corps is comprised of civil servants employed by the INS. Immigration Judges are employed by the Department of Justice, and are not answerable to the INS. Asylum applicants not granted asylum will be placed in removal proceedings, and their claim will be adjudicated by an Immigration Judge, who grants a *de novo* hearing with significant procedural protection. Either the claimant or the INS can appeal the Immigration Judge's determination to the Board of Immigration Appeals (US BIA) and to a federal court thereafter.

The process before the Asylum Officer is relatively informal. Legal aid is not universally available, though some legal clinics do serve asylum claimants. Claimants are responsible for supplying their own interpreters, who are frequently relatives or friends. Consequently, the competence of interpreters varies. The Asylum Officer conducts an interview and takes notes, which form the only record of the proceedings. Lawyers may make submissions, but their role is relatively limited. The US Considerations apply only to this process. Immigration Judges and the Board of Immigration Appeals are not subject to the US Considerations, although they may choose to be guided by them. In the recent case of *In re Kasinga* (US BIA 1996), the BIA explicitly took note of the Considerations in rendering a decision in favor of an applicant fleeing female genital mutilation (FGM). The Considerations do not apply to the overseas selection process.

The Australian Guidelines were developed by the Department of Immigration and Multicultural Affairs (DIMA), and apply to the officers employed by the Department who assess refugee claims. Applicants for refugee status who are already in Australia seek a "protection visa." Officers conduct an interview at which counsel may be present, but the role of counsel at this stage is limited. The officer must issue written reasons for decisions. Claims that are refused may be appealed to the Refugee Review Tribunal (RRT), upon payment of a fee of $1,000. The applicant's appeal may be granted upon a review of written documentation, but it cannot be rejected without an oral hearing. The RRT, like the IRB is an independent tribunal composed of government appointees, and its hearing process is relatively formal. The Australian Guidelines do *not* apply to the RRT, although one can reasonably assume that RRT members may find their contents persuasive.

Overseas applicants for refugee status apply under the offshore Humanitarian Programme. They may be assessed under the refugee class in accordance with the Convention refugee definition, or under various nonrefugee categories for nationals from designated countries, persons for whom there are compelling humanitarian reasons to admit them to Australia, or persons suffering hardship or disadvantage who have close links to Australia.

The Australian Guidelines are unique in applying to both the inland and overseas selection process, and even to nonrefugee humanitarian classes. Officers are encouraged to recall that "women may experience not only persecution but also discrimination, disadvantage, or hardship in a manner qualitatively different from men as a result of their gender" (Australian Guidelines 1996, par. 4.2.). The drafters recognize that the Guidelines are meant to function in "different operational decision making environments," and should be adopted "as far as practicable" (Australian Guidelines 1996, par.1.6).

Institutional Factors

Neither the Canadian Guidelines nor their American or Australian counterparts constitute binding law. They are drafted in a manner that encourages decision-makers to apply them, but they stop short of dictating adherence. Most Members of the IRB are mindful of their independence, and are particularly sensitive to real or perceived pressure to decide cases in a particular way. As civil servants, Australian officers are answerable to their government department and ultimately to their Minister. Thus, they are more amenable to implementing government policy than members of the RRT who, like members of the IRB, are formally independent of government. For its part, the US Asylum Corps has been roundly criticized for its lack of independence and apparent eagerness to align its decisions with US foreign policy interests of the day, to the detriment of victims of repression by US-sponsored regimes. Ironically, this very lack of independence may redound to the benefit of claimants seeking the benefit of the Considerations, since Asylum Officers are effectively mandated to apply them, while IRB Members cannot be compelled to do likewise.

Whether directives are formally binding or otherwise, institutional incentives to abide by them have an effect. While the pressure to conform may be more explicit when the decision-makers are employees of a government department, few IRB Members explicitly reject the Guidelines in their decisions. Moreover, even the obligation to apply the US Considerations or Australian Guidelines cannot determine outcomes. Decision-makers must still apply the Considerations to the facts and rule on credibility, the availability of state protection, and a range of other issues. The fact that rape is recognized as a form of persecution does not prevent a decision-maker from being predisposed to disbelieve women who say they were raped.[5]

It is too soon to pronounce definitively on the relative impact of the Australian and Canadian Guidelines and the US Considerations. However, Anker, Kelly, and Willshire-Carrera (1996a: 616) suggest a disappointing trend among the INS lawyers who represent the INS before the Immigration Judges and the Board of Immigration Appeals. Since the Considerations apply only to Asylum Officers, some INS lawyers adopt positions diametrically opposed to the Considerations, apparently on grounds that since they are not formally bound, they are entitled to reject them. The irony is that the very agency whom these lawyers ostensibly represent promulgated the Considerations. Why the INS tolerates this is unclear.

In Canada, the IRB committees on refugee women have been dismantled, ostensibly to maximize Members' time in the hearing rooms. A subsidiary rationale has been that the Guidelines' apparent success has rendered these committees superfluous. Their demise will almost certainly mean that less institutional attention will be paid to implementation of the Guidelines, emerging issues, and ongoing sensitization of personnel.

There are several reasons why it is not yet possible to measure the impact of the Guidelines and Considerations on the number or proportion of gender-related refugee claims that are successful. The number of women who claim and obtain refugee status will fluctuate yearly according to many factors, especially country of origin. Second, while cynics have suggested that the Guidelines invite women to concoct gender-related claims, women alternatively may now claim gender-related grounds precisely because the Guidelines legitimate their experience. Finally, it is very difficult to specify precisely what constitutes a gender-related claim. During my tenure at the IRB, Members were expected to identify gender-related claims in order to generate comparative statistics. However, there turned out to be no consensus on what constituted a gender-claim. Was it any claim involving a woman? Any claim in which the form of persecution was uniquely or predominantly inflicted on women (e.g., rape)? Did it include situations in which women were persecuted to retaliate against, humiliate, or pressure male family members? Could it include situations in which men were persecuted in gender-specific ways? Without greater clarity on precisely what constitutes a 'gender claim', statistics cannot convey meaningful information within a single jurisdiction, let alone between Canada, the US, and Australia. Thus, any putative correlation between the existence of the directives and the number of applicants raising gender-related claims is unreliable.

It does, however, appear safe to assert that the Canadian Guidelines did not lead to a 'flood' of women seeking asylum in Canada. Nor has the comparative acceptance rate of female and male claimants changed dramatically; this observation facilitated the subsequent issuance of directives in the US and Australia.

Procedural and Evidentiary Issues

Procedural issues focus on the process of decision-making, such as the personnel present and how those people conduct themselves at the hearing or interview. Evidentiary issues involve the evaluation of credibility and the use of documentary sources. All three sets of directives counsel decision-makers to be sensitive to the variety of religious, cultural, and personal reasons why women might experience pain, trauma, humiliation, or shame in recounting certain incidents, especially those of a sexual nature. The Canadian Guidelines indicate that decision-makers should be familiar with the UNHCR Executive Committee *Guidelines on the Protection of Refugee Women*, which in turn provides practical suggestions on how to conduct interviews in a sensitive manner (UNHCR EXCOM 1991, par. 72).[6] Unfortunately, the Canadian Guidelines do not refer to the UNHCR Executive

Committee's 1995 publication, *Sexual Violence Against Refugees: Guidelines on Prevention and Response* (UNHCR EXCOM 1995), which contains more extensive discussion and guidance regarding interviews of women who have been sexually violated. In general, the Canadian Guidelines rely on reference to external sources and do not focus on the actual conduct of decision-makers in the hearing room.

In contrast, the US Considerations and the Australian Guidelines devote significant attention to hearing room practice. The former call on Asylum Officers to be aware that most claimants come from countries where they have good reason to distrust people in authority. As claimants may be traumatized, officers should create a rapport with the claimant, move gradually into sensitive areas of questioning, and confine questioning about sexual assault to confirming that it happened and to the motives of the perpetrator. The Considerations also suggest how trauma may affect the claimant's testimony and lead to erroneous negative inferences about her credibility. Similar comments are made about culturally specific body language.

The Australian Guidelines include the items highlighted in the Considerations and go even further, focusing as much on what the interviewer can do to diminish a claimant's discomfort as on why the claimant may be uncomfortable. The frequent use of adjectives such as "sensitive," "sympathetic," "neutral," "supportive," and "compassionate" in the Australian Guidelines conveys a strong message about decision-makers' responsibility to interact sensitively and respectfully. Along these same lines, the Australian Guidelines also discuss arranging the physical environment to put claimants at ease and promote confidentiality. They contain practical advice about the interviewer's body language and "active listening" skills to minimize intimidation and reassure the claimant that she is in a safe space to speak. With admirable candor, the Australian Guidelines acknowledge that "no matter how supportive the interviewing officer and the environment may be, the interview process (because of the imbalance of power between participants) will impact on how women respond" (Australian Guidelines 1996, par. 3.21).

Indeed, the comportment of decision-makers in the hearing room can have a profound impact on the willingness of women to disclose evidence and on the quality of evidence disclosed. In *Yusuf v. Canada (Minister of Employment and Immigration),* the Federal Court of Appeal overturned an IRB decision because of the offensive, sexist, and condescending behavior of the Members toward the female claimant (Canada [1992] 1, FC 629 (FCA)) and ordered a new hearing before a differently constituted IRB panel.

The fact that refugee hearings before the IRB are recorded means that transcripts can be produced for purposes of judicial review, such as they were in *Yusuf*. In INS interviews, the only written record of the proceedings are in the notes of the Asylum Officer (and possibly the lawyer). One can file a complaint with the Asylum Office on the grounds that the Asylum Officer behaved inappropriately, but it is not clear how effectively one might mount a challenge when the record consists only of handwritten notes and one person's word against another's. At the same time, if an asylum application is not accepted, the claim will be referred to an Immigration Judge for a rehearing, where all proceedings are recorded. Similarly, a rejected applicant in Australia who alleges unfair treatment by the officer may appeal to the RRT, where she must receive a formal, recorded hearing. In effect, while there is no direct remedy in the US and Australia for inappropriate behavior by officers, the unsuccessful applicant can nevertheless appeal on the merits of her case. The Canadian system does not provide for an appeal on the merits of a negative decision by the IRB, and judicial review is limited to errors of procedure or law.

The Canadian Guidelines do not address whether gender-related claims should be conducted with all-female personnel. Some counsel representing women claimants before the IRB have requested female panels, refugee hearing officers, and interpreters, arguing that this will minimize the claimant's reticence and enable her to present her claim more fully. No consistent policy addresses these requests, and they are dealt with on an ad hoc basis. Resistance to such a policy did emerge from some Members and RHOs who believed it suggested that male Members or RHOs were inherently less competent and sensitive in dealing with gender-related claims. Others expressed concern about the burden that would be placed on female personnel if they were to deal with all such claims, as gender-related cases can be particularly demanding and draining. While the revised Guidelines maintain silence on the question, in my personal experience, when counsel does request all female personnel, their requests are usually accommodated whenever possible.

Both the US Considerations and Australian Guidelines are more assertive on this issue, and encourage assigning a female interviewer to cases where particularly sensitive or traumatic evidence may arise. They also acknowledge the reluctance of a woman to speak through a male interpreter, especially if he is a relative or friend from the same cultural community, as women may legitimately fear the negative repercussions of divulging certain facts in front of a person who may stigmatize her, or reveal her story to family and community.

Unlike Canada and Australia, in the US the claimant is responsible for providing the interpreter, and that person may not necessarily be someone the claimant would otherwise trust. The US Considerations offer no constructive suggestions here, and expressly state that "interviews should *not* generally be canceled and rescheduled because women with gender-based asylum claims have brought male interpreters" (US Considerations 1995: 704). In light of this limitation, the Considerations, caution about the inhibitory effect of male interpreters rings rather hollow.

Substance of Refugee Determination

Slight variations in how Canada, the US, and Australia interpret the refugee definition have emerged through the years. These variations form the background against which gender directives are drafted, constraining certain interpretive moves and enabling others. In general, the elements of any refugee claim (including one involving gender) can be disaggregated as follows:

1. Does the treatment feared constitute persecution?
2. Is the fear objectively "well-founded"?
3. If the persecutor is not an agent of the state,[7] is the state able and willing to protect the claimant from the persecution?
4. Is the reason for the claimant's fear one of the listed grounds (race, religion, nationality, membership in a particular social group, or political opinion)?

The Australian and US directives closely track the questions posed above. In doing so, decision-makers are implicitly reminded that a gender-sensitive interpretation of the refugee definition does not require a departure from the general principles that apply to all refugee claims. This is an important message to convey, because critics may be inclined to dismiss the Guidelines and Considerations as "special treatment" for women and a capitulation to external political pressure, rather than a legitimate application of existing principles. In contrast, the Canadian Guidelines commence with a series of questions that randomly incorporate various elements of the refugee definition (Canadian Guidelines 1996: 1). While the net effect is to cover the terrain of the refugee definition, this approach gives the Canadian Guidelines the appearance of being a separate scheme. This is both confusing to decision-makers and strategically unwise, inasmuch as it fosters the impression that a different, less stringent standard applies to gender-related claims.[8]

Persecution

All three directives recognize that the following forms of persecution may be inflicted exclusively or more commonly on women: sexual abuse, forcible abortion, forced marriage, and genital mutilation. The Canadian Guidelines also list compulsory sterilization (Canadian Guidelines 1996: 7), and the Canadian and US directives identify domestic violence (US Considerations 1995: 708; Canadian Guidelines 1996: 7). The Canadian Guidelines make the point that the pervasiveness of the harm—such as rape or domestic violence—does not detract from their persecutory character (Canadian Guidelines 1996: 7). The Australian Guidelines explain that rape may be used to punish the victim, to pressure or humiliate others, or as part of a campaign of 'ethnic cleansing' (Australian Guidelines 1996: par. 4.7–8).[9]

Recognition of rape as persecution has proved problematic in the United States, in part because certain courts conflate the question of whether the harm is serious enough to constitute persecution with whether the persecution due to a Convention reason. Some have ruled that this analytical short circuit was encapsulated under the rubric "private harm." For instance, in *Klawitter v. INS* (US 1992: 149–52), a case involving sexual harassment by a colonel in the Polish secret police, the court ruled that "harms or threats of harm based solely on sexual attraction do not constitute persecution" (152). Leaving aside its retrograde understanding of sexual harassment, the court here fails to keep the question of whether the harassment constituted persecution analytically distinct from whether the harassment was motivated by a Convention reason.

In *Lazo-Majano v. INS* (US 1987), a Salvadoran military officer physically and sexually abused and enslaved the claimant. The court asserted that this putatively "private harm" took on a public character only because the officer falsely denounced her for alleged political subversion when she resisted. The court was then able to characterize the claim as persecution for imputed political opinion. On the other hand, in *Campos-Guardado v. INS* (US 1987), the gang rape of female kin of politically active males was treated as the unlawful expression of sexual desire—a "private harm." The Considerations attempt to distance themselves from this decision, though they eschew open criticism of it. Recently, in *Matter of Krome* (US BIA 1993), the Board of Immigration Appeals determined that gang rape and beating in retaliation for political activities constituted persecution, and the US Considerations emphasize that the "appearance of sexual violence in a claim should not lead adjudicators to conclude automatically that the claim is an instance of purely physical harm"

(US Considerations 1995: 708). It remains to be seen whether this clear recognition in the Considerations that "severe sexual abuse does not differ analytically from beatings, torture, or other forms of physical violence that are commonly held to amount to persecution" (US Considerations 1995: 708) will necessarily mitigate the practice of viewing the motivation for rape as apolitical "sexual desire."

This is even more problematic with regard to domestic violence, which the Considerations refer to as "private actions" (US Considerations 1995: 718). While the Considerations identify domestic violence as a form of persecution, they are silent on why it should not be characterized as "private harm." Indeed, in the sole case cited involving domestic violence (*Matter of Pierre* 1975*)*, the Board of Immigration Appeals ruled that spousal abuse by a Haitian legislator, whom the state would not restrain, did not constitute persecution (US BIA *Pierre* 1975). The case is more than twenty years old, and the Considerations do not refer to more recent jurisprudence or even suggest a more contemporary analysis of the issue. Ironically, while the Australian Guidelines do not declare domestic violence to be a form of persecution, the jurisprudential environment in Australia seems more receptive to it in practice than does the United States.

As if to preempt complaints that labeling as persecutory such practices as forcible sterilization or female genital mutilation amount to cultural imperialism, the Canadian Guidelines provide that "[w]hat constitutes permissible conduct by a state toward women may be determined ... by reference to international instruments" (Canadian Guidelines 1996: 7). The Australian Guidelines adopt a similar approach (Australian Guidelines 1996: par 2.2, 4.4), and explicitly assert that rape, forced abortion, and female genital mutilation constitute cruel, inhuman, and degrading treatment contrary to the *Convention Against Torture* (Australian Guidelines 1996: par 4.6). A range of relevant human rights instruments are identified by name in the Guidelines.

The US Considerations briefly mention international human rights instruments at the outset, but then quickly turn inwards, relying instead on American case law (Anker, Kelly, and Willshire-Cerrera 1996a: 609). Indeed, the Considerations in general interpret "persecution" to mean inter alia, "threats to life, torture, and economic restrictions so severe that they constitute a threat to life or freedom." The Considerations in general focus heavily on jurisprudence from the Board of Immigration Appeals (BIA) and the federal courts; as such they seem to provide less of an overview of the various issues that could arise in future claims of gender-related persecution than a digest of cases that have already been decided.

Given that the Considerations are presented as the state of existing law, it is relatively easy to argue that Asylum Officers who deviate from them are departing from settled law. The disadvantage of this retrospective format, however, is that the Considerations are less able to advance the state of the law.

One of the most common media profiles of women refugee claimants involves a woman from a theocratic Muslim state who rejects proscriptions imposed on her dress, behavior, educational opportunities, ability to marry, divorce and obtain custody, etc. In media reports, this resistance is often telescoped into a refusal to wear a headscarf or *chador*. More generally, this scenario exemplifies situations in which a woman objects to laws or policies which discriminate against, impose burdens upon, or otherwise disadvantage women. In refugee law, persecution is distinguished from prosecution for breach of a legitimate law. The Canadian Guidelines advise that discriminatory laws may constitute persecution under the following circumstances:

(a) the policy or law is inherently persecutory; or

(b) the policy or law is used as a means of persecution for one of the enumerated reasons; or

(c) the policy or law, although having legitimate goals, is administered through persecutory means; or

(d) the penalty for non-compliance with the policy or law is disproportionately severe.

Arguably, the cumulative effect of the web of discriminatory laws, policies, and practices restricting women could therefore amount to persecution. In practice, Canadian decision-makers most often focus on the severity of penalties for noncompliance. Thus, in *Namitabar v. Canada (MEI* [1993]*)*, the Federal Court of Canada found that seventy-five lashes for breach of the Iranian law governing women's dress was so severe that it constituted persecution. Such an approach circumvents judgments about the legitimacy of the law itself, and focuses instead on the penalty as persecutory in relation to its purpose: even if a law requiring a woman to don a veil is (arguably) not persecutory, flogging her forty-seven times to achieve compliance is.[10]

The US Considerations explore this issue chiefly through case law involving the strictures imposed on women's dress and behavior in Iran. Quoting *Fatin v. INS* (1993: starting at 1233), the Considerations caution that "the concept of persecution does not encompass all treatment that our society regards as unfair, unjust or even unlawful or unconstitutional" (1240).[11] Nevertheless, as noted in *Fatin*, "the concept of persecution is broad enough to include governmental measures that compel an individual to engage in conduct that is not physically painful or harmful but is abhorrent to that individual's deepest beliefs" (1241–2).[12] The evidence in the case also indicated that the penalty for flouting the morality code in Iran would be flogging and imprisonment, leading to possible rape and death, and the Court found that these penalties would also constitute persecution. Thus, the Considerations extract from the case law two principles: first, that compelling obedience to a law could constitute persecution if it required a person to renounce or violate deeply held religious or other fundamental beliefs; second, certain penalties for violating discriminatory laws might constitute persecution. Interestingly (but perhaps not surprisingly), the Court in *Fatin* ultimately rejected the applicant on grounds that it did not believe that obeying the rules would be "profoundly abhorrent" to her.

The Australian Guidelines adopt a diffident tone regarding women who violate or object to the discriminatory norms of their society. They advise that restrictions on women's behavior, be it through exclusion from public life, forcible marriage, or abuse of their sexual/reproductive capacities, may "vary from mere inconvenience to oppression" (Australian Guidelines, par. 4.9). Decision-makers are advised to consider the severity of the restrictions, along with the penalties for disobedience, in deciding whether they constitute persecution. In a recent decision, the Australian Refugee Review Tribunal (RRT) (Australian RRT V97/05699 1997) affirmed the rejection of an Iranian applicant who objected to the generalized oppression of women in that country and feared being subjected to a forced marriage and being punished for violating Iranian dress codes. In a radical departure from prior rulings, the Tribunal extrapolated from the UNHCR position that dress codes are not in themselves persecutory to the conclusion that the entire network of norms, policies, laws, and practices constraining Iranian women cannot constitute persecution.

Certainly, no member of the RRT is bound by decisions of other Members. Nevertheless, in order to explain the discrepancy between this decision and earlier RRT cases, I suggest that one must go beyond the apparently divergent opinions on the status of Iranian laws relating to women. It is interesting to note that in an earlier case where the applicant was accepted, the decision-maker concluded that the applicant "has strong objections to the Islamicization of Iranian culture which she sees as subsuming her own religious and cultural practices. The Tribunal considers that the depth of the applicant's beliefs and feelings is such that she would deliberately flout the dress codes thus exposing herself to severe penalties" (Australian RRT N94/03738 1995). Conversely, in the case cited previously, the Tribunal asserted that the "applicant has shown no history of willfully flouting Islamic regulations nor any credible reason to believe that she would do so in the future." (Australia RRT V97/ 05699 1997). Evidently, the decision-maker doubted the sincerity of the claimant's opposition to the strictures imposed on her as a woman. This is similar to the ultimate conclusion drawn by the US court in *Fatin*. It is worth commenting, however, that a person is not normally required to deliberately undergo persecution in order to validate her convictions.[13] The Tribunal also asserted that the associated persecutory penalties could be avoided by obeying the laws in question. This finding would presumably defeat the claim of any applicant, regardless of the authenticity of her opposition to the laws in question.

Objective Basis

It is not enough for a woman to fear persecution. She must also establish that her fear is well founded. In Canada, the courts require that there be a "reasonable chance" or "real risk" of persecution should the claimant be returned to her country of nationality. In Australia, the applicant must demonstrate a "real chance" of future persecution, unless she proves that she has been persecuted in the past, in which case the burden shifts to the officer to establish a "substantial and material change in circumstances in the country of origin" (Australian Guidelines 1996: par. 4.17–4.20). Evidence regarding the objective basis to a claimant's fear may be located in her experience or the experience of similarly situated women. Documentary evidence about the human rights situation in the country of origin often furnishes the objective basis to a claimant's subjective fear of persecution. This type of documentary information is typically gathered and reported by various NGOs, human rights monitors, media, and governmental bodies, which now increasingly see 'women's rights as human rights', whereas they once largely did not.

In Canada, most documentation about country conditions used in the hearing rooms is assembled and generated by the IRB Documentation Centre. Since the advent of the Canadian Guidelines, the Documentation Centre has diligently sought and gathered information about the condition of women in many countries, and has produced a range of country profiles. The US INS recently set up a Resource Information Center (RIC) modeled after the IRB, and the Considerations indicate that the "RIC will be working on a number of projects in an attempt to assure that information concerning violations of the rights of women are distributed regularly and systematically" (US Considerations 1995: 706–7). The Australian Guidelines encourage officers to conduct their own research into country of origin conditions, using both departmental resources and UNHCR data.

Despite these efforts, physical and sexual violence against women tends to be underreported at all levels, and the type of detailed information capable of substantiating individual claimants' narratives regarding gender-related persecution may not be readily available. Decision-makers in Canada and Australia (Australian Guidelines 1996: par. 3.6; Canadian Guidelines 1996: 9–10) are cautioned to be sensitive to these limitations.

State Protection

All three directives address state responsibility for persecutory acts committed by nonstate actors. All proceed from the basic premise that the state owes a duty to protect citizens' basic rights, not only from abrogation by the state itself, but from private actors as well. A person is entitled to seek protection in the form of asylum if her government violates her fundamental rights for a Convention reason, or proves unwilling or unable to protect her from the violation of those rights by others. This principle evolved with no particular attention to gender. However, it resonates with particular force in gender-based claims, as Crawley observes in this volume. Domestic violence is the paradigmatic example of gender-specific abuse committed by "private actors." It has long been consigned to the 'private' sphere and is thus allegedly beyond the reach of state intervention. Its invisibility in the arena of international human rights follows almost axiomatically. And, of course, inattention and inaction by the state tacitly condone and sustain the practice of domestic abuse.

In recent years, however, the international community has begun to accept that domestic violence has international human rights implications, as evinced by the UN *Declaration on the Elimination of Violence Against Women*. When taken together with refugee law's recognition that the state may be responsible for its failure to protect individuals, it *should* follow that domestic violence is a form of persecution from which the state is obliged to protect its women nationals.

Even so, prior to the issuance of the Guidelines, Canadian decision-makers sometimes dismissed domestic violence as a crime that, though deplorable, was not within the purview of refugee law; even if it constituted persecution, the abuse was not connected to a Convention reason. The notion that domestic violence is a "private harm" still figures strongly in Australian and American jurisprudence. Though this rationale has faded from Canadian jurisprudence, significant hurdles remain with respect to the question of state protection in the context of domestic violence. The complexity of the issue can best be introduced by comparing two IRB cases. The most revealing features of these cases are the indicia that decision-makers deem proof of a state's ability and willingness to protect a woman from domestic violence. The first decision concerned a Jamaican woman known as "E.R.M." (Canada IRB T95–04279, 1996), who claimed refugee status on grounds that she feared violent retaliation by an abusive ex-husband in Jamaica. Her ex-husband was a policeman who, inter alia, had been convicted in 1989 for beating up criminal suspects.

The panel's analysis can be summarized as follows: first, the panel notes that assault/battery causing bodily harm is a criminal offense, and describes the legal remedies that are available. Later, and in the same vein, the panel draws attention to the passage of Jamaican legislation specifically aimed at domestic abuse. The description is entirely theoretical, and there is no discussion of what actually happens if a woman complains to police about spousal assault. The question "is state protection both *real* and *effective?*" is neither asked nor answered. The only resulting commentary on the efficacy of the law is that it is "mixed." The panel infers from this one-word assessment that protection is indeed effective, noting that it often takes time for new legislation to achieve its objective. It is unclear why the possibility that legislative measures may be effective in the future is sufficient to render state protection adequate at present, since the failed refugee claimant presumably faces return to her country of origin within a reasonably short time.

Secondly, the panel notes that new legislation may not be immediately effective in Canada either. The tacit message is that if systemic defects also exist in Canada, they are not indicative of a failure of state protection, but of a 'normal' fluctuation in law enforcement. It is important to recognize the resort here to Canada as a normative referent against which other states will be judged: if Canada does it (or does not do it), it cannot be a problem. The more general underlying assumption is that Canada both can and will provide effective state protection to women trying to escape physically abusive relationships. It is a proposition that many in Canada would dispute.[14]

Thirdly, the panel catalogues a variety of Jamaican services typically offered by private nonprofit agencies, such as shelters for battered women, legal aid clinics, and women's crisis centers, and treats them as components of *state* protection. Thankfully, the revised Guidelines clarify that "the fact that the claimant did or did not seek protection from non-government groups is irrelevant to the assessment of the availability of state protection" (Canadian Guidelines 1996: 9).

Finally, the panel concludes by remarking that where a government can be shown to be taking steps to protect women, absent evidence to the contrary, "it must be presumed that these steps will be effective." The effect of this presumption is to alchemize legislative enactments into real protection, and to mask the dearth of meaningful information about actual state protection by rendering such evidence superfluous.

At the same time, it would be misleading to suggest that claims by women fleeing domestic violence are routinely rejected. The following factors appear to incline panels toward a finding that the state is able and willing to protect: the country of nationality is a democracy; spousal abuse is punishable under a specific law; services (governmental or nongovernmental) are available to assist battered women; the claimant did not make vigorous attempts to seek police protection. On the other hand, factors militating in favor of the claimant include: undemocratic country of nationality; repeated unsuccessful attempts to elicit police response; assailant holding an influential position (through wealth, employment, politics, etc.) that shields him from police intervention; and the claimant belonging to an ethnic group or social class that would lead authorities to ignore or denigrate her requests for assistance.

It is not uncommon for different IRB panels to come to opposite conclusions regarding the availability of state protection for claimants from the same countries. Decisions of one panel do not bind others, and no two factual situations are identical. State protection may be more forthcoming for some than for others. And, of course, attitudes vary among decision-makers about what constitutes a genuine ability or willingness to protect women from domestic violence, or what 'adequate' protection really means. Yet these explanations do not tell the whole story, for sometimes the same decision-maker will draw opposite conclusions from very similar evidence. For example, the same decision-maker who wrote the decision referred to above concluded five months *earlier* in the case of a claimant known as "R.R.P.":

> In assessing the effectiveness of state protection in the present case the panel has considered [her spouse's] position in the ————— reserves, the claimant's past experiences in soliciting protection from the police against persecution by [her spouse], and the documentary evidence noted above which corroborates the claimant's allegation that effective

state protection from further aggression by ———— is not available to her in Jamaica. We therefore find that the claimant can not avail herself of effective state protection in Jamaica. (Canada, IRB T95–01010/11/12, 1996)[15] [Footnotes and citations omitted; data that may identify claimant have been sanitized.]

Can one reconcile these two rulings on state protection in Jamaica? Both men against whom the allegations of abuse were made held positions that arguably made police less likely to intervene on the women's behalf. The first was a police officer, the second, a member of a civilian militia. The most salient factual difference between the two cases is that R.R.P. had attempted in various ways to obtain police protection, whereas E.R.M. had not. R.R.P. was also able to summon evidence from a Jamaican source indicating that, despite the existence of legislation and legal remedies for abused women, the reality is that the problem is immense and police do not take it seriously. Thus, battered women have little prospect of obtaining meaningful protection. In principle, the fact that E.R.M. did not seek state protection should not matter, if it was reasonable for her to believe that protection would not be forthcoming. The fact that her husband was a policeman, which made seeking police protection futile, should not, in principle, damage her claim.

Why would a decision-maker first concur with the conclusion that Jamaica fails to provide adequate protection to victims of domestic violence, then in a *subsequent* case come to the opposite conclusion? Certainly, there is nothing in the documentation supplied in the later case that challenges the information supplied in the earlier one. While one may hypothesize that the women were differently situated with respect to the availability of state protection, there is no evidence to validate this hypothesis. My experience as a decision-maker leads me to speculate that two extrinsic factors often play a significant role–albeit unconsciously–in generating divergent outcomes where the relevant facts appear similar. The first is the complex interaction between a panel of two decision-makers. Each two Member panel has its own dynamic, and inasmuch as a positive decision by either Member determines the final result,[16] a Member who might otherwise be inclined to reject the claim may simply defer to his or her colleague.

Second, the assessment of credibility can be crucial. In the larger offices of the IRB, panel Members typically specialize in a few countries or regions. They may hear many similar claims from the same country, and over time become more discerning and/or skeptical (perhaps even cynical) regarding the authenticity of the narratives they are hearing. Canadian refugee jurisprudence, nevertheless, makes it clear that a claimant cannot be rejected for lack of credibility simply because of a decision-maker's 'gut feeling'. A decision-maker must be able to point to serious inconsistencies or implausibilities in the claimant's evidence in order to justify a finding that a claimant is fabricating her story. It is not uncommon for a decision-maker to doubt the claimant's credibility but lack sufficient proof of contradiction or implausibility necessary to substantiate those doubts. The appropriate course of action is to render a positive decision, despite one's doubts.

This can be a hard pill for some Members to swallow. I believe that some resist by deploying alternative strategies to reject such claimants. In this regard, the ruling referred to earlier–that women could avoid the persecutory penalties associated with breach of the Iranian dress code by wearing the prescribed garments–may have been invoked to supplement the decision-maker's suspicions about the sincerity of the applicant's objection to the dress code. In the context of domestic violence, a common alternative to explicitly disbelieving that the claimant was persecuted is the finding that even if the claimant has been battered in the past, the state is able and willing to provide adequate protection in the future.

Something of this sort may well have occurred in the case of E.R.M., who in contrast to R.R.P. may have appeared incredible because she had no evidence corroborating the abuse. The only evidence of abuse that E.R.M. presented was her own testimony. R.R.P. produced letters from witnesses, medical personnel, and a crisis center to substantiate the pattern of abuse. Moreover, E.R.M. arrived in Canada in 1988, and did not file a refugee claim until 1994; R.R.P. did so almost immediately. The panel questioned whether E.R.M. subjectively feared her ex-husband in Jamaica since she waited six years to file her refugee claim. While R.R.P.'s claimed abuse was in her immediate past, at the time of her refugee hearing E.R.M. had not seen her ex-spouse in eight years, and the last incident of abuse allegedly occurred nine years earlier. No one in her family had heard from her ex-husband in four years, and the panel found it unlikely that her ex-husband would want to kill her if she returned to Jamaica after all those years. In other words, the panel also questioned the objective basis to her fear of persecution in Jamaica.

While each such negative inference drawn by the panel is equivocal, it seems clear that the panel had doubts about whether E.R.M. was indeed battered. In this context, adding an analysis which concludes that state protection is both available and adequate effectively seals the negative decision and further insulates it from judicial review by a higher court. Distilled down to its essence, the panel's decision consists of the following: we doubt the claimant was abused; even if she was abused, it happened so long ago that her ex-husband would no longer be interested in her; even if he was still interested in her, adequate state protection is available. Amply documented, recent, and demonstrating an attempt to seek protection, R.R.P.'s case produced a different response: the panel explicitly ruled that "In light of the claimant's testimony and the corroborating evidence she provided, the panel believes that [R.R.P.] was abused in the manner alleged." The panel then described how the Jamaican state was *unable* to provide effective protection to the claimant.

The Australian Guidelines remain curiously silent on the topic of domestic violence, although the discussion about state protection seems drafted with domestic violence in mind. The Australian Guidelines begin by admitting that claims of "gender-based persecution often involve persecution committed by non-state agents," and note that "particular types of violence against women may be officially condemned or illegal but in fact be so endemic that local authorities turn a blind eye to its occurrence" (Australian Guidelines 1996: par. 4.11, 4.12). The Australian Guidelines also acknowledge that it may not always be reasonable or possible for a woman to approach the authorities for protection and that an inability to request protection may itself be indicative of a failure of state protection (Australian Guidelines 1996: par. 4.14). Critically, the Guidelines counsel officers to "research accepted norms of the relevant societies to determine how they operate both through legislation and in terms of actual practice in order to determine the degree of protection available to women" (Australian Guidelines 1996: par. 18), noting that state protection should be effective, realistic, and accessible to a woman of the claimant's culture and position.

A review of decisions by the Australian RRT related to domestic violence nevertheless indicates variation in the assessment of state protection in situations of spousal abuse,[17] and I have been unable to locate any such decisions that refer explicitly to the Australian Guidelines. However, as noted earlier, the RRT is not formally subject to the Guidelines, and relatively few cases involving domestic violence have been decided and reported since the issuance of the Guidelines. The US Considerations say little about state protection that applies to the situation of domestic violence, save the following:

> [T]he persecutor might also be a person or group outside of the government that the government is unable or unwilling to control. If the applicant asserts a threat of harm from a non-government source, the applicant must show that the government is unwilling or unable to protect its citizens. It will be important in this regard, though not conclusive,

to determine whether the applicant has actually sought help from government authorities. Evidence that such an effort would be futile would also be relevant.

The Considerations do not address evidentiary issues regarding state protection or the standard of 'adequacy' that citizens are entitled to expect.

Nexus to Convention Ground

In order to succeed in a refugee claim, one must also prove that the reason for the persecution relates to one of the enumerated grounds: race, religion, nationality, particular social group, or political opinion. The list does *not* include gender, and none of the directives add it. Instead, they encourage decision-makers to let gender inform their assessment of persecution on the basis of race, religion, nationality, or political opinion. In the final resort, 'women' (or a subcategory thereof) might qualify under the residual category of "particular social group."

Enumerated Grounds and Gender

The Australian and Canadian Guidelines attempt to illustrate the interaction between gender and each of the enumerated grounds. With respect to race, the Australian Guidelines refer to "ethnic cleansing" and state that a "persecutor may choose to destroy the ethnic identity and/or prosperity of a racial group by killing, maiming or incarcerating the men while the women may be viewed as capable of propagating the ethnic identity and persecuted in a different way, such as through sexual violence" (Australian Guidelines 1996: par. 4.29). The Canadian Guidelines remark that "a woman from a minority race in her country may be persecuted not only for her race, but also for her gender" (Canadian Guidelines 1996: 3). The US Considerations are silent on the intersection of race and gender.

With respect to nationality, the Australian and Canadian Guidelines mention that a woman who marries a foreign national may lose her citizenship. They both caution, however, that it is not loss of citizenship per se that constitutes persecution, but the consequences that flow from loss of citizenship that may amount to persecution (Canadian Guidelines 1996: 3; Australian Guidelines 1996: par. 4.31). The US Considerations do not discuss nationality as a ground of persecution in a gender context.

With respect to religion, the Canadian Guidelines propose that freedom of religion encompasses the right to practice—or not practice—a prescribed religion or a version of a religion. Thus, in a patriarchal theocracy where "the religion assigns certain roles to women," a woman who "does not fulfil her assigned role and is punished for that ... may have a well-founded fear of persecution for reasons of religion" (Canadian Guidelines 1996: 3). Strangely, the US Considerations do not articulate religion as a ground of persecution in such cases, but rather incorporate it into the definition of persecution. The Considerations quote *Fisher v. INS* (US INS 1994, 1371) regarding the proposition that "when a person with religious views different from those espoused by a religious regime is required to conform to, or is punished for failing to comply with, laws that fundamentally are abhorrent to that person's deeply held religious convictions, the resulting anguish should be considered in determining whether the authorities have engaged in extreme conduct that is tantamount to persecution" (1994: 1379; quoted in the Considerations at 709). The Considerations do not mention that this persecution may be on grounds of religion.

All three directives do indicate that persecution caused by a woman's resistance to institutionalized gender discrimination, as manifested by her speech or conduct, may also be framed as persecution on grounds of political opinion (Australian Guidelines 1996: par. 4.25–4.28; Canadian Guidelines 1996: 4; US Considerations 1995: 710–11). That political opinion may be labeled feminist; certainly, political opinion would be the preferred choice where the laws or practices in question are putatively justified not by "religion," but by "culture."

The Canadian Guidelines go somewhat further than their counterparts in noting that "where women are 'assigned' a *subordinate status* and the authority exercised by men over women results in a general oppression of women," political protest and activism engaged in by women may manifest differently from the familiar modes expressed by men. For instance, a refusal to wear the veil in a fundamentalist Islamic state; setting up communal kitchens and cooperative nurseries under the fascist Pinochet regime; or providing food, shelter, and sustenance to those engaged in 'public' forms of politics could all be seen as types of political resistance carried out within the cultural confines of the roles assigned to women (Greatbatch 1989: 518).[18]

The United States has sporadically taken a more expansive view of political opinion than Canada or Australia. For example, in *Lazo-Majano v. INS* (1987: 1432), the Court ruled that a Salvadoran domestic worker who was beaten, raped, and enslaved by her military employer was persecuted on account of political opinion in the sense that her persecutor was "asserting the political opinion that a man has a right to dominate." He persecuted her allegedly "to force her to accept his opinion without rebellion" (1987: 1435). Her employer threatened to denounce her as a political subversive if she resisted him, though, the record seems to indicate that he did not genuinely believe her to hold subversive political opinions. The court's analysis was designed to overcome the assertion that the harm inflicted was merely "personal," and thus it strained to find that she had a political opinion in relation to the Salvadoran government. It would not suffice to suggest that the nexus to the Convention ground was the *persecutor's* political opinion regarding the role of women because, as the US Supreme Court stated in *INS v. Elias-Zacarias* (1991:812; quoted in the Considerations at 709), the persecution must be "on account of the victim's political opinion, not the persecutor's."

The US Considerations do not elaborate on the potential scope of political opinion in relation to gender claims. However, on 30 September 1996, just over a year after the INS issued the Considerations, Section 601(a) of the *Illegal Immigration Reform and Immigrant Responsibility Act of 1996*[19] amended the refugee definition of section 101(a)(42) of the *Immigration and Nationality Act*, 8 USC. s 1101(a)(42) (1994), to compel recognition of forcible abortion and sterilization as persecution on account of political opinion. Presumably, the political opinion in question is the belief that people ought to be free to choose the size of their family. In Canada, forcible sterilization is usually characterized as persecution on account of membership in a particular social group, variously described in terms such as "Chinese parents with more than one child who face forcible sterilization," "parents of more than one child," or "parents." In Australia, the High Court ruled in *Anor v. Minister for Immigration and Ethnic Affairs* (1997) that there is no particular social group to which the targets of forcible sterilization belong but has not considered political opinion as an alternative ground.

In theory, women ought to be the main beneficiaries here, because it is women who typically suffer forcible sterilization and abortions. This is not because the Chinese state prefers to sterilize women over men, but because the "choice" of which spouse will be sterilized is made by the couple, with the unsurprising result that it is the woman who almost always ends up being sterilized. Ironically, the leading cases from the highest courts of Canada (*Chan v. Canada (MEI)* 1995),[20] the US (BIA *Matter of Chang* 1989) and Australia (*Anor* 1997) all involve *male* claimants allegedly escaping forcible sterilization, perhaps because men are more likely than women to have the resources to flee.

The phenomenon of domestic violence is perhaps the paradigmatic manifestation of women's relative powerlessness in the 'private sphere'. As with forcible sterilization, a divergence appears to be emerging with respect to the treatment of domestic violence in the United States, on the one hand, and Canada and Australia on the other. The trend in American jurisprudence appears to favor characterizing successful claims based on domestic violence as persecution on account of political opinion. Canada and Australia treat them as persecution for reasons of membership in a particular social group. In order to appreciate the implications of each approach, I describe and compare them together in the next section.

Particular Social Group

In many, if not most, cases involving women claimants, decision-makers can link the persecution to race, religion, nationality, or political opinion. Where individual women are persecuted because of their male relatives' activities or political opinions, tribunals have recognized the 'family' as a particular social group, and have accepted that women may be targeted because of their membership in it. The Canadian Guidelines and the US Considerations endorse this approach (Canadian Guidelines 1996: 5; US Considerations 1995: 714–15), while the Australian Guidelines address the same scenario as persecution on account of imputed political opinion. This is based on the assumption that persecutors impute to women the political opinions of their male kin and persecute them for that reason (Australian Guidelines 1996: par. 4.24, 4.26).

When it comes to actually defining a particular social group by reference to gender, decision-makers have generally demonstrated a preference for using the enumerated grounds wherever possible. For example, in a case not mentioned in the Considerations, an Immigration Judge accepted a woman asylum-seeker fleeing domestic violence (US Department of Justice 1994). The applicant was a woman married to a prominent businessman with connections to the Jordanian royal family. He beat her over the course of thirty years. His power and influence insulated him from legal intervention. In accepting the applicant, the judge ruled that the claimant was persecuted because of her belief in Western values as expressed through her actions consisting, in the main, of attempting to obtain her high school equivalency and resisting the abuse inflicted on her (over the course of thirty years). Thus, the woman was persecuted allegedly because "she seeks to have her own identity ... [and] believes in the 'dangerous' Western values of integrity and worth of the individual"; the abuse was inflicted "to achieve her submission into the society's mores" (US Department of Justice 1994: 14).

It is curious and not a little ethnocentric to presume that a belief that one should not be beaten is a distinctively 'Western value'. If a belief that women should not be abused by their male partners really was a fundamental 'Western value', one would expect domestic violence to be rare in the West. It is, of course, pervasive in the United States, Canada, and other 'refugee receiving' countries, and none of the states adequately protect women from domestic violence. Indeed, the Immigration Judge describes an episode of abuse where the applicant and her husband were living together *in the US* (he subsequently returned to Jordan), in which the applicant's husband "was terrorizing his wife and sons" (US Department of Justice 1994: 8).

Ethnic chauvinism aside, it seems bizarre to characterize a man's reason for beating his spouse as *her* real or imputed political opinion about her role and status in society. Among other things, it begets potentially invidious and artificial inquiries into men's motivation for beating their intimate partners.[21] The issue is not the proximate reason for the violence, but the underlying assumption that men are entitled to beat women. This attitude is merely another manifestation of their proprietary view of women.

Moreover, I find it more plausible, and closer to reality, to suggest that men who beat women do so because of what men believe about women, not what women believe about themselves. Indeed, to suggest that men beat women because of what women believe (or are imputed to believe) as manifested by their actions might support an inference that the abuse would stop if women only "behaved," a proposition which is offensive and untrue. It would be odd to argue that South African whites oppressed blacks because blacks held the political opinion that they were entitled to be treated as human beings (though they presumably did hold that belief). Apartheid existed because of the racist beliefs of whites—in other words, blacks were persecuted because of their racialized identity, not because of what they believed. By the same token, domestic violence is not about what a woman believes, but about her gender identity—and the sexist beliefs of the man who abuses her. This cannot be captured under the rubric of political opinion because, as noted earlier, political opinion refers to the victim's beliefs, and not those of the persecutor.

Most Canadian and Australian decision-makers concede that the reason for domestic violence is linked in some meaningful way to gender, but gender (or sex) is not listed as a ground of persecution. This has forced the consideration of 'women', or 'women subject to domestic violence' as a particular social group. In *Ward*, the Supreme Court of Canada recognized that a particular social group may be defined by inter alia, the fact that members share an innate or immutable characteristic. The Court listed gender as an example of such a characteristic. The revised Canadian Guidelines incorporate this aspect of *Ward* into the text (Canadian Guidelines 1996: 4), but contain no practical guidance on how to circumscribe or identify a particular gender-based social group. The Australian Federal Court has not explicitly considered whether gender may define a particular social group. It has, however, confirmed that a particular social group cannot be constituted by a common fear of a particular form of persecution. In *Matter of Acosta* (US BIA 1985; cited in US Considerations 1995: 712), the Board of Immigration Appeals remarked that sex could be the type of shared characteristic relevant to constituting a particular social group. As in Canada, however, this observation has not yielded further precision in the US, and, as the US Considerations note, various appellate courts have proffered different opinions on whether and how gender may form the basis of social group ascription.

The Considerations discuss gender and "particular social group" in the context of women who resist the norms of fundamentalist Islamic regimes because those are the fact patterns contained within the jurisprudence. None of the three directives address "particular social group" in reference to domestic violence. This is unfortunate, because domestic violence is probably the commonest and most challenging context wherein decision-makers must articulate a "particular social group."

Upon examination of case law, the actual choices made by Australian and Canadian decision-makers of what "particular social group" is relevant usually range from 'women from country X', to 'women from country X who are victims of domestic violence'.[22] In the United States, some have constructed a particular social group along the lines of "women who fail to conform to the subservient role assigned to women" (Anker, Kelly, and Willshire-Carrera 1996b: 1181). This last approach derives from the UNHCR's Executive Committee's *Conclusion No. 39* that "women asylum-seekers who face harsh or inhuman treatment due to their having transgressed the social mores of the society in which they live may be considered as a 'particular social group' within the meaning of Article 1 A(2) of the 1951 United Nations Refugee Convention." To the extent that their transgression consists of resistance to being beaten, this is more or less a restatement of the political opinion rationale and is problematic for the same reasons.

With respect to the choices of 'women' or 'women who are victims of domestic violence', none of the directives offers explicit advice on selecting definitively from among the options, although they do contain some useful general comments. The Considerations indicate that some appellate courts reject the category 'women', because it is "overbroad." Even when courts have endorsed in principle the category 'women' or a subset of women, applicants have ultimately failed because they could not prove to the Court's satisfaction that they fell within the group. Understandably, the Considerations emphasize the general principles that emerge from these cases, rather than the somewhat dispiriting outcomes on the facts.

Meanwhile, various Canadian and Australian decision-makers, including the Australian High Court (*Anor* 1997), have ruled that it is tautological to define a particular social group simply by reference to the form of persecution feared. The cumulative effect of the critiques is that 'women' is too broad a category to form a particular social group, and 'women who are victims of domestic violence' is circular. The result puts women in a 'no-win' situation.

The revised Canadian Guidelines incorporate *Ward* (Canadian Guidelines 1966: 4) and advise that women may form a particular social group. While they add that a subgroup of women may be identified by reference to other innate or unchangeable characteristics (such as age, race, marital status, economic status, etc.), they do not expressly exclude the form of persecution feared as an appropriate factor (Canadian Guidelines 1996: 5). In fact, some Canadian and Australian decision-makers do accept women claiming to flee persecution in the form of domestic violence. Since positive decisions are rarely challenged, some decision-makers construct the particular social group however they see fit and ignore the criticisms; others adopt one or both of the objections to a gender-based particular social group and reject claimants on grounds that their fear of persecution cannot be linked to a Convention ground. Often the latter conclusion is misstated as a finding that the claimant fears 'personal harm' rather than persecution.

In my view, the critique of women who are victims of domestic violence without state protection as a particular social group is cogent. In the context of the refugee definition, it *is* circular. At the same time, the contention that 'women' cannot constitute a particular social group without making all women refugees is not, I submit, a valid criticism. The impetus to reject the category 'women' emanates, I suggest, from two related anxieties: first, some believe that gender alone is not an attribute sufficient to 'bind' such a large population into a particular social group; second, some subscribe to a 'floodgates' fear that recognizing women as a particular social group would mean that all women are automatically entitled to refugee status.

Partial responses to these objections can be found in jurisprudence and the Canadian Guidelines. In *Chan v. Canada (MEI)* (1995,

La Forest J [diss.]), the court emphatically rejected the floodgates argument, stating that this was "not an appropriate legal consideration" (par. 57). Concurring, the Guidelines state: "The fact that the particular social group consists of large numbers of the female population in the country concerned is irrelevant–race, religion, nationality, and political opinion are also characteristics that are shared by large numbers of people."

The notion that calling women a particular social group leads inexorably to designating all women as refugees is implicitly refuted in the Guidelines by the clear statement that only being a woman is not likely to ever be enough to earn one refugee status, anymore than being a family member (another commonly used "particular social group") or a member of an ethnic/racial minority automatically makes one a refugee. Yet it remains that some people are persecuted because of their family or on account of their race/ethnicity, just as some women are persecuted because they are women. Simply stated, elements of the refugee definition apart from the ground of persecution perform what is, in essence, a filtering function.

Perhaps the easiest way to approach the issue is to understand "particular social group" in the context of the other grounds of persecution and the antidiscrimination principles animating the refugee definition. The refugee definition requires that persecution be linked to "race, religion, nationality, membership in a particular social group, or political opinion." As noted above, *Ward* described the criteria for particular social group as innate or unchangeable characteristic, voluntary association for reasons fundamental to human dignity, or past association for the same reasons. The antidiscrimination orientation of the refugee definition implies that, like other grounds of persecution, a particular social group is also characterized by a marginal or disadvantaged status in society that makes them vulnerable to oppression, including (but not limited to) the actual persecution feared by the claimant.

Close examination of the grounds of persecution that precede and follow "particular social group"–race, religion, nationality, and political opinion–in my view reveal that they are essentially specific applications of the criteria for designating a particular social group agreed upon by the international community. If this is correct, then it follows that the approach to defining other particular social groups should be comparable. Thus, for example, refugee discourse describes a claimant who flees anti-Semitism as one who fears persecution on account of her religion (Judaism), not as "a Jewish person who had been subject to anti-Semitic harassment and discrimination amounting to persecution." A finding that a claimant was persecuted because of her religion (Judaism) is not tantamount to a finding that all Jewish people are refugees. So too with a finding that a woman has been persecuted because of her membership in a particular social group (women).[23]

The Australian Guidelines state that the RRT "has found that whilst being a broad category, women nonetheless have both immutable characteristics and shared common social characteristics which may make them recognisable as a group and which may attract persecution" (Australian Guidelines 1996: par. 4.33).[24] Unfortunately, some Australian Members of the RRT still reject the contention that women constitute a particular social group (RRT N96/12294, 1997),[25] so one cannot assume a consistent gender-sensitive analysis from Australian officers on this issue.

Future Challenges

The Australian and Canadian Guidelines and the US Considerations represent bold and courageous initiatives by national agencies to address the specificity of women's experiences of persecution within the context of the Convention refugee definition. The UNHCR has played a critical role by promoting gender awareness in various aspects of the refugee phenomenon from the refugee camp to the hearing room, despite the fact that the UNHCR exerts no formal authority regarding the interpretation of the refugee definition by States Party. In the end, a constellation of forces within Canada precipitated the Canadian Guidelines, which was then instrumental in motivating similar action in the United States and eventually Australia. In effect, the transmission of ideas regarding the interpretation of an international instrument in this case began vertically, then proceeded horizontally. Canada, by demonstrating what could be achieved, politically and legally, in one jurisdiction, made it politically feasible for other states to follow suit. Ultimately, this may give the UNHCR additional leverage in encouraging other States Party to adopt their own gender Guidelines. Ultimately, however, it is probably the perceived success (or failure) of the Guidelines and the Considerations, as seen through the lens of domestic political concerns, that will have the greatest impact on the direction taken by other States Party.

The Canadian and Australian Guidelines and the US Considerations may appear as final resolutions to the problems surrounding the application of the Convention to the particular circumstances of women and girls. They are not. Identifying an issue of concern and formulating a response rarely 'solves' a problem with finality. Instead, some responses do not work and/or generate unwanted 'side effects'. Responses are not comprehensive, leaving various 'loose ends' unaddressed. Also, higher authorities (such as courts or politicians) will exercise their power to interpret or alter the law, necessitating amendment or revision by subordinate bodies such as tribunals and government agencies. Other times, resolving problems at one level exposes a deeper set of issues that might not have come to the fore but for the fact that the initial response cleared enough conceptual space to problematize those deeper issues. Finally, without ongoing training and sensitization of those who apply them, the best laid guidelines will lead nowhere.

The treatment of domestic violence in the directives, or lack thereof, furnishes one example of these limitations. Each directive was drafted at a fairly high degree of generality and in language that is always equivocal enough to avoid the appearance of fettering the discretion of decision-makers. To the extent that the US Considerations rely heavily on restating existing American jurisprudence, issues that have been sparsely considered by the courts (such as domestic violence) receive relatively little attention. The Australian Guidelines do not even name domestic violence, though significant components of the Guidelines seem directly applicable. The Canadian Guidelines deal more explicitly with the phenomenon, but the advice offered is too equivocal (and confusing at times) to provide much concrete guidance.

While these patterns may be understandable, key questions–What is the nexus to the definition in cases of domestic violence? What are the criteria for assessing the ability or willingness of the state to protect? What constitutes adequate protection?–remain unacknowledged and unaddressed. Thus, while I have disagreed strongly with the use of political opinion in domestic violence cases, it is understandable that counsel will employ whatever strategy is most likely to succeed. The US Considerations, through their retrospective focus on existing jurisprudence, miss the opportunity to suggest new avenues that may be preferable both in theory and practice. This means that political opinion (or its particular social group proxy) is likely to become more entrenched as the vehicle of choice in the United States.

I harbor similar concerns about the directives' treatment of state protection. In fairness, each of the directives do acknowledge the issue, which may well be too complex to address meaningfully in administrative guidelines. In the context of domestic violence, one of the thorniest problems is the absence of any standard against which to assess the ability or willingness of the state to protect women. Again, one of the symptoms of women's marginalization is the failure of the state to take seriously harms inflicted on women of a so-called "private nature," be they sexual or physical. If one accepts that women occupy a subordinate and vulnerable status in a wide range of places and to a greater or lesser degree all over the world,[26] there is no extant standard against which one might measure the adequacy of protection in a particular state, unless one resorts to the fiction that Canada, the US, or Australia adequately protect women from domestic violence. Having said that, it may be useful to compare how effectively the state protects women as compared to other groups in society.

At this juncture, it might be useful for domestic decision-makers to turn their search for guidance back to the international arena. Early in 1996, Radhika Coomaraswamy, UN Special Rapporteur on violence against women, issued a report on violence against women in the family (United Nations Economic and Social Council 1996). The report describes domestic violence as a violation of human rights, details its worldwide various manifestations, compares existing legal mechanisms for addressing it in various countries (United Nations Economic and Social Council 1996: 31–38), and issues recommendations for action at the national and international level. An addendum to the report contains a framework for model legislation on domestic violence (United Nations Economic and Social Council 1996: Add.2), but the Report is clear in insisting that effective protection must take the form of action, not words. Strategies to confront domestic violence must include not only law, but education (of state personnel and the public), health/social services, and campaigns to eradicate female poverty (United Nations Economic and Social Council 1996: 38–40). The Report also appears to take a cue from Canada and the US[27] in recommending that states broaden their refugee and asylum laws "to include gender-based claims of persecution, including domestic violence" (United Nations Economic and Social Council 1996: 40).

The work of the Special Rapporteur illustrates yet again the symbiotic relationship between the international and domestic spheres. The existence of the Canadian Guidelines and US Considerations provides the Special Rapporteur with concrete examples she can use to exhort other countries to follow, while her research and recommendations regarding the eradication of domestic violence can help local refugee decision-makers articulate a standard of adequate state protection in the context of domestic violence. In this way, national and international human rights regimes can reinforce and propel one another forward. Ultimately, an idealized process might be depicted as dialogic. International actors, including the UNHCR and the Special Rapporteur on women, communicate with national actors regarding the interpretation of the Convention in a gender-sensitive manner. Different states learn from one another's example about the options. National bureaucracies listen to nongovernmental actors, academics, activists, and their own internal sources about the need for change and how to go about it. Bureaucracies then engage their decision-makers in the critical process of listening to women tell their stories. However well intentioned the UNHCR, however committed the activists, and however good or bad the directives, whatever else happens, nothing counts unless actual decision-makers open their hearts and minds to women who have risked all to flee their home and seek refuge in a new country. The success of the directives should be judged solely by the extent to which they enhance decision-makers' ability to genuinely listen to the stories of women who are persecuted as, or because, they are women, and to hear them as the stories of refugees.

Notes

1. I wish to thank Penelope Mathew and Deborah Anker for their helpful comments, and Doreen Indra for her editorial work and guidance.

2. Although the UNHCR encourage states to adopt favorable policies and practices, it is not in a position to dictate to States Party. Indeed, as Crawley explains (this volume), in 1996 the British Home Office asserted that the Executive Committee's *Conclusion No. 39* imposed no obligation on States Party to recognize women as a social group.

3. In the event that panel Members disagree on the outcome, the split decision is treated as a positive decision in virtually all instances.

4. In Nova Scotia, Prince Edward Island, and New Brunswick, legal aid is denied to refugee claimants, who often appear unrepresented.

5. In the US, it appears that some immigration judges are requiring scientific corroboration of claims based on rape, justifying on grounds that "anyone can come in and claim rape" (Anker, Kelly and Willshire-Carrera 1996a).

6. For instance, the UNHCR Guidelines advise against questioning in detail about sexual abuse, since what matters is simply that it occurred. In my experience as a Member, the UNHCR Guidelines were not actually distributed to Members.

7. Canada, the US, and Australia accept that the state is responsible not only for persecution that it commits, but also for persecution committed by others in situations

when the state cannot or will not protect the victim. Other countries, such as France, confine the application of the refugee definition to acts perpetrated by the state.

8. There is some attempt at reintegrating in the "Framework of Analysis" at the end, which relates the preceding discussions back to the refugee definition (Canadian Guidelines 1996: 12–13).

9. The Canadian Guidelines advert to rape in the context of ethnic cleansing at section 65(3).

10. As Blackstone wrote in 1670, "Where the evil to be prevented is not adequate to the violence of the prevention, a sovereign that thinks seriously can never justify such a law to the dictates of conscience and humanity."

11. Quoted in Considerations, at 709.

12. Quoted in Considerations, 709. To pick another example, forcing a devout Jew or Muslim to eat pork would not be physically painful but could surely inflict genuine anguish.

13. For example, a conscientious objector is not normally required to demonstrate that he has been punished for refusing to serve in order to substantiate his convictions.

14. I have written elsewhere on the implications of this assumption for refugee law. In brief, using Canada as the normative referent against which the adequacy of state protection elsewhere will be judged reinforces Canada's self-understanding as a refugee acceptor/nonrefugee producer, but only by misrepresenting (and prettifying) the situation of battered women in Canada.

15. Although Then presided, and the presiding member usually writes the decision, this decision was written by Kelley. Then concurred.

16. If one Member decides positively and the other negatively, the decision is positive.

17. For examples, see the negative decisions rendered in RRT N94/06342 (Fiji), 28 June 1995 (R. Layton); RRT N96/11892 (Ghana) 16 October 1996 (R. Smidt); for positive decisions, see RRT N94/06730 (Philippines), 14 October 1996 (M. Tsamenyi); RRT V96/04260 (Lebanon), 30 May 1996 (A. Borsody)

18. The Canadian Guidelines thus attempt to respond to the concern expressed by Thomas Spijkerboer (1994) that the women's activities in the so-called "private sphere" may not be recognized as political.

19. Enacted as Division C of the Departments of Commerce, Justice, and State, and the Judiciary Appropriations Act for 1997, Pub. L. No. 104–208, 110 Stat. 3009 ("IIRIRA").

20. The majority of the Supreme Court of Canada refused to rule on whether forcible sterilization constitutes persecution and based its decision on other grounds. The dissent did rule that it constitutes persecution. In *Cheung v. MEI* (1993), 19 Imm. LR (2d) 181 (FCA), a unanimous Federal Court of Appeal ruled that forcible sterilization did constitute persecution. The refugee claimant in *Cheung* was a woman.

21. For example, in the course of his decision, the Immigration Judge remarked that if a man beats his partner because he believed she was having an extramarital affair, "her claim would not, by itself, qualify as a ground for granting asylum" (US Department of Justice 1994: 18). In fact, many abusive men are very jealous and possessive, and frequently accuse their intimate partners of infidelity.

22. On occasion, one also sees "women who are victims of domestic violence and cannot obtain state protection."

23. See the argument of Lesley Hunt, Member of the Australian RRT (RRT N93/00656, 1994: 15–18), for an excellent analysis of the appropriate use of "women" as a particular social group.

24. This proposition is extracted from a superb decision by then RRT Member Lesley Hunt. In a case involving a Filipina survivor of decades of spousal abuse, Hunt carefully sets out the degraded status of women around the world to establish that women comprise a particular social group. Hunt cites numerous facts, including socially imposed gender roles, sex discrimination in law and employment, women's relative lack of economic and political power, and women's vulnerability to male violence and the absence of state protection from it. These indicators are taken as evidence that "[w]hilst there does exist separation in lifestyles, values, political leanings, etc., women share a defined social status and as such are differentially dealt with by society as a group" (RRT N93/00656, 3 August 1994: 18).

25. In a recent case, a Member of the RRT accepted that women may, in principle, constitute a particular social group on account of shared marginalization, but found that Mauritian women were not marginalized: "The attitude of Mauritius and Mauritian society as a whole is not indicative of the systemic marginalization of women at all levels, which, in my view, is a necessary precondition to the acceptance of 'women in Mauritius' as a particular social group" (RRT N96/12294).

26. I do not dispute, of course, that other factors (race, economic status, nationality, sexual orientation, etc.) may all affect a particular woman's vulnerability.

27. Australia had not issued its Guidelines at the time the Report was written.

17

Women and Refugee Status

Beyond the Public/Private Dichotomy
in UK Asylum Policy

Heaven Crawley

Introduction

> Both the structures of international law making and the content of the
> rules of international law privilege men; if women's interests are ac-
> knowledged at all they are marginalized. International law is a thor-
> oughly gendered system. (Charlesworth et al. 1991: 614–5)

While the rules of international law are commonly assumed to be
abstract, objective, and gender-neutral, feminist jurisprudence has
emerged over the past decade as a systematic critique of the practice and profession of law, with its central theme that law is an
inherently gendered system reinforcing male domination. It has
been argued that the impact of 'neutral' laws is not always equal
and that laws based on men's lives do not effectively incorporate
women's experience: "Asking the 'woman question' means examining how the law fails to take into account the experiences and values that seem more typical of women than of men, for whatever
reason, or how existing legal standards and concepts might disadvantage women" (Roach Anleu 1992; Romany 1993; Binion 1995).
In this context, a feminist perspective, with its concern for gender as
a central category of analysis and its commitment to equality between the sexes, provides a substantial challenge to international

refugee law as it is institutionally understood, and asks fundamental questions about the processes by which human rights are defined, adjudicated, and enforced.

International refugee law, as enshrined in the *1951 Convention Relating to the Status of Refugees* (hereafter "the Convention") and implemented by signatory states, has generally assumed that all refugees–irrespective of their sex–face the same problems and will be treated equally in the process of asylum determination. My aim here, however, is to expose some of the underlying gendered assumptions upon which international refugee law is based and to examine their implications for refugee women seeking asylum in the UK. Drawing upon research with lawyers, practitioners, and refugee women themselves, I argue in this chapter that the process of becoming, *and being recognized as,* a refugee is gendered, and that Convention refugee law, as interpreted through asylum policy in the UK, presents significant difficulties for many women whose fears of persecution arise out of forms of protest or ill-treatment not considered 'political' or deserving of international protection. Women are often denied refugee status for reasons that have to do less with refugee law itself than with gender (see also Spijkerboer 1994).

Although international instruments for protection make no distinction between male and female refugees,[1] I argue that the interpretation of refugee law in the UK, as elsewhere, has evolved through an examination of male asylum applicants and their activities, and that this both reflects and reinforces existing gender biases within states. It is *men* who have been considered the principal agents of political resistance and therefore the legitimate beneficiaries of protection from resulting persecution; thus, "the law has developed within a male paradigm which reflects the factual circumstances of male applicants, but which does not respond to the particular protection needs of women" (Kelly 1993: 674; see also Bhabha 1993; Goldberg and Kelly 1993). This approach suggests to me that the 'problem' is not so much the actual invisibility of women but rather how their experiences have been "*represented and analytically characterized*" (Indra 1987: 4, emphasis in original). In this context, my conceptual focus is not on women per se but *gender*, and the ways in which societally and culturally constructed ideas about gender roles have conditioned the normative structures of international refugee law. Unpacking these categories and relationships, which typically have been seen as natural, self-evident, and ungendered, is a critical first step toward gaining a deeper understanding of relations of power and process in asylum determination.

The Normative Structures of International Refugee Law

Nothing explicitly precludes a woman from being recognized as a Convention refugee. Indeed, as Bhabha (1993) notes, the gender-blindness of the refugee definition may not present a problem for women who flee 'traditional' persecution, such as torture and imprisonment, for reasons similar to those of their male counterparts.[2] Furthermore, the fact that gender is not included as an enumerated ground for persecution (see Macklin, this volume) does not necessarily lead to the conclusion that a woman will be denied refugee status on that basis and *cannot* be protected. Nonetheless, women are less likely than men to appear directly involved in political activity, and are frequently involved in supportive roles or in gendered forms of resistance to oppression by the state, community, or family (see Nordstrom, Matlou, and Giles, this volume). In this context, the task of framing a claim to gender-related persecution in the absence of gender as a prohibited ground in the Convention remains problematic in the UK chiefly because of the normative framework within which women's claims to asylum are assessed.[3]

It has been argued that when gender becomes central to the analysis of international refugee law, "international law ... dissolves into a normative struggle whose outcome is determined largely by power" (Strizhak and Harries 1993: 6). Charlesworth et al. (1991) maintain that it is this normative structure that has allowed issues of particular concern to women (including refugee women) to be either ignored or undermined. In particular, modern international law (including asylum law) rests on and reproduces various dichotomies between the public and private spheres; a distinction is made between matters of international 'public' concern and matters 'private' to states that are considered within their domestic jurisdiction, and in which the international community has no recognized legal interest. These authors suggest that at a deeper level this public/private dichotomy is gendered; the two spheres are accorded asymmetrical value, with greater significance being attached to the public, 'male' world than to the private, 'female' one. As a result, many issues of concern to women are conceptually relegated to the private realm, a domain regarded as inappropriate for legal regulation. Although international law is gender neutral in theory, in practice it interacts with gender-based domestic laws and social structures that partially relegate women and men to separate spheres of existence (Thomas and Beasley 1993). Even though the basis of the public/private distinction has been thoroughly attacked and exposed as a culturally constructed, highly politically potent ideology, it continues to have a strong grip on legal thinking.[4] The result is that while the refugee definition does not intrinsically exclude women's experiences, in practice the public/private distinction leads to situations in which much of what women do, and what is done to them, is seen as irrelevant to refugee law.

Clearly, there is no such thing as a private or a public act per se; what is critical for this analysis is the way in which such distinctions are made and responded to by the determining authorities in the UK. Only by challenging these 'practical' distinctions can they be shown to be ideological constructs rationalizing the exclusion of women from sources of power. In this context, my argument supports Greatbach's (1989) proposal for an alternative feminist critique that takes into account historical and cultural context, and places the question of gender within a broader analysis of the limitations of the refugee definition. I suggest that women are not less likely to be granted asylum than men in the UK primarily because of the absence of explicit recognition of gender-related persecution; rather, it is because of the social and political context in which the claims of women are adjudicated. The problem lies primarily in the fact that, in applying the refugee definition, asylum adjudicators have largely failed to incorporate the gender-related claims of women in the interpretation of the grounds already enumerated in the Convention. Neither have they acknowledged the state's responsibility for persecutory acts involving non–state agents. The material I present in this chapter suggests that "[t]he consequences for women of this dichotomous perspective are fundamental and profound" (Binion 1995: 519).

Privatizing 'Persecution'

The phrase, a 'well-founded fear of persecution', is central to the definition of a refugee and is said to exist if the applicant can establish, to a reasonable degree, that her continued stay in her country of origin has become intolerable (UNHCR 1979b, para. 42). However, there is no universally accepted definition of 'persecution', and various attempts to formulate one have met with little success. Some suggest that this is a deliberate omission, in order to permit a case-by-case determination of whether any given conduct constitutes a persecutory act (Grahl-Madsen 1966; Hathaway 1991). At the same time, the lack of any agreed-upon definition makes the objective assessment of individual refugee women's claims for asylum highly problematic. Given the perpetual challenges of appropriately interpreting and applying the refugee definition, and in particular the central concept of persecution, a comprehensive gendered critique is needed.

'Serious Harm' and the Violation of Women's Human Rights

Hathaway (1991) insists that the concept of persecution requires two distinct determinations: firstly, whether harm apprehended by the claimant is sufficiently serious to amount to persecution; and secondly, whether the state can be held accountable in some measure for the infliction of that harm. Both elements are critical to any assessment of whether 'persecution' can be said to have taken place, yet rarely in practice are they distinguished and analytically addressed. Refugee women seeking asylum in the UK have often suffered physical harm or abuses that are specific to their gender, but 'persecution' has not been widely interpreted to include these experiences. According to Hathaway (1991), "Persecution is most appropriately defined ... in relation to ... the core entitlements which [have] been recognized by the international community," and he constructs a hierarchy of rights based upon existing human rights instruments.[5] While the use of such a framework is appealing, the focus on international human rights, which might ordinarily be viewed as a strength, is problematic from a feminist perspective for several reasons.

The first of these relates to a general theme in recent literature centered around the idea that human rights–commonly assumed to be immutable and universal–have not always been women's rights (Bunch 1990; Bunting 1993; Cook 1994; Peters and Wolper 1995). Clearly, there are certain human rights that are considered so fundamental as to be nonderogable, such that any violation of those rights is considered egregious. In this regard, Macklin (1995) suggests that the linkage between persecution and the abrogation of basic human rights compels an articulation of what authoritatively constitutes a 'human right'. She also notes that, while international human rights instruments provide a reference point for assessing the seriousness of the harm inflicted on the claimant, *all rights are not created equal.* The fact that discriminatory violations of rights such as the right to work and the right to basic education, which conceivably might be more likely to affect women, are placed lower in the hierarchy lends support to the conclusions of Charlesworth et al. (1991) that human rights law on which the definition of persecution is based offers little redress in cases where there is pervasive, structural denial of rights. Interpreting 'serious harm' to include gender-based discrimination and social mores becomes problematic, because the structure and content of international legal discourse are gender biased at a number of levels, not the least of which is the ordering of priorities (Macklin 1995).

A further problem is that of a perceived conflict between the rights of the individual (in this case, the rights of individual women) versus the rights of each sovereign state or culture. The debate typically is over which rights should 'prevail' in such a situation, especially given that the 'universal' human rights upon which refugee law is based are essentially Western constructs: are human rights values indeed *universal* or can *cultural relativism* legitimately be factored into human rights policies? As the following extracts from UK determinations suggest, one of the strongest objections to recognizing state-specific, pervasive social mores and gender discrimination as constituting persecution has been that states should not be critical of other cultures, values, and practices. In this way, violence against women is often 'legitimated' by the refugee determination process through reference to the social or cultural 'order' of the country from which such women have fled:

> It is clear that a very large number of women in Iran do not agree with the emancipation of women. It seems to me one is on dangerous ground if you attempt to interfere with a person's customs or religious beliefs and on even more dangerous ground if you do so ... on a national or a worldwide scale.[6]

In the case of *Ranjbar* (1994), the Tribunal explicitly stated:

> No doubt the standards which would be applied by the authorities in Iran would differ from those in some other countries: no doubt the status of women and children will be differently regarded. The Convention however is not designed to give relief to all those who live under a less liberal social order than that in some Western countries.[7]

Both cultural relativism in human rights scholarship and antiessentialism in feminist theory have challenged the assumptions of the respective discourses. One critical question arising from these debates is how universal human rights might become legitimized in radically different societies without succumbing to either homogenizing universalism or the paralysis of cultural relativism.[8] However, even outside this debate, the fact remains that one can provisionally take the model on its own terms and still find massive derogation of the so-called higher order human rights of women that are not addressed by refugee determination procedures in the UK or elsewhere. A particularly clear example of this can be seen in the interpretation of sexual violence.[9]

The occurrence of sexual violence in refugee-producing situations has been well documented (Amnesty International 1991; Thompkins 1995), and its use would appear to be a major factor in forced migration. The true scale of sexual violence against refugee women is as yet unknown, since numerous incidents are never reported (UNHCR EC 1995). Sexual violence including rape occurs in a variety of situations. It may be explicitly politically motivated (for example, as a method of interrogation or as part of a process of 'ethnic cleansing') or can occur in situations of generalized violence such as civil war:

> One day the soldiers came in our office and they killed two of my brothers who were working with me. I was showered with their brains and blood ... then my mother–our house was not far from there–when she heard she rushed in and came in. So then the soldiers raped me and my mother. And then I lost my mind. I used to shout and run away but I don't know what I was running away from. I got a bad depression. My mother and my family used to tie me up so I don't run away.[10]

> People are dying in Kabul every day. Even when the rockets stop, then the fighters will rape, loot, smuggle ... if the fighting gets more we feel more secure. If there is peace for two or three days then they are everywhere and if there is a woman they will rape and kidnap her. (Woman from Afghanistan)

Women who are on their own may be particularly vulnerable to this kind of abuse, as are women targeted because of the political activities of absent husbands or other (usually male) family members:

> We have strong values in our culture. Your father can't see you wearing a thin night-dress so that they know that that is not respectable. So this is why they used to torture us. In front of my father they took off my clothes, and they ask your brother to do sex with you in the presence of your mother or father. They know that it hurts them more than physical torture. (Ms. A. from Zaire)[11]

Sexual violence including rape involves the infliction of both physical and psychological harm. It may also carry traumatic social repercussions, which may be affected by a woman's cultural origins or social status. Women who have been raped or sexually abused are often unwilling to report the abuse because they feel degraded or ashamed and/or fear that they would suffer social stigma should they disclose what has been done to them. Thompkins (1995) suggests that the key to understanding the injury of sexual violence including rape is to recognize that, although in many cases the insult may have been intended *for* men *through* women, it is internalized *by* women in three ways. Firstly, women bear the physical injury; secondly, they blame themselves for being raped and feel ashamed; and thirdly, in cultures where men view rape as a stain on their honor and that of the family, women internalize this guilt. In many cultural contexts the experience of sexual violence may lead women to fear being ostracized by their family and the wider community:

> I would prefer to kill myself rather than for my family to know. In my country men do everything but then they want to marry a virgin girl. It is a very strong culture and the girl must be a virgin until she is married ... she can't see anyone until she is married. I can't tell my father or my two sisters. My father lived all his life with the belief that he has four girls who are all virgins, so they can live a good Iranian life.... Even if my brother finds out he will kill me. (Woman from Iran)[12]

Theoretically, sexual violence should be one of the least controversial examples of 'serious harm' in the context of a definition of persecution. Sexual violence is after all a grave breach of the well-institutionalized human right not to be subjected to cruel, inhuman, or degrading treatment or punishment.[13] These rights are so fundamental that no circumstance whatsoever justifies their derogation under international law. It is not, in my view, possible to make a meaningful legal distinction based on clear principles between the sexual violence used against women and other tortures inflicted upon men. In practice, however, things are quite different. Sexual violence has frequently been characterized as the random expression of spontaneous sexual impulses by *individual men* toward women or as the common (and by implication, acceptable) fate of women caught in a war zone. Kelly (1993), for example, citing case law from the US courts, notes that the refusal to accept rape and other forms of sexual abuse *as violence*, instead of as passion or lust gone wrong, is a pervasive problem in evaluating the asylum claims of women.[14] As Macklin suggests, "[s]ome decision makers have proven unable to grasp the nature of rape by state actors as an integral and tactical part of the arsenal of weapons deployed to brutalize, dehumanize, and humiliate women and demoralize their kin and community" (1995: 226).

In the UK, problems in investigating allegations of sexual violence (which are exacerbated by procedural difficulties that are not acknowledged by the determining authorities)[15] can significantly undermine the credibility of female asylum applicants. This was clearly the case for the Iranian woman who earlier described her fears of family reprisals: "They didn't accept my case ... they refused my application. I am appealing because they don't accept it. They want proof, evidence, but I don't have any. Nobody saw me arrested.

Nobody saw me abused and they told me that if I told anyone, they would kill my family." Moreover, even when relevant information is revealed to the Home Office at an early stage, recognition of sexual violence as sufficiently serious to constitute persecution has been inconsistent. For example, a letter from the Home Office refusing the claim of a Kenyan woman who was twice arrested, detained, and tortured by the authorities because of her involvement with the Safina party states boldly that "rape is a criminal matter and as such not the basis of a claim to asylum under the 1951 United Nations Convention." In the case of a woman from Ethiopia who had been refused asylum and appealed against the decision, medical evidence supporting her claims to have been raped and otherwise maltreated by uniformed men of the ruling party, was dismissed by the adjudicator: "It seems reasonable to suggest that they [the scars] could also be compatible with numerous innocent activities.... It is my view that the appellant's emotional response to the doctor was calculated and false ... [and that] the appellant's rape is a complete fabrication."[16]

The problem here does not lie with the refugee definition itself, which does not require decision-makers to view sexual violence as inherently private. Spijkerboer instead suggests that what is at issue is a particular conceptualization of sexual violence that effectively legitimates and normalizes it. In this context, what we need to address is the way in which a nonlegal conception of violence is used to distort sexual abuse. That sex is generally seen as pleasurable (and this is what makes it so different from other forms of torture) is irrelevant. This has finally been recognized in the US, where decision-makers are now reminded that "sexual abuse does not differ analytically from beatings, torture, or other forms of physical violence that are commonly held to amount to persecution. The appearance of sexual violence in a claim should not lead adjudicators to conclude automatically that the claim is an instance of purely personal harm."[17] In this view, whether sexual violence forms the basis for an asylum claim depends upon the *context* in which the abuse took place, the motives of the abuser, and the level of protection available from the state.

Engendering the Concept of State Protection

There is a theoretical distinction in international refugee law between conduct that can be attributed to the state, and for which the state will be held responsible by the international community, and the conduct of private persons that does not implicate the international obligations of the state. In regard to this distinction, a decision on whether an individual faces a risk of 'persecution' must also assess the state's ability and willingness to respond effectively to that risk. In order to constitute persecution, violations of a woman's human rights must be at the hands of the state or of a force that the state is unwilling or unable to control. The state may be said to have failed in its duty to protect when it is actively involved in the persecution or when it offers active assistance to, or condones, persecution through a nonstate agent. Insofar as it is established that meaningful state protection is available to the claimant, protection under the Convention will not be granted.

The obstacles many female refugee claimants face in proving a failure of state protection epitomize the critique leveled by feminist scholars against the public/private dichotomy in international human rights law. Because the distinction between 'common crime' and 'persecution' turns on the role of the state (Macklin 1995), paradigmatic examples of persecution typically involve the state actively engaging in the proscribed conduct (Charlesworth et al. 1991; Macklin 1995). And yet, much of the violence committed against women on a global scale occurs in the 'private sphere' and is perpetrated by husbands, boyfriends, fathers, brothers, and in-laws:

> The abuse was so severe and so much of it ... at least one thousand incidents of abuse, on a daily basis practically since I was born ... sometimes just my father and then other men my father allowed in to abuse me, and abuse by my siblings and family friends.... My father went from abusing me to beating me, and he set a precedent for the whole family on how to treat me...like a piece of dirt, someone you could go to at night to relieve yourself, excrement on, urine on, dogs ... all of this.... I was like a little rabbit they hunted down every day. I was like a prostitute, a whore to be spat on, shat on. (Woman from Zimbabwe awaiting a decision on her claim)

The UNHCR *Handbook on Procedures and Criteria for Determining Refugee Status* is the principle source of guidance for states on the interpretation of the Convention. It acknowledges that the denial of protection by the state against violence may confirm or strengthen the applicant's fear of persecution and that this denial itself may indeed be an element of persecution (UNHCR 1979b: para. 98). Commentators have consistently supported this approach to the failure of state protection (Grahl-Madsen 1966: 191). In recent years, however, a number of countries including the UK have narrowed their interpretation of the Convention and restricted the application of the concept of agents of persecution (UNHCR 1995b).[18] In some cases, states have been held responsible for serious harm only when their designated agents are directly implicated in persecutory measures. In others, states have not been considered responsible if they maintain a legal and social system in which violations of physical and mental integrity are endemic.

Violence within the family is a widespread and often gender-specific form of abuse that can constitute 'serious harm' and, in some cases, rises to the level of persecution. Such violence has begun to be recognized as a human rights concern; nonetheless, it remains on the margins of asylum law.[19] This results primarily from the fact that violence within the family tends to be viewed as a 'personal', 'private', or 'family' matter. Its goals and consequences are obscured, and its use justified as chastisement or discipline: "It is still considered different, less severe, and less deserving of international condemnation ... than officially sanctioned violence" (Copelon 1994: 117). Yet in many of these cases, it is apparent that the protection of the state is not available. As the woman from Zimbabwe just quoted observes:

> In Zimbabwe [my father] would be laughing because the police don't get involved and there is nothing in the law to protect me. He would have the right to do anything he wished.... I'm his property, his daughter and he can do what he likes. The Zimbabwean state endorses this.... If I was ever safe I would go back but I know now that it will never be safe.

Several women from Ghana whom I met during the course of my research had been subjected to this kind of abuse and had received no protection from the Ghanaian state:

> My husband started chasing girls after my son was born. He wouldn't come home. If I said something about it he would beat me, with his hands, his belt. I had a very swollen face. He beat me for three years. He said if I tried to stop him he would cut me with knives and kill me. He didn't want me to divorce and his family has to divorce me. (Ghanaian woman in detention)

> My husband was a very rich man and had a large business in the capital. He was very influential and had many friends within the police. On many occasions my husband forced me to sleep with him and he hit me and my son. Once when he was trying to rape me I hit him on the back of his head and ran away to another town. He reported me to the police so I moved to another town but I thought they would find me there also. (Another Ghanaian woman in detention)

The abuse facing these women was so severe that they fled Ghana leaving their children behind. Even so, they were detained on arrival in the UK, and their claims for asylum were dismissed as 'frivolous'. The adjudicator at one appeal hearing argued that *as he understood the law* "being beaten up by your husband is not a ground for asylum however deplorable it might be." Both women were subsequently deported.

Until recently there has been no substantial discussion in the UK of whether women fleeing from violence within the family can claim protection under the Convention.[20] Moreover, when women have been allowed access to the asylum determination process, case law in the UK has almost invariably gone against them because the failure of the state to protect women against violence within the family has been disputed. For example in *Ranjbar* (1994),[21] the Secretary of State appealed against the decision of an adjudicator to grant Convention refugee status to an Iranian woman who had been beaten by her father. In the grounds for the appeal, it was argued that the applicant could look to the state of Iran for protection against maltreatment and that such violence is not condoned by state authorities.[22] The Immigration Appeal Tribunal upheld the appeal and refused asylum, stating that "there is no acceptable evidence in our view that the authorities in Iran would not accord protection to those severely ill-treated within a family." Similarly in *Jamil* (1996),[23] the Tribunal upheld the decision of the adjudicator to refuse asylum to a Pakistani woman threatened with a death sentence (*jirga*) following a divorce from her husband. It is clear from these and other examples from recent UK case law that, while international refugee law recognizes that persecution can take the form of governmental *inaction* as well as action,[24] the normative conceptualization of persecution in the UK determination process is that persecution occurs chiefly in the public sphere. This has important ramifications.

Firstly, because traditional human rights law (and virtually all other discourses except feminism) has so sharply distinguished the public sphere from the private sphere of the home, courts are likely to characterize familial violence as a 'personal dispute' unless the applicant can demonstrate a strong and consistent pattern of the government's inability or refusal to protect women from such abuse. Yet as Kelly (1993) points out, there is little to differentiate the position of a man who is locked in a torture cell from that of a woman who is repeatedly abused within the confines of her own home. Further, the state connection to persecution required in the definition of a refugee may be difficult to see, since the state never actively commits and seldom overtly condones violence against women. In addition, establishing a state connection is exacerbated by the fact that there is often little documentary evidence available concerning violence against women. In many countries, even the most basic statistics regarding violence within the family are unavailable.

For international refugee law to respond to the protection needs of women whose human rights are violated, the concept of state responsibility must be expanded in practice and doctrine to include more effectively the systematic failure of states to prosecute acts of harm inflicted by nonstate agents. To accomplish this, breaking down the public/private dichotomy is critical (Stairs and Pope 1990). So also is the more effective appreciation that "[t]he widespread absence of state intervention in crimes against women is not merely the result of government's failure to criminalize a class of behavior (since the violent acts themselves usually *are* crimes), but rather is the result of governments' failure to enforce laws equitably across gender lines" (Thomas and Beasley 1993: 46). This kind of 'institutionalized misogyny' (Cipriani 1993) resulting in the nonprosecution of private individuals then becomes a human rights issue, because the state's failure to protect can be shown to be rooted in discrimination along prohibited lines. Moreover, given that the state clearly does regulate the private sphere in other respects—most notably in the areas of family law, social assistance law, and criminal law—it is spurious to claim that there is no relationship between the two (Stairs and Pope 1990).

Understanding how the state can be seen to condone or even promulgate violent activities within the home in turn lays the basis to connect the state to that persecution. As Goldberg (1993) points out, the state has an affirmative obligation to prevent, investigate, prosecute, and punish violations of human rights. The failure or refusal to act—the omission—is equivalent to the commission of the act itself in assessing culpability because, in its failure to respond, the state gives the abuser freedom to act with impunity: "These failures are acts of persecution, accomplished with the acquiescence, if not overt complicity, of the state" (Goldberg 1993: 588).

Depoliticization and Problems in Grounding the Asylum Claim

To be recognized as a Convention refugee, an asylum applicant in the UK, as elsewhere, has to have a well-founded fear of persecution, a fear that must be related to one of the five statutory grounds that are norms of nondiscrimination. Only when harm is inflicted on discriminatory grounds can a claim to the protection of refugee law be recognized. There are, of course, many women who are politically active in the (C)onventional sense, and whose claims for asylum in the UK can be framed within the Convention as it is currently interpreted. At the same time, in some contexts the penalties for political participation may be more severe for women because of cultural and social norms that proscribe their involvement in politics. Political women who are imprisoned by the authorities consequently run the risk of 'double punishment'. They are punished not only because they oppose the regime in some way, but also because they shirk the traditional role of women by being politically active at all: "In the case of political activists, women are not only [sexually] assaulted on the basis of their political opinion, but also because, as women, they should not participate in the political arena" (Spijkerboer 1994: 25). Eventually granted exceptional leave to remain in Britain (as opposed to refugee status) due to her *husband's* political activities, a Kurdish woman from Turkey states:

> I was also involved in political activity. I used to work in a factory as a representative and steward, and I was a supporter of the party.... They arrested forty people and I was the only female. They treated me very badly ... they beat me and asked me if I was ashamed as a woman participating in such events. It is more difficult and more humiliating because of their narrow minds ... the authorities and the police. They try to put women aside in politics.

When this concern combines with dominant gender roles and responsibilities, women are often less likely than men to be directly involved in stereotypically political activity. Instead, women are often involved in 'low level' supportive roles or in sustaining people that the state deems to be 'antagonistic'. Women's political protest and activism often occurs within, or is framed by, the 'private' sphere: "Women who offer political resistance by carrying out 'odd jobs' often do not label their actions as political resistance, and asylum-granting countries may not judge these activities by their political merits, underestimating the political dimensions of these acts" (Spijkerboer 1994). In addition, many women are persecuted or face persecution because of the status, activities or views of their (usually male) family members. The political opinions of these family members are then imputed to women by the persecuting agent, as illustrated by the experience of a Kurdish woman from Turkey, who was denied refugee status but granted leave to remain in the UK on compassionate grounds:

> I also had some problems when my husband was not at home. The gendarme, he said bad words to us. Once he put a gun on my child's head to threaten me ... to push me to say where my husband was.... They captured my husband. He was arrested and they tortured him terribly. The police captured me and the children. I was pregnant and they beat me up.

This is also reflected in the words of another Kurdish woman from Turkey who is awaiting a decision on her claim for refugee status in the UK: "After my husband came here the police came to my house looking for my husband and to ask me where he was, and in order to find out where he was they harassed me and my children. Once they came and beat us and took away our passports." As Macklin (1995) suggests, women's identities, beliefs, and status are frequently subsumed under those of their male kin; there is a societal assumption that women defer to men on all significant issues and that their political views are aligned with those of the dominant members of the family. Thus it seems reasonable to infer that a woman's kinship tie to men could precipitate her persecution on the basis of imputed political opinion regardless of what she herself believes. This logic, however, is not reflected in the UK, where claims for asylum on this basis are often refused. For example, a woman from Zaire and her young sister were refused refugee status:

> I was living with my father and sister. He is a politician and a member of a political party. Because of his activity with the party he had problems with the government so he escaped and hid. Then the local government came and threatened me and asked where my father was hiding.... The soldiers came to our house. They came and threatened me and shot in the air. They kept me in prison for about one month ... but they [the Home Office] told me that my case has been refused. They told me that it's because it's not really me who has suffered ... it was my father ... so it was my father's case not mine. But I appealed because in Africa the way of thinking is different. If one member is hurt it affects all members.

Moreover, female applicants for asylum in the UK are more likely than their male counterparts to be granted Exceptional Leave to Remain (ELR) on compassionate or humanitarian grounds.[25] Not only does ELR provide substantially fewer rights and privileges than Convention refugee status, but it also reflects a particular conceptualization of women as 'victims' and depoliticizes their experiences of persecution. This kind of thinking can be seen in several recent appeal cases, including the case of a Ugandan woman whose husband, father, and grandfather had been politically active and who was arrested and subsequently tortured and raped. She was kept in a cell with three or four others, and each was tortured and raped in front of the others. They were also urinated on and made to drink the urine. When she refused, she was pushed against a piece of broken glass, and her leg was injured to the extent that she could not walk. Although the adjudicator accepted her story and evidence that other members of her family had been persecuted because of the family's political connections (her father's wife had been beheaded and her eldest child's hand had been cut off, with the result that the child died), the (woman) adjudicator did *not* accept that what the applicant had suffered was persecution for a Convention reason and instead made a recommendation that ELR be granted.[26]

In this context, feminist scholars and advocates have increasingly criticized both the Convention itself and the asylum laws of individual countries for their failure to incorporate the gender-based persecution claims of women into one of the existing enumerated grounds. To date, much of this analysis has centered on 'membership of a particular social group'; that the experiences of women generally, or particular subsets of women, can be explained by reference to their social group membership has been the dominant position within the existing literature (Neal 1988; Greatbach 1989; Stairs and Pope 1990; Castel 1992; Goldberg 1993; Fullerton 1993; Kelly 1993; Kelly 1994; Binion 1995). It is the position taken by Hathaway, who insists that "[g]ender-based groups are clear examples of social subsets defined by an innate and immutable characteristic" (1991: 591), and it also finds strong support in the pronouncements of the UNHCR and other governmental bodies.[27] By contrast, the UK response to the social group issue is indicative of its overall approach to gender-related persecution claims:

> The UK Government interprets paragraph (k) of EXCOM 39 as indicating *no obligation* to grant asylum on the basis of women being a social group ... in the United Kingdom gender is taken into account in the assessment of individual asylum claims where this is relevant. However, casework experience suggests that in practice few, if any, asylum applications made in the UK by women turn solely on the question of gender-based persecution ... [our] approach is not to define in the abstract whether women, or any other set of people, might or might not be regarded as a social group. Each individual claim is considered on its merits.[28]

The evidence which has been presented in this chapter disputes this assertion.

While the argument that women's asylum claims can best be responded to by a more liberal interpretation of the 'social group' ground has its merits, it is also strategically and politically problematic from a feminist perspective. The first difficulty concerns the perceived size of the social group itself, and the implications often drawn from it in the UK:

> It is submitted that the appellant belongs to a more narrow category of the social group consisting of abused wives.... However this would mean that the whole of the female population of such countries as adopt Islamic

law in a fundamentalist or extreme version would automatically acquire the right of asylum or at least those who could show some abuse by their partners would fall into a defined category ... an innocent wife who has been abused or may suffer abuse, does not in my view form part of a social group within the meaning of the Convention.[29]

As is noted in the Canadian *Guidelines*, "the fact that the particular social group consists of large numbers of the female population in the country concerned is *irrelevant*–race, religion, nationality and political opinion are also characteristics that are shared by large numbers of people."[30] Moreover, recognizing that *some* women constitute a 'particular social group' does not lead inexorably to the consequence that *all* women are automatically entitled to refugee status. The applicant will still be required to establish that the fear of persecution was well founded, that the nature of the harm inflicted or anticipated rises to the level of serious harm, and that there was a failure of state protection. The unfortunate reality is that the *perceived* size of the prospective social group of women *is* important in the UK, where there is an overall trend toward reducing the number of asylum-seekers and limiting recognition rates.

The most critical problem, however, with the social group approach arises with the proposed addition of gender as an enumerated persecution ground; *there is an implicit assumption that the persecution of women takes place simply or predominantly because of their gender status.* 'Women' are not a cohesive social group; even within individual countries, women fall into their own subgroups–economically, socially, and culturally. While there are clearly cases where gender alone is the basis for persecutory treatment (for example, in some cases involving female genital mutilation), more often the persecutory treatment is not applied equally to *all* women. The assumption that women have common experiences that can be explained by reference to their gender alone undermines the argument. Moreover, subsuming the claims of refugee women into a gender-defined social group category risks depoliticizing women's experiences.

This problem is reflected in, and reinforced by, the failure of some commentators to adequately conceptualize the relationship between the *fact* of the persecution and its *form*.[31] All too often, efforts to frame women's experiences within the Convention resort to arguing that the group is defined by the persecutory treatment itself. Regardless, the *form* that persecution takes cannot explain the *fact* that it happened. The UK position is that a statistical grouping based on a description of the persecution suffered or feared, even if the victims coincidentally share a particular characteristic, will not be seen to constitute a particular social group within the meaning of the Convention.[32]

For many years, the only authority in the UK regarding the possibility for claims to be made on the basis of a gender-defined social group was that of *Gilani* (1987), which concerned a woman fleeing discrimination in Iran.[33] Although the Immigration Appeal Tribunal accepted that the penalties for transgressing against the social mores of dress and behavior could amount to persecution, it did not accept that a woman from Iran ran the risk of persecution solely for being a woman. Women were not considered to be a social group because "many women in Iran seem content with their lot." This Tribunal also considered whether "Westernized women" constitute a social group in the Iranian context and concluded that they do not: "The opposition to the dress and other aspects of the Islamic approach adopted in Iran remains individually based and there is no evidence that there is any recognition that those opposing look upon themselves as a group distinguished from other women." More recently, two relevant cases have been taken to the High Court, both of which involve women from Pakistan.[34] In the case of *Islam* (1996),[35] the Immigration Appeal Tribunal had ruled that a social group could not be defined by the persecutory treatment alone:

> We do not consider that Pakistani women subject to violence within the family are a social group within the Convention. That they are simply women does not make them a social group: the only common characteristic identified is that they are subject to violence within marriage: the only common feature, beyond their sex, is the persecution to which they are alleged to be subject within marriage—that is the persecution itself.

In *Shah* (1996),[36] a battered woman from Pakistan was finally forced to flee from her husband and her country and came to the UK with her six children. On arrival, she found that she was pregnant and feared that if forced to return she would be accused by her husband of conceiving the child adulterously and would be exposed to the *Sharia* statute law prescribing stoning to death as punishment. The Special Adjudicator initially dismissed her appeal, stating that the persecution feared did not fall within the terms of the Convention; women who suffer domestic violence in Pakistan were not a legitimate definable group. In the High Court, this was recast as women who are perceived to have transgressed Islamic mores. The judge quashed the decision of the Immigration Appeal Tribunal by which leave to appeal from the Special Adjudicator's decision was refused, and allowed the case to be reheard. He did not explicitly accept that women could constitute a particular social group in these circumstances.

Given that current jurisprudence is undecided but that *Savchenkov* (1996)[37] recognizes gender as an immutable characteristic, the potential for pursuing a gender-defined social group argument in the UK is unclear. What is apparent is that while this decision may provide a 'safety net' for some refugee women, it also reflects a particular static conceptualization of gender that rests on, and ultimately replicates, the existing and paradigmatically masculine normative structures of international refugee law. As Johnsson (1989) suggests, the 'social group' argument does not address the core issue of discrimination on grounds of gender as a violation of fundamental rights, or the problems of violence directed against women as women. Even more critically, it depoliticizes refugee women's experiences and, by defining them as passive 'victims', undermines the validity of their actions.

This evidence further suggests that decisions on whether or not a refugee claimant falls within the political opinion ground have been strongly informed by the male experience of overt political activity and that women's private sphere activities are viewed largely as apolitical. One of the most critical contributions of the state to the construction of the underlying public/private dichotomy is the shaping of institutions and cultural norms, including the definition of politics itself. In the UK as elsewhere, "the state constitutes itself as the realm of political action and promotes a definition of politics that narrowly construes power relations" (Peterson 1992: 44). Activities and actions are not inherently political or apolitical but depend upon their context; whether or not they can result in an acknowledged claim to refugee status depends both on the reaction of the authorities in the country of origin of the claimant and on the ways in which those experiences are conceptualized by the receiving state.

By more rigorously investigating the relationship between the *fact* and the *form* of persecution, and by reconceptualizing gendered power relations to better reflect the experiences of refugee women, it becomes clear that in many cases these experiences *are* grounded in politics. Similarly, going beyond the public/private dichotomy facilitates the revisioning of women who refuse to oblige with or who transgress social mores, not because they are women per se, but because they are opposing, or are assumed to be opposing, the dictates of a political or religious system that institutionally discriminates against women (Spijkerboer 1994). Women in many countries have to maintain certain restrictive dress codes or are denied education, access to professions, or paid work; they are forced to marry, or are denied important civil and political rights. The nature and extent of such discriminatory measures is sufficient in some cases to be deemed persecution, as is the gendered punishment for violation of particular social mores:

When I came [to the UK] I saw the man who is now my husband ... we fell in love and I decided to marry him because I will live just one time. But my family did not agree. They were disappointed. My father and my brother said they would kill me if I went back to the Sudan. Because of the tradition. I embarrass them. Then my father sent me a letter like I told you. It said, "[Y]ou are not our daughter. If you come to Sudan we will kill you. Forget us." I have brought shame on the family.[38]

Feminists have long recognized the political nature of seemingly private acts that transgress customary norms. Yet as Bhabha (1993) suggests (and this is reinforced by case law from the UK), these challenges to social norms have typically not been categorized as political, and women persecuted for such transgressions have met with great difficulties when seeking the protection of refugee law.

Macklin (1995) maintains that there is a strong argument that 'political opinion' should include women's opposition to these extreme, institutionalized forms of oppression. Political opinion as a ground of persecution does not suffer from the same particularity as does persecution on the grounds of religion or race. While it does not address a single topical aspect of persecution experienced by women claimants, it does have the potential to equate resistance to gender oppression with a political opinion. In effect, it can use the language of liberal democratic rights discourse and refashion it for feminist use: "Identifying women's resistance to gender subordination as political opinion ... [is] profoundly feminist, if indeed one believes that 'the personal is political', and that patriarchy is a system constituted primarily through power relations, not biology" (Macklin 1995: 260). In the end, politics is about power, and women who oppose institutionalized discrimination or express views on the social or cultural dominance of men should be recognized as having been persecuted because of their political opinions and the threat they pose to gendered hierarchies of power.

The strength of this approach is particularly clear in the case of women's refusal to wear the veil or other highly symbolic, constraining dress. The veil can be a major site of struggle for religious and political freedom, and it has been noted with regard to Iranian *hejab* that a woman refusing to wear the veil is looked upon as disloyal to both faith and regime and condemned as "instrumental in the foreign-inspired plot to undermine revolutionary puritanism" (Afshar 1985: 266, cited in Neal 1988: 219). Accordingly, religious leaders command the faithful to resist these 'subversives' with the same vigor as they oppose others who have sought to undermine the revolution: "Clearly in this instance women are not being punished solely because they are women–those women who wear the veil are

not punished—but because their actions are not accepted" (Spijkerboer 1994). When seen in this context, such an act of defiance is an
expression of a political and/or religious opinion:

> The intimidation of women has a political meaning … it's not only intim-
> idating them in a political way but to make them subordinate. But amaz-
> ingly women's consciousness is very strong, and [they are] the only group
> in Iran who has maintained their opposition regardless of the oppression,
> the level of oppression. They are still a force that the government has to
> reckon with.[39]

As Spijkerboer further suggests, much of the difficulty in recognizing
these acts as persecution stems not from refugee law per se, but from
its gendered interpretation by states and the narrow way in which
women's resistance is often conceptualized. Thus, "[i]f a woman
refuses to oblige with a social practice she finds oppressive, be it a
dress code or a denial of education, then that is a political issue. The
demarcation of public and private spheres at stake here is a political
issue of significance to international refugee law" (Spijkerboer 1994:
66). Moreover, conceptualizing (actual or imputed) political opinion
in a way that goes beyond the public/private dichotomy pervasive in
the normative structures of international refugee law has the potential to better reflect the *agency* of those represented; it privileges more
what women *do* and sanctions less the preordained, paradigmatically
masculine categories (Macklin 1995).

The approach is more sensitive to refugee women themselves
and avoids innovative or highly liberal interpretations of the refugee
definition. What *is* required is further work on the implications of
framing acts as 'public' and 'private'. Questions of whether or not a
woman is free to choose to wear a veil, to be circumcised, to exercise
the human right to be educated, or to be free from male violence
"are about the demarcation of the public and private sphere. Conflicts concerning the demarcation of privacy are conflicts of a most
essentially political nature, and should be considered as such in evaluating a claim to refugee status" (Spijkerboer 1994: 46).

Beyond the Public/Private Dichotomy in British Asylum Policy?

In this chapter, I have argued that at a number of different levels the
normative structures of international refugee law are based upon a
public/private dichotomy and that this is reflected in a paradigmatically masculine interpretation of the *1951 UN Convention Relating to*

the Status of Refugees. I have suggested that while the experiences of refugee women are highly varied, both individually and regionally, a gendered analysis of the asylum determination process in the UK reveals a wide variety of assumptions that effectively serve to exclude the experiences of many women seeking protection.[40] Although the implications of the processes involved are complex and sometimes contradictory, several important conclusions can be drawn in regard to the way in which the state conceptualizes violence and discrimination against women.

Firstly, the interpretation of persecution in the UK frequently negates the significance of violations of women's basic human rights. Women's experiences are conceptualized as 'private'– *private to personal relationships, private to cultures, and private to states*–and therefore beyond the scope of international protection efforts. In addition, women's *resistance* is depoliticized, in part because it frequently occurs within the geographically and conceptually 'private' sphere of the home, the family, or the community. This leads to significant difficulties in linking the fear of persecution to a recognized Convention ground, especially because of the reluctance in the UK to protect women fleeing gender–related persecution as members of a particular social group. While the more effective inclusion of women as members of a particular social group would provide a safety net for many refugee women, I believe that actual or imputed political opinion is a preferable way to frame cases involving the discrimination and the violation of social mores: both strategically, insofar as it is a more accepted ground for refugee status, and politically, in that it recognizes the diversity of women's experiences and locates them in their political and social context. Moreover, it could be argued that advocating the social group approach contradicts the fundamental aim of many advocates for women's rights who want human rights to be recognized as women's rights and not for women's rights to be somehow separate and distinct.

The substantive problems of interpretation faced by refugee women in the UK asylum determination process that have been the focus of my analysis are reflected in, and reinforced by, a number of procedural difficulties. It seems clear that the UK is now actively trying to limit the extent of its obligation under international asylum law by using arguments of state sovereignty to justify a particularly narrow interpretation of the Convention. In this environment, those whose experiences of persecution do not fit rigidly defined categories and stereotypical expectations will be the first to be refused protection,[41] as the evidence presented in this chapter suggests.

In this hostile UK context, incorporating a more gendered approach to the asylum determination will take time and considerable effort. It will also meet with both passive resistance, because it disrupts routines and the comfortable assumption of stereotypes, and active opposition, because it challenges dominant gender roles and relations. As Macklin explains in this volume, however, formal efforts to challenge the public/private dichotomy in international refugee law have recently been implemented in Canada, the US, and Australia.[42] While such guidelines do not resolve all problems raised in this chapter, they represent an acknowledgment of the particular difficulties that refugee women face in benefiting equitably from protection and assistance efforts. Given that the UK claims to not yet even have identified a need to issue separate guidance on dealing with applications from female asylum seekers,[43] it is clear that academics, advocates, and practitioners will face many challenges before significant changes occur. In the light of international developments and demands that women's human rights be protected, the failure of the determining authorities to address this issue only provides further compelling evidence, if it is needed, that international law, including international refugee law, is a thoroughly gendered system that marginalizes women's interests.

Notes

1. Johnsson (1989) notes that to the extent that gender surfaces in these legal texts, the language used suggests that male refugees were in the mind of the drafters.
2. As Kelly (1993) notes, here there may be gender-related aspects to the case that cause particular difficulties in establishing the facts sufficient to lead to the granting of refugee status. Many of these problems are procedural and are particularly evident in cases involving sexual violence.
3. As used in this analysis, 'normative' refers to an accepted standard of behavior within a society of, or pertaining to, a norm. It is prescriptive in the sense that it lays down (unwritten) rules or directions for behavior and policy.
4. As Indra (1993) suggests, "This dichotomy of private and public spheres remains deeply grounded in discourse about refugees and leads to many ironies concerning notions of rights, privacy and culture." It can lead to the tendency to valorize refugee family life through reference to an idealized, historical traditional culture, even when it encodes profound gender and other disparities.
5. These include the Universal Declaration of Human Rights, the International Covenant on Civil and Political Rights and the International Covenant on Economic, Social and Cultural Rights.
6. Appeal No. TH/9515/85 (1986) subsequently upheld in *Secretary of State for the Home Department v. Gilani*, Immigration Appeal Tribunal 25th February 1987 (5216) (unreported).

7. *Secretary of State for the Home Department v. Ranjbar*, Immigration Appeal Tribunal 28th June 1994 (11105) (unreported). Despite growing opposition, this argument continues to be made in the UK. For example in *Islam v. Secretary of State for the Home Department*, Immigration Appeal Tribunal 2nd October 1996 (13956) (unreported), the Tribunal stated that "we do not think that the purpose of the Convention is to award refugee status because of a disapproval of social mores or conventions in non-Western societies."

8. For further discussion see Bunting (1993), Spijkerboer (1994), Cook (1994), Macklin (1995), and Peters and Wolper (1995).

9. The term sexual violence as defined by UNHCR (UNHCR EC 1995: 1) covers "all forms of sexual threat, interference and exploitation including 'statutory rape' and molestation without physical harm or penetration."

10. Testimony of a woman from Somalia during an interview with the author held shortly after her arrival in the UK. The Home Office decision regarding her case is unknown. All quotes from refugee women in the UK that follow that are otherwise unreferenced are derived from interviews with the author.

11. Ms A. was arrested when she arrived in the UK and detained for two weeks. Several attempts were made to deport her. She is still awaiting a decision in her case five years later.

12. These fears were reflected in her refusal to reveal her experiences of sexual violence to her lawyer. She has been denied refugee status and now fears deportation.

13. Sexual violence including rape is a grave violation of the right to security of person, including the right not to be subjected to torture or other cruel, inhuman or degrading treatment or punishment. This right is laid down in, inter alia, Articles 3 and 5 of the Universal Declaration of Human Rights, Article 7 of the International Covenant on Civil and Political Rights and in the Convention Against Torture and Other Cruel, Inhuman or Degrading Treatment or Punishment.

14. *Campos-Guardado v. Immigration and Nationality Service* [1987] 809 F.2d 285 (5th Circuit) has been widely cited as an example where rape was interpreted by the judge as being 'personal' rather than politically motivated (see Castel, 1992 and Macklin, this volume, for further details). More recently in *Klawitter v. Immigration and Nationality Service* [1992] 970 F.2d 149 (6th Circuit), in which the applicant feared the unwanted sexual advances of a colonel in the Polish secret police, the Court decided: "Although the petitioner's testimony recounts an unfortunate situation, harm or threats of harm based solely on sexual attraction do not constitute persecution."

15. For example, no special provision is made for female interviewing officers and interpreters, despite considerable evidence that the presence of men may prevent women from fully presenting their case.

16. Appeal No. HX/73584/94 (1995) (unreported). This decision was overruled in *Gimhedin v. Secretary of State for the Home Department*, Immigration Appeal Tribunal 21st October 1996 (14019) (unreported).

17. INS *Considerations for Asylum Officers Adjudicating Asylum Claims from Women* (June 1995).

18. See UNHCR (1995b).

19. See for example *Declaration on the Elimination of Violence Against Women* (1993).

20. Several feminist critiques of international asylum law, however, have focused specifically on the issue of familial, domestic, and intimate violence. See, for example, Stairs and Pope (1990), Goldberg (1993), and Thomas and Beasley (1993).

21. *Secretary of State for the Home Department v. Ranjbar*, Immigration Appeal Tribunal 28 June 1994 (11105) (unreported).

22. More generally, Pettman (1996) has noted the irony of expecting women to appeal to a masculinist state for protection against the violence of individual men.
23. *Jamil v. Secretary of State for the Home Department,* Immigration Appeal Tribunal 25th June 1996 (13588) (unreported).
24. According to UNHCR (1979b: para. 65), "Where serious discriminatory or other abusive acts are committed by the local populace, they can be considered as persecution if they are knowingly tolerated by the authorities, or if the authorities refuse, or prove unable, to offer protection."
25. According to statistics obtained from the Home Office but not publicly available, in 1995, 26 percent of female applicants were initially granted ELR compared with 14 percent of male applicants.
26. Appeal No. HX/80191/95 (24 January 1996) (unreported). This case also illustrates that merely being female does not guarantee adjudicator gender sensitivity. Female decision-makers are often no more likely than male decision-makers to interpret the Convention in a way that deeply considers women's experiences of persecution, perhaps because they too are working within the same patriarchal ideology and normative framework. It should also be noted that recommendations that ELR be granted are increasingly ignored by the Home Office, who may instead decide to deport the applicant.
27. In 1984, the European Parliament adopted a resolution calling upon states to accord refugee status to women within the particular social group category in certain circumstances, a position reflected in the policies of the Dutch Refugee Council (Schilders et al. 1988).
28. UK response to a questionnaire to governments participating in the *UNHCR Symposium on Gender-Based Persecution* Geneva, February 1996 unpublished (emphasis in original).
29. Appeal No. HX/75169/94 (1996) (unreported).
30. Canada CIRB *Guidelines on Women Refugee Claimants Fearing Gender-Related Persecution: UPDATE* November 1996: 8 (emphasis in original).
31. An example of this can be seen in Goldberg's (1993) work on domestic violence. Specifically, to describe a social group of women who are battered does not explain why such harm occurred; it simply notes that there are characteristics common to a number of individuals. As a result, it provides no specific grounds for the persecution by itself, as required by the Convention definition.
32. See the ruling in *Secretary of State for the Home Department v. Savchenkov* [1996] Imm AR 28 (Court of Appeal).
33. *Gilani v. Secretary of State for the Home Department,* Immigration Appeal Tribunal 3 June 1987 (5216) (unreported).
34. These cases were heard on 20 May 1997. At the time of writing, the judges' determination had not been released.
35. *Islam v. Secretary of State for the Home Department,* Immigration Appeal Tribunal 2 October 1996 (13956) (unreported).
36. *Regina v. Immigration Appeal Tribunal and Secretary for the Home Department* ex parte *Shah,* Queen's Bench Division 25 October 1996 (unreported).
37. *Secretary of State for the Home Department v. Savchenkov* [1996] Imm AR 28 (Court of Appeal).
38. Testimony of a refugee woman from the Sudan during an interview with the author. At the time of interview her application for leave to remain in the UK through marriage had been refused and she was considering making an application for asylum on the basis that she could not now return to the Sudan and was effectively a refugee *sur place.*

39. Comment made by Minoo Jalali, an asylum advocate and practitioner who is herself a refugee from Iran, during an interview with the author.

40. See also Crawley (1997) for more detailed analyses of procedures and case law and their implications for women seeking asylum in the UK.

41. The UK is explicit about its aim of restricting refugee inflows and often asserts that the vast majority of asylum seekers are 'bogus' because they do not fit into a very narrow interpretation of the Convention. These views are reflected in several very significant new pieces of legislation, including the 1996 Asylum and Immigration Act, which, among other measures, restricts the availability of welfare support for many refugees and makes it illegal for them to work while their claim for asylum is being processed. Virtually all applications are now refused in the first instance, and many applicants face a lengthy appeals procedure.

42. According to the CIRB *Guidelines on Women Refugee Claimants Fearing Gender-Related Persecution: UPDATE* (November 1996: 5), "[A] woman who opposes institutionalized discrimination of women, or expresses views of independence from male social/cultural dominance in her society, may be found to fear persecution by reason of her *actual political opinion or a political opinion imputed to her (i.e. she is perceived by the agent of persecution to be expressing politically antagonistic views*" (emphasis in original). The Australian *Guidelines on Gender Issues for Decision Makers* (July 1996, paragraph 4.25) also note that "the fact that a woman may challenge particular social conventions about the manner in which women should behave may be considered political by the authorities and may attract persecutory treatment on this basis."

43. UK response to a questionnaire to governments participating in the *UNHCR Symposium on Gender-Based Persecution Geneva*, February 1996, unpublished.

18

The Problem of Gender-Related Persecution

A Challenge of International Protection

Lisa Gilad

Refugees leave their country because they fear serious violations of their basic human rights due to their civil or political status, or because of danger arising from external or internal aggression.[1] Their states cannot or will not protect them. Under certain conditions, enlightened interpretation of the UN definition of a Convention refugee can also protect women who are persecuted simply because they *are* women by including them under one of five enumerated grounds of "membership in a particular social group" facing oppression by the state or its agents.[2] In fact, the Supreme Court of Canada has defined a particular social group (among other criteria) to embrace those persons who share a fundamental, immutable characteristic from which disassociation is impossible.[3] The Supreme Court of Canada has specifically identified gender and sexual orientation as grounds to claim international protection, both of which are analogous to the unalterable characteristics of race and nationality (ethnic origin). Application of the *ejusdem generis* principle in Canada challenges other states to follow, given that precious few states acknowledge an obligation to protect women because they are women. This chapter explores how the protection of refugee women because they are women came about in Canada; it invites anthropologists to participate in the effort to protect women from gender-based persecution.

It must be recalled that 80 percent of the refugees in the world are women and children, though few make their way to North America or Western European states. The vast majority of refugee women languish in camps or are displaced within their own countries, living in dismal conditions. Refugeehood brings its own set of problems: sexual and physical assault are chronic problems in most refugee camps, compounding the socioeconomic and psychological upheaval that typifies the refugee experience.

The history of acknowledging the claims of women to be Convention refugees on the basis of their gender through membership in a particular social group category is brief indeed. In 1984, the Dutch Refugee Council and the European Parliament passed resolutions suggesting that persecution on the basis of sex falls under the particular social group category.[4] In 1985, the United Nations High Commissioner for Refugees (UNHCR) recommended that women who violate the social mores of their society might be considered members of a particular social group.[5] In 1987, one of the first claims acknowledged on the basis of gender was recognized by the Canadian Immigration Appeal Board (IAB), which offered protection to a Turkish widow who had been sexually assaulted by young men and harassed on a daily basis by such men, and was the object of an abduction attempt. The Turkish authorities had not protected her because it found it was inappropriate for her to live without a male relative. The IAB subsequently found that sexual assault was a form of persecution.[6]

In 1989, the Canadian Immigration and Refugee Board (IRB) was created. It soon became a tribunal with about 230 Members. A subgroup in which female members were particularly represented became very active in searching for ways to routinize the acceptance of women as Convention refugees, if such women could reasonably prove that they faced a chance of persecution because they were women. These Members, many of whom had worked on women's human rights issues in previous careers, also recognized the unique problems women had in testifying about the persecution they had experienced or feared might happen to them.

In 1990, IRB working groups for refugee women claimants were formed in Toronto, and later in Montreal. Much discussion took place regarding how the law could encompass the protection of women from types of harm not typically seen as persecution by what had been a male-structured history of refugee jurisprudence. Materials were collected internationally and shared with members. Seminars were held by legal experts from the nongovernmental, academic, and UNHCR communities. Videos were produced in which

Sri Lankan, Somali, and Iranian women talked about cultural barriers to testifying in a Canadian hearing room, including the shame of revealing details of sexual abuse.

In March 1993, the Chairperson of the IRB issued *Guidelines for the Convention Refugee Determination Division* on gender-related persecution, using her power in this regard under the *Canada Immigration Act*.[7] The issuance of these detailed *Guidelines* indicated the priority given to this issue among members of the IRB. Our model has been internationally acclaimed, and so have some of our practices in promoting a comfort zone for claimants in which to testify. Women–*if* they get to Canada–can now be protected from: forced sterilization, forced abortion, forced marriage, domestic and societal violence, bride burning, rape and other forms of sexual torture, genital mutilation, and serious violations of other fundamental human rights. Most of these types of persecution are more often or exclusively experienced by women, but of course we try to extend sensitivity to victims of torture and oppression regardless of their gender.

While the *Guidelines* are not mandatory, fairness dictates that if a Member departs from them in her reasoning, she must justify in writing why the *Guidelines* do not relate to the case at hand. The Federal Court of Canada has also firmly dealt with some relevant issues of bias based on gender: members must refrain from the use of sexist and culturally judgmental language. Perhaps most importantly, the Supreme Court of Canada has laid to rest the question of whether or not gender is an appropriate grounds for protection, as indicated at the beginning of this chapter.

The Convention Refugee Determination Division (CRDD) attempts to provide a 'user-friendly' hearing room environment for gender-related claims. When a gender claim is noted in a Personal Information Form (PIF),[8] it might be expedited if there is a prima facie case, enabling women to be interviewed in an informal setting by an officer of the IRB, rather than testifying before the tribunal. In the case of an expedited claim, a Refugee Hearing Officer (RHO) may recommend that a Member accept the woman as a Convention refugee without a formal hearing. We rely on counsel to inform us of sensitive cases, but the competence of legal counsel to recognize gender-related claims varies considerably.

Frequently, a panel specializing in gender issues will be assigned to a case. Female interpreters who will not be culturally judgmental are sought. Sometimes a less formal setting will be provided in the hearing room, including sitting very close to the claimant–rather than distantly, behind large tables. Special hearing rooms are being constructed for this purpose. Sometimes counsel will provide, or members will request, detailed affidavits to avoid oral testimony about very upsetting matters. Members will also attempt to test credibility around the traumatic events rather than requiring women to discuss details of sexual assault.

The members of the CRDD are constantly working on improving their skills and analytical abilities to adjudicate gender-related claims fairly. The IRB promotes gender and cultural training. The fact that our decisions are reviewable by the Federal Court of Canada Trial Division (on errors of law or capricious findings of fact) provides the accountability necessary in implementing the *Guidelines* and in applying the Supreme Court of Canada's inclusion of gender in the definition of particular social group.

Gender-related claims are becoming more common. In 1994 alone I adjudicated at least twenty such claims out of a couple of hundred cases. One case involved a victim of gang rape for whom there was no effective state protection in her home country;[9] others involved long-term victims of domestic violence, including one who had been held hostage in Canada by her husband, who has since returned to his home country. Still others involved women who were persecuted on account of imputed political opinion because their family members were viewed as subversives by state authorities. Some of these claims were not detailed in PIFs, but these women had the strength to tell their lawyers about their true fears once they learned that Canada has options to protect women because they are women.

Anthropological Data

In Canada, anthropologists have become conventional sources of information to understand the cultural contexts of claims before the IRB and other deciding bodies. I cannot stress too much how important this is. It is my strongly held position that each practicing anthropologist has the responsibility under international human rights law to protect persons from human rights violations, as these are set out in international human rights instruments.[10] Of course, the debate surrounding the legitimacy of group rights over individual's rights come into play at this point, but that is the subject of another paper.[11] Here, I want to relate the expert evidence we received via affidavit from Professor Sidney Waldron and to discuss some of its effects. I do not think he will mind being named in this context. He should be very proud of his contribution in providing the evidentiary basis to protect from serious harm an 'Issa woman from northern Ethiopia.

The history of the claimant's sojourn in Canada is worth relating. She left Ethiopia in fear for her life in February 1991. She arrived in Canada later that month and made a claim to be a Convention refugee. That claim was rejected by the Refugee Division, and the claimant was deported in March 1993. She returned to Canada in December 1993 and made another claim to be a Convention refugee. On 16 August 1994, the claim commenced in Ottawa, Ontario. There was a lengthy prehearing conference with counsel, during which the panel learned that the claimant had a serious hearing impediment resulting partially from a blow to her ear by a rifle butt. Counsel was not at all certain that the claimant would be able to hear the questions put to her. During the hearing conference, the panel discussed in an open fashion the difficulty the claimant would have in asserting her claim for the reasons that she originally left Ethiopia; at that point in time there was no systemic violence against 'Issa, who are ethnic Somalis, although particular 'Issa might be at risk for reasons other than those set out in the claimant's PIF. Counsel and the panel discussed at some length the implications of the claimant's status as a never-married woman, of whether there would be a reasonable possibility of marriage, and what would happen to her in the absence of male relatives. One brother had been murdered, and another had disappeared in the fall of 1990. The Presiding Member suggested that counsel contact at least one of three anthropologists who worked in Ethiopia to see if they could provide relevant cultural evidence that might or might not assist the claimant to establish her claim.

At the opening of the hearing, it became clear that the claimant could barely hear the interpreter sitting next to her, let alone the Presiding Member. She was very frustrated and began to cry. After a recess, the Presiding Member asked that the claimant be equipped with a hearing aid so that she could have a full and proper asylum hearing. The RHO indicated that, having observed the claimant's hearing difficulties, he was not so concerned about discrepancies from her previous hearing. The hearing adjourned until 5 October 1994. So that the claimant would not have to face two more strangers at the next sitting, the panel assigned itself to the case.

At this October sitting before the CRDD, the claimant clearly heard and understood what was going on for the first time. Although the claimant had her hearing aid at the 16 August hearing, she was ashamed to wear it. In the medical report of 14 September 1994, the doctor outlined the claimant's history of hearing difficulties and treatment, including surgery in Canada in January 1992. In March 1992, she had been equipped with a hearing aid. She returned to the doctor twice after that with an infected right ear. At the second visit of May 1994, she indicated to the doctor that she did not wear the hearing aid because it did not work. The hearing aid was tested and found to have good sound quality, and the doctor advised her to use it full time. The restoration of her hearing is significant in light of her experiences.

The story she presented illustrates a number of themes characteristic of gender-based oppression. The claimant's father was killed by the regime of Haile Selassie in 1960, when the claimant was seven years old. Her mother and sister died of natural causes in the early 1980s. The claimant then lived with her niece and two of her brothers, and worked in a market until 1986 in an area called the 'Issa Village. She described in her PIF a series of problems faced by ethnic Somalis at the hands of Ethiopian soldiers. One of the claimant's brothers failed to report for military service in August 1990. He fled Ethiopia, and the claimant had not seen him since. After he fled, soldiers came to their home several times in a week. On one occasion, after telling the soldiers she did not know the whereabouts of her brother, she was beaten with a rifle butt on both ears. The right ear bled and became swollen and infected, leaving her partially deaf in that ear. The claimant feared going to the police because she could have been jailed.

Another brother of the claimant was arrested at the end of June 1990 while in the center of town. The claimant did not know why he was arrested. Her younger brother had looked for him and learned that he was at the police station, where he was kept for three days and then transferred to Galshire prison. The claimant was notified by a family friend that he was killed in prison in September 1990. Several days later, three men came to the claimant's house in civilian dress looking for documents. The claimant indicated that she had no documents. Her house was confiscated, and the claimant was asked to sign a letter. She is illiterate and had no idea what she signed under protest, with a gun to her head.

The claimant and her fifteen-year-old niece then went to stay with a friend of the brother who had been killed. They could not stay there permanently, however, and this person helped the claimant and her niece to leave the country by paying for passports and airfare. The claimant maintained that she continued to fear persecution in Ethiopia because of the circumstances that caused her to leave. It was not clear at the hearing whether her brother was killed because of his nationality or because of his political opinion. Her other brother had not been heard of since he fled the country, and could therefore offer no evidence. She feared returning at this point also because she would have nowhere to live and no one to protect her. She did not know why she never married, attributing it to her fate. She feared that she would be raped or killed, citing the case of a woman she knew who had lived alone and was raped and murdered. The shame of a rape would be insufferable. The claimant could not imagine returning, particularly with her hearing impediment.

Despite the fact that the circumstances that forced the claimant to flee were held to no longer obtain in 1994, the claim was well established on the basis of membership in a particular social group–gender. This claimant is particularly vulnerable as an unmarried 'Issa woman. It also appears that at this point in her life, her unmarried status is also immutable. Several documents before the tribunal provided an independent basis for the claimant's fears, beyond that to which she testified. A background paper on the status of women in Ethiopia, while dated in 1987, was deemed still relevant when read in conjunction with other articles.[12] The paper indicated that women who do not have the protection of male relatives are often forced to migrate to urban areas "in search of an income: uneducated, unskilled, and destined to live in abject poverty." Abject poverty resulting from the social status of an unmarried woman constitutes persecution, insofar as it connotes a serious deprivation of economic rights.

Also to the point, and ultimately persuasive of the well-foundedness of this claim, was the expert evidence provided by Professor Waldron (see following chapter, this volume), who has done research in Ethiopia since the early 1960s. Having evaluated Professor Waldron's curriculum vitae, I believe there are few people so well qualified to speak to the cultural context and potential risk of persecution this claimant might face should she return to her country of nationality. The following is taken from his detailed letter concerning the circumstances of this claim, as relayed to him by the claimant's lawyer:

> … a woman in [this] situation … would be in grave trouble. Indeed, if my experience is pertinent, I believe that a woman in her position would be in risk of losing her life….
>
> First, it is unusual to the point of abnormality for a woman of forty not to have been married. Whatever the explanation–whether she is deformed, whether she comes from an extremely poor family, or even if she had not undergone the traumatic female circumcision operation–it would still be considered extremely unusual in her society that she had never been married. This fact places her in a very vulnerable position. Most Somali survive times of hardship, which are a recurrent probability in 'Issa Somali life, by sharing food and getting support of all kinds from relatives and clan members. A married woman would always be supported by her natal relatives, but, as a matter of honor, her husband's relatives–even if he were deceased–would aid her.
>
> A single woman with no family is in the worst possible predicament….

... the only way that a Somali woman might seek to provide necessities for herself would be to market goods, or more rarely, to gain employment based on marketable skills. Without these possibilities, begging or prostitution would be the only recourses in the attempt to survive. Frankly, the prospects of survival as a beggar, these days in Dire Dawa, would be poor....

I last visited this region in 1992. I was shocked to see old women trying to sell soiled and ripped rags. I had never seen this in my years of experience....

There are no welfare institutions in Ethiopia.... Her group of origin, the 'Issa, are primarily a poor pastoralist group, with little political clout or wealth. There would be, in all likelihood, no aid for her.

My conclusion is that a woman with the attributes described, who is even too old for prostitution, might well die of a malnutritionally-related disease or worse, were she to attempt to survive in Dire Dawa in 1995.

Professor Waldron has unequivocally set out the risk of persecution to this claimant. She has good grounds to fear persecution in the form of a serious deprivation of her socioeconomic and food rights, potentially threatening her life, should she return to Ethiopia today.

Hundreds of refugees and their stories have compelled my commitment to refugee protection. Let Professor Waldron's example deepen your commitment that anthropology has a serious contribution to make to the protection of human rights generally, and women's rights in particular.

Notes

1. The views expressed in this chapter are those of the author and do not necessarily reflect the views of the Canadian Immigration and Refugee Board (IRB).

2. The definition of a Convention refugee is set out in section 2(1) of the *Canada Immigration Act.*

3. *Canada (Attorney General) v. Ward* [1993] 2 S.C.R. 689.

4. See the *Guidelines* issued by the Chairperson pursuant to section 65(3) of the *Immigration Act,* "Women Refugee Claimants Fearing Gender-Related Persecution," 9 March 1993, at Footnote 6, page 13. It should be noted, however, that it is rare for a claimant to successfully argue a case on the basis of gender in any European state.

5. See in particular *Conclusion No. 39 (XXXVI) Refugee Women and International Protection,* 1985, UNHCR; "Note on Refugee Women and International Protection," UNHCR Executive Committee EC/SCP/50 (28 August 1990) and UNHCR EC

(1991). There is expanding legal and anthropological literature on gender-related persecution. For a recent and comprehensive source, see Macklin (1995).

6. *Incirciyan, Zeyiye v. Minister of Employment and Immigration* (IAB M87–1541X, M87–1248).

7. See *Guidelines* issued by the Chairperson pursuant to section 65(3) of the *Immigration Act*, "Women Refugee Claimants Fearing Gender-Related Persecution," and Macklin (this volume).

8. This is a form filed with the IRB in advance of a hearing that sets out basic demographic and familial information, the route(s) taken to Canada, the possession and details of authentic or fake documents, and a detailed statement of why the person fears persecution in her (or his) home country.

9. It should be reiterated that a claimant must show good grounds for fearing persecution on the basis of a Convention ground, and also that there is an absence of state protection for that person. See Macklin (this volume).

10. See for example, the Preamble to the *International Covenant on Civil and Political Rights,* 16 December 1966, which states: "*Realizing* that the individual, having duties to other individuals and to the community to which he belongs is under a responsibility to strive for the promotion and observance of the rights recognized in the present Covenant...."

11. There is increasing anthropological and legal literature on this subject, but for an exposition in the area of gender and refugee determination, see Gilad (1996).

12. Exhibit R–5, Response to Information Request ETH18259 dated 13 September 1994, an attachment written by Ruth Anne Fellows, a consultant for the Canadian Embassy in Addis Ababa.

19

Anthropologists As 'Expert Witnesses'

Sidney Waldron

When I first saw Lisa Gilad's chapter, I was quite surprised to learn of the importance of my testimony (in the form of an affidavit) in shaping the fate of an 'Issa Somali woman applying for refugee status. Given the reported facts of the woman's case, I thought she would be in desperate straits, should she be returned against her will to Dire Dawa, Ethiopia. Anthropologists are not trained to reach conclusions on the basis of minimal, secondhand reports, and I was aware of several questions I would have liked to investigate if this were possible and if the case were not a matter of urgency, but I did not hesitate to respond. Was this an ethical compromise?

Neither my experience nor the body of anthropological literature on the Somali was sufficient to fully answer these questions. For instance, was it meaningful to speak of a woman 'with no family', given the pervasiveness of the Somali extended lineage, which would link all 'Issa in a patrilineal system extending back over twenty generations? Both my observations in refugee contexts in Somalia and my conversations with English-speaking Somali convinced me that reference to a coresidential 'core' family is not unusual, and that sociologically this group can be identified as a regularly interacting, very important social unit, however different it is from a North American nuclear family, which exists separately from other relatives. Although research would be needed to corroborate this, I am convinced that an urban Somali woman would rely heavily on her coresidential family, and that certainly this family could be wiped out, as it had in the claimant's case. Ultimately, it was my judgment that the extended lineage into which the claimant was born might not provide minimum life-supporting essentials, given the dire economic and political circumstances of the region.

Might not another reasonably competent anthropologist reach opposite conclusions? An anthropologist who was less acquainted with urban life in this region and more influenced by published reports of the all-pervasive functions of the lineage system might well have disagreed with my conclusions. If, as some literature suggests, the domestic economy of Somali pastoralists is channeled through lineage connections, and if all Somali are born into one or another lineage system, then logic insists that all persons have lineage protection, or so the analyst might conclude. I, of course, maintain that my opinion is sound, at least until contradicted by further research. Presumably, so would be the expert anthropological witness who might disagree. I was aware of the limits of my 'expertise', but I wondered how a judge and jury might evaluate contradictory 'experts'. I was not aware, at the time of my affidavit, that Lisa Gilad, well respected as an anthropologist, was also the judge of the case. The combination of her cross-disciplinary and cross-cultural training was a rare combination, perhaps unique in Lisa Gilad.

Non-anthropologists would face, I believe, the general quandary of evaluating expert witnesses in legal proceedings: how does one verify expertise in an esoteric realm of knowledge? I hope I was correct in my opinion, but the only true experts here are the Somali themselves. I am relieved that my information was not used to bar the applicant from refugee status. I am also sadly aware that another letter, written on behalf of a Somali professional who was a good friend, did not help his claim for refugee acceptance in the US.

A final note on expertise in the context of Somali culture. In 1981, I encountered the Norwegian anthropologist Ian Haakonsen, who had considerable experience in Somalia and obviously communicated fluently with his Somali colleagues. I congratulated him on his knowledge, which exceeded mine by far. He replied that he did not speak the language, "since the language, properly spoken, is poetry, and this is more than I can do." Such humility is rare among expatriates.

If Anthropologists Are Often Inexpert 'Experts', Why Are They Required?

The reply here is simple. The social and cultural ignorance of others who design and implement plans that affect non-Western peoples is appalling, just as their power is immense. While academic anthropologists debate the ethics of intervention, and while they debate the threat to scientific purity raised by the premature application of 'anthropological' knowledge, uninformed intervention proceeds untrammeled. We worry, very justifiably, about delicate cultural systems being damaged irreparably by interventions informed by our necessarily incomplete knowledge. While these debates take place, projects and programs based on obvious error are funded and imposed. We now realize, for instance, that one of the most serious forces for massive dislocation of human communities in Asia is development in the form of dam-building (see Colson, this volume, for an African case).

Anthropologists who have not worked on teams otherwise made up of non-anthropologists have an eye-opening experience awaiting them. While in Somalia in 1981–82, I heard an American NGO project director state that the daily food requirement of Somali was much lower than "ours," because they "had evolved that way." Many assertions about refugee conditions in Somalia were based on hasty impressions and other partial information that circulated, often with embellishment, until the 'truth' available to expatriates, and accepted by many, was simply a kind of urban rumor. Food consumption figures, published by the UN agencies responsible, were statistical fallacies, dangerous because they asserted satisfactory performance while, in fact, severe malnutrition was going unnoticed. Expatriates had no regular and trustworthy way of knowing what the problems of refugees might have been, nor how the ideas of these refugees might have contributed to solutions. They accepted fallacy and exaggeration along with fact more often than not. I shared the reluctance expressed by many anthropologists to inform powerful outsiders about the inner workings of a local culture. But what was needed was not particularly sensitive material. Basically, I felt that an anthropologist could serve as a constant source of day-to-day, routine information from the Somali concerning camp conditions and problems. The ability to communicate was essential as was the ability to understand the cultural context. A clear role of an anthropologist in such a setting is to function as a bridge between two bodies of cultural information, and thus to act as an antidote to rumor. Another routine but important duty of an anthropologist in refugee contexts is to simply and clearly relate ideas and materials from the literature (anthropological, cultural, and historical) to inform the nonspecialist practitioner.

In the Somali refugee crisis of the 1980s, another clear need was the independent assessment of relief efforts, including food supplies and agricultural and other development projects. For instance, in 1982, after a policy declaration of the Somali government, a massive effort was enjoined by the UN, USAID, and NGOs to make the hundreds of thousands of refugees more independent of donated food by developing local refugee agricultural projects. Any economically oriented anthropologist would have seen, as I did, that this was merely window dressing, which may have diverted attention from the precariousness of the donated food supply. Much was made of self-sufficiency in refugee agriculture. In fact, if all the land available for this had been fully and efficiently devoted to food production, it could have served only one-tenth of the total food demand. However, the anthropologist-as-investigative-reporter must realize that, in the efforts to show that the 'Emperor has no clothes', one may bring down his wrath.

In these examples, as far as the ethics of involvement are concerned, most of the information that an anthropologist might have provided would have been on a very basic level. It must, however, be the responsibility of the anthropologist to decide on the ethics of the investigation. When an anthropologist is asked to gather information that reeks of surveillance or intelligence work, that anthropologist must have the ability to judge the matter, and to make his or her own determination. I once refused a project director's request to provide him with a detailed account of lineage affiliations of each person.

Basically, the role of anthropologists in the context of refugee work is usually to point out glaring errors, obvious facts, and absurd claims. There is always an ethical caveat when one cultural group (refugee aid workers) is administering and perhaps changing another (Somali refugees). Paramount, I believe, is the warning given to medical practitioners, "First do no harm." Sometimes, however, it is important to do something.

Advocacy and Human Rights

The legal significance of Lisa Gilad's case lies in its reasoned extension of Canada's interpretation of the body of international law as it applies to refugees, so that it can include persecution based on gender as one of its principles of acceptance.[1] Lisa Gilad was unusual, to say the least, among those with power of adjudication over refugees in that she sought, as an anthropologist, an understanding of their condition, and was able to effectively incorporate this in her legal decisions. In her cases, as we have seen, she sought to critically evaluate anthropological expertise as a major source of information.

Presumably, most court cases involving refugees are judged by non-anthropologists. As all experienced anthropologists realize, convincing others of the reality and humanity of people in non-Western cultures is as much an art as a science. In the case at hand, I responded with confidence that I would be understood. How far would an anthropologist go, as 'expert witness', in intentionally selecting evidence that advocates the position of the appellant? To state this somewhat more dramatically, if we, as anthropologists, have considerable experience and perhaps similar understanding of a region and its people, and if we are seriously convinced that people in this region are undergoing virtually unreported and serious human rights abuses, do we have the ability, the right, or perhaps the duty to make these serious abuses known to the outside world? Are we the advocates of those who have allowed us to live among them, or are we scientific observers of patterns and processes, observing from a distance? Does one who has experienced, from the fringes, the decimation of the Dinka in the Southern Sudan, and who realizes the world is virtually oblivious to this holocaust, seek widespread publicity and action, or do ethics constrain one to professional publications?

The range of replies would probably reflect the range of personalities and professional ethics among the full body of anthropologists. A Berkeley professor, whom I hold in respect, once remarked before I presented a paper on Somali refugees that perhaps there were some subjects that anthropologists should not explore. Although this may be a valid ethical position, it is not mine.

We who are anthropologists and who work in development or emergency situations have a professional perspective on the affected peoples that we cannot expect to find among medics, economists, logistical specialists, etc. We are thus in a unique position to speak with people, to understand their problems, to understand the range of abilities in the population, and consequently to develop both empathy and an informed analytic understanding. It is our duty to convey this understanding to other professionals. My experience is that this is seldom routine. Our understanding of local specifics depends on our acceptance of the basic lessons of anthropology: that humans are not subdivided into separate species with major biological and intellectual abilities; that local people, such as Somali pastoralists, know a great deal about a way of life adapted to their environmental possibilities (rather than representing a lower evolutionary stage); that refugees belong to cultural communities, have knowledge, and are fellow humans. The acceptance of specifics, by a non-anthropological audience, depends partially on one's ability to summarize undergraduate anthropology, and it is an endless process.

In a courtroom, one may have the same task, without control over the proceedings. One does not control the direction of questioning, or have the hours of a Somali evening to make one's points. I believe that the ethically most acceptable position here is also the most effective: if one has a reasonable command of the salient information, and if one can summarize a valid interpretation, then a fair court will reach a just decision. I have explained above that I chose to emphasize certain aspects because I felt my interpretation was warranted. I have a bias, however, which is not necessarily a professional attribute. I know almost as many people in eastern Africa as I do in North America, and I have seen the lives of many good people ruined by war, poverty, and dislocation. If I am inclined to present a favorable case, it is with the belief that this may counteract false impressions and negative stereotypes. I am inclined to believe that a refugee claim is based on fear of persecution rather than simply the desire to get a better income. In the case at hand, this may have influenced my emphasis on the local, coresidential family, rather than the lineage.

In the greater arena outside the courtroom, the question of anthropologists as advocates exceeds the range of this consideration. If the world media ignores the holocaust in the Southern Sudan, perhaps those of us who have direct awareness need to lobby for coverage, to show videos, and to write exposés. We do this informed by anthropological knowledge, but, I believe, in this advocacy role we must make clear that these are personal statements rather than professional acts. The serious human rights investigations and the resulting reports of *African Rights*, directed by Alex de Waal and Rukiya Omar, are means of publicizing perceived human rights violations. Although the investigative reporting involved in such publications is itself controversial in the eyes of some, these publications provide a clearly defined forum for discussing the kinds of horrors that anthropologists too frequently encounter.[2] In the case at hand, I think it is important for non-lawyers such as myself to realize that the specifics of the threat to survival of the female applicant were considered in reaching a decision; the case was not based on identifying 'gender (female)' as a dangerous category per se. I point this out because I am very skeptical of single-issue, sweeping campaigns to abolish or prohibit specific types of behavior adjudged cross-culturally as rights violations.

As for advocacy within the profession of anthropology, when acting in the role of anthropologist-cum-expert, I am optimistic that the facts clearly presented will make the case.[3] We can only hope for a reappearance, somewhere, of the rare combination of jurist and anthropologist represented by Lisa Gilad. Meanwhile, we mark her loss.

Notes

1. International law is strengthened through refinement and extension in practice. It is weakened through the neglect and abuse of basic principles. While Canada was expanding its refugee coverage, the US, with ten times Canada's population, was simultaneously weakening the bases of refugee conventions by proclaiming all Cubans intercepted at sea as "refugees," while all intercepted Haitians were categorized as illegals, intercepted, and refouled (forcibly returned).

2. *African Rights* reported that Belgian troops had dragged corpses of Somali through the streets of Kismayo months before the North American media reported Somali dragging a US airman's corpse through the streets of Mogadishu. The report related Somali anger and upset about the dragging of corpses, including Somali worries that something might happen in reaction. Neither these incidents nor the torture by Canadian Armed Forces personnel of a young Somali man in Belet Weyne was reported by the network news in the US.

3. I used to espouse my undergraduate college's motto, "Veritas vos liberatit" (the truth shall make you free). When I discovered that this motto was emblazoned on the CIA's entrance in Langley, I realized that even grand phrases can be warped by interpretation–a problem familiar in the courtroom.

Notes on Contributors

Marleen Boelaert is a medical doctor with training in tropical medicine and epidemiology. She has working experience in East and Central Africa as a district doctor and is currently an instructor and researcher at the Prince Leopold Institute of Tropical Medicine, Antwerp, Belgium. Her research interests are in perceptions of health services and health care utilization in postemergency contexts. Her co-authored *Refugee Relief Rations* appeared in *The Lancet* in 1997, followed by *The Effects of a Refugee-Assistance Programme on Host Population in Guinea* (1998).

Diana Cammack is an American freelance research consultant working for The Redwood Partnership in Lilongwe, Malawi. Originally trained as an African historian, she held a SSRC-MacArthur Fellow on Peace and Security in a Changing World at St. Antony's College, Oxford, and now writes about human rights and refugees, relief and development, gender and aid, and democratic transitions. She is the author of *The Rand at War* (1990) and numerous academic articles and NGO/UN reports. She has lived, studied, and worked in the UK and in Asia and Africa for eighteen of the past twenty years.

Elizabeth Colson is a social anthropologist whose field research has been carried out in North America among Native Americans (Pomo, Makah, Navajo), in Australia (the city of Darwin), and in Africa (Plateau and Gwembe Tonga). For the past forty years her primary focus has been an ongoing, in-depth study of the Gwembe Tonga, who were resettled in 1958 after the building of the Kariba Hydroelectric Dam on the Zambezi River. This longitudinal research program has been shared with Thayer Scudder and, more recently, Jonathan Habarad, Sam Clark, Rhonda Gillett-Netting, and Lisa Cliggett. Colson's many authored and co-authored books include her *Social Consequences of Resettlement* (1971), the first ethnography of developmentally forced migration. Colson has held academic positions at Manchester University, Goucher College, Boston University, Brandeis University, Northwestern University, and the University of California, Berkeley.

Heaven Crawley is the author of *Women As Asylum Seekers: A Legal Handbook*. She is a member of the Gender Guidelines Drafting Committee of the UK Refugee Women's Legal Group, and is currently completing doctoral research at the University of Oxford on the politics of protection in the UK.

Tine Dusauchoit is a medical doctor trained in tropical medicine with extensive experience in Honduras, Uganda, former Zaire, and Mozambique. Her main interest is in mother and child health, and she was a technical adviser at the Medical Department of Médecins Sans Frontières at the time her chapter was written. Dusauchoit is the author of *MSF-CIS, Mozambique: A Data Collecting System Focused on Food Security and Population Movements*.

Khadija Elmadmad is Professor of Public Law and English, Faculty of Law, University of Casablanca, Morocco. She has long been involved in research on international and refugee law, human rights, forced migration, and African studies. Elmadmad has been a consultant for the UNHCR, the International Committee of the Red Cross, and many other national and international organizations. She teaches regularly at the Refugee Studies Programme, University of Oxford.

Lisa Gilad was an accomplished social anthropologist and member of Canada's Immigration and Refugee Board when a tragic automobile accident ended her life in 1996. She was author of *Ginger and Salt: Yemeni Jewish Women in an Israeli Town* (1989), *The Northern Route: An Ethnography of Refugee Experiences* (1990), and many other works on refugees, immigrants, and ethnic relations.

Wenona Giles is an Associate Professor in the Social Sciences Department, Atkinson College, York University, Canada. She is the coordinator and principal researcher in the international *Women and Conflict Zones* research project, and formerly was Coordinator of the Gender Unit at the Center for Refugee Studies, York University. She is the co-editor of *Development and Diaspora: Gender and the Refugee Experience* (1996) and the author of many publications on migration and gender.

Inés Gómez is a Lecturer in Elementary Education at San Francisco State University. Her research centers on Chilean women in exile and on participatory research.

Barbara Harrell-Bond is a social anthropologist whose work on kinship, family, and law in West Africa led to her authoring *Modern Marriage in Sierra Leone* (1975), co-authoring *Family Law in Sierra Leone* (1975) and *Community Leadership and the Transformation of Freetown (1801–1976)* (1978), and co-editing *The Imposition of Law* (1979). She founded the Refugee Studies Programme at the University of Oxford in 1982, and was its Director until 1996. Her *Imposing Aid: Emergency Assistance to Refugees* (1986) has initiated many new research domains in refugee studies.

Doreen Indra is a Professor of Anthropology, University of Lethbridge, Canada. Her most recent work has been involved with environmentally forced migrants in Bangladesh and with the construction and culture of disasters. She is co-author of *Continuous Journey: A Social History of South Asians in Canada* (1985), co-editor of *Ten Years Later: Indochinese Communities in Canada* (1988) and *Uprooting, Loss and Adaptation: The Resettlement of Indochinese Refugees in Canada* (1987), and author of many academic journal articles in the area of forced migration.

Natalya Kosmarskaya is a sociologist at the Institute of Oriental Studies, Russian Academy of Sciences and at the Moscow Center for Gender Studies. She has researched and published widely on post-Soviet ethnic migration, the position of Russian speakers in the New Independent States, and forced migrant adaptation in Russia, focusing on a range of gendered aspects of these phenomena.

Audrey Macklin is an Assistant Professor of Law at Dalhousie University, Canada. She has written extensively on gender in refugee determination, and has served as a member of Canada's Immigration and Refugee Board.

Peter Marsden is with the Refugee Council in London, and serves as the Information Coordinator of the British Agencies Afghanistan Group. He is the author of *The Taliban: War, Religion and the New Order in Afghanistan* (1998).

Patrick Matlou is Chief Director, Migration, Department of Home Affairs, Pretoria. The child of parents involved in the liberation struggle in South Africa who were forced to flee, he grew up as a forced migrant in southern, East, and West Africa. He did postgraduate studies in England on African refugee camp organization. Matlou is a pioneer in the study of sub-Saharan refugee policies and the social organization of refugee assistance.

Atsuko Matsuoka is an Associate Professor of Social Work, York University, Canada. Her research focuses on the elderly, multiculturalism, ethnicity and social work, program evaluation, ethics, and aging and social policy. She is currently doing a study of gender, ethnicity, and nation building in Eritrea with John Sorenson.

Lucia Ann McSpadden is the Director of Research, Life, and Peace Institute, Uppsala, Sweden. She has published extensively on gender dynamics in the resettlement of Eritrean women and men in Sweden and the US.

Carolyn Nordstrom was recently cross-appointed to the Department of Anthropology and to Peace Studies at Notre Dame University, having previously been a visiting scholar and research associate at the Peace and Conflict Studies Program at the University of California, Berkeley. She has carried out extensive fieldwork in South Asia and southern Africa. Her current research interests include the culture of conflict, internal guerrilla and low intensity warfare, communal conflict resolution, and complex medical systems. She is the author of *A Different Kind of War Story* (1997), co-editor of *Fieldwork Under Fire* (1995), and co-editor of *The Paths to Domination, Resistance, and Terror* (1992).

Charles David Smith teaches in the Sociology Department of Moi University, Eldoret, Kenya. He has done extensive research on Haya women in the Kagera region of Tanzania.

John Sorenson is an Associate Professor and Chair of Sociology at Brock University, Canada. His interests include race, ethnicity and nationalism, development studies, cultural studies, and social theory, particularly in the areas of representation and colonial discourse. Currently, he is writing on diaspora, transnationalism, and ethnic identity, focusing on the process of settlement and adaptation of Eritrean, Ethiopian, and Somali refugees and immigrants in North America and on gender equity issues in Eritrea. He is the author of *Imagining Ethiopia: Struggles for History and Identity in the Horn of Africa* (1993), editor of *Disaster and Development in the Horn of Africa* (1995), and co-editor of *African Refugees* (1994).

Wim Van Damme, is a medical doctor and has a masters degree in public health. He has worked extensively as a physician and researcher for Médecins Sans Frontières in Latin America and West and East Africa. Van Damme is currently a researcher at the Department of Public Health in the Prince Leopold Institute of Tropical Medicine, Antwerp, Belgium. His research interests in forced migration and health care organization have led to publications in *The Lancet* and other important journals. He is currently doing doctoral research in social anthropology at Oxford.

Monique Van Dormael, Ph.D., is a sociologist doing research and teaching sociology at the Department of Public Health in the Prince Leopold Institute of Tropical Medicine, Antwerp, Belgium. Her main research interest is in the role behavior and motivation of health care providers in the first line of the health service.

Fabienne Vautier has a M.S. degree in nutrition, and has several years of experience working for relief programs of the humanitarian agency Médecins Sans Frontières. She was the coordinator of the relief program in Hagadera Camp, Kenya, for several months and provided technical guidance over the period 1992–96.

Sidney Waldron is a social anthropologist at SUNY-Cortland with more than thirty-five years of research involvement in the Horn of Africa. He is the author of the pioneering urban ethnography *Social Organization and Social Control in the Walled City of Harar, Ethiopia* (1974) and *Somali Refugees in the Horn of Africa* (1995).

References

Abadan-Unat, N. 1977. Implications of migration on emancipation and pseudo-emancipation of Turkish women. *International Migration Review* 11(1):31–57.

Aberle, D. 1993. The Navajo-Hopi land dispute and Navajo relocation. In *Anthropological approaches to resettlement*, ed. M. Cernea and S. Guggenheim. Boulder, Colo.: Westview Press, 153–200.

Abitbol, E., and C. Louise. n.d. *Up in arms: The role of young people in conflict and peacemaking*. London: International Alert.

Abu-Lughod, J., and G. Lutz, eds. 1991. *Language and the politics of emotion*. New York: Cambridge University.

Adeji, A., ed. 1990. Breaking the vicious circle: Refugees and other displaced persons in Africa. In *The African social situation*. ACARTSOD Monograph Series. London: Hans Zell.

Adelman, H., and J. Sorenson. 1994. *African refugees*. Boulder, Colo.: Westview Press.

Adepoju, A. 1982. The dimension of the refugee problem in Africa. *African Affairs* 81(332):21–35.

Adepoju, A., and C. Oppong, eds. 1994. *Gender, work, and population in Sub-Saharan Africa*. London: James Currey.

Afghan Refugee Information Newsletter (ARIN). 1992. Report of the Women in Development seminar held in London on 25 April. *ARIN* 38 (Nov.).

Afkhami, M. 1997. Promoting women's rights in the Muslim world. *Journal of Democracy* 8(1):57–166.

Afsar, H., ed. 1991. *Women, development and survival in the Third World*. London: Longman.

Aga Khan, Prince Sadruddin. 1981. *Study on human rights and massive exoduses*. Geneva: UN Economic and Social Council, Commission on Human Rights.

Agarwal, B. 1986. Women, poverty and agricultural growth in India. *Journal of Peasant Studies* 13(4):165–219.

———. 1994. *A field of one's own: Gender and land rights in South Asia*. Cambridge: Cambridge University Press.

Agency Coordinating Body for Afghan Relief (ACBAR). 1990. *Overview of NGO assistance to the people of Afghanistan*.

Ager, A., W. Ager, and L. Long. 1995. The differential experience of Mozambican refugee women and men. *Journal of Refugee Studies* 8(3):265–87.

Agosin, M. 1987. Metaphors of a female political ideology: The cases of Chile and Argentina. *Women's Studies International Forum* 10(6):571–7.

———. 1987/88. *Scraps of life, Chilean arpilleras*. Trenton, N. J.: The Red Sea Press.

Ahearn, F., and J. Athey, eds. 1991. *Refugee children: Theory, research and services*. Baltimore: Johns Hopkins.

Ahmadi, F. 1997. The problem of identity crisis among female Iranian refugees. Paper presented to the Third European Feminist Research Conference, Shifting bonds, shifting bounds: Women, mobility, and citizenship in Europe. University of Coimbra, Portugal, 8–12 July.

Ahmed, I., ed. 1984. *Technology and rural women*. London: George Allen Unwin.

Alegria, F., and J. A. Epple. 1987. *Nos reconoce el tiempo y Silva su Tonada*. Santiago: Literatura Americana Reunida.

Alexander, M., and C. Mohanty. 1997. Genealogies, legacies, movements. In *Feminist genealogies, colonial legacies, democratic futures*, ed. M. Alexander and C. Mohanty. New York: Routledge, xiii–xlii.

Allison, D. 1992. *Bastard out of Carolina*. New York: Plume.

———. 1994. *Skin: Talking about sex, class, and literature*. Ithaca: Firebrand Books.

Allman, E., O. Cass et al., eds. 1989. Refugee women. *Canadian Women Studies* 10(1).

Almaz Eshete. 1991a. Women, development, and education reform: An Ethiopian perspective. Lecture given at the Mary Ingraham Bunting Institute, Radcliffe Research and Study Center, Cambridge, Massachusetts, 5 November.

———. 1991b. Perspectives on gender and development. In *Gender issues in Ethiopia*, ed. Tsehai Berhane-Selassie. Addis Ababa, Ethiopia: Institute of Ethiopian Studies, Addis Ababa University. Nov., pp. 1–5.

Alot, M. 1981. OAU clarion call for ICARA [International Conference on Assistance to Refugees in Africa]. *ICARA REPORT.* No. 3 (12 March):1. Geneva: UNHCR.

Amadiume, I. 1987. *Male daughters, female husbands: Gender and sex in African society*. London: Zed Books.

Amare, T. 1994. *Eritrea and Ethiopia*. Trenton, N.J.: Red Sea Press.

Amnesty International. 1991. *Women on the front line: Human rights violations against women*. New York: Amnesty International.

———. 1995a. *Women in Afghanistan: A human rights catastrophe*. May. New York: Amnesty International.

———. 1995b. *Afghanistan: International responsibility for human rights disaster*. Nov. New York: Amnesty International.

———. 1995c. *Amnesty International: Report 1995*. London: Amnesty International.

Anker, D., N. Kelly, and J. Willshire-Carrera. 1996a. Rape in the community as a basis for asylum: The treatment of women refugees' claims to protection in Canada and the United States (Part II). *Bender's Immigration Bulletin* 2:608–16.

———. 1996b. The BIA's new asylum jurisprudence and its relevance for women's claims. *Interpreter Releases* 73, 1180.

Anor v. Minister for Immigration and Ethnic Affairs. 1997. High Court of Australia. (24 Feb.).

Armstrong, A. 1991. Refugees and agricultural development in Tanzania. In *Migrants in agricultural development*, ed. J. Mollett. London: Macmillan, 206–21.

Arnaout, G. 1986. *L'asile dans la tradition arabo-islamique*. Geneva: UNHCR.

Arutyunyan, Y. 1992. *Russians: Ethno-sociological essays*. Moscow: Nauka Publishing House.

Ashworth, G. 1986. *Of violence and violation: Women and human rights*. London: Change.

Asia Watch and The Women's Rights Project. 1993. *A modern form of slavery: Trafficking of Burmese women and girls into brothels in Thailand*. New York: Human Rights Watch. Dec.

Australia. Department of Immigration and Multicultural Affairs (DIMA). 1996. *Guidelines on gender issues for decision-makers.* July.

Australian Refugee Review Tribunal. 1994. RRT N93/00656. (3 August). (L. Hunt).

——. 1994. RRT N94/06342 (Fiji) (28 June). (R. Layton).

——. 1995. RRT N94/03738. (4 June). (Ransome).

——. 1996. RRT N94/06730. (Philippines). (14 October). (M. Tsamenyi).

——. 1996. RRT N96/11892.(Ghana). (16 October). (R. Smidt).

——. 1996. RRT V96/04260. (Lebanon). (30 May). (A. Borsody).

——. 1997. RRT N96/12294. (18 June). (R. Mathlin).

——. 1997. V97/05699. (21 July). (Hudson).

Bach, M. 1993. Uncovering the institutionalized masculine: Notes for a sociology of masculinity. In *Men and masculinities: A critical anthology,* ed. T. Haddad. Toronto: Canadian Scholars' Press.

Bader, Z. 1975. Women, private property and production in Bukoba district. M.A. Thesis, University of Dar es Salaam, Tanzania.

Baitenmann, H. 1990. NGOs and the Afghan War: The politicisation of humanitarian aid. *Third World Quarterly* 12(1):62–85.

Bakhtin, M. 1981. *The dialogic imagination,* trans. C. Emerson and M. Holquist. Austin: University of Texas Press.

Balch, J., P. Granstedt, and K. Kenny. 1996. *Consolidation of democracy and human rights in emerging democracies: Focus on newly-elected politicians.* Occasional Papers, Series 1. Brussels: The African European Institute and Association of European Parliamentarians for Africa.

Beneria, L. 1995. Towards a greater integration of gender in Economics. *World Development* 23(11):1839–50.

——. ed. 1982. *Women and development: The sexual division of labor in rural societies.* New York: Praeger.

Benjamin, W. 1973. *Illuminations.* London: Fontana.

Bennett, M. 1993. Towards ethnorelativism: A developmental model of intercultural sensitivity. In *Education for the intercultural experience,* ed. R. M. Paige. Yarmouth, Me.: Intercultural Press, 21–71.

Ben-Tovim, D. 1987. *Development psychiatry: Mental health and primary health care in Botswana.* London: Tavistock.

Bereket, H. 1980. *Conflict and intervention in the Horn of Africa.* New York: Monthly Review Press.

——. 1989. *Eritrea and the United Nations.* Trenton, N.J.: Red Sea Press.

Berhane Woldemichael. 1992. Rural development in post-conflict Eritrea: Problems and policy options. In *Beyond conflict in the Horn of Africa,* ed. M. Doornbos, L. Cliffe, A. Ghaffar, M. Ahmen, and J. Markakis. Trenton, N.J.: Red Sea Press, 171–7.

Bernal, V. 1988. Losing ground – women and agriculture in Sudan's irrigated schemes: Lessons from a Blue Nile village. In *Agriculture, women and land: The African experience,* ed. J. Davison. Boulder, Colo.: Westview Press, 131–56.

Berry, J. 1991. Refugee adaptation in settlement countries: An overview with emphasis on primary prevention. In *Refugee children: Theory, research, and services,* ed. F. L. Ahearn Jr. and J. L. Athey. Baltimore: The John Hopkins University Press, 20–39.

Berthiaume, C. 1995. Do we really care. *Refugees: Refugee Women* 2(100):10–13. Geneva: UNHCR.

Bhabha, H., ed. 1991. *Nation and narration.* New York: Routledge.

———. 1993. Legal problems of women refugees. *Women: A Cultural Review* 4(3):240–9.

Bhattacharjee, A. 1997. The public/private mirage: Mapping homes and undomesti-cating violence work in the South Asian immigrant community. In *Feminist genealogies, colonial legacies, democratic futures*, ed. M. Alexander and C. Mohanty. New York: Routledge, 308–29.

Binion, G. 1995. Human rights: A feminist perspective. *Human Rights Quarterly* 17:509–26.

Boelaert., M., M. Englebert, G. Hanquet, W. Van Damme, and P. der Stuyft. 1997. Refugee relief rations. *Lancet* 349:1775.

Boesen, J. 1973. Peasants and coffee export: A coffee exporting region in Tanzania. In *Dualism and rural development in East Africa*. Copenhagen: Institute for Development Research.

Boothby, N., E. Ressler, and D. Steinbock. 1988. *Unaccompanied children: Care and protection in wars, natural disasters, and refugee movements*. Oxford: Oxford University Press.

Bordo, S. 1990. Feminism, postmodernism and gender-scepticism. In *Feminism/postmodernism*, ed. L. Nicholson. New York: Routledge, 133–56.

Boserup, E. 1970. *Women's role in development*. London: George Allen and Unwin.

Bourdieu, P. 1977. *Outline of a theory of practice*. London: Cambridge University Press.

Brah, A. 1996. *Cartographies of diaspora*. London: Routledge.

Brain, J. 1976. Less than second-class: Women in rural settlement schemes in Tanzania. In *Women in Africa: Studies in social and economic change*, ed. N. Hafkin and E. Bay. Stanford, Calif.: Stanford University Press.

Breckenridge, C., and A. Appadurai. 1989. On moving targets. *Public Culture* 2(1):i–iv.

British Agencies Afghanistan Group. 1996a. *Afghanistan Report: 30 January*. British Agencies. London: British Refugee Council.

———. 1996b. *Report on a study on coping strategies of refugees from, and returnees to Afghanistan: Visit of Information Coordinator to Iran, Afghanistan and Pakistan from 17 June to 5 July*. London: British Refugee Council.

———. 1996c. *Afghanistan report: 1 October*. London: British Refugee Council.

———. 1996d. *Afghanistan report: 15 November*. London: British Refugee Council.

———. 1996e. *Visit of Information Coordinator to Afghanistan and Pakistan from 19 November to 2 December*. London: British Refugee Council.

———. 1996f. *Living in exile: Report on a study of economic coping strategies among Afghan refugees in Pakistan*. (Dec.). London: British Refugee Council.

———. 1997a. *Afghanistan report: 30 April*. London: British Refugee Council.

———. 1997b. *Afghanistan report: 31 May*. London: British Refugee Council.

———. 1997c. *Afghanistan report: 26 June*. London: British Refugee Council.

Brittain, V. 1996. Rwanda's plight is far from over. *Mail and Guardian* (Johannesburg) 12, No. 13 (29 March to 3 April):23.

Britzman, D., K. Santiago-Válles, G. Jiménez-Munoz, and L. Lamash. 1993. Slips that show and tell: Fashioning multiculture as a problem of representation. In *Race identity and representation in education*, ed. C. McCarthy and W. Crichlow. New York: Routledge.

Brochmann, G. 1991. The significance of gender relations in international migration. *Forum for utviklingsstudier* 1:113–124.

Brown, R. 1989. *Social science as civic discourse: Essays on the invention, legitimation, and uses of social theory*. Chicago: University of Chicago Press.

Bryceson, D. 1990. *Food insecurity and the social division of labor in Tanzania, 1919–1985.* New York: St. Martin's Press.

Buckley, S. 1996. African grandparents are forfeiting their status and age-old privileges. *Diamond Fields Advertiser* (Kimberley), 21 May, p. 5.

Buijs, G., ed. 1993. Introduction in *Migrant women. Crossing boundaries and changing identities.* Oxford: Berg Publishers.

Bunch, C. 1990. Women's rights as human rights: Towards a re-vision of human rights. *Humanitarian Rights Quarterly* 12(4):486–98.

Bunting, A. 1993. Theorizing women's cultural diversity in feminist international human rights strategies. *Journal of Law and Society* 20(1):6–22.

Burton, E. 1982. *Transpacific odyssey: Vietnamese women refugees in United States and Asia.* Amherst, Mass.: Hampshire College.

Cairns, E. 1987. *Caught in the crossfire: Children in Northern Ireland.* Syracuse: Syracuse University Press.

———. 1995. *Children and political violence.* London: Basil Blackwell.

Caldwell, J., P. Caldwell, and P. Quiggin. 1989. The social context of AIDS in Sub-Saharan Africa. *Population and Development Review* 15(2).

Callaway, H. 1987. Women refugees: Specific requirements and untapped resources. *Third World affairs,* ed. Gaunar Altaf. London: Third World Foundation for Social and Economic Studies, 320–5.

Campos-Guardado v. U.S. Immigration and Naturalization Service (INS). [1987]. INS. 809 R.2d 285 (5th Cir.).

Camus-Jacques, G. 1989. Refugee women: The forgotten majority. In *Refugees and international relations,* ed. G. Loescher and L. Monahan. Oxford: Oxford University Press, 141–57.

Canada. Immigration and Refugee Board (IRB). 1993. *Guidelines on women refugee claimants fearing gender-related persecution.* Issued by the Chairperson of Canada's IRB pursuant to Section 65(3) of the *Immigration Act.* (9 March).

———. 1996. T95–01010/11/12. (30 July). (Then, Kelley).

———. 1996. T95–04279. (30 December). (Then, Wolman).

———. 1996. Women refugee claimants fearing gender-related persecution: Update. Guidelines Issued by the Chairperson of Canada's IRB Pursuant to Section 65(3) of the *Immigration Act.* (13 Nov.).

Cantril, A. H., and C. W. Roll, Jr. 1971. *The hopes and fears of the American people.* New York: Universe Books.

Carmichael, W., and S. Berresford. 1983. *Refugees and migrants: Problems and program responses.* Aug. New York: Ford Foundation.

Carrigan, T., B. Connell, and J. Lee. 1985. Towards a new sociology of masculinity. *Theory and Society* 14(5):551–603.

Castel, J. 1992. Race, sexual assault and the meaning of persecution. *International Journal of Refugee Law* 4(1):39–56.

Cecelski, E. 1984. *The rural energy crisis, women's work and family welfare: Perspectives and approaches to action.* Geneva: ILO.

Center for Applied Linguistics. 1981. *Ethiopians.* Refugee Fact Sheet Series No. 1. Washington, D.C.: Center for Applied Linguistics.

Center of Demography and Human Ecology. 1995. *Population and Society.* Information Bulletin No. 5. Moscow: Center of Demography and Human Ecology.

Centers for Disease Control and Prevention. 1992. Famine-affected, refugee, and displaced populations: Recommendations for public health issues. *Morbidity and Mortality Weekly Report: Surveillance Summary* 41:1–76.

Cernea, M. 1985. Knowledge from social science for development policies and projects. In *Putting people first: Sociological variables in rural development*, ed. M. Cernea. Oxford: Oxford University Press, published for the World Bank, 1–41.

Cernea, M., and S. Guggenheim, eds. 1993. *Anthropological approaches to resettlement: Policy, practice, and theory*. Boulder, Colo.: Westview Press.

Chakravorty Spivak, G. 1987. *In other worlds: Essays in cultural politics.* New York: Methuen.

Chambers, R. 1969. *Settlement schemes in tropical Africa: A study of organizations and development*. London: Kegan Paul.

———. 1979. Rural refugees in Africa: What the eye does not see. *Disasters* 3(4):381–92.

Chan v. Canada (Minister of Employment and Immigration). [1995] 3 SCR 593.

Charlesworth, H., et al. 1991. Feminist approaches to international law. *American Journal of International Law* 85:613–64.

Cheung v. Canada (Minister of Employment and Immigration) [1993] 19 Imm. LR (2d) 181 (FCA).

Chilvers, E. 1992. Women cultivators, cows, and cash crops in Cameroon. In *Persons and powers of women in diverse cultures*, ed. S. Ardener. Oxford: Berg, 105–34.

Chowdhury, M., and R. Bairagi. 1990. Son preference and fertility in Bangladesh. *Population and Development Review* 16(4):749–57.

Christensen, H. 1990. *The reconstruction of Afghanistan: A chance for rural women*. Geneva: United Nations Institute for Social Development.

Christensen, H., and W. Scott. 1988. *Survey of the social and economic conditions of Afghan refugees in Pakistan*. Geneva: United Nations Institute for Social Development.

Cichon, D., E. Gozdiak, and J. Grover. 1986. *The economic and social adjustment of non-Southeast Asian refugees*. 2 vols. Falls Church, Va.: Research Management Corporation.

CIMADE. 1981. The influence of political repression and exile on children. In *Mental health and exile*. London: World University Press Service, 22–34.

Cipriani, L. 1993. Gender and persecution: Protecting women under international law *Georgetown Immigration Law Journal*, 511–48.

Clements, K. 1992. Introduction. In *Peace and security in the Asia Pacific region*, ed. K. Clements. Tokyo: United Nations University Press.

Clifford, J. 1997. *Routes: Travel and translations in the late twentieth century*. Cambridge, Mass.: Harvard University Press.

Colson, E. 1960. *Social organization of the Gwembe Tonga*. Manchester: Manchester University Press.

———. 1966. Land law and land holdings among valley Tonga of Zambia. *Southwestern Journal of Anthropology* 22(1):1–8.

———. 1969. Spirit possession among the Tonga of Zambia. In *Spirit mediumship and society in Africa*, ed. J. Middleton and J. Beaties. London: Kegan Paul, 69–103.

———. 1971. *Social consequences of resettlement*. Manchester: Manchester University Press.

———. 1977. A continuing dialogue: Prophets and local shrines among the Tonga of Zambia. In *Regional cults*, ed. R. Werbner. New York: Academic Press, 119–39.

Colson, E., and T. Scudder. 1975. New economic relationships between the Gwembe Valley and the line of rail. In *Town and country in Central and Eastern Africa*. London: Oxford University Press for the International African Institute, 190–210.

——. 1988. *For prayer and profit: The ritual, economic, and social importance of beer in Gwembe District, Zambia, 1950–1982.* Stanford, Calif.: Stanford University Press.

Colville, R. 1995. The difficulty of educating Leyla. *Refugees* 100.

Community Aid Abroad, Australia, and OXFAM, UK and Ireland. 1994. *UN interventions in conflict situations.* Feb.

Connell, R. 1971. *The child's construction of politics.* Melbourne: Melbourne University Press.

Cook, R., ed. 1994. *Human rights of women: National and international perspectives.* Philadelphia: University of Pennsylvania Press.

Copelon, R. 1994. Surfacing gender; Re-engraving crimes against women in humanitarian law. *Hasting's Women's Law Journal* 5(2):243-266.

Cornwall, A., and N. Lindisfarne, eds. 1994a. *Dislocating masculinity: Comparative ethnographies.* London: Routledge.

——. 1994b. Dislocating masculinity: Gender, power, and anthropology. In *Dislocating masculinity: Comparative ethnographies,* ed. A. Cornwall and N. Lindisfarne. London: Routledge, 11–47.

Cory, H., and M. Hartnoll. 1971. *The customary law of the Haya tribe.* London: Frank Cass.

Crawley, H. 1997. *Women as asylum seekers: A legal handbook.* London: Immigration Law Practitioners Association.

Creevey, L., ed. 1986. *Women farmers in Africa: Rural development in Mali and the Sahel.* Syracuse, N.Y.: Syracuse University Press.

Crisp, J., and C. Nettleton. 1984. *Refugee Report.* London: British Refugee Council.

Crosby, F., and K. Jasker. 1993. Women and men at home and at work: Realities and illusions. *Gender issues in contemporary society,* ed. S. Oskamp and M. Costanzo. Newbury Park: Sage, 143–71.

Cuenod, J. 1967. The problem of Rwandese and Sudanese refugees. In *Refugee Problems in Africa,* ed. S. Hamrell. Uppsala: The Scandinavian Institute of African Studies.

Daley, P. 1991. Gender, displacement, and social reproduction: Settling Burundi refugees in Western Tanzania. *Journal of Refugee Studies* 4(3):248–66.

Das, V., ed. 1991. Our work to cry: Your work to listen. In *Mirrors of violence: communities, riots and survivors in South Asia.* Oxford: Oxford University Press.

Dauber, R., and M. Cain, eds. 1981. *Women and technological change in developing countries.* Boulder, Colo.: Westview Press.

Davies, J., comp. 1990. *Displaced peoples and refugee studies: A resource guide.* New York: H. Zell.

Davies, R. 1997. Humanitarian aid: Economic consequences and implications. *Refugee Participation Network,* No. 23. Oxford: Refugee Studies Programme.

Davis, A. 1996. Targeting the vulnerable in emergency situations: Who is vulnerable? *Lancet* 348:868–71.

Davis, J. 1992. The anthropology of suffering. *Journal of Refugee Studies* 5(2):149–61.

Davison, J., ed. 1988. *Agriculture, women and land: The African experience.* Boulder, Colo.: Westview Press.

de Alwis, M. 1996. *Motherhood as a space of protest: Women's political participation in contemporary Sri Lanka.* Paper presented at the Women in Conflict Zone Workshop. November, York University.

——. 1997. Women in Conflict Zone Network (WICZNET). E-mail communication. 23 June.

de Certeau, M. 1988. *The practice of everyday life.* Berkeley: University of California Press.

De Vos, P. 1993. The silent majority: Women as refugees. *The Women and International Development Annual* Vol. 3., ed. R. Gallin, A. Ferguson, and J. Harper, Boulder, Colo.: Westview Press.

de Waal, A., and R. Omar. 1994. Humanitarianism unbound? Current dilemmas facing multi-mandate relief operations in political emergencies. *Africa Rights* vol. 5.

Decimo, F. 1997. *Living in the city: The urban integration of Somali women in Naples.* Paper presented to the Third European Feminist Research Conference, Shifting bonds, shifting bounds: Women, mobility, and citizenship in Europe. University of Coimbra, Portugal, 8–12 July.

Del Mundo, F. 1995a. Do we really care? *Refugees* 100:10–13.

———. 1995b. Foster families in Rwanda. *Refugees: Refugee Women* 2(100):14–15. Geneva: UNHCR.

Deleuze, G., and F. Guattari. 1987. *A thousand plateaus: Capitalism and schizophrenia.* Minneapolis, Minn.: University of Minnesota Press.

Delgado-Gaitán, C., and H. Trueba. 1991. *Crossing cultural borders: Education for immigrant families in America.* London: Falmer.

di Leonardo, M. 1991. *Introduction.* In *Gender at the crossroads of knowledge: Feminist anthropology in the postmodern era*, ed. M. di Leonardo. Berkeley: University of California Press.

Dixon, R. 1980. *Assessing the impact of development projects on women.* Washington, D.C.: USAID.

Dupree, N. 1988. Demographic reporting on Afghan refugees in Pakistan. *Modern Asian Studies* 22(4):855.

———. 1991. Constitutional requirements for Afghan women. *Writers Union of Free Afghanistan* 6(2):54–55.

Dwyer, M. 1995. Trading the work of children. *Financial Review*, 26 July.

Eastmond, M. 1993. Reconstructing life: Chilean refugee women and the dilemmas of exile. In *Migrant women, crossing boundaries and changing identities*, ed. G. Buijs. Oxford: Berg.

Eisenstadt, S. 1954. *The absorption of immigrants.* London: Routledge and Kegan Paul.

Ekejiuba, F. 1995. Down to fundamentals: Women-centred hearth-holds in rural West Africa. In *Women wielding the hoe: Lessons from rural African for feminist theory and development practice*, ed. D. Bryceson. Oxford: Berg Publishers, 47–61.

Elmadmad, K. 1991. An Arab convention on forced migration: Desirability and possibilities. *International Journal of Refugee Law* 3(3):461–81.

———. 1993. L'asile dans les pays afro-arabes avec une référence spéciale au Soudan, thèse de Doctorat d'Etat en Droit Public, University of Casablanca, November (in collaboration with the Refugee Studies Programme of Oxford University).

Enloe, C. 1989. *Bananas, beaches, and bases.* London: Pandora.

———. 1993. *The morning after: Sexual politics at the end of the cold war.* Berkeley, Calif.: University of California Press.

Escriva, A. 1996. *Control, composition and character of new migrations to south-west Europe: The case of Peruvian women in Barcelona.* Paper presented to the Second International Conference, New migration in Europe: Social constructions and social realities. Utrecht, The Netherlands, 18–20 April.

European Forum of Left Feminists. 1993. *Confronting the fortress: Black and migrant women in the European community.* Report presented to the Eighth Conference of the European Forum of Left Feminists, *Nationalism, racism and gender in Europe*, Amsterdam, 19–21 November.

Fahim, H. 1981. *Dams, people, and development: The Aswan High Dam case.* New York: Pergamon.

———. 1983. *Egyptian Nubians: Resettlement and years of coping.* Salt Lake City: University of Utah Press.

Fair, D. 1995. War and Africa's children. *Africa Insight* 25(4):212–15.

Fatin v. INS. [1993] 12 F.3d 1233 (3d Cir.).

Federal Migration Service of the Russian Federation (FMS) 1995. *Forced migrants in Russia.* Statistical Bulletin No. 5. Moscow: Federal Migration Service of the Russian Federation.

Feldmeier, H., G. Poggensee, and I. Krantz. 1993. Gender-related biases in the diagnosis and morbidity assessment of schistosomiasis in women. *Acta Tropica* 55(3):139–69.

Ferris, E. 1992. Refugee women and family life. In *The psychological well-being of refugee children: Research practice and policy issues,* ed. M. McCallin. International Catholic Child Bureau.

Fetherston, A. 1995. UN peacekeepers and cultures of violence. *Cultural Survival Quarterly* (Spring):19–23.

Fetherston, A., and C. Nordstrom. 1995. Overcoming *habitus* in conflict management: UN peacekeeping and war zone ethnography. *Peace and Change* 20(1):94–119.

Filippova, E. 1997. Factors influencing stability of forced migrants' families. In *Family, gender, culture,* ed. V. Tishkov. Moscow: Institute of Ethnology and Anthropology.

Fincher, R., L. Foster, W. Giles, and V. Preston. 1994. Gender and migration policy. In *Immigration and refugee policy: Australia and Canada compared,* ed. H. Adelman, A. Borowski, M. Burstein, and L. Foster. 2 Vols. Melbourne: Melbourne University Press, 149–86.

Firebrace, J., with S. Holland. 1985. *Never kneel down.* Trenton, N.J.: Red Sea Press.

Fisher v. INS. [1994] 37 F.3d 1371, 1379. (9th Cir.).

Forbes-Martin, S. 1991. *Refugee women.* London: Zed Books.

Fortmann, L. 1982. Women's work in a communal setting: The Tanzanian policy of *Ujamaa.* In *Women and work in Africa,* ed. E. Bay. Boulder, Colo.: Westview Press.

Foucault, M. 1972. *The Archaeology of Knowledge and the Discourse on Language,* trans. A. Sheridan Smith. New York: Pantheon.

Freire, M. 1995. The Latin American exile experience from a gender perspective: A psychodynamic assessment. *Refuge* 14(8):20–25.

Freire, P. 1994. *Paulo Freire and higher education,* ed. M. Escobar, A. Fernandez, and G. Guevara-Niebla. Albany: SUNY.

French, M. 1992. *The war against women.* New York: Summit Books.

Frisch, M. 1981. The memory of history. *Radical History Review* 25:9–23.

Fullerton, M. 1993. A comparative look at refugee status based on persecution due to membership in a particular social group. *Cornell International Law Journal* 26(3):505–64.

Ganguly, K. 1992. Migrant identities: Personal memory and the construction of selfhood. *Cultural Studies* 6(1):27–50.

Geisler, G. 1993. Silences speak louder than claims: Gender, household, and agricultural development in Southern Africa. *World Development* 12(12):1965–1980.

Gennet Zewdie 1991. Women in primary and secondary education. In *Gender issues in Ethiopia,* ed. T. Berhane-Selassie. Addis Ababa, Ethiopia: Institute of Ethiopian Studies, Addis Ababa University. Nov., pp. 89–98.

Gilad, L. 1990. *The northern route.* St. John's: Memorial University of Newfoundland.

———. 1996. Cultural collision and human rights. In *Development and diaspora: Gender and the refugee experience*, ed. W. Giles, H. Moussa, and P. Van Esterik. Halifax: Fernwood Press, 74–86.

Giles, W. 1996. *Reinventing boundaries: State discourse and definitions of community among Portuguese women in Toronto.* Paper presented at the Women and Citizenship Conference. Greenwich University. London, 16–18 July.

———. 1997. Re/membering the Portuguese household in Toronto: Culture, contradictions and resistance. In *Women's Studies International Forum. Special Issue: Concepts of Home* 20(3):387–96.

Giles, W., H. Moussa, and P. Van Esterik. 1996. Introduction. In *Development and diaspora: Gender and the refugee experience*, ed. W. Giles, H. Moussa, and P. Van Esterik. Dundas, Ontario: Artemis, 11–28.

Gilmore, D. 1990. *Manhood in the making: Cultural concepts of masculinity.* New Haven, Conn.: Yale University Press.

Giorgis, T. 1984. Cross-cultural counseling of Ethiopian refugees. Paper prepared for the Ethiopian Community Development Council Workshop on Refugee Mental Health. San Francisco, Calif.

Giroux, H. 1988. *Schooling and the struggle for public life: Critical pedagogy in the modern Age.* Minneapolis: University Press.

Gladwin, C., ed. 1991. *Structural adjustment and African women farmers.* Gainesville, Fla.: University of Florida Press.

Glick-Schiller, N., L. Basch, and C. Blanc-Szanton. 1992. Transnationalism: A new analytic framework for understanding migration. In *Towards a transnational perspective on migration: Race, class, ethnicity, and nationalism reconsidered*, ed. N. Glick-Schiller, L. Basch, and C. Blanc-Szanton. New York: The New York Academy of Sciences, 1–24.

Goldberg, D. P. 1972. *The detection of psychiatric illness by questionnaire.* London: Oxford University Press.

Goldberg, P. 1993. Any place but home: Asylum in the United States for women fleeing intimate violence. *Cornell International Law Journal* 26(3):565–604.

Goldberg, P., and N. Kelly. 1993. International human rights and violence against women: Recent developments. *Harvard Humanitarian Rights Journal* 6:195–209.

Gómez, I. 1974. Mapuche Indians of Chile: The culture of resistance. *Indigena* 1(2).

———. 1993a. Disruption and relocation: Chilean women in exile, a participatory research. Unpublished Doctoral Diss. University of San Francisco, San Francisco, California.

———. 1993b. Qualitative research with special populations: Studying within and across difference. Paper presented at the Qualitative Research Internet Group Conference, January. University of Georgia, Athens.

Graburn, N. 1987. Severe child abuse among the Canadian Inuit. In *Child Survival*, ed. N. Scheper-Hughes. Dordrecht: D. Reidel.

Grahl-Madsen, A. 1966. The status of refugees in international law. Leyden: Sijhoff.

Greatbatch, J. 1989. The gender difference: Feminist critiques of refugee discourse. *International Journal of Refugee Law* 1(4):518–27.

Grewal, I. 1996. *Home and harem: Nation, gender, empire, and cultures of travel.* Durham: Duke University Press.

Grewal, I., and C. Kaplan, eds. 1994a. *Scattered hegemonies: Postmodernity and transnational feminist practices.* Minneapolis: University Press.

———. 1994b. Transnational feminist practices and questions of postmodernity. In *Scattered hegemonies: Postmodernity and transnational feminist practices*, ed. I. Grewal and C. Kaplan. Minneapolis: University of Minnesota Press, 1–33.

Guggenheim, S. 1993. Peasants, planners, and participation: Resettlement in Mexico. In *Anthropological approaches to resettlement*, ed. M. Cernea and S. Guggenheim. Boulder, Colo.: Westview Press, 201–28.

Gupta, A. 1992. Beyond "culture": Space, identity, and the politics of difference. *Cultural Anthropology* 7(1):6–23.

Guyer, J. 1986a. Intra-household processes and farming systems research: Perspectives from anthropology. In *Understanding Africa's rural households and farming systems*, ed. J. L. Moock. Boulder, Colo.: Westview Press, 92–104.

———. 1986b. Women's role in development. In *Strategies for African development*, ed. R. Berg and J. Whitaker. Berkeley, Los Angeles: University of California Press.

Habte-Mariam, Z. 1989. Methodology and perspectives in research on the teaching of mother tongue. *Language Issues* 3(1):24–26.

Hall, S. 1990. Cultural identity and diaspora. In *Identity: Community, culture, difference*, ed. J. Rutherford. London: Lawrence & Wishart.

Hammer, J., and M. Mabry. 1996. Liberia–a deadly quiet. *Newsweek*, 8 July, p. 16.

Hansen, A. 1981. Refugee dynamics: Angolans in Zambia, 1966 to 1972. *International Migration Review* 15(1–2):175–94.

Harding, S., ed. 1987. *Feminism and methodology*. Bloomington: Indiana University Press.

Harrell-Bond, B. 1969. Conjugal role behaviour. *Human Relations* 22(1).

———. 1975a. The influence of legislative change on behaviour: A case study on the status of illegitimate children in Sierra Leone. *Verfassung und Recht in Ubersee* 3–4. Quartall.

———. 1975b. *Modern marriage in Sierra Leone: A study of the professional group*. The Hague: Mouton.

———. 1981. *The struggle for the Western Sahara: A three-part series*. American Universities Field Staff Reports, Hanover, N. H. Part I: The Background, No. 27. Part II: The Legal/Political Milieu, No. 38. Part III: The People, No. 39.

———. 1982. *4 June – A Revolution Betrayed*. Nigeria: Ikenga.

———. 1985. Humanitarianism in a straitjacket. *African Affairs* 84(334):3–11.

———. 1986. *Imposing aid: Emergency assistance to refugees*. Oxford: Oxford University Press.

Harrell-Bond, B., and U. Rijnsdorp. 1975. *Family law in Sierra Leone*. Leiden, Holland: Africa-Studiecentrun.

Harrell-Bond, B., and D. Skinner. 1977a. The distinction between "native" and "non-native" in Sierra Leone law. *Commonwealth Law Bulletin* 3(4).

———. 1977b. Misunderstandings arising from the use of the term "Creole" in the literature on Sierra Leone. *Africa* 47(3).

Harrell-Bond, B., A. Howard, and D. Skinner. 1977. *Community leadership and the transformation of Freetown, 1801–1976*. The Hague: Mouton.

Harrell-Bond, B., and S. Burman, eds. 1979. *The imposition of law*. New York: Academic Press.

Harrell-Bond, B., and D. Harrell-Bond. 1980. Tourism in the Gambia: A "development" plan for creating dependency. In *La dependence de l'Afrique et les moyens d'y remedier*. Etabli par V.Y. Mudimbe. Agence de Co-operation Culturelle et Technique, Berger-Lebrault.

Harrell-Bond, B., and A. Smith. 1983. Dispute treatment in an English town. In *Disputes and the law*, ed. M. Cain and K. Kulcsar. Budapest: Akademiai Kiado.

Harrell-Bond, B., and E. Voutira. 1992. Anthropology and the study of refugees. *Anthropology Today* 8(4):6–12.

Hathaway, J. 1991. *The law of refugee status.* Toronto: Butterworth.

Hitchcox, L. 1989. Vietnamese refugees in transit: Process and change. Ph.D. diss., University of Oxford, Oxford.

Hoerz, T. 1995. *Somali clans and their relevance to refugee assistance in Kenya.* Submitted to Identity: Nationalism, regionalism and ethnicity in the explanation of human displacement. Unpublished document.

Hoffman, D. 1996. Culture and self in multicultural education: Reflections on discourse, text, and practice. *American Educational Research Journal* 33(3):545–69.

Hollands, M. 1996. *Of crowbars and other tools to tackle Dutch society: The integration of refugees and the multicultural society.* Paper presented to the Second International Conference, New migration in Europe: Social constructions and social realities. Utrecht, 18–20 April.

Hudelson, P. 1996. Gender differentials in tuberculosis: The role of socio-economic and cultural factors. *Tubercle and Lung Disease* 77:391–400.

Hyden, G. 1969. *Tanu yajenga nchi: Political development in rural Tanzania.* Nairobi: East African Publishing.

Hyman, A. 1992. *Afghanistan under Soviet Domination, 1964–91.* Basingstoke: Macmillan.

Hyndman, J. 1996. *Organizing women: UN approaches to gender and culture among the displaced.* Paper prepared for the Women in Conflict Zone Network Meeting, November. York University, Toronto, Ontario.

Hyndman, M. 1996. Geographies of displacement: Gender, culture, and power in UNHCR refugee camps, Kenya. Ph.D. diss., Faculty of Graduate Studies, Department of Geography, University of British Columbia.

Igoa, C. 1995. *The inner world of the immigrant child.* New York: St. Martin Press.

Indra, D. 1987. Gender: A key dimension of the refugee experience. *Refuge* 6(2):3–4.

———. 1989a. Ethnic human rights and feminist theory: Gender implications for refugee studies and practice. *Journal of Refugee Studies* 2(2):1–22.

———. 1989b. Resettlement and gender differences: A Lethbridge community study. *Canadian Woman Studies* 10(1):63–66.

———. 1993. Some feminist contributions to refugee studies. Paper presented at a joint plenary session of Gender Issues and Refugees: Development Implications and Exploring Knowledge, Power and Practice in Society (CASCA Annual Meetings), York University, Toronto, Ont., 9–11 May.

———. 1996. Not a "room of one's own": Engendering forced migration knowledge and practice. Paper presented at the International Society for the Study of Forced Migration first annual meeting. Moi University, Kenya, 9–12 April.

Indra, D., and N. Buchignani. 1997. Rural landlessness, extended entitlements and inter-household relations in South Asia: A Bangladesh case. *Journal of Peasant Studies* 23(3):25–64.

International Centre for Humanitarian Reporting. 1996. *Crosslines Global Report* 4(4/5), Issues 22/23. Aug. Cambridge, Mass.: International Centre for Humanitarian Reporting.

Jack, S. 1996. Continent in conflict: African women must play a vital role. *New Nation* 8 (Nov.):11.

Jennings, J. 1990. *Friday Times* (Pakistan), 17–28 May.

Jetter, A., A. Orleck, and D. Taylor, eds. 1997. *The politics of motherhood: Activist voices from left to right.* Hanover, N.H.: University Press of New England.

Jiggins, J. 1986. Women and seasonality: Coping with crisis and calamity. *IDS Bulletin* 17(3):9–18.

Johnsson, A. 1989. International protection of women refugees: A summary of principle problems and issues. *International Journal of Refugee Law* 1(2):221–32.

John-Steiner, V., and H. Mahn. 1996. Sociocultural approaches to learning and development: A Vygotskian framework. *Educational Psychologist* 31(3/4):191–206.

Jordan, G. 1989. *Peasants and nationalism in Eritrea.* Trenton, N.J.: Red Sea Press.

Kabeer, N. 1988. Subordination and struggle: Women in Bangladesh. *New Left Review* 168:95–121.

———. 1990. Poverty, purdah and women's survival strategies in rural Bangladesh. In *The food question: Profits versus people*, ed. H. Bernstein, B. Crow, M. Macintosh, and C. Martin. London: Earthscan, 134–48.

———. 1991. Gender dimensions of rural poverty: Analysis from Bangladesh. *Journal of Peasant Studies* 18(2):241–62.

Kamuf, P., and N. Miller. 1990. Parisian letters: Between feminism and deconstruction. In *Conflicts in Feminism*, ed. M. Hirsch and E. Keller. New York: Routledge.

Kandiyoti, D. 1988. Bargaining with patriarchy. *Gender and Society* 2(3).

Karadawi, A. 1983. *Constraints on assistance to refugees: Some observations from the Sudan.* World Development 2(6):537–47.

Kayigamba, J. 1997. African women call for peace-making role. *Citizen*, 11 March, p. 11.

Kearney, A. 1996. Tactical withdrawal. *Crosslines Global Report.* Aug. Cambridge, Mass.: International Centre for Humanitarian Reporting.

Kelly, N. 1993. Gender-related persecution: Assessing the asylum claims of women. *Cornell International Law Journal* 26(3):625–74.

———. 1994. Guidelines for women's asylum claims. *International Journal of Refugee Law* 6(4):517–34.

Kibreab, G. 1987. *Refugees in Africa: The case of Eritrea.* Trenton, N.J.: Red Sea Press.

———. 1990. *The Sudan from subsistence to wage labor.* Trenton, N.J.: Red Sea Press.

———. 1995. Eritrean women refugees in Khartoum, Sudan, 1970–1990. *Journal of Refugee Studies* 8(1):1–25.

Klawitter v. INS. [1992] F 970.2d: 149 (6th Cir.).

Kleinman, A., and J. Kleinman. 1991. Suffering and its professional transformation: Toward an ethnography of interpersonal experience. *Culture, Medicine and Psychiatry* 15(3):275–301.

Koenig, D. 1992. Involuntary resettlement and gender. Paper given at the meeting of the American Anthropological Association, San Francisco, Dec.

———. 1995. Women and resettlement. In *The women and international development annual* 4:21–49, ed. R. S. Gallin, A. Ferguson, and J. Harper. Boulder, Colo.: Westview Press.

Komarova, O. 1997. Socio-demographic characteristics and major problems of the forced migration in Russia. In *Forced migrants: Integration and return*, ed. V. Tishkov. Moscow: Institute of Ethnology and Anthropology.

Kondo, D. 1996. The narrative production of "home," community, and political identity in Asian American theater. In *Displacement, diaspora, and geographies of identity*, ed. S. Lavie and T. Swedenburg. Durham, N.C.: Duke University Press.

Korac, M. 1996a. Ethnic-nationalism, identity politics and women in the former Yugoslavia: Rethinking differences. Paper presented at the Annual Conference of the American Anthropological Association, San Francisco, November.

———. 1996b. Ethnic conflict, rape and feminism: The case of Yugoslavia. *Research on Russia and Eastern Europe* 2:247–66.

Kosmarskaya, N. 1995. Women and ethnicity in present-day Russia: Thoughts on a given theme. In *Crossfires: Nationalism, racism and gender in Europe*, ed. H. Lutz, A. Phoenix, and N. Yuval-Davis. London: Pluto Press.

———. 1996. *A micro-level study of forced migrants adaptation in Central Russia.* Interim report for the INTAS project seminar. Moscow, 1–5 June.

———. 1997. "I have a feeling of being exiled here …" women migrants in central Russia: Reefs of adaptation. In *Gender and catastrophe*, ed. R. Lentin. London: Zed Books.

Kruefeld, R. M. 1992. Cognitive mapping and ethnic identity: The changing concepts of community and nationalism in the Laotian diaspora. In *Selected papers on refugee issues*, ed. P. DeVoe. Washington, D.C.: American Anthropological Association.

Kuhlman, T. 1990. *Burden or boon?: Study of Eritrean refugees in the Sudan.* Amsterdam: VU University Press.

Lamphere, L. 1993. The domestic sphere of women and the public world of men: The strengths and limitations of an anthropological dichotomy. In *Gender in cross-cultural perspective*, ed. C. Brettell and C. Sargent. Englewood Cliffs, N.J.: Prentice-Hall.

Landry, D., and G. Maclean. 1993. *Materialist feminisms.* Oxford: Blackwell.

Lankshear, C., M. Peters, and M. Knobel. 1996. Critical pedagogy and cyberspace. In *Counternarratives: Cultural studies and critical pedagogies in postmodern spaces*, ed. H. Giroux, C. Lankshear, P. McLaren, and M. Peters. New York: Routledge.

Lather, P. 1991. *Getting smart: Feminist research and pedagogy with/in the post-modern.* New York: Routledge.

Lazo-Majano v. INS. [1987] 813 F.2d 1432 (9th Cir.).

Ledeneva, A. 1998. *Russia's economy of favours: Blat, networking and informal exchange.* Cambridge: Cambridge University Press (forthcoming).

Lee, R., and I. Devore, eds. 1968. *Man the hunter.* Chicago, Ill.: Aldine.

Lele, U. 1986. Women in structural transformation. *Economic Development and Cultural Change* 34(2):195–221.

Levine, D. 1965. *Wax and gold: Traditions and innovations in Ethiopian culture.* Chicago, Ill.: Chicago University Press.

———. 1974. *Greater Ethiopia: The evolution of a multiethnic society.* Chicago, Ill.: Chicago University Press.

Levine, R., and D. Campbell. 1972. *Ethnocentrism: Theories of conflict, ethnic attitudes and group behavior.* New York: John Wiley.

Linton, S. 1971. Woman the gatherer: Male bias in Anthropology. In *Women in perspective*, ed. S. Jacobs. Urbana, Ill.: University of Illinois Press, 9–21.

Lipsky, S., and K. Nimol. 1993. Khmer women healers in transition: Cultural and bureaucratic barriers in training and employment. *Journal of Refugee Studies* 6(4):372–88.

Loizos, P. 1981. *The heart grown bitter: A chronicle of Cypriot war refugees.* Cambridge: Cambridge University Press.

Luig, U. 1992. Besessenheit als Ausdruck von Frauenkultur in Zambia. *Peripherie* 47–48:111–28.

Lungu, G., and I. Sinyangwe, eds. 1987. *Women and development in Africa*. Lusaka: Professors World Peace Academy, South Central Africa.

Lutheran World Federation. 1978. *Annual Report 1978*. Gaborone: Lutheran World Federation.

——. 1980–1989. *Annual Reports 1980–1989*. Gaborone: Lutheran World Federation.

Lutz, C. 1982. The domain of emotion words on Ifaluk. *American Ethnologist* 9:113–28.

Machel, G. 1996. *Impact of armed conflict on children*. New York: United Nations and UNICEF.

Macklin, A. 1995. Refugee women and the imperative of categories. *Human Rights Quarterly* 17:213–77

Magaia, L. 1988. *Dumba nengue (Run for your life): Peasant tales of tragedy in Mozambique*. Trenton: Africa World Press.

Malkki, L. 1992. National geographic: The rooting of peoples and the territorialization of national identity among scholars and refugees. *Cultural Anthropology* 7(1):24–44.

——. 1995. Refugees and exile: From "refugee studies" to the national order of things. *Annual Review of Anthropology* 24:495–546.

Maloney, C. 1988. *Behavior and poverty in Bangladesh*. Dhaka: University Press Limited.

Maluwa, T. 1996. Changing power relations between men and women in southern Africa: Some recent legal developments. Paper presented at a workshop on Transformation of Power and Culture. CAAS, University of Michigan, Ann Arbor, 11–20 Nov.

Malysheva, M. 1996. Women's identification in the post-war and post-communist Russia. In *People's destinies: Russia of the twentieth century. Family biographies as an object of sociological research*, ed. V. Semenova and E. Foteeva. Moscow: Institute of Sociology.

Mankekar, P. 1995. To whom does Ameena belong?: Towards a feminist analysis of childhood and nationhood in postcolonial India. Paper presented at Stanford University, 25 June.

Markakis, J. 1987. *National and class conflict in the Horn of Africa*. Cambridge: Cambridge University Press.

Marsden, P. 1996a. Repatriation and reconstruction: The case of Afghanistan. Paper presented at the International Society for the Study of Forced Migration first annual meeting. Moi University, Kenya, 9–12 April.

——. 1996b. *Crisis in Afghanistan: The future of aid*. European Institute for Asian Studies. (19 Nov.).

Marshall, R. 1995. Refugees, feminine plural. *Refugees: Refugee Women* 2(100):3–9.

Martin, S. 1993. *Refugee women*. London: ZED Books.

Mascarenhas, O., and M. Mbilinyi. 1983. *Women in Tanzania: An analytical bibliography*. Uppsala: Scandinavian Institute of African Studies.

Matlou, P. 1992. Refugee policy in Botswana (1958–1989): The interaction between state security, refugee agency interests, and refugee needs. Ph.D. Diss., University of Essex, Colchester.

Mazur, R. 1987. Linking popular initiatives and aid agencies: The case of refugees. *Development and Change* 18(3):43–60.

——. 1988. Refugees in Africa: The role of sociological analysis and praxis. *Current Sociology* 36(2):437–61.

McCall, M. 1987. Carrying heavier burdens but carrying less weight: Some implications of villagization in Tanzania. In *Geography of gender in the third world*, ed. J. Momsen and J. Townsend. State University of New York Press: Hutchinson.

McCloy, M. 1997. Dongo v. Flame. *Mail and Guardian* (Johannesburg) 13(18), 9–15 May:28.

McDowell, C., eds. 1996. *Understanding impoverishment: The consequences of development-induced displacement.* Oxford: Berghahn.

McLaren, P. 1995. *Critical pedagogy and predatory culture: Oppositional politics in a postmodern era.* New York: Routledge.

McMillan, D. 1995. *Sahel visions: Planned resettlement and river blindness control in Burkina Faso.* Tucson: University of Arizona Press.

McSpadden, L. 1987. Ethiopian refugee resettlement in the western United States: Social context and psychological well-being. *International Migration Review* 21(3):796–819.

———. 1989a. Ethiopian refugee resettlement in the western United States: Social context and psychological well-being. Ph.D. Diss., University of Utah.

———. 1989b. *Ethiopian refugees in the United States.* Immigration and Refugee Program Briefing Paper for Sponsors of Ethiopian Refugees. New York: Church World Service.

———. 1991. Cross-cultural understandings of independence and dependence: Conflict in the resettlement of single Ethiopian males. *Refuge* 10(4):21–25.

McSpadden, L., and H. Moussa. 1993. "I have a name": The gender dynamics in asylum and resettlement of Ethiopian and Eritrean refugees in North America. *Journal of Refugee Studies* 6(3):203–25.

———. 1996. Returning Home? The decision-making processes of Eritrean women and men. *Development and diaspora: Gender and the refugee experience,* ed. W. Giles, H. Moussa, and P. Van Esterik. Dundas, Ontario: Artemis.

Médecins Sans Frontières. 1997. *Refugee health: An approach to emergency situations,* ed. G. Hanquet. London: Macmillan.

Meijer, M., and M. Weeda. 1990. *Travel report: Pakistan.* Dutch Interchurch Aid. Nov.

Mencher, J., and A. Okongwu, eds. 1993. *Where did all the men go? Female/headed, female/supported households in cross-cultural perspective.* Boulder, Colo.: Westview Press.

Mercer, K. 1988. Diaspora culture and the dialogic imagination: The aesthetics of black independent film in Britain. In *Blackframes: Critical perspectives on black independent cinema,* ed. M. Cham and C. Andrade-Watkins. London: MIT Press.

Merton, R. 1957. Social structure and anomie. In *Social theory and social structure,* ed. R. Merton. Glenco, Ill.: The Free Press, 185–214.

Millett, K. 1994. *The politics of cruelty.* New York: W. W. Norton.

Minh-ha, T. 1989. Woman, native, other: Writing postcoloniality and feminism. Bloomington: Indiana University Press.

———. 1992. *Framer framed.* New York: Routledge.

Minnich, E. 1990. *Transforming knowledge.* Philadelphia, Pa.: Temple University Press.

Mitchneck, B., and D. Plane. 1995. Migration patterns during a period of political and economic shocks in the former Soviet Union: A case study of Yaroslavl *oblast. Professional Geographer* 47(1):17–30.

Mohanty, C. 1997. Under western eyes: Feminist scholarship and colonial discourses. In *Dangerous liaisons: Gender, nation, and post colonial perspectives,* ed. A. McClintock, A. Mufity, and E. Shohat. Minneapolis: University of Minnesota Press.

Molefe, R. 1996. Children—victims of war. *Sowetan,* 19 Nov., p. 11.

Moore, H. 1988. *Feminism and anthropology.* Minneapolis: University of Minneapolis Press.

———. 1994. *A passion for difference: Essays in anthropology and gender.* Cambridge: Polity Press.

Morokvasic, M. 1984. Birds of passage are also women. *International Migration Review* 18(4):886–907.

Moser, C. 1989. Gender planning in the Third World: Meeting practical and strategic gender needs. In *World Development* 17(11):1799–1825.

———. 1993. *Gender planning and development theory, practice and training.* London: Routledge.

Moussa, H. 1993. *Storm and sanctuary: The journey of Ethiopian and Eritrean women refugees.* Dundas, Ontario: Artemis.

———. 1994. Sowing new foundations: Refugee and immigrant women and support groups. *Refuge* 13(9):3–7.

Myerhoff, B. 1986. Life not death in Venice: Its second life. In *The anthropology of experience,* ed. V. Turner and E. Bruner. Chicago, Ill.: University of Illinois Press, 261–86.

Mÿnz, R. 1996. A continent of migration: European mass migration in the twentieth century. *New Community* 22(2):201–26.

Nabaity, J., C. Bachengana, and J. Seely. 1994. Marital instability in a rural population in Southwest Uganda: Implications for the spread of HIV1 infection. *Africa* 64(2).

Naficy, H. 1991. The poetics and practice of Iranian nostalgia. *Diaspora* 1(3):285–302.

Namitabar v. Canada (Minister of Employment and Immigration) [1993] FCTD Action No. A-1252–92. (5 Nov.) (Tremblay-Lamer J.)

Neal, D. 1988. Women as a social group: Recognizing sex-based persecution as grounds for asylum. *Columbia Human Rights Law Review* 20(1): 203–57.

Nordstrom, C. 1992a. The backyard front. In *The paths to domination, resistance, and terror,* ed. C. Nordstrom and J. Martin. Berkeley, Calif.: University of California Press, 260–74.

———. 1992b. The dirty war: Culture of violence in Mozambique and Sri Lanka. In *Internal conflicts and governance,* ed. K. Rupesinghe. New York: St. Martin's Press, 27–43.

———. 1992c. War: Intricacies and complications. *Life and Peace Review* 6(4):6–8.

———. 1994. *War zones: Cultures of violence, militarisation and peace.* Working Paper No. 145, Peace Research Centre. Canberra: Australian National University.

———. 1995. Creativity and chaos: War on the frontlines. In *Fieldwork under fire: Contemporary studies of violence and survival,* ed. C. Nordstrom and A. Robben. Berkeley, Calif.: University of California Press.

———. 1996. *Rape: Politics and theory in war and peace.* Working Paper No. 146, Peace Research Centre. Canberra: Australian National University. [Reprinted in *Australian Feminist Studies* 11(23):147–62].

O'Laughlin, B. 1995. Myth of the African family in the world of development. In *Women wielding the hoe: Lessons from rural Africa for feminist theory and development practice,* ed. D. Bryceson. Oxford: Berg Publishers, 62–91.

Ogundipe-Leslie, M. 1996. Recreating ourselves: Gender issues for African women today. Paper presented at the School of Oriental and African Studies, University of London, 8 February.

Okbazghi, Y. 1994. *Eritrea, a pawn in world politics.* Gainesville, Fla.: University of Florida Press.

Ong, A. 1988. Colonialism and modernity: Feminist re-presentations of women in non-Western societies. *Inscriptions* 3(4):79–93.

———. 1996. Cultural citizenship as subject-making: Immigrants negotiate racial and cultural boundaries in the United States. *Current Anthropology* 37(15):737–51.

Oslon, A. 1997. The last year of Russia: Chronicle of public opinion, July 1996–March 1997. *Nezavismaya Gazeta*, 10 April 1997, pp. 4–5.

Panarin, S. 1997. Involuntary ethnic migration and human security: Experiences of Russia and the CIS. *Migration*, in press.

Pankhurst, R. 1990. *A social history of Ethiopia.* Addis Ababa: Institute of Ethiopian Studies, Addis Abab University.

Papanek, H. 1990. *To each less than she needs, from each more than she can do: Allocations, entitlements, and value.* In *Persistent inequalities: Women and world development*, ed. I. Tinker. New York: Oxford University Press, 162–84.

Parada, E. 1990. Culture and community filling the gap in Chilean education: Saturday community schools in London. *Refugee Participation Network* 8 (May):18–19.

Passerini, L. 1987. *Fascism in popular memory: The cultural experience of the Turin working class.* Cambridge: Cambridge University Press.

Patai, D. 1987. Ethical problems of personal narratives, or, who should eat the last piece of cake? *International Journal of Oral History* 6(1):5–27.

Pateman, R. 1990. *Even the stones are burning.* Trenton, N.J.: Red Sea Press.

Peri Rossi, C. 1988. *Cosmogonias.* Barcelona: Editorial Laia.

Permanent Peoples' Tribunal of the International League for the Rights and Liberation of Peoples. 1984. *The Eritrean case.* Rome: Research and Information Center on Eritrea.

Peters, J., and A. Wolper, eds. 1995. *Women's rights, human rights: International feminist perspectives.* London: Routledge.

Peterson, V. 1992. *Gendered states: Feminist (re)visions of international relations theory.* London: Lynne Rienner.

Pettman, J. 1996. *Worlding women: A feminist international politics.* London: Routledge.

Phillips, B. 1994. Mozambique: Teenage sex for sale. *BBC Focus on Africa* 15(2).

Pinar, W. 1993. Notes on understanding curriculum as a racial text. In *Race identity and representation in education*, ed. C. McCarthy and W. Crichlow. New York: Routledge.

Pitterman, S. 1985. International responses to refugee situations: The UNHCR. In *Refugees and world politics*, ed. E. Ferris. New York: Praeger.

———. 1987. Determinants of international refugee policy: A comparative study of UNHCR material assistance to refugees in Africa, 1963–1981. In *Refugees: A Third World dilemma*, ed. J. Rogge. Totowa, N.J.: Rowan and Littlefield.

Poats, S., M. Schmink, and A. Spring, eds. 1988. *Gender issues in farming systems research and extension.* Boulder, Colo.: Westview Press.

Pool, D. 1980. Revolutionary crisis and revolutionary vanguard: The emergence of the Eritrean People's Liberation Front. *Review of African Political Economy* 19:33–47.

———. 1982. *Eritrea, Africa's longest war.* London: Anti-Slavery Society.

———. 1983. Eritrean nationalism. In *Nationalism and self-determination in the Horn of Africa*, ed. I. Lewis. London: Ithaca Press, 175–93.

Poston, M. M. 1994. *Guns and girls: UN peacekeeping and sexual abuse in the context of gender and international relations.* M.A. Thesis., School of Development Studies, University of East Anglia, Norwich, U.K.

Potten, D. 1976. Etsha: A successful resettlement scheme. *Botswana: Notes and records* 8:105–117.

Pryer, J. 1990. Hunger and women's survival in a Bangladesh slum. In *The food question: Profits versus people*, ed. H. Bernstein, B. Crow, M. Mackintosh, and C. Martin. New York: Monthly Review Press, 125–33.

Quillet, C. 1994. Equal chances for all children enrolled in supplementary feeding program? Report of a project submitted in part fulfillment of the regulations for the degree of Master of Science in the Faculty of Medicine, University of London.

Radcliffe, S. 1993. Women's place/*el Lugar de mujeres*: Latin America and the politics of gender identity. In *Place and the politics of identity*, ed. M. Keith and S. Pile. London: Routledge.

Raikes, P. 1978. Rural differentiation and class formation in Tanzania. *Journal of Peasant Studies* 5(3).

Rathgeber, E. 1990. WID, WAD, GAD: Trends in research and practice. *Journal of Developing Areas* 24:489–502.

Refugee Studies Programme. 1995. Code of conduct for the International Red Cross and Red Crescent Movement and NGOs in disaster relief. *Refugee Participation Network (RPN)*. 19(May). Oxford: Refugee Studies Programme.

Reiter, R. 1975. Men and women in the south of France: Public and private domains. In *Toward an anthropology of women*, ed. R. Reiter. New York: Monthly Review Press.

Reynell, J. 1989. *Political pawns: Refugees on the Thai-Kampuchea border*. Oxford: Refugee Studies Programme.

Reynolds, P. 1991. *Dance civet cat: Child labor in the Zambezi valley*. Athens, Ohio: Ohio University Press.

Richards, A. 1932. *Hunger and work in a savage tribe*. London: Routledge.

———. 1939. *Land, labour and diet in Northern Rhodesia*. London: Oxford University Press.

Roach Anleu, S. 1992. Critiquing the law: Themes and dilemmas in Anglo-American Feminist Legal Theory. *Journal of Law and Society* 19(4):423–40.

Rogge, J. 1985. Africa's resettlement strategies. In *Refugees and world politics*, ed. E. Ferris. New York: Praeger.

Rogge, J., and J. Akol. 1989. Repatriation: Its role in resolving Africa's refugee dilemma. *International Migration Review* 23(2): 184–200. New York: Center for Migration Studies.

Romany, C. 1993. Women as aliens: A feminist critique of the public/private distinction in human rights law. *Harvard Humanitarian Rights Journal* 6:87.

Rossiter, J., and R. Palmer. 1991. *Northern NGOs in Southern Africa: Some heretical thoughts*. Oxford: OXFAM.

Rumbaut, R. 1985. Mental health and the refugee experience: A comparative study of Southeast Asian refugees. In *Southeast Asian mental health: Treatment, prevention, services*, ed. T. Owan. Rockville, Md.: U.S. Dept. of Health and Human Services, National Institute of Mental Health, Public Health Service, Alcohol, Drug Abuse, and Mental Health Administration in collaboration with Office of Refugee Resettlement, Social Security Administration.

Rutherford, J., ed. 1990. *Identity: Community, culture, difference*. London: Lawrence & Wishart.

Saharso, S. 1996. *Gender, ethnicity and public identity: Migrant women in Dutch policy on women and minorities*. Paper presented to the Second International Conference, New migration in Europe: Social constructions and social realities. Utrecht, 18–20 April.

Salem-Murdock, M. 1989. *Arabs and Nubians in New Halfa: A study of settlement and irrigation*. Salt Lake City: University of Utah Press.

Salinas, M. 1989. Report on the First International Consultation on Refugee Women. Ecumenical Centre, Geneva, Switzerland, 14–19 Nov. 1988. *Journal of Refugee Studies* 2(2):292–302.

Sapir, D. 1993. Natural and man-made disasters: The vulnerability of women-headed households and children without families. *World Health Statistics Quarterly* 46:227–33.

Savane, M. 1986. The effects of social and economic changes on the role and status of women in Sub-Saharan Africa. In *Understanding Africa's rural households and farming systems*, ed. J. L. Moock. Boulder, Colo.: Westview Press, 124–32.

Sboros, M. 1997. Women try and find the road to recovery. *Star*, 23 May, p. 15.

Schilders, N., et al. 1988. *Sexual violence: You have hardly any future left.* Amsterdam: Dutch Refugee Council.

Scott C. 1985. *Domination and the arts of resistance: Hidden transcripts.* New Haven, Conn.: Yale University Press.

Scott, J. 1992. Experience. In *Feminists theorize the political*, ed. J. Butler and J. Scott. New York: Routledge.

Scudder, T. 1962. *The ecology of the Gwembe Tonga.* Manchester: Manchester University Press.

———. 1969. Relocation, agricultural intensification, and anthropological research. In *The anthropology of development in Sub-Saharan Africa*, ed. D. Brokensha and M. Pearsall. Society for Applied Anthropology Monograph 10:31–39. Lexington, Ky.: University Press of Kentucky.

Scudder, T., and E. Colson. 1972. The Kariba Dam project. In *Technology and social change*, ed. H. Bernard and P. Pelto. New York: Macmillan, 39–70.

Searle-Chattergee, M. 1981. *Reversible sex roles: The special case of Benares Sweepers.* Oxford: Pergamon Press.

Segal, M. 1986. Islam, feminism, and Afghan refugee women. *ARIN* (London) 23 (Winter).

Sen, A. 1976. Famines as failures of exchange entitlements. *Economic and Political Weekly* 11:1273–80.

———. 1977. Starvation and exchange entitlement: A general approach and its application to the great Bengal Famine. *Cambridge Journal of Economics* 1:33–59.

———. 1981. *Poverty and famines: An essay on entitlement and deprivation.* Oxford: Clarendon Press.

———. 1983. Economics and the family. *Asian Development Review* 1(2):14–21.

———. 1988. Family and food: Sex bias in poverty. In *Rural poverty in South Asia*, ed. T. Srinivasan and P. Bardhan. New York: Columbia University Press, 453–72.

———. 1990. Gender and cooperative conflicts. In *Persistent inequalities: Women and world development*, ed. I. Tinker. Oxford: Oxford University Press, 123–49.

Serrill, M. 1996. Slaves: On sale now. *Time*, 1 July, p. 28.

Shawcross, W. 1984. *The quality of mercy: Cambodia, holocaust and modern conscience.* London: Andre Deutsch.

Shelley, T. 1990. Development: NGOs. *West Africa*, 9–15 April, p. 590.

Sherman, R. 1980. *Eritrea the unfinished revolution.* New York: Praeger.

Simon, R. 1994. Forms of insurgency in the production of popular memories: The Columbus quincentenary and the pedagogy of counter-commemoration. In *Between borders: Pedagogy and the politics of cultural studies*, ed. H. Giroux and P. McLaren. New York: Routledge.

Simon, R., and C. Brettell, eds. 1986. *International migration: The female experience.* Totawa, N.J.: Rowman and Allanheld.

Slim, H. 1995. The continuing metamorphosis of the humanitarian practitioner: Some new colours for an endangered chameleon. *Disasters* 19:10–126.

Smith, C. 1994. Sustainable development reconsidered: Rich farmers of Kagera Region, Tanzania. In *Labor Capital and Society* 27(1).

Smith, D. 1991. *Reflections on feminist scholarship.* Vancouver: University of British Columbia Centre for Research in Women's Studies and Gender Relations.

Smith, N., and C. Katz. 1993. Grounding metaphor: Towards a spatialized politics. In *Place and the politics of identity,* ed. M. Keith and S. Pile. London: Routledge.

Sommers, M. 1995. Representing refugees: The role of elites in Burundi refugee society. *Disasters* 19:19–25.

Sorenson, J. 1993. *Imagining Ethiopia.* New Brunswick, N.J.: Rutgers University Press.

———., ed. 1995. *Disaster and development in the Horn of Africa.* Houndmills, U.K.: Macmillan.

Southall, A., and P. Gutkind. 1957. *Townsmen in the making: Kampala and its suburbs.* Kampala: East African Institute of Social Research.

Spencer-Nimmons, N. 1994. *The emergence of refugee women as a social issue: 1978–1988.* Ph.D. Diss., York University (Canada).

Spijkerboer, T. 1994. *Women and refugee status: Beyond the public/private distinction.* The Hague: Emancipation Council.

Spring, A. 1979. Women farmers and food in Africa: Some considerations and suggested solutions. In *Food in Sub-Saharan Africa,* ed. A. Hansen and D. McMillan. Boulder, Colo.: Lynne Rienner, 332–48.

———. 1982. Women and men as refugees: Differential assimilation of Angolan refugees in Zambia. In *Involuntary migration and resettlement: The problems and responses of dislocated people,* ed. A. Hansen and A. Oliver-Smith. Boulder, Colo.: Westview Press, 37–48.

Stairs, F., and L. Pope. 1990. No place like home: Assaulted migrant women's claims to refugee status and landings on humanitarian and compassionate grounds. *Journal of Law and Social Policy* 6:148–225.

Starr, P. 1992. Social categories and claims in the liberal state. *Social Research* 59(2).

State Statistical Committee of the Russian Federation (SSCRF). 1996. *Numbers of Population and Its Mobility in the Russian Federation in 1995.* Statistical Bulletin. Moscow: Committee of the Russian Federation.

———. 1997. *Numbers of Population and Its Mobility in the Russian Federation in 1996.* Statistical Bulletin. Moscow: State Statistical Committee of the Russian Federation.

Staudt, K. 1982. Women farmers and inequities in agricultural services. In *Women and work in Africa,* ed. E. Bay. Boulder, Colo.: Westview Press.

———. 1990. *Women, international development, and politics.* Philadelphia, Pa.: Temple University Press.

Stephens, S., ed. 1995. *Children and the politics of culture.* Princeton, N.J.: Princeton University Press.

Stevens, L. 1995. Bananas, babies and women who buy their graves: Matrifocal values in a patrilineal Tanzanian society. *The Canadian Journal of African Studies* 29(3).

Stewart, K. 1988. Nostalgia: A polemic. *Cultural Anthropology* 3(3):227–41.

Strizhak, E., and C. Harries. 1993. *Sex, lies, and international law.* New York: Women's Commission for Refugee Women and Children.

Suárez-Orozco, M. 1987. The treatment of children in the "dirty war": Ideology, state terrorism, and the abuse of children in Argentina. In *Child Survival,* ed. N. Scheper-Hughes. Boston: D. Reidel.

———. 1996. California dreaming: Proposition 187 and the cultural psychology of racial and ethnic exclusion. *Anthropology and Education Quarterly* 27(2):151–67.

Summerfield, D. 1996. When women become killers. *Lancet* 347:1817.

Sutton, C. 1992. Some thoughts on gendering and internationalizing our thinking about transnational migrations. In *Towards a transnational perspective on migration: Race, class, ethnicity, and nationalism reconsidered,* ed. N. Glick-Schiller, L. Basch, and C. Blanc-Szanton. New York: The New York Academy of Sciences, 241–50.

Swantz, M. 1985. *Women in development: A creative role denied?* London: C. Hurst.

Swift, R. 1995. B. Harris interviewed by R. Swift. *New Internationalist* (July):31.

Taft, J. 1987. *Issues and options for refugee women in developing countries.* Washington, D.C.: Refugee Policy Group.

Tebeje, A. 1989. *Cultural interaction between Canadians and Ethiopian newcomers in Canada.* Ottawa: Employment and Immigration Canada.

Tekie, F. 1983. The international dimensions of the Eritrean question. *Horn of Africa* 6(2):7–24.

Thangaraj, S. 1996. Impoverishment risks analysis: A methodological tool for participatory resettlement planning. In *Understanding impoverishment: The consequences of development-induced displacement,* ed. C. McDowell. Oxford: Berghahn Books, 223–32.

Thomas, D. Q., and M. Beasley. 1993. Domestic violence as a human rights issue. *Human Rights Quarterly* 15:36–62.

Thompkins, T. L. 1995. Prosecuting rape as a war crime: Speaking the unspeakable. *Notre Dame Law Review* 70(4):845–90.

Thompson, C. 1985. *Challenge to imperialism: The frontline states in the liberation of Zimbabwe.* Harare: Zimbabwe Publishing.

Tibaijuka, A. 1984. *An economic analysis of smallholder banana-coffee farms in the Kagera Region, Tanzania.* Uppsala: Swedish University of Agricultural Sciences.

Tinker, I. 1990. *Persistent inequalities: Women and world development.* New York: Oxford University Press.

Toole, M. 1996. Vulnerability in emergency situations. *Lancet* 348:840.

Trevaskis, G. 1960. *Eritrea, a colony in transition.* London: Oxford University Press.

Turnbridge, L. 1995. Children accused of genocide in Rwanda. *Sunday Times.* 17 December, p. 10.

Turner, V. 1967. *The forest of symbols: Aspects of Ndembu ritual.* Ithaca, N.Y.: Cornell University Press.

———. 1986. Dewey, Dilthey, and drama: An essay in the anthropology of experience. In *The Anthropology of Experience,* ed. V. Turner and E. Bruner. Chicago, Ill.: University of Illinois Press.

Turner, V., and E. Bruner, eds. 1986. *The anthropology of experience.* Chicago, Ill.: University of Illinois.

Umoren, R. 1995. Civilian daily victims of landmine blasts. *Citizen,* 27 September, p. 6.

UNICEF 1995a. *The state of the world's children 1995.* Oxford: Oxford University Press.

———. 1995b. *1995 Annual Report.* Geneva: UNICEF.

———. 1996a. *Study on the Impact of Armed Conflict on Children.* Geneva: UNICEF.

———. 1996b. *The state of the world's children 1996.* Oxford: Oxford University Press.

United Arab Emirates (UAE). 1994. *The Sharjah Declaration: Recommendations of the International Conference on Uprooted Muslim Women,* 12–15 Nov. United Arab Emirates.

United Nations. 1951 *Convention relating to the status of refugees ("the Convention,"* *throughout this volume)*. UNTS 189: 2545. Entered into force 22 April 1954.

———. 1990. *The rights of the child*. Fact Sheet No. 10. Geneva: UN.

———. 1995. *The world's women, 1995: Trends and statistics*. Social Statistics and Indicators Series, K, No. 12. New York: United Nations.

United Nations Development Program (UNDP). 1992. *Young women: Silence, susceptibility, and the HIV epidemic*. New York: United Nations.

United Nations Economic and Social Council, Commission on Human Rights. 1996. *Report of the Special Rapporteur on Violence Against Women*. E/CN.4/1996/53:5. (February).

United Nations High Commissioner for Refugees (UNHCR). 1979a. *Collection of international instruments concerning refugees*. Geneva: UNHCR.

———. 1979b. *Handbook on procedures and criteria for determining refugee status*. Geneva: UNHCR.

———. 1991. *Rapid nutrition survey among populations in emergency situations*. Draft. Geneva: UNHCR, MSF, and WFP.

———. 1993. *The state of the world's refugees, 1993*. New York: Penguin.

———. 1994. *Population statistics for Dadaab area camps, 19 September*.

———. 1995a. *Reproductive health in refugee situations. An inter-agency field manual*. Geneva: UNHCR.

———. 1995b. *An overview of protection issues in Western Europe: Legislative trends and positions taken by UNHCR*. European Series No. 3:27–30.

———. 1996. Household food economy assessment of Ifo, Dagahaley and Hagadera camps, Garissa District, Northeastern Kenya. (October). Unpublished Report of an Assessment undertaken by SCF UK on Behalf of WFP Kenya and UNHCR Kenya.

United Nations High Commissioner for Refugees (UNHCR). Executive Committee (EXCOM). 1985. *Conclusion No. 39 on refugee women and international protection; Conclusions on the international protection of refugees*. In *Report of the Thirty-sixth Session of the Executive Committee of the High Commissioner's Programme*. 36th Sess. (7–18 October), at 36, UN Doc. A/AC 96/673, par. 115(4)(k).

———. 1990. *Conclusion No. 39 on refugee women and international protection; Conclusions on the international protection of refugees*. Geneva: UNHCR, 84–85.

———. 1991. *Guidelines on the protection of refugee women*. EC/SCP/67. (22 July). Geneva.

———. 1995. *Sexual violence against refugees: Guidelines on prevention and response*. Geneva.

United Nations Office for the Coordination of Humanitarian Assistance in Afghanistan (UNOCHA). 1996. *Desperate situation in Kabul*. Briefing note. (29 Jan.).

United States Board of Immigration Appeals (BIA). 1975. *Matter of Pierre*. 15 I & N Dec. 461. Cited in US *Considerations* (1995), p. 716.

———. 1985. *Matter of Acosta*. 19 I & N Dec. 211, 222. Cited in U.S. *Considerations* (1995), pp. 707, 712.

———. 1989. *Matter of Chang*. BIA Interim Decision 3107. (12 May).

———. 1993. *Matter of Krome*. (25 May).

———. 1996. *In re Kasinga*. Int. Decision, p. 3278.

United States Committee for Refugees. 1991. *Refugee reports*. Washington, D.C., Dec.

United States Office of Refugee Resettlement, Health and Human Services. 1993. *Monthly Data Report for September 1992 and 1992 FY Summary*. Feb.

United States. Department of Justice, Executive Office for Immigration Review, Office of the Immigration Judge. 1994. *In the matter of A and Z*. A 72-190–893, A 72-793–219.

United States. National Security Archive. 1983. Confidential from U.S. Embassy Islamabad to Secretary of State, 2 Sept. Washington, D.C.: National Security Archive.

United States *INS v. Elias-Zacarias.* [1991] 112 S. Ct. 812.

United States. Immigration and Naturalization Service (INS). 1992. *Statistical yearbook of Immigration and Naturalization Service, 1991.* Washington, D.C.: U.S. Government Printing Office.

———. 1995. Considerations for asylum officers adjudicating asylum claims from women. Memorandum by P. Coven, Office of International Affairs, to all INS Asylum Officers and HQASM Coordinators, 6 May. *International Journal of Refugee Law* 7:700.

van Amersfoort, H. 1996. Migration: The limits of governmental control. *New Community* 22(2):243–57.

Van Prang, N. 1986. From Ethiopia to the USA: A difficult transition. *Refugees* 25 (Jan.): 15–6.

Vasquez, A. 1981. Adolescents from the Southern Cone of Latin America in exile: Some psychological problems. In *Mental health and exile.* London: World University Press, 22–34.

Vishnevsky, A., ed. 1994 *Population of Russia. Second Annual Demographic Report.* Moscow: Eurasia Publishing House.

Vitkovskaya, G. 1995. Travelling willy-nilly: Migrating women. *Russkoye Obozreniye (Russian Survey)* 9 (1 March 1995):5–6.

Voutira, E. 1995. *A strategic action plan for making WFP's policy and practice more gender sensitive: Recommendations for operational policy development.* Oxford: Refugee Studies Programme.

Voutira, E., M. Mahmud, and E. Oestergaard-Nielsen. 1995. *Improving social and gender planning in emergency operations.* A World Food Programme Report prepared by the Refugee Studies Programme, Queen Elizabeth House, University of Oxford. Oxford: Refugee Studies Programme.

Wali, A. 1989. *Kilowatts and crisis: Hydroelectric power and social dislocation in Eastern Panama.* Boulder, Colo.: Westview Press.

Walsh, M. 1990. Strained mercy: A "relief agency" dispenses propaganda. *Progressive.* May.

Warren, K., and S. Bourque. 1991. Women, technology and international development ideologies: Analysing feminist voices. In *Gender at the crossroads of knowledge: Feminist anthropology in the postmodern era,* ed. M. di Leonardo. Berkeley: University of California Press, 278–311.

Weaver, M. 1995. Children of the Jihad. *The New Yorker,* 12 June.

Weiss, B. 1993. Money, movement and AIDS in Northwest Tanzania. *Africa* 63(1).

Weissbrodt, D. 1977. Human rights legislation and U.S. foreign policy. *Georgia Journal of International and Comparative Law* 7:231.

West, J., and S. Pilgrim. 1995. South Asian women in employment: The impact of migration, ethnic origin and the local economy. *New Community* 21(3): 357–78.

West, S. 1987a. Bay Area Ethiopian refugee pushed to suicide. *Oakland Post,* 3 June.

———. 1987b. Helplessness and hopelessness behind refugee suicide. *Oakland Post,* 10 June.

White, L. 1990. *The comforts of home: Prostitution in colonial Nairobi.* Chicago, Ill.: University of Chicago Press.

Wickstead, D. 1996. Staying in. *Crosslines Global Report.* Aug. Cambridge, Mass.: International Centre for Humanitarian Reporting.

Wilkes, S. 1993. Don't let the sun go down. *Refugees* (Dec.):36–37.

Williams, R. 1977. *Marxism and literature*. Oxford: Oxford University Press.

Wilson, K. 1992. *Internally displaced, refugees and returnees from and in Mozambique*. Report No. 1 (Nov.) for SIDA Studies on Emergencies and Disaster Relief. Stockholm: Swedish International Development Authority.

Wolpe, H. 1989. Oppressive stalemate. *Southern African Review of Books* 3(1,11):8–10.

Yanagisako, S. 1987. Mixed metaphors: Native and anthropological models of gender and kinship models. In *Gender and kinship*, ed. J. Collier and S. Yanagisako. Stanford, Calif.: Stanford University Press, 86–118.

Young, M., and P. Willmott. 1957. *Family and kinship in East London*. London: Routledge.

Young, R. 1990. *White mythologies*. New York: Routledge.

Yusuf v. Canada (Minister of Employment and Immigration). [1992] 1, FC 629 (FCA).

Zarjevski, Y. 1988. *A future preserved: International assistance to refugees*. Oxford: Pergamon Press.

Zetter, R. 1988. Refugees, repatriation, and root causes. *Journal of Refugee Studies* 1(2):99–106.

Zolberg, A., A. Suhrke, and S. Aguayo, eds. 1989. *Escape from violence: Globalized social conflict and the refugee crisis in the developing world*. Oxford: Oxford University Press.

Index